THE VERSE BOOK
OF INTERVIEWS

THE VERSE BOOK
OF INTERVIEWS

27 POETS ON LANGUAGE, CRAFT & CULTURE

EDITED BY
**BRIAN HENRY &
ANDREW ZAWACKI**

VERSE PRESS, AMHERST MA

Published by Verse Press

Ten-digit ISBN: 0-9746353-5-9

Thirteen-digit ISBN: 9780974635354

Verse Press titles are distributed to the trade by Consortium Book Sales and Distribution, 1045 Westgate Drive, St. Paul, Minnesota 55114.

Library of Congress Cataloging-in-Publication Data:

The verse book of interviews : 27 poets on language, craft and culture
/ edited by Brian Henry & Andrew Zawacki.-- 1st ed.
     p. cm.
  ISBN 0-9746353-5-9 (pbk. : alk. paper)
  1. Poetry--History and criticism. 2. Poets--Interviews. I. Henry,
Brian, 1972- II. Zawacki, Andrew, 1972-
  PN1064.V47 2005
  809.1--dc22
                                   2004020262

Composition by Brian Henry. Set in Electra and Copperplate.
Cover design and photograph by J. Johnson.

Printed in the United States of America

9 8 7 6 5 4 3 2 1

FIRST EDITION

Contents

Tomaž Šalamun

Tomaž Šalamun was born in Zagreb, Croatia, in 1941, and raised in Koper, Slovenia. He was educated in art history at the University of Ljubljana, and he worked as a conceptual artist from 1968 to 1970. He has published 30 books of poetry in Slovenian, as well as eight collections in English: the chapbooks *Turbines* (Windhover Press, 1973) and *Snow* (Toothpaste Press, 1974); a volume of *Selected Poems* (Ecco Press, 1988; reprinted in the UK as *Homage to Hat & Uncle Guido & Eliot: Selected Poems*, Arc Publications, 1997), edited by Charles Simic with an introduction by Robert Hass; *The Four Questions of Melancholy: New and Selected Poems* (White Pine Press, 1997), edited with an introduction by Christopher Merrill; *Feast* (Harcourt, 2000); *A Ballad for Metka Krasovec* (Twisted Spoon Press, 2001); *Poker* (Ugly Duckling Presse, 2003), and *Blackboards* (Saturnalia Books, 2004). Šalamun has received numerous honors for his writing, including the Preseren Fund Prize, the Mladost Prize, a fellowship to the International Writing Program at the University of Iowa, residencies at Yaddo and the MacDowell writing colonies, and a Fulbright grant to Columbia University. He was the Cultural Attaché to the Slovenian Consulate in New York City from 1996 to 1999. Brian Henry conducted this interview on March 4, 1998, in a bistro in Adelaide, Australia, where Šalamun was a featured writer at the Adelaide Festival. The interview appeared in Volume 15, Number 3 / Volume 16, Number 1 of *Verse*.

Is it important to you for your work to enter other languages, countries, and traditions?

Definitely. Especially English, of course. I'm completely satisfied with Slovenian as a language; I think it's an absolutely complete language, and I never felt frustrated in terms of the Slovenian language. It's a language with all the possibilities. In my language I don't miss anything which I would in English or French. I had a weird moment after a year and a half in Iowa when, with my bad English, I started to dream my childhood in English, and it was a completely schizophrenic moment. At that time I went to see Czeslaw Milosz at Berkeley, asking him for advice, and he said, "Go back, young man. Tito is not Stalin; and you're absolutely too old to be able to change language." And I took his advice, and I'm grateful for it because I would not be able to write in English.

But still the public in Slovenia is small: we are two million. And I've been on the scene for thirty years and I've published 26 books, and there are really moments when everyone is fed up with me, not many people are reading me at the moment. I was most popular when I didn't write for four years, so it's important to have friends around the world. I remember, when Yugoslavia still existed, I had many books translated in Serbian and Croatian: this was a wonderful public, it was a much broader public. And you always like when you see somebody, a young poet, who really liked your work and was touched by it. I tremendously enjoy meeting younger American poets who tell me that they've read me and that they liked me and some of them had a dialogue with the work.

Was the first edition of your Selected Poems *[Ecco, 1988] a shock for you?*

No, I had two small chapbooks before. One was published by Windhover Press in '73, and the next chapbook was called *Snow* and it was published by Toothpaste Press in Iowa, which later became Coffee House Press. I was absolutely amazed and stunned when Kevin Hart, for example, told me he had read *Snow* in the Brisbane library; and when I met Mark Doty, I was completely stunned that he liked *Snow*.

But this was '72, '73, '74, then I was not in touch with ... I didn't have any new translations. I came to Yaddo in '79, at a time when I didn't publish—nobody knew anything about me. So when the Ecco Press book came out, I somehow didn't really realize what it was all about—what this means—and I needed about two years to realize that this meant a lot, that this really broadened my public.

What happens to a Šalamun poem when it crosses from Slovenian into English? When you read it in English, do you even feel like you're reading your own work—a diluted or skewed version of it, maybe?

No, I feel that I am reading complete Šalamun, only that when I pronounce the words, I cannot reach them as I would like to reach them. When I pronounce them, I seem somehow before a glass [pushes against an invisible wall in front of him] and I'm not sure, really, if I reach my audience or not. But I'm comfortable as I'm reading myself in English—I'm comfortable with it, I like it.

So you recognize yourself?

Absolutely, absolutely. But there are segments which cannot be translated because they are too much in the language—maybe thirty or forty percent of my poems—which I hope one day will be translated. They seem too minute, too tiny, too … they seem strange and minimal when they're in English, and they should be lucid and powerful, as I hope they are in Slovenian. But I didn't succeed in translating them well.

It's clear that wordplay is important to your work: do your translators approximate that in English, or do they take the Slovenian flavor and carry it in English?

I believe more in almost literal translations: just strictly translate the meaning and then things will come out. Unlike what the French are doing; they are transposing it. French poetry has a tradition of translations which are not very literal. Their tradition is different compared to Germans, who are more literal—the French are more free and also much less literal than the American tradition.

But only the short poems don't survive well, also because of the tradition of narrative in American poetry. It's very hard to compete with that with small poems.

Do you like giving readings in English? Is it difficult?

In a way it's difficult, but in a way I like it, because, for example, at the reading in Massachusetts, in Northampton [April 1997], I would never dream that there are so many buyers for this book [*The Four Questions of Melancholy: New and Selected Poems*]. This was a very magical moment for me. And I was amazed today in the tent at 12:30—I thought people would go to lunch or go see the other writers who were really famous, but no, they stayed there and there were two, three hundred people and they just watched. These poems are quite complicated and metaphysical, confused and strange—they liked them, apparently, because there was total silence.

Your poetry has various international affinities, or allegiances; you're not working solely in the Slovenian tradition. Which non-Slovenian poets affected you when you were young?

When I was young, I was formed for sure by French poets, especially Rimbaud. I was hit by Rimbaud before I considered myself a poet—I never wanted to be a poet.

Weren't you a conceptual artist?

I wasn't a conceptual artist before being a poet. I published two of my books and then I became a conceptual artist for two or three years; and this was a break—at the time I didn't write—between '68 and '70 I didn't write at all, I only did conceptual art.

Was it difficult for you not to write?

No, not at all. The social experience of being a conceptual artist—we were doing it in a group, called OHO—was tremendous, was wonderful. I joined the four other younger persons and made them more known, socialized them for the foreign galleries. This was how I first came to America. The Museum of Modern Art invited me, and this blew my mind. I spent July 1970 in New York, and this was a tremendous experience for me.

Have you translated American poetry into Slovenian?

No, I mostly translated what I had to do for bread, and I translated from French and from Italian—basically novels and a kind of encyclopedia. This was because I had to fight very strongly to be published, to publish my poems. I was not in the position to choose what I wanted to translate. Slovenia is very small, and you have the translator for English poetry, you have the translator for French poetry ... It wasn't a question of the Tito regime or Communism, it's just that the place is small and everything was set, and I didn't want to make more trouble for myself by eating other people's bread. So I just translated Simone de Beauvoir, some Walter de la Mare stories, some history—nothing that stayed with me, except for a little bit of Stevens, a little bit of Williams. But I didn't publish them by book, I published translations of American poets only in magazines.

Which other American poets, of any century—

It started with Eliot, with Pound—Pound was a big shock to me. I read it in Italian, also I discovered Williams through Italian translations. And it went gradually: Pound, Williams, then Stevens. And then the really big transformation for me was Ashbery. I read *Three Poems* and I was changed—it was something that completely fit my chemistry. The way he was using language was very close to me. He changed me, he changed my perception. Everything else after I went through *Three Poems* was completely normal, easy. For me at that time, Ashbery had the clues of the language, of the American language, in his hands. He was the major force.

What about poets younger than Ashbery?

I tremendously admire Jorie Graham—she has some kind of intensity, intensity from different layers, like French culture, Italian ... She has tremendous power for me.

And now, I'm completely taken by Kevin Hart. And Charlie Simic—I needed a long time before I got his whole ... really got his importance for the English language and American language. For a long time I considered him somehow a French poet in English, and I needed a decade to realize that he travelled in the heart of the heart of the English language and transformed English. It's a very special, mysterious story—how Charlie Simic travelled in the heart of the heart of the American tradition.

Well, many, many poets. Bob Perelman when I was young—the first poems of Bob Perelman I loved. James Tate strikes me as somebody I'm very close to. We have many things in common, only that he's more crazy and more playful, and historically more secure (being an American, not having Fascism and Communism and concentration camps there in this century). In a way, therefore, he was able to play with language and he was able to dare more. In [*Worshipful Company of*] *Fletchers*, I admire his immense courage in going toward madness, challenging the borders of madness. There is a religious part in going through this, which is wonderful and which saves this civilization—those bits which stay are enough to have a perfectly sane and wonderful civilization, even if it seems there are crumbs.

Very different poets: Leslie Scalapino, two books of Leslie's I like very much. Michael Palmer, Mark Levine's book *Debt*, Phyllis Levin, Mary Ruefle.

There is only one younger Slovene poet who hit me completely, and this is Aleš Debeljak. When I returned from two years in Mexico in winter '81, I read four lines, and this was a total hit for me, something which came from unknown space, something definitely outside of my range. Ales practically didn't read me. But after four lines of his poetry, I sensed that a new era was coming for Slovene poetry. At that time I was completely imbued with Spanish poetry, especially Vallejo. My mind was part of the Spanish world at that moment. But with Ales it was one sentence: " ... astonished the thought after the scream moves into the speech." It was like he would shoot me [mimes the motions of a bow and arrow], he would throw [mimes a javelin thrower] ... This sentence marked a new age. Four lines marked the territory as his territory, so with his first poems he was immediately the owner of the powerful position in ... in everything. Basically he's the strongest poet of the '80s in Slovenia.

The American poets you mentioned seem to have in common an obsession with revitalizing language, revitalizing the lyric, whether through the anti-lyric or through working against closure, eloquence, lyricism. Is that something you sympathize with in your work?

I'm always afraid of ... for example, I'm afraid of the language poets. At the end of the seventies, I was a language poet in Slovenia myself, and came to a dead end.

But still ... At the moment I wake up in the night — it started about three years ago, in November '95, I guess, after I didn't write at all for four and a half years, when my kids had problems, war was going on in Yugoslavia. I came to a border at Yaddo in '89, and everything somehow was as if my head would explode, and I was afraid of poetry. There was this terrible sorrow of the war, and I was not able to write anything about the war, I was just silent for four and a half years. Then I started to write again, in spring '94, and I wrote *Ambergris*, which is selected in this book [*The Four Questions of Melancholy*]. For the last three years, I woke up at 3 o'clock or 4 o'clock in the night, in Ljubljana, and I went to my studio, because I need a special place to be comfortable, to write, and I always was writing between 5 and 7 in the morning. I was doing this in Ljubljana, then I went to Paris and spent December '95 in Paris, in Maison des Artistes Internationals. At my right hand was my brother, who's a painter, in the same institution, but I didn't know ... I knew he was applying, because for painters it's easier — Slovenian painters have a place there, but to be accepted as a writer at this Maison you have to have a book in French — and at my left hand was rue des Rosiers, which is a Jewish street in Paris. So on one side I read Zohar constantly, and on the other side I read Giordano Bruno and Saint

John of the Cross (the place which interests me the most, I guess, is fifteenth-century Spain, where there was this incredible mixture and power of Jewishness and Catholicism). This is something which really torments me, where these two traditions come together—Zohar, and on the other side, Giordano Bruno. Giordano Bruno is something completely mysterious to me, though I can read and enjoy him, as Artaud was a very strong influence for me, and I still like to go to Artaud at his utmost craziest. Another poet who influenced me a lot and I love very much is Attila József, the Hungarian poet who committed suicide in the '30s. And of course Czeslaw Milosz was also one of my fathers. And I haven't mentioned Dane Zajc, who was the poet who started me as a poet, at the beginning—he came to read when I was a student, I was 22, and he had such a magical presence, an angel jumped out of his shoulders.

What aspects of your poetry do you consider to be distinctly Slovenian? Is it a certain kind of pathos or melancholy? In your poem"Versailles," for example, you write, "You are Slovenian, therefore sad"; the title of your book is The Four Questions *of* Melancholy; *and in his introduction to that collection, Christopher Merrill says "if Slovenia has a national disease, it is melancholia." But you don't seem like a poet of sadness, and your work is often humorous and warm. Is there a certain emotional tenor in your poetry that can be identified as Slovenian?*

I don't know about that, because I think I'm very anti-Slovenian in my general status. But for sure, a lot of rural imagery comes through, because Slovenia is quite a rural place. I'm a city person, but I spent many summers of my early childhood in the country, my great-grandparents had a house there, in a small village, so I mixed with country boys. I remember when I was translated into Italian, somebody said that it seems to him I come from the woods and from the mountains—not a nature poet, but a pastoral poet, which I'm definitely not!

What is Edvard Kocbek's role for you? You wrote that poem for him on his birthday—

He's probably the biggest poet—as Slovenians consider him now, he's the biggest poet of the second part of the twentieth century—and he was tremendously important as a political figure, as a thinker, as an essayist, and to a certain degree he was an incredible burden to me, and in that poem ["To Edvard Kocbek on his 70th Birthday"] it shows. Also he was a friend of my father, and I experienced him in person, when I was twelve or thirteen, when he was a dissident and was very sad, in political terms. But he doesn't seem like a sad poet—he seems a very vital, very outgoing poet.

You mentioned that you feel like an anti-Slovenian poet in a way. There's that now-famous Charles Simic quote where he points out that at some point everyone's tribe will ask him to assent to murder. In your poem "Folk Song," you've written that "Every true poet is a monster. / He destroys people and their speech." And in "Eclipse," "I grew tired of the image of my tribe / and moved out"—

This was actually my first line in my life, this is the line where I started as a poet. It was a gesture of how to get rid of the claustrophobia of Slovenia, the cage of smallness there, being entrapped in a small nation.

Do you think the poet has to break out of that cage in order not to be partisan—

Yes, yes—I always wanted to go as far as possible ... to be free. This is the reason why I enjoyed Mexico so much, why I enjoyed the States so much. And I felt the freest when I was far away.

So do you feel like the Slovenian poet has to work against the tribe yet still represent it?

Of course, but every young poet has to break the common pattern. To become a poet is to step into the void, to jump into the dark, to make some kind of treason toward your education, toward your parents.

You mentioned Artaud and Saint John of the Cross, and I find a visionary, or mystical, current in your work, as well as an ontological one: in a way you're arguing with God and in some poems you replace God. What is your idea of God, and how does it affect your poetry?

When I was very young, I had written 'Poetry is because man is not God himself,' and this is what is the most difficult to bear ... . It's constant drama for me, because I was raised a little bit as a Catholic, but ... to go to the mosque or to go to Catholic church, or to be part of Jewish rituals is tremendously moving, and I become dizzy, many times I'm on the verge of crying, and still I'm not a believer, I'm not a member of any confession. So I basically don't know what happens. As Kevin Hart said today, religion has incredibly dark powers: God can crush you, if you, as I do with language, try to reach the borders of everything possible, the borders of language, to go to total transgression, to go to total blasphemy—it can happen, and it happened to me in '89. It was as if God took everything out of me, it was as if my head would explode, as if my brain would melt, and I was left in a completely dark, cold place, in total terror and feeling guilty and not being able to help myself, and I was not able to write for four and a half years after this happened to me. But still, I envy Kevin Hart's … God, because it's a God who comes with great gifts to him. I'm constantly escaping God, quarreling with Him, and making terrible gestures, terrible blasphemies. I'm a cannibal against God, sometimes, and still I'm crushed in total humility and … Also at Yaddo I experienced a presence … this was the presence of God, a presence of total whiteness, and total gentleness, and total tenderness, and it was a presence that didn't have shape, didn't have physical presence, but it was there, and it was probably a warning sign … that I should stop in my search of total transgression and total blasphemy.

So you feel like you were punished for being defiant? In some poems, like "History," "Proverbs," and "Who's Who," you seem to mythologize, or, at least, immortalize yourself, deify yourself—

But it was constantly an ironic line—that "Who's Who" poem is a poem about how to crush your own ego, how to make it so pathetical and so exposed that you break it … you just crush it.

But you seem like a rebellious poet—

Well, I hope not, I hope I am also a tender, and gentle, and subdued, and happy poet.

I can see what you mean about crushing your own ego, because in "Drums" you say "I am the people's point of view," and in "Homage to Hat & Uncle Guido & Eliot," you mention the "song of songs of the Pan-Šalamunian religion / terribly democratic people's institution," In one of your untitled poems from Arena, you say, "I am the food of great masses." But just as you move out of your tribe, you also embrace it.

Yes. One of the biggest obsessions for me as a Slovenian is that I don't have ancestors who are known in the world. France Preseren was—is—our greatest poet and no one else knows him. Now I'm more comfortable because Plecnik has become very famous and because what Ales is doing will travel, it will go through. I tried to share my American experience and also this kind of spirit to just go—go west—with some other younger poets in Slovenia before, but nobody was fit enough, until Ales.

How did Slovenia's independence in 1991 affect you personally?

The fact that Communism collapsed was something which really made me relaxed—it was a wonderful moment. When Communism as a system collapsed, the body really relaxed, the skin got shinier, and you felt relieved. Things which made you paranoid before, because of the completely irrational possibility that the Communist repression could squeeze you, was something which made you sick and tired and … unhappy. When this collapsed, we were on our own and were not in the hands of some power outside of ours and we could arrange our lives as we were fit to.

At the moment, Slovenia is somewhat shy, somehow insecure—it lacks tradition. There are many things which were done in other European nations in the 17th, 18th, 19th centuries which were not there—there are many lacunas, and we need time to balance all these things. But I do acknowledge a much higher energy among young people and a much more daring way of life, and they have more power to go out and to mix with the rest of the world.

What is your view of the role of play—humor, wit, absurdity, parody, mockery—in poetry? Many American poetry critics, and even poets, seem blind to the seriousness of much humor, but it seems a crucial element of any subversive poetry.

I don't have any views on it, and I don't think of it. It comes as part of my body, my movement, my dance. I enjoy it … . Play and irony: this is not enough. Irony is good to destroy authority or power; it's subversive, but it's not enough for poetry. At the end it's not a very important thing. At the end, it's a very important thing how in the center you are, how you are able to be there where you are needed to be, in the heat of the language. There is always a place in how language historically develops that is the frontier, and there is a center of a frontier, and this is the position that is the highest point of the technology of the language—it's like a moment of supreme power.

The question—the interrogative—seems central to your work. In "Car le vice," you write, "Such are the incredibly pathetic questions / Tomaž Šalamun puts to his soul to get / to the bottom of things. But there is no thing. Or / bottom." And several of your poems—"Jonah," "The Difference," "Let's Wait"—are in the form of a series of questions and responses. And of course you have "The Four Questions of Melancholy." Why are there so many questions for Tomaž Šalamun?

No idea ... Well, the four questions of melancholy is probably a kabbalistic question ... The way questions are like screws, screws in heaven, they are like powers that break through the horizon and they want to go as far as possible, and they are the way to get as far as possible. They are tools to get as high as possible, as *in* as possible.

But the questions are "incredibly pathetic."

The questions *are* pathetic, many of them are completely, outrageously insane. But this is like making love, making the ground fecund—these are my sperm, this is sperm, sperm—in heaven and everywhere around to make the world fecund.

CHARLES WRIGHT

Charles Wright's most recent books of poetry are *A Short History of the Shadow* (Farrar, Straus and Giroux, 2002) and *Buffalo Yoga* (Farrar, Straus and Giroux, 2004). *The Grave of the Right Hand* (1970), *Hard Freight* (1973), *Bloodlines* (1975), and *China Trace* (1977) were collected in *Country Music: Selected Early Poems* (Wesleyan University Press, 1982); *The Southern Cross* (1981), *The Other Side of the River* (1984), *Zone Journals* (1988), and *Xionia* (1990) were collected in *The World of the Ten Thousand Things: Selected Poems 1980-1990* (Farrar, Straus and Giroux, 1990); and *Chickamauga* (1995), *Black Zodiac* (1997), which won the Pulitzer Prize and the National Book Critics Circle Award, and *Appalachia* (1998) were collected in *Negative Blue: Selected Later Poems* (Farrar, Straus and Giroux, 2000). He is also the author of two books of essays and interviews, *Halflife* (1988) and *Quarter Notes* (1995), both published by the University of Michigan Press. He has taught at the University of Virginia since 1983. This interview was conducted by Andrew Zawacki at Wright's home in Charlottesville, Virginia, on January 19, 1998. It appeared in Volume 16, Number 2 of *Verse*.

Black Zodiac *was published very quickly after* Chickamauga. *Have you been more productive than usual in the last three or four years?*

I did have quite an intense spell between the end of *Chickamauga* and the end of the book I've just finished, *Appalachia*, during which, I think it was about three years and four months, I wrote two books. That's sort of an unheard-of situation for me. It took me five years to write *Chickamauga* and then it took three years and, as I say, four months to do *Black Zodiac* and *Appalachia*. Since *Appalachia*, which was finished in August of '97, I haven't really written anything; we're now in January, January the nineteenth of '98. I attribute that, I hope, to the finishing-up of a long project that I'd started back in 1971, when I got the idea for a series of books. I didn't know it was going to take twenty-seven years, but I think the wind kind of went out of my sails when I finished the last two books. I got speeded up toward the end, because I felt that I saw the end in sight, and I wanted to make sure that I got it done. Part of the impetus, also, is psychological, because my old friend Larry Levis had died at the age of forty-nine, dropped dead of a heart attack, and I said, "Jesus, I'd better get this thing finished; you never know." So that's part of it. The other part is that I had in mind what I wanted to do. The only other time that I had a writing spurt like that was years ago when I did *Bloodlines* and *China Trace* in a quick spurt of time—not quite as quickly as *Black Zodiac* and *Appalachia*, but then again I feel as though I knew what I wanted to do this time, knew how I thought I could do it, and always at my back I'd hear ...

In Black Zodiac *you speak of "journal and landscape" as "discredited form" and "discredited subject matter." Why do you feel that the journal form specifically has been discredited?*

Well, perhaps I didn't choose my word as accurately as I should have. I thought of the journal form being discredited as a conveyor of serious literary ambition. Usually the journal form is thought to encompass shut-in women, old guys trying to make sense of or justification for what they've done or haven't done in their lives, and so on. What I was trying to do was to make the journal form and the idea of a serious look at landscape, which is thought of as a kind of Sunday painterly occupation—I was trying to make both of those into a serious vehicle for saying something that exists possibly beyond each. Since neither is generally thought of as a repository for poetic seriousness, but as poetic gesture, I wanted to take them both and see what I could do with them vis-à-vis ... this sounds pretentious, but the spiritual journey that I felt I've been on for the last thirty years, when I've been trying to write these poems. And I was trying to imbue them, or endow them, or at least inject them with the kind of seriousness that I thought they could contain and could regenerate in poetry. One never knows whether one has done that or not. It's the sort of thing that everyone tells you not to do: don't write a poem about the sunset, and quite properly so, because you can't beat the sunset. Well, probably one shouldn't write serious poems in a journal form, or write landscape that is imbued with something beyond the landscape. But since you're not supposed to, that seemed to be a good reason to try to do it. And since I like looking at landscape, and since my mental faculties seem better equipped for notation and observation rather than flow-through narrative, I thought perhaps these are good vehicles for me to try to get in and drive, and so I did.

Do you keep a journal, and have the journal poems grown out of journal entries? The reason I ask is that you've written that a poet's life consists only of those things not good enough to go into his poems. Has that somehow put an extra burden on the journal poems?

I think writing itself puts an extra burden on anything you try to put down, just because of the fact that you're putting it down, and once you've put it down, it's ineradicable to a certain extent. I don't keep a journal. I used to keep a little book of notations that weren't even interesting enough to be called *pensées* that I collected in *Halflife*; it was sort of a commonplace notebook, just things I would think of from time to time, and I did that for about ten years or so and then got tired of it; I thought it was rather pretentious and what I was saying wasn't very interesting really. So I don't keep a journal, and the journal poems do not come out of or exist previously in any kind of journal form. And I don't do them any more: I did that series of *Zone Journals* and *Xionia* as both a technical experiment in the long line and the idea that you could get anything into a journal form and get it in there accurately and unrandomly if you organized it right. So even though they are journals, they are journals perhaps conceptually, but they are poems technically and actually, which is to say that they partake of the beginning, middle, and end of a poem, rather than a journal where everything is kind of in the middle. They take as their structures the seasonal changes, which is maybe not a brilliant structure, but at least it's workable. They allow, it seems to me, so much more of a possibility for inclusion of material. As I said before, they seem to fit the processes of my mental capacities, which are notational and schematic and impressionistic, as opposed to logical and mapped-out. The idea of a journal—it's sort of like Scott Fitzgerald in the fountain outside The Plaza—the idea of the journal seemed like a good idea at the time. Anything that you've stopped doing seems sort of old-hat, but I think that the way the journals operated, and the way they contributed to the structural assembly of my poems, continues to this day. Which is to say that the poems I'm writing now, and the longer poems I wrote in *Black Zodiac* and the one in *Chickamauga*, "Sprung Narratives," partake of that idea I generated in the journals. And one always likes to think that one is doing something that either hasn't been done before or hasn't been fully explored before, and at the time I thought that the idea of the poem as journal, rather than the journal as poem, hadn't been really explored as far as it might have. Of course journals have been explored and poems have been explored, but trying to get a finite poem into a kind of infinitely open form, which a journal is, I found seductive. One of the reasons I don't write prose or a memoir or that sort of thing is because—at least as far as my project has been for the last twenty-seven years, these series of books, series of trilogies that I've been doing—to me, anything that's been interesting in my life or that my life has generated has wormed its way into the poems in one way or another. The husk, or the narrative shell of that, would be what I would then go over and try to fill in with artificial material if I were going to do some kind of narrative about it. The heart of it, or for lack of a better word, the soul of it, is all contained in the poems. And again, that's another way that the journal poems were interesting, because I could say things in a journal that one would never let oneself say perhaps in a poem quite so openly. Because you could always say, oh well, this is a journal, people admit everything in their journals, why not be more open in this poem. Anything that I've had to say about my life, that was of any interest to me, has been said in my poems. And God knows if it's not of any interest to me, it won't be of any interest to anyone else, so I, you know, sweep the husks away and chew on the kernels.

There's a fairly explicit struggle in Black Zodiac *as to whether memory redeems or not. What is your hope, however skeptically you check it, for the role of memory in language or poetry?*

It's the case of the disillusioned lover. For years and years I thought memory was the golden ladder to heaven, and it may still be. But as I get older, memory tends to become memories, and memories are not memory. Memory is a tactile, tensile thread along which our whole lives have passed; memories are little snapshots that are pleasing or displeasing, but you have to work very hard to make them into something whole. The painter David Hockney has a process with photography where he takes snapshots, hundreds of snapshots, of a really banal or everyday scene or event, and then puts them together to make a narrative out of it. He calls them "joiners." They are actually layerings: he layers these photographs together to re-create the narrative that was there, and by re-creating the narrative, he lets you look at it from different points of view, and it's a fascinating visual experimentation. Now, what he's done is taken the snapshots and made the event into something whole again, with different refractions. I suppose one could do the same thing with memories and make them into memory, which is, as I say, the line that runs between the beginning and the end. So I am of two minds now that I see there are different ways to do this, and so I often think, well, maybe I shouldn't be doing it this way, maybe I should be doing it some other way. So when I say it's best not to remember at all, I mean it's best not to just have isolated snapshot kind of memories; I don't mean that it's best not to believe in the efficacy and the inevitability of the line of memory that connects us to our past and to our future. I guess when I feel that I've fallen into the memories pit, that I have then tried to reconstruct it in the way that Hockney reconstructs a photograph, in the ways that Paul Cézanne reconstructs the visual scene through the nonlinear approaches that he used to make his narratives and his representational paintings.

But it's probably a battle that's of no interest to anyone but me, but when I'm writing the poem, it is of supreme interest to me, because I am trying to make something out of something, which is harder than making [laughs] something out of nothing, actually, because the somethings that you pick have to end up being the something that you see. Whereas if you make it up out of nothing, you have no obligation to anybody; otherwise, you have a great obligation to yourself, which is always the worst obligation to have and the one that's hardest to bring to fruition.

Regarding that obligation to oneself: in Black Zodiac *you write, "Before you bear witness, / Be sure to have something that calls for a witnessing ... / Don't shine what's expendable." Is this a personal issue, or does it also have historical or aesthetic components? Is it being shrugged in contemporary American poetry?*

Yes. One always likes to think that one occupies a certain high ground, be it an imagistic highground, a narrative highground if you write narrative, a technical highground. What you don't want to occupy is the moral highground, because the moral highground is so full of people that there's no high ground there, because everybody thinks he has the right answer, and nobody does of course. If you have it for yourself you're lucky. I guess what I was talking about ... I was talking to myself—I never talk to anybody else. One, I found it fruitless. Two, the best advice I ever got was when I was fifteen years old and a man named Jim Perry at the little school I went to in North Carolina called Sky Valley (there were eight of us in this school one year; it was a farm, and they had a school one year)—he said, "People are always going to believe what they want to believe, you can't tell them anything." And he was right. So I talk to myself in my poems. I speak to myself, I give myself instructions, I try to carry them out. Any kind of injunction, any kind of nudging, any kind of moral password that I give in a poem, is to myself alone, and I don't pretend to speak for anyone else. One has to keep oneself alert, one has to try to keep one's own standards. If one's own standards aren't higher than what one perceives the standards of the rest of the situation are, then one is in trouble. That's why the moral highground is always so crowded [laughs], because everybody thinks he's got this answered, but of course they don't—you do, right [laughs]? So I said yes because yes, I feel that way, but only personally. I would never dream of telling anybody out loud what they should do. Like everybody else, I tell everybody what they should do, under my breath.

How is it, given the fact of your work, let alone its thematic concerns, that "the unexamined life's no different from the examined life"?

Well, that's kind of a tongue-in-cheek statement, I guess. I meant only that your life is your life, and whether you examine it or don't examine it, it rolls along, or it doesn't roll along. If you spend your life examining your life, as I do, obsessively, and probably ridiculously so, then there's no such thing as the unexamined life. Therefore, the unexamined life is the same as the examined life. One doesn't go about saying: I'm now going to examine my life and see what this comes to. It's a daily process, I think, if you write out of your life, as most people do. Even Eliot, as we found out, wrote almost exclusively out of his own life. So since there's no such thing for a writer as the unexamined life, then like all statements, it's both a true and a false statement. It was probably a little cuter than I meant it to be when I put it down.

In one of your newer poems, you say that "the dream of a reclusive life, a strict, essential solitude, / Is a younger hermit's dream." Was that your dream once, and how has it changed?

Yes, in my fantasy life I have dreamed of the perfect reclusion being the best way to think and to write about what one was thinking about. As one gets older, that becomes less and less of an attractive option, and more and more of a possible necessity. Any time it becomes a possible necessity, instead of a choice, anything starts to lose its luster a little bit. My ambition now is to be what John Ashbery once termed himself to be, "a well-known recluse about town."

How often do you return to Italy now, and why?

For some years, I didn't go back at all. After my son was born in 1970, I didn't go back for fifteen years, until 1985, because I really didn't want to go around with a kid on a backpack, that sort of thing, because Italy was still an aesthetic continuum for me. In '85, Mark Strand and his family and I and my family rented a house in northern Italy, and we went back for two months. My son was fifteen at the time, and so that was OK. Since then, my wife and I have gone back almost every year. It gets shorter and shorter each year, because I like less and less to be away from home, as it turns out. It used to be I wanted to go for two years, then it was two months, now it's two weeks. I go because it still remains the start of everything for me, as far as writing, looking, thinking. I have a very good friend there, Gaetano Prampolini, who has a little house in the town of Spello in Umbria, and we go visit him usually every other year, and then we go somewhere the intervening year. I like to go eat the food and look at the landscape, and I like to see Gaetano [laughs], I guess that's the reason, more than anything else. Also, the world is divided into two kinds of people: those who want to go somewhere new every time they go somewhere, and those who want to go back to the same place. I want to go back to the same place. Monet wanted to go back to the same place. Bruce Chatwin always wanted to go somewhere different. Also, Italy is the only country except England where I speak a little bit of the language, so it's easier to get around.

You've spoken of the inclusiveness of the journal and of the long line. Have you ever considered returning to the prose poem, which you abandoned after The Grave of the Right Hand, *as an equally inclusive strategy?*

I've thought a lot about the prose poem and going back to the prose poem, and I thought for years that just to effect a kind of, if not perfect, at least not imperfect, circularity, I should end this project, the coda, with five prose poems, the way I started [laughs]. But the reason I haven't is because somewhere along the line, no pun intended, I became married to the idea of the line of the poem, and it's a marriage which I don't want to break up. I got to the point in extending the line, after *China Trace*, that there didn't seem to be much purpose in then pushing it one more step and going back into prose, because I had come all the way from prose. Ultimately, I guess I agree with what Eugenio Montale, whose work I translated some thirty years ago, said about poetry. He said that all poetry rises out of prose and longs to return to it. Like all great writers, he didn't explain that image, but I think what he means is that it's in that tension of trying to go back to prose that the poetic line gets its vibrancy and its electricity. But once it goes back into prose, then it becomes just prose, even if it's good prose, it becomes just prose, and, in that case, something lesser. Once I accepted that fact, I never really wanted to go back to the prose poem, although I too love the prose poem still, and it was a great … it was a great what? It was a great opening for me when I first tried to do them many years ago, and I still have a great affection for them, and I like to read them, and I like to see them, I like to see what other people are doing with them. It's just that I feel that if I went back to the prose poem, I would be going back to something rather than forward to something. Maybe it's like saving the best thing on your plate til last, because you think it'll taste better. Maybe someday, but at the moment I'm too much under the sway of that comment by Montale to ever try to do it.

You've translated Montale and Campana. Do you translate much any more, if not for publication, then as an exercise between poems or between books?

That's how I got into translating in the first place, when I couldn't write my own poems. Again, I bring up my friend Strand, he and I were in school together, and this was what he said, "Well, if you can't write your own poems, why don't you try translating? You speak a little Italian." So that's how I got into it. Then I translated Montale and got very deeply into that, and I did do Campana back in 1984, after I finished *The Other Side of the River*. I didn't know what I was going to do, and so I translated Dino Campana. Boy, was it a lot of work, and I realized that I was not quite up to this endeavor any more. My Italian had deteriorated to such an extent that I was looking up every word, instead of every other word. Since then I haven't really done much. I translated five poems by a guy named Franco Buffoni, whom I met at a Montale conference in 1996 in Florence. He was a nice fellow, and he said, "Hey, if you ever want to translate any of my stuff ..." He sent me a little thing that had five poems. So I tried that. They were really quite easy to translate, or should have been, and they were quite difficult for me, so I realized that I've got to give this up. The reason I did Campana was he was one of the two important early Italian influences on me, Montale being the other. There was no stylistic influence by Campana, it was just his legend as the Italian Rimbaud, the *poet maudit* and all of that sort of thing, and so I thought I'd translate him, and it was fun. But as Minnie Pearl used to say when she was finished playing: "We're through playin' now." I'm through translating now, I think.

The last year has witnessed the deaths of many American poets: most recently Larry Levis, as you've mentioned, Denise Levertov, James Laughlin, William Matthews. Before that, Amy Clampitt, Allen Ginsberg, James Dickey, Jane Kenyon, James Merrill ... Do you have a sense that there's a generation of American poetry waning?

That's actually a hard question to answer, because I never thought of it in generational terms. Were I in my twenties, I would think about it in generational terms. Now that I'm sixty-two, it's for the most part friends who have died. I knew most of those people, I'd met them all, several of them were very good friends of mine. It's true that the generation above me, the generation of Merrill and Levine, Justice, Hollander and Merwin and Kinnell, all of those people—a huge generation born in the twenties, is now entering their seventies, and they are going to be dropping out as time goes by. One of the reasons I don't think in terms of generational loss is because my generation seems somehow caught between the generation of those born in the twenties and those born in the forties, which is another huge generation that's coming on behind us. Those of us born in the thirties, there are very few of us. Mark Strand once said, "Charles, we're a generation of three: me and you and Simic." Well, that's not true, it's just that we're all good friends and so he was joking. But in that joke is a kernel of truth, in that those of us in the thirties are kind of squeezed in. We don't really have a generation: we're either tacked onto the end of the twenties or tacked onto the beginning of the forties. If I were an ambitious young poetry climber, I would say, well, that generation is passing away and our generation is coming. But I can't say that, because I'm not sure we have a generation. But I do feel that there is, as there hasn't been perhaps for the last ten or fifteen years, a movement upward, a generation of movement, and I believe that people born in the forties are starting to muscle their way up. The thing about the generation of the twenties is that there were so many of them; it's going to be a long time muscling them out, as far as that sort of attitude goes. But yes, I guess I do have a feeling that there is a slight movement going on, although I'm not sure what the movement is, other than what I just said.

Your new poems include quite a bit of technological lingo: downloads, on-lines, printouts, meta-optics, and so on. To what extent does a spiritual poetry, in order to be legitimate now, need to accommodate this language of the time?

Part of the fact of using them is that I don't really know what they mean. I mean, I know how they operate, but I do not do computers, and I certainly don't do optics in any kind of scientific way. The words seem, when I use them, to have a specific reference to what I'm talking about, outside their sphere of influence, and so I do use them. It's not really an attempt to be "modern," as Hart Crane would have had it, when he had, you know, "a rip-tooth of the sky's acetylene," that sort of thing, and would write about cars and trains and so on. I don't feel that I have to write about computers and what all of that business is going to signify to my life, or to you-all's life, I guess. But I don't want to try to avoid it either, so when it pops into my head, I use it, if it seems specific to the moment. I'm not trying to drag it in, I'm not trying to do it to show off, and I'm not trying to fit the language of the times into my poems, because I think my poems use the language of the times, they just may not use as many scientific allusions as other people. Because I'm not a scientific kind of guy.

*In one new poem, you speak of "our landscape, / Bourgeois, heart-breakingly sub-
urban." Do you ever feel the heart-breakingly suburban is a kind of privilege?*

I was talking about my back yard, and the exterior life one lives; I feel that
my interior life is anything but that. I think that there is a … I don't want to
say a school or a branch or a movement, but there are an awful lot of people
who write, as my mother's friend malapropped all the time, "heart-render-
ingly" suburban poems, which is to say they're trying to make nothing out of
something, and they too often succeed. That's another *genre* that I've taken
on, the back yard poem, trying to make it more than just the back yard poem:
"Sitting on the back stoop with a can of Bud Light watchin' my bird dogs
and the john-boat leaned up against the garage …" I think there is too much
outer suburban concentration these days. When I say that, you're right, it was
slightly tongue-in-cheek, because I can be anywhere and write the same poem. I
mean, I can be in the Taj Mahal or I can be, you know, down on the riverbank
under a lean-to, and I'm still going to be writing the same poem, because my
poem doesn't openly depend on where I am. That may spark the beginning
of it, but it's not where the poem goes. I live a fairly typical American life, I
have a house and a back yard. It's middle class, I'm middle class, I make no
apologies for that; I don't know what else to do. Phil Levine's mother once
cracked that he's the only person she knows who started out in the middle
class and worked desperately down to the lower classes in his work. I've just
sort of sat and spun around where I started. That doesn't mean that my mind
has sat and spun in east Tennessee, or as it is now, in central Virginia. I don't
know, I don't find any long-term disease in being middle class, it's what you
do with what you've got. You can take the back yard and move it anywhere,
just as long as it doesn't stay the back yard.

*You were enrolled in a creative writing program, and now you teach in one.
What are some of the responsibilities of teaching creative writing? How much
involves directing students, and how much is a case of what Thoreau said, that
that government is best which governs least?*

Well, I think Thoreau was right about his comment on writing classes in general
[laughs]. It depends on whether you're teaching an advanced graduate group or
whether you're teaching an undergraduate group. There's more "You shouldn't
do this, you shouldn't do that" that goes on in the undergraduate, because
they've been around it less. If you're lucky and get a good graduate group, you
should just do the blocking for them and get out of the way, and that's what

often happens. There are … how do I say this? When I teach, I only talk about their poems. I don't talk about what they should *do* in them, where they should *go* next, unless they ask me—of course, I never know where anybody should go next, I don't even know where I'm going next, how can I tell anybody else where they should go next in their work? The question that's usually asked most often is: Should I try a long poem? Well, I say, sure, try a long poem, you know. If you don't like it, go back to writing short poems. Again, I'm talking about graduate students, because the battle that started out in the fifties and sixties to get writers into teaching courses has been won many, many years ago, and the students who come to graduate classes now know so much more than any of the students did earlier on, because they've been through many undergraduate workshops with good writers. There are just a few things that you can tell someone or teach someone: Donald Barthelme has said prayer was one of them, self-laceration was another, and "notions of the lousy" was a third, and I think that's about all you need to be able to teach them. If you can teach them notions of the lousy, there's no other job you need to do. Almost everybody who gets into a graduate writing program is competent, or they wouldn't get in the program. Now, going from competence to occasional brilliance is a large step, and you don't get that many who can make that step. But that doesn't mean it's not fun to talk about their poems to see what they're doing, to encourage them—to let them imitate whomever they want to, because eventually if they're any good, they'll realize that's what they're doing and then they'll stop, and as they go along they will have learned something by doing the imitation. So I think the first time a poem comes up in a workshop and somebody says, "God, that sounds just like W.S. Merwin!" and "Jesus, that's Galway Kinnell!" or "Adrienne Rich already said …"—so what? I'm of two minds, of course, about teaching in a writing program. I think there are too many people out there writing, but there are too many people out there doing everything, so I don't know that that's such a bad thing. The good stuff always rises to the top. The bad stuff will rise to the top too [laughs], so you have to be selective when you look at what's arisen. But I don't think anyone has ever been damaged by going to a creative writing class or workshop. I guess the one thing I really think is that you should try as hard as possible not to encourage people to write the way you do. I mean, if they want to, fine, they'll get out of it, but don't make them, and that's what happens in more cases than I think it should in workshops. And as Clint Eastwood said in *High Plains Drifter*: "It's what's inside them that makes them do that, teach that way." So I say: go to a place that doesn't have that stuff inside of the teacher.

Does your wife Holly's work as a photographer have any impact on yours?

Not really. Holly is much more intellectually attuned to her art than I am to mine. Mine seems to be, as I've said before, more impressionistic, more nota-tional, more language-oriented, more follow-the-image-and-see-where-it-will-take-you. Holly is much more conceptual: she gets ideas for these large series, which I find just amazingly beautiful and amazingly brilliant, because I can't do that, and we always love what we can't do, you know, if what we can't do is something that's good, and I feel that about her work. I have been influenced by a lot of the books that she has on photography. By looking at the pictures and seeing certain set-ups, in the early days I would write poems from certain photographs. There was one: I used a picture by an Italian photographer named Ugo Mulas, it's called "Bar Jamaica, 1953-54," which is a bar in Milano that I used to go to in 1959 and 1960, and I put my own people into the positions that he had his people in in the same scene. Manuelo Alvarez Bravo, the great Mexican photographer, I've looked at his work from time to time, in the early days, and have not exactly used things from it but been influenced by his way of looking at landscape. But for the most part, not really. It's a different kind of enterprise, even though they're both imagistic, they're a different kind of enterprise. We seem to be working on the same spool perhaps, but at different ends of that spool.

The Wallace Stevens Journal is publishing a special issue on apocalyptic language in Stevens. Is the encroaching millennium making its way into your work?

Haven't thought about it at all, other than getting ready to call my next book *Millennium Falcon* ... No, seriously, I haven't really thought about it, except that I'm hoping that my third and last trilogy, which will be comprised of *Chickamauga, Black Zodiac,* and *Appalachia,* plus this illusory coda that I'm trying to write now, and which will be called, I think, *Journeyman,* will come out in 2001 probably—one of my favorite movies. So that's the only millennial concern that I have, other than to be as far away from Times Square on the first of January 2000 as I can possibly get. It really hasn't. My language has been apocalyptic since 1961. Why should I try the prophet now, for just the millennium? There'll be another one.

AUGUST KLEINZAHLER

August Kleinzahler has published numerous books of poetry, most recently *The Strange Hours Travelers Keep* (2003), *Live from the Hong Kong Nile Club* (2000), and *Green Sees Things in Waves* (1998), all from Farrar, Straus and Giroux. In Spring 1999, he was a visiting professor of poetry at the University of Texas' Michener Center for Writers. Andrew Osborn conducted the first session of this interview on a bright early-April afternoon in the back yard of the small house Kleinzahler had rented in Austin. Ten days later, they looked over the first session's transcript in his living room and taped a few more questions and answers. This interview appeared in Volume 17, Numbers 2 and 3 / Volume 18, Number 1 of *Verse*.

In the introduction to Live from the Hong Kong Nile Club, *you mention that by 15 or 16, you were already committed to poetic pursuits.*

I remember very vividly. We were reading the Romantics—Keats and Shelley and Wordsworth—and, like a lot of adolescent boys, I was transported by Keats' odes. One day I was just sitting on the grass, cutting study hall, and—it was an early spring day—I wrote a poem about the late-winter/early-spring grass. ABAB, roughly pentameter, maybe blended pentameter-tetrameter. Class-time passed in an instant. It was one of the most pleasurable, diverting experiences of my life. I got a neuromuscular ... not ecstasy, but intense pleasure.

This was from the writing itself or from reading the finished poem back to yourself?

From writing it. As I wrote, I read it; I would get caught up in a cadence and continue on, sustain it as best I could at the time, got very caught up in the voluptuous possibilities of word sound, imagery, all kinds of tonalities and variations thereof. Gee whiz! This was hot stuff. And also, I was, as now, a fairly solitary person. It suited me temperamentally.

What's your relation to the schoolboy in your poem "16"? Were you even then like him in thinking Shelley a "prink"? Or was it only later that you wanted to write lyrics that lurch like the El?

Well that's pretty much a straight autobiographical poem about what I was like as a schoolboy, or what I seemed like to myself twenty years later. Shelley would have seemed like a fancy, rather fey character to me—very far away from the IRT local making its way up to the Bronx. I had then, as I do now, something of a grudge toward those who didn't have to go to work in the morning and were in exotic locales doing poetic things. I was jealous. I probably still am. These are the people I was reading and being moved by in various ways, but I didn't identify with them. In a crude, cross-historical, distorted way, it probably had something to do with social class. And I think it still does.

You've ranged quite a bit yourself, traveling as much, perhaps, as Shelley. But then you always worked at your various destinations.

Yes, and I was traveling steerage the whole way. There's nothing wrong with Shelley. I was just cross at his having so much fun out there with Mary and Lord Byron on the beach while I was dragging my wretched self up the hill to 11th or 12th grade.

Are you also skeptical about Romanticism? Shelley is often particularly, as you say, fey. There's an interesting implicit contrast in "16" between that sense of "Romantic" and the "romantic comics" that your "plump domestics" read on the public transit.

I inherited a skeptical nature. Shelley would have seemed particularly strange and mildly preposterous to me, in the way that Keats and Wordsworth did not. Byron, too, was much too exotic for me to get close to. That poem involves an older person talking about the younger person. I was conflicted because I also didn't know how I could go about *being* a poet. I was barely cut out for the university, much less scholarship, and I didn't have independent means. I was a little bewildered by it all—how one would do such a thing, have those powerful feelings, and still be obliged to ride the subway to school or work.

What was the first occasion for you to share your poetry with others?

There was an English teacher there who was a bit daft ...

There being?

There being Horace Mann in New York City, which was a very good school for instruction of the traditional canon of literature, for learning to write, sentence structure, diagramming, and so forth. That was all very useful. But the teacher was strange, and after the fact—well, I know too much about him after the fact—he was mildly encouraging. For a while, he would let me come in and show him these things and he didn't discourage me. Probably suggested that I read this or that. It seemed that I had entered into an area that was magical or sacrosanct. It was an overwhelming feeling. Around that time I got interested in Rimbaud in translation, probably Louise Varèse's New Directions translations, *The Illuminations* and *A Season in Hell*. And I read what was probably a very cornball book by a fellow named Ullman, I think, which was called *Day on Fire*, a biography of Rimbaud. It electrified me and confirmed me in my notion that this was my vocation, and avocation, as Frost talks about.

Did you grapple with Rilke's advice in Letters to a Young Poet *to avoid being a poet if possible? He warns, if you can imagine living without writing, you should not attempt it. Run for your life.*

Well, he's right. He's a strange character. I've never really cottoned to Rilke, but it has been very difficult, in more ways than I can remember. But there wasn't anything else I was interested in. I would have liked to be center fielder for the Yankees or on the American Davis Cup tennis team. But that wasn't in the cards; I wasn't good enough. One thing about poetry, this wasn't the era of creative writing; there wasn't a rush of people to challenge me for the mantle. I was able to walk around, intoxicated by the notion that I was a *poet*.

Did you have a public persona as a poet when you were in high school, or later in college?

No. I was regarded in high school as a stupid jock, a scholarship boy from New Jersey—literally. And in college, I think I fancied myself a Beatnik, in the sense that I had short hair, smoked pot, and listened to blues and jazz. But I was just your basic young jerk.

What acted for you back then as the seeds of your creative germinations? And how has that changed over the years? Do poems grow out of overheard speech, as I sometimes suspect? Out of images, as your evident interest in Pound's ideogrammatic method would suggest? Out of rhythms? Has there been a trend over your several decades of writing?

I think it has been different; I'm trying to remember. I certainly would have been influenced by translations of Chinese and Japanese poetry, very heavily, and then also from poets along the lines of Gary Snyder and some of the Beats. Probably like a lot of young people, I had a heroic sense of myself. I don't know if I was involved in a quest for the Truth. I would do things: everybody dropped acid in those days (or it seemed everyone did) and I'd go off by myself with a notebook and write madly until my pen turned into a mostacelli noodle or something.

Are there specific poems that are the products of acid-dropping in the way that some recent poems are, ostensibly, written out of dreams?

Well, I had thousands of pages of poetry. I threw it all out as soon as I began studying with Bunting because I realized it wasn't any good. Which was a mistake. Not that it *was* any good. But I should have just buried it for twenty years until I became another person and then …

Harvest it?

Harvest it. See who I was and if there was anything worth taking out. But I was so self-loathing and disappointed in myself, in not being this or that, I couldn't bear to look at that work. I don't know what I wanted. I probably wanted to be a cross between James Bond, Frank Sinatra, and, uh, Thomas Nashe.

Most would-be Beatniks would not have been reading or seeking to be like Thomas Nashe. Were you continually reading not just fairly marginalized poets but canonical work throughout your younger years?

Well sure, but it wasn't all that unusual then. I have a lot of friends who are not at all literary *per se*, in the sense that they're not writers or teachers, who perhaps don't read the more remote Elizabethan long poems, but they read. In the earlier couple of generations, there was a much healthier tradition of the lay reader, delving deep into what's come to be called canonical literature. And because one was outside of academe, one wasn't specialized, so one could read or go see *Henry IV*, then go see a Godard movie or go listen to Iron Butterfly play badly *In-a-Gadda-Da-Vida*, and everyone would take off their clothes. These things weren't separate from each other; they weren't considered unconnected.

Am I right in recalling that you concentrated in something Asian-related in college?

Yes, that's very important. I majored in Asian studies at the University of Wisconsin at Madison and it had a wonderful department, probably the best in the country after Berkeley and Columbia. In particular, there was a professor originally from Winnipeg named Richard Robinson, whose area of expertise was Madhyamika Buddhism, which is a Northern Chinese Buddhism, a Mahayana Buddhism. He was a remarkable figure, who died only a year after I left Wisconsin in a tragic accident. I used to take all his courses. I didn't always know what he was talking about, but he was a brilliant character. I finished that major apart from my language, and it involved studying Asian philosophy, Asian history, Asian art, and Asian literature. So through college, apart from my own reading, most of what I read was Asian: works like *Dream of the Red Chamber* and *Monkey*, *Tales of Genji*, the *Mahabarata*, the *Bhagavad Gita*, along with various poems, sutras, and texts about painting and sculpture.

Do you have a feel today for what attracted you to Asian philosophy and literature?

I had been exposed to it in high school. There was an unusual course, which one of the more enlightened teachers created—Asian History or something; I remember we read Lao-tzu's *Tao Te Ching* and that absolutely knocked me on my rear-end. I felt I understood it perfectly. I have no feeling whatsoever for Western philosophy. I can't read it: my eyes cross, I find it unbearable. And yet intellectually, temperamentally, I find Asian philosophy—primarily Buddhist philosophy and Taoist and some Confucian philosophy—very interesting. I don't know why someone from a relatively provincial Jewish family in New Jersey would take to this sort of thing, but I still find it interesting. It's become popularized. People now take aspects of it and turn it into a New Age phenomenon. But I read more deeply than that; I really did have feeling for it. It affected me and how I look at the world.

Are there really no Western philosophers who speak to you? In an essay on George Oppen and other minimalist late-modernist poets, you make fun of his influence by Heidegger, quoting Günter Grass's send-up of Heideggerian mannerisms. But I would have thought you'd have a taste for Nietzsche or Emerson.

Of that group, I've read a bit of Schopenhauer. This is just one area—one of numerous areas—in which I'm deeply ignorant. I'm certainly a great fan and devourer of Camus, as a writer … also as a thinker. I've always regarded Sartre as a charlatan. But I'm sure I'm out of my depth.

You mentioned you didn't fulfil your language requirement for Asian studies at Wisconsin. You eventually ended up at the University of Victoria on Vancouver Island, I think, taking classes with Basil Bunting and writing your thesis about him.

Right.

What attracted you to his work and how did it influence your own?

It was very much *Briggflatts.* The poems I encountered in Pound's anthology were mildly interesting to me but didn't turn my engine over. I would imagine the concentrated music with its very strong and various rhythms along with a concentration of imagistic detail were all working together. The music and density, the fabric of the whole just took my breath away. Very strong. There was no way of faking language and feeling at that level of observation. Then as now, I have a pretty good dowsing rod for identifying what's contrived or dishonest—an effect gone after and not found or won.

In Earthquake Weather, *you present four tercets of* Briggflatts *as an epigraph:*

It tastes good, garlic and salt in it,
with the half-sweet white wine of Orvieto
on scanty grass under great trees
where the ramparts cuddle Lucca.

It sounds right, spoken on the ridge
between marine olives and hillside
blue figs, under the breeze fresh
with pollen on Apennine sage.

It feels soft, weed thick in the cave
and the smooth wet riddance of Antonietta's
bathing suit, mouth ajar for
submarine Amalfitan kisses.

It looks well on the page, but never
well enough. Something is lost
when wind, sun, sea upbraid
justly an unconvinced deserter.

Why this passage? Who is the "unconvinced deserter"?

I chose that passage because it's probably my favorite passage in that extraordinary poem, and one of the most beautiful passages in poetry that I know of. If you say very carefully and slowly "submarine Amalfitan kisses," you might have the notion of what it's like kissing a girl underwater. It really manages to reproduce the physical situation through sound, the muscular articulation of sound. Terrific. The bit at the end, the "unconvinced deserter," is a complication that just comes along with that particular passage. But I think he is talking about leaving off a poem before it adequately captures all the complexity of the experience, abandoning it … which, of course, we do more often than we like to admit.

You've mentioned that part of your poetic pursuit is to hit Truth. That surprises me; more and more, people believe only in a lowercase truth that has to be made, not found. And yet I've read … I think you wrote that Bunting often started off, maybe even Briggflatts, *with a structure already in mind instead of one he discovered through the process.*

Oh very definitely. I'm an improvisational writer; he's not in the slightest.

That doesn't get in the way of Truth?

No, that's just the method. I can't speak for Bunting, but with *Briggflatts* he envisioned a long poem along the lines of a sonata. He had a structure in mind and had been gathering material for a reflective, autobiographical poem while he wasn't writing. He was doing menial journalism work on his return from Persia. When he was ready, when he felt it, when the fire was lit under him, he had the material and had the structure to pour it into.

Was he a good teacher? In asking this, I'm also asking what you think a good poetry teacher does? Of late, you've made your way into the creative writing workshop circuit. You've sometimes called it silly.

Well, the notion of teaching creative writing, teaching people to write poetry, is preposterous. You can't do it. As I've just written in a public letter, it's like teaching someone to be kind or amusing or a wizard at languages. It's hard-wired. Language as poetic expression is hard-wired. Then there has to be a strange psychological setup in there as well to trigger it. And then to sustain it in this society—or in any society, really—long enough to where you develop originality and expertise is really too much to ask of a normal person. It doesn't fit into an institutionally-friendly place. It's a strange, not particularly healthy brew that makes a poet.

Having said that, I think one can teach poets to read ... to listen. You can encourage them in habits of mind, methods of execution. You can give them exercises to familiarize them with different ways of writing so that they have those arrows in their quiver. You can even suggest techniques whereby they can learn to edit themselves. I think a successful teacher sends his students off knowing more and caring more for poetry than when they came in. Now, many people come into a program caring not very much for poetry, or reading. They've been somehow seduced into believing that it's a glamorous life or whatnot. They're ambitious for the life, or for the attention. I'd say that's the case far more often than not. These people are invariably disappointed. That's not my fault. And I think that sometimes to those students I'm a disappointment. I try not to discourage them from writing their own poetry, but I do try to suggest that poetry has its resistances, as any other medium does. And they have to learn about the form by reading and practicing and ... sailing on open water. In the current environment where students, instead of being taught, have been encouraged in self-esteem—we're at an impasse. I think most teachers of creative writing often go in there and just confirm the students in their self-esteem. I find that disgusting and irresponsible.

What made Bunting's teaching enjoyable?

It was rather unconventional, and nowadays it'd be impossible: he simply read to us. He read us poetry he valued, often by heart and often not in English—poems in German, Italian, and Persian—to see if we could get a sense of them without knowing the meanings of the individual words. I think most students got fed up with him and that way of teaching. He couldn't bear photocopying student poems and talking about them. He looked like he was about to keel over in despair or illness whenever he'd get one of these poems. (I know the feeling.) We wound up, three or four of us, meeting at his house. He had a little bungalow down by the water. And he'd give us a beer. I remember he had Toby's Beer, and I remember he had bacon, cheese, and bread in the refrigerator—very spartan—and beer. He had plenty of beer. And he'd read to us and he'd play us music. He played us Byrd and Purcell, Dowland; he played Bach's Goldberg Variations. Every so often he'd tell us a story if he was reading something which reminded him of something else. He was fascinating to listen to. Although we were untrained listeners and, you know, silly kids, I think some of it slipped through. I think reading aloud is a far more valuable exercise than having students critique their own work. But you could never get away with that now. And he didn't do too well getting away with it then. He had a very stormy stay there in Victoria.

The Irish poet Nuala Ní Dhomhnaill read here recently and commented that the memorization of poetry is a dying art; she very much values the emphasis her parents and teachers placed on it. Do you value memorization?

I have mixed feelings about it. For some reason, I have great difficulty memorizing things. And when I was a high school student, for instance, a teacher wanted me to memorize five soliloquies from *Hamlet,* which set me to weeping wretchedly that night. But I think I got a couple of them down. And every year we had to memorize a poem. Because the teachers changed, I was able to reproduce the same poem every year, which was "A Noiseless Patient Spider" by Walt Whitman. It happens to be a very good poem—emblematic of Whitman's structures and cadences and so forth. And I'm absolutely certain, because that was the only poem I had that sort of familiarity with, it has affected my own work.

I think it's wonderful to memorize poetry. It's a pleasurable thing, if one is able to do it, and especially if it is fostered in the home. What I find very widespread and repulsive is the sort of pissing contest one encounters at literary gatherings, where people begin quoting bits and pieces of this and that at each other. There's an element of brinkmanship in it, and joylessness. It's a very common, dreary parlor trick. I'm awfully tired of it.

Do creative writing programs in today's academic institutions fill a gap left when critical scholars abdicate themselves from responsibility for the last fifty years or so of poetry, everything since, say, modernism?

No. That may happen and that's a nice way of looking at it. But it's a business.

It's a quarter billion dollar business. It's not simply a business; it's a Ponzi scheme—you can look that up.

Tell me about your course, "The Poet in the City." You've taught it several times at various programs.

I resolved a few years ago that if I was ever to go on the road teaching—this was before anyone invited me—I'd teach a course titled "The Poet in the City" and maybe avoid workshop classes. I'd teach "The Poet in the City" to writers or a combination of creative writing and English students. It covers a period, 1850s to 1960s or so, that I have a little knowledge of and a great interest in. I'm also very much interested in the arts related to poetry and their evolution during that era. Just so much happened: photography, realist painting, Impressionism, Cubism, and so forth, all the way up to Abstract Expressionism. Jazz. Cinema. And how the environment of the modern city and the technologies which were coming into being, one after another, changing everything yearly, pushed the arts into new modes of expression to accommodate all that sudden change—a very dynamic, exciting time. I'm interested in the city, the development of the city, the physical nature of the modern city and how it has changed.

When you say "physical nature," do you mean architecture? Or the way communities are forced together?

The whole bit: what happens if you put a freeway right through the middle of things; what happens if you have a subway, or don't; the urban planning; Haussmann's remaking of Paris, the boulevards and so forth; the appearance of the skyscraper in Chicago and New York; a new kind of mobility, an accelerated mobility that followed the introduction of the locomotive. There are just so many facets to it. This is the third time I've taught the course, but it seems infinitely various to me. And I enjoy having the students give presentations and finding out what aspects they're interested in. For instance, one young woman wrote an interesting piece on advertising in the twentieth century. These things are all very much related to poetry and the other arts. In other words, poets *do* go to the movies. Baudelaire was photographed by Nadar; so was Nerval. Whitman was terrifically interested in photography. It changed the way they conceived of the world around them, and it changed the way they wrote a line and how their lines interrelated. It had to. It *had* to. The medium had to change. I realize many people resist that. But it changes and changes, until it loses its shape and function. Then it looks to its origins to rediscover and revitalize itself.

Would you speak a little about some of the poets who have influenced you most? Catullus? Pound? Williams?

Williams had a great deal of influence. O'Hara and Schuyler, of the New York poets. Denby a bit. Lots and lots of influences. Browning. Hopkins. Wyatt and George Gascoigne maybe the most among the Elizabethans. Herrick very much. And I've read an awful lot of poetry in translation, which has been a great treasure to people of my generation. It wasn't always available in good translations, and now you can pick up a Penguin and read Horace in eighteenth-century versions, twentieth-century versions, nineteenth-century versions, each wonderfully introduced. Blaise Cendrars was very important to me.

When you read such work, do you listen mostly for rhythms and cadences or—I wouldn't suspect subject matter—maybe rhetorical tone?

In translation?

Well that's why I ask. When you read something in translation, you can't always trust that the original rhythms have been maintained.

You can forget the rhythms. Someone like Pound, whose translations have been very influential, installs his own rhythms. How close they are to the original I don't know; they probably in some cases are. With translated texts, I would say I focus on the treatment of the subject. I don't have too much interest soundwise and in the kind of textures one gets—all that's lost in translation. When I read someone like Gascoigne, it's the movement and the diction and the syntax. Likewise Wyatt. Overlooking a few exceptions like Surrey, there wasn't the appetite for regularity then. That developed further on, especially in the eighteenth century. Shakespeare's very irregular, as well, in his blank verse and his sonnets.

Do you see any general trends in your poetry over the years? For example, without seeming any less smitten with street-level city life, you're dedicating a larger proportion of recent poems to relationships, dreams, the products of your eclectic scholarship.

A lot of it depends on what's happening during my life in the span of five years or so it takes to write a book. *Red Sauce* was very involved with the beginning and end of a significant relationship. With *Green Sees Things* I got interested in dreams—maybe because the rest of my life was less interesting. Whatever intrigues me at the time I chase down. And it's affected by my reading. Also, I try not to beat a dead horse. I've written a great deal about street life; I'll probably write some more. But I'm disinclined to go to the same place. I've written a great deal about my cat. I knew, or it was suggested to me at a certain point, to give that a rest. Now people who've read the last book think I write about dogs all the time. I'd probably be well advised not to write about dogs in the near future. But generally I write about whatever claims my attention most vividly. That appetite changes, from my reading and so forth.

Do you write poetry in part to discover who you are? How consistent is your lyric "I"?

No, I have no interest in who I am. Maybe when I was younger. But I have no interest in self-knowledge … beyond what's required to live in the world and behave in a reasonable fashion. The "I" in my poems would be a rather elusive "I." It would have to depend; you'd have to ask me about a specific poem. It would probably have something to do with an identifiable me. There are probably multitudes of shadings or personae. I'm never one of Napoleon's generals.

You don't write persona poems, dramatic monologues?

I *have* done. "The Sausage Master of Minsk" was a dramatic monologue. And I'm very fond of Browning's "Andrea del Sarto," which is a poem I read in high school and still think is extraordinary. I usually make my writing classes endure it. I have a recording by James Mason—the same one that was played to me in high school, which was very good. It's a great poem. And it's a good exercise: both a blank verse exercise and a dramatic monologue exercise. In fact that's this week's assignment here at UT [the University of Texas].

Do you make a distinction between lyric and poem? Helen Vendler calls you an epigrammatic poet. What do you take her to mean by that? Do you agree?

I don't think about poems I write in relation to genre. I don't think I'm an epigrammatic poet, *per se*. She quoted a rather uncharacteristic poem of mine. I'm glad she did and I'm glad she found epigrammatic qualities in it. But I think of someone like Martial as an epigrammatic poet. I think of myself usually as a lyric poet with a broad and rather vague definition: something sung or having to do with a strong emotion—rather short. I write all sorts of poems. I think most of what I do falls into the category of modern lyric.

I think of Zukofsky's integral: upper limit music, lower limit speech. That's how I might define your lyric.

Yes. I think that's very good. He's an interesting, irritatingly difficult poet and writer about poetry—a brilliant mind.

You've mentioned that you think the writing of long poems is overrated or over-emphasized, that a great poet needn't write a Paterson *or a "Notes Toward a Supreme Fiction." Would you explain your reasoning?*

I think it's awfully difficult to write a long poem in the twentieth century. Obviously, Eliot wrote a couple of dandies. I actually think *Briggflatts* is the great long poem of the century ... because Bunting had a very firm structure in mind, a musical structure that was able to accommodate lots of shifts in tone and subject matter, speed, register, and so forth. *The Cantos* is a mess, a mess full of glories. But I'd never recommend it to anyone to read straight through. It would be useful to read it through, but you'd be slogging through a lot of junk. *The Song of Myself* is full of junk. But one would be depriving oneself if one didn't read it in its entirety. I can't imagine an American poet not reading it with profit. (Although I'm well aware that many don't, but that's another problem.) I think Eliot's great success with *The Waste Land*, and being taken seriously, threw a gauntlet down for a lot of other poets. Someone like Williams, for instance, who felt very competitive with Eliot and was much neglected, probably felt that he should come up with a big poem, a large poem, for which he was not suited. *Paterson* is a mess. Not in the way *The Cantos* is a mess. *The Cantos* is a great—I don't know what you'd call it—an encyclopedia of modern poetry and a crazy man's view of culture and history and economics. However flawed it is, it is a critical document in our literature. *Paterson* is not.

What's the great William Carlos Williams for you?

The poems a few years after the Armory Show, the poems he wrote in the 20s, 30s, and 40s, are his best work. I consider him a great man, working in that isolation in the 1940s, achieving what he was achieving. It's extraordinary. He's really a giant.

Eliot's great success, as you call it, his domination of American poetry for several decades, could be attributed perhaps to his critical writings. He taught people to read with his criteria and The Waste Land *fit nicely. Do you think a poet, in order to establish himself or herself, needs to write prose?*

I think poets really should write about poetry—not their poetics, which I find ridiculous. They should write criticism and try to write intelligently about poetry. Very few can. I'll be very blunt. Most of our *well-known* poets are idiots or frauds, and you find it out as soon as you look at their prose. It's really a test of a writer's intelligence to argue compellingly about the medium he's working in. I think there's also a moral responsibility, especially now when there's almost no good criticism being written by poets who are disaffected with the state of things; they should do something about it. It's also a gutless time. No one's willing to take shots at certain prominent characters.

When you say that a lot of esteemed poets these days are idiots, I think of the etymology of that word in relation to the notion of voice. *One can be an idiot in the sense of speaking with a unique voice, an idiom. Is it necessary for poets to hear and appreciate other voices?*

Whether they hear other voices or not (whether they hear voices in the night) is immaterial. No matter how original a voice they have, that voice has to be contained in verse lines that are structured to highlight and shade and move along in certain ways that reflect what the poet is trying to get across. But I think people confuse voice with personality. There's a great deal of personality out there. One could go out with a shovel and dig and dig and dig, like Hercules in the Augean stables, and not put a dent in all the personality out there. But there's very little poetry out there.

What's your take on poetic schools or coteries? Living in the Bay Area, you've no doubt had a lot of exposure to the Language poets. You have published poems in many of the same venues.

I really have no interest in schools. People like the Language poets have merchandised themselves very aggressively as a school. So did Creeley and Olson, in conjunction with Cid Corman. But with the Black Mountain crowd, there was quite a bit of first-rate poetry. Self-promotion works. The Surrealists were successful; the Futurists were successful, even though they were ripping off Apollinaire left and right. Schools of poetry don't come into being naturally. They're invented.

Okay, but you seem fairly comfortable with the idea of Cubism and Abstract Expressionism. Is there something that differentiates poetry from the visual arts in relation to community and schools?

That's a good question. Just looking at some of the poets we've talked about: Baudelaire wasn't in a school; Whitman wasn't in a school (no school could *contain* him). Apollinaire and Cendrars knew one another. They were both deeply affected by the Cubists—by the painters who weren't necessarily called Cubists then—but they never thought of themselves as a school. They might go to the same bar or the same parties. But they would have spit at the notion of a school. The so-called Objectivists … that was a phony name, invented so they could be represented in a magazine. None of them took it seriously at the time. Williams, certainly, was not of a school. Pound was not of a school. He and Eliot and Williams—well, Eliot and Williams hated each other, but Pound was very much involved with both and they never considered themselves a school. Bunting was not of a school. O'Hara, Ashbery, and Schuyler were not of a school. I asked Denby about that. I knew Edwin Denby for a little bit—not well, but we spent a little time together. The "New York School" was about interesting, bright, young, talented people being introduced to each other. And in that case I think Denby was hooking them up with some of the New York painters, like de Kooning.

To return to your earlier question, there isn't one poet identified with the Language group that is at all interesting to me. And in many cases, they've really behaved in a shameful fashion and been terribly destructive to what had been a very fragile, heterogeneous environment, particularly in the Bay Area. There, as much as anything, they were like a virus taking over a healthy cell. It destroyed what was left of the poetry scene in San Francisco. The professionalization and institutionalization of reading series, arts councils, the gender and ethnicity scam all contributed to its demise. But when I came to San Francisco, it was in the last days of the good reading venue Intersection, at a church in North Beach. You got big, healthy, diverse crowds, even though a lot of people couldn't stand each other or what others were doing. But what happened subsequently was a disaster, and I think the Language people are very much implicated in that—there and in New York as well. No one any good identifies with a school or a scene. Someone like Ginsberg, who was a very important American poet—a number of his friends were important figures—did use it as a successful merchandising device. I don't know that he didn't get himself and his friends hoisted on their own petard. They got famous, but they all got a lot less interesting as writers.

So you think their later poetry, once they became identified as Beats, is less interesting, more homogenized?

I think almost that entire generation we encountered in Donald Allen's tremendously useful 1960 anthology was effectively finished by 1965. Creeley, Dorn, Ginsberg, and others. Some of them were finished because they were dead. O'Hara was finished before he died.

Skipping over a question I had about the New Formalism, let me ask instead: Is there a danger involved in polish, or what, in Earthquake Weather's *"Art & Life" you call "that high finish"?*

Don't you want me to address the New Formalists? [laughter]

Go ahead.

There's nothing among the younger writers identified with that movement, or the critics, which is any goddamned good at all. If possible, they're even more boring than the Language poets. And there's a political subtext which is rather creepy. As for polish, "Art & Life" is really talking about another kind of poet, really a kind of—

Ashberian poet, I imagine.

An Ashberian poet.

Is that whose poetry you were thinking of as "the origami of an exiled prince"?

An Ashbery kind of poet or a Michael Palmer kind of poet. I'm a great admirer of Ashbery's poetry; I'm less interested in his epigones, his imitators. If poems are not driven by emotional subject matter of some kind, they're doodles.

Whether it's Ashbery or whoever.

Unlike many published poets, you've worked predominantly outside academic institutions. What is the work of being a poet? Are there blue-collar and white-collar aspects? (I'm thinking of Philip Levine's "What Work Is.")

I don't know what the hell Phil was talking about. It's not a job. It's hard work, but it's not a way to make money, not something one does regularly. To me, a job is something you do to make money so you can buy food, pay rent, and put clothing on your back or on your family's back. Poetry's more like an obsession or a disease, something you have to do. And usually it's very inconvenient. It's a form of madness. It's very difficult to fit it into one's life. A lot of people have died trying to—died from booze or suicide or what have you. Not a job. I've done a lot of jobs.

When you call the drive to make poetry a madness or disease is that because, while its products can be pleasurable, often the obsession is the opposite?

Right. It produces great pleasure, maybe the ultimate pleasure. That and the heights of sexual love are the great pleasures I'm acquainted with. But one doesn't work at it as one works at a relationship. You're overcome, you're visited, you're interfered with, you're intruded upon. And then you have to wrestle with it, as Jacob wrestled with the angel. It's serious business. I'm not accustomed to talking about it. Certainly I don't talk about it with students, because [laughing] why the hell would you talk about anything like that.

Seems to me it might be singularly unhelpful to explain one's own process of struggling since it's certainly not going to be the same process as what will be helpful to another.

Well, I would tell a young person who's into it part of the way that it's going to be difficult and there will be struggles along the way. Her struggle won't necessarily be like mine, almost certainly, just as—of course, I'm not the one to ask, but—if someone came to me and was struggling through a difficult time in a relationship, I would say, "It's okay, you'll have a lot of difficult times."

Do you draw a line between poetry and politics? Do you think poetry can make things happen?

Absolutely not. Guns and money or lack of it make things happen.

Do you not think that representing, as you often do in your poetry, a wide range of humanity, segueing between high and low dictions, attending to the underside of the city in a social realist way—does that not have any impact?

On the politics of the day?

Not on President Clinton necessarily, but—

There's no *political* impact. I think probably some of my political feelings are evident, certainly my sociopolitical feelings are evident. We're all political creatures. Every gesture we make—the way we walk, the way we talk—is political. And I'm someone deeply interested in political life, how it affects social life. The poems I write affect nothing. They give pleasure or they don't give pleasure. I'm always amused, well, I don't know if I'm really *amused*—people always characterize me as writing about the underside, the life of the street. But I think I talk about what novelists like Balzac have been talking about for 150 years. I talk about the whole canvas. Poetry has restricted itself, to put it metaphorically, to the garden, which is now the suburb. Perhaps the subject of most contemporary poetry is the personality in the suburb—the personality experiencing discomfort in the suburb. Maybe that's the subject matter of 95% of poetry now.

I think of Ashbery's "The Picture of Little J.A. in a Prospect of Flowers," but I don't think that's the kind of poem you're talking about. You're talking about the modern-day confessionals. Which of the non-literary arts do you think have the greatest impact on poetry today?

Not only are 95% of our poets infantile clucks, they don't read books, they don't look at paintings, they don't listen to music. So many people write poetry now. Someone was telling me there's a union in Canada now that has 45,000 members.

That's twice the population of Canada's new Inuit state.

That's how many Kosovars are leaving Kosovo every day, being driven into Macedonia and Albania. You have an artificial population now of several thousand new MFAs a year, who identify themselves as poets. They have the life-span of mayflies, really. They almost all disappear. They're not writers;

they can't write. They're certainly not poets. They're usually young people between gigs, trying to find a little time for themselves to figure out what they want to do, which can be very useful. It's very hard for young people in the current culture, much harder than for people my age when they were in their early twenties. We were able to fake it somewhat. Nowadays, kids can't. So any friendly port is useful. But as I said, these kids aren't really listening to interesting music or looking at paintings or mixing with other artists. A lot of them are actually in bands themselves, but they play garbage.

What about the not-so-young poets, the more established, who I thought you were saying also don't read or respond to the arts enough?

They're on the phone all day. They're like fundraisers for the Democratic National Committee. They're trying to get on committees, trying to make sure other people are on committees, trying to accumulate power. They're low-grade ward politicians. They don't have time to do anything else. Look to the committees and you'll find the gangsters.

Writing poetry's a contemplative art. One isn't required to dutifully go to the ballet and the opera and the theater, all three of which I have no interest in at all. In all three areas, I'm a philistine. I do very much like music. And I do have an appetite for painting. I was very fortunate in my growing up to have a father who loved objects of art: paintings, sculpture … The house looked like the collections room of a museum. No little boy from New Jersey logged more hours in the Museum of Modern Art in the 1950s than I did, unless his father was working in the museum. I'd be dragged in almost every weekend, to the Modern and the Frick and the Whitney. And my father had only a high school education.

What did he do?

He was always a businessman: he was a haberdasher, then he was a stock-broker, then a real estate broker. But he wrote and he painted and collected art, antiques—that was his great hobby and his mother's hobby. So I was exposed to a lot of wonderful stuff, and in an environment that wasn't at all self-consciously arty, that was probably contemptuous of people in the arts. Which maybe explains some of the way I am. I hate arty types and I'm rather uncomfortable being an artist.

I remember hearing you read "The Conversation." Of course that poem ends

with the French phrase objet d'art. *But you pronounced it like a pirate:* arrghhh.
Like the Scotsman on the Simpsons.

Yeah, maybe I am the Scotsman on the Simpsons. My family were great read-
ers. That's really a gift.

*Would you speak to your musical influences? Your poetry is rife with indications
of a deep devotion to a wide range of musics: classical, jazz, blues, and so on.*

I'm very much affected by the blues. I've been writing some reviews recently
and replaying some of these things, stuff I began listening to when I was 17 or
so. Very strong influence. The lines where they drop the last part of the line
and substitute a glissando on the slide guitar or what have you. The phrasing.
The simplicity and power and succinctness—all those things. Jazz, really later.
I'd always listened to it and enjoyed it, but really in my late twenties or thirties,
I jumped in with both feet, got a bit crazed about it. And I very much like the
piano trios, the very percussive piano—that comes out of Monk especially, Bud
Powell, Elmo Hope, Herbie Nichols, the Catalan Teté Montoliu. I like the
drive, complexity, and polyrhythms of bebop. I would say the vintage I like best
in jazz is late-50s, early-60s. But all the way back to the 20s, I hear great things.
It's all slipped into my work. Poems about jazz—and I have several—don't really
work, and I left a couple out of *Hong Kong Nile Club*. I might end up leaving
another couple out. But it's certainly gotten into my notion of movement and
probably into my ideas of improvisation. More recently, I got very much into
a lot of twentieth-century, so-called contemporary music, and have listened
to that for two or three years. I don't know how it's affected me as a writer; it
passes through a lot of filters. It's probably in there somewhere.

*Your desire that your poems give pleasure might be allied with the aesthetics of the
beautiful. I wonder if you ever aim for a contrastive aesthetics of the sublime.*

Well, it's been about 27 years since I read Longinus. And regarding the aes-
thetics of the beautiful, I'm not quite sure what they are, but it sounds like
a porcelain dish, a rather Victorian notion of beauty, like an overwrought
porcelain dish. I do believe Truth is Beauty and Beauty is Truth … at least a
goodly share of Beauty.

In a back-cover blurb, Allen Ginsberg calls you "a loner, a genius," and Helen

Vendler has commented on a loneliness pervading your work. You live alone and move or travel fairly frequently. Does it surprise you that people who don't know you except through your poetry perceive this?

Yeah, it did. I guess it doesn't anymore. They both wrote that before they met me, so there must be something in the work. I think I was living in those days with a woman, so I wasn't really alone. Sometimes I live alone. My normal, my healthy state of being is as a couple. I'm not a couple at the moment and miss it. But even as a couple, I'm private. I have lots of friends, but my closest friends are spread pretty widely across the continent so I don't get to see them too often. But I do spend a lot of time by myself and I'm usually comfortable.

I could probably go through the poems and identify the suggestions of loneliness. You know, listening to fog horns or this or that. But in that poem [*Earthquake Weather*'s "Bay Lullaby"], I'm in bed at the time not only with my partner but with my pussycat, both of whom are no longer with me. Maybe as a poet—you can't really share that with other people, even when you're living happily with someone else. Which is upsetting sometimes to them—to some, not to others. But one's always an outsider because you have this other part of your life which is rather strange and extreme. It's not like *I've got to go disappear now and commit an act of pedophilia*. But one does disappear.

How do you approach your critical writing? How do you decide what you're going to write about, for example?

Well, usually with dread. And usually at the prompting of Wendy Lesser [editor of *The Threepenny Review*], who has been a friend and supporter I'd never want to let down.

The dog Stoltz mutters, "I simply have to knock off that essay on Sassoon."

It's become a part of my life. That poem, incidentally, came out whole. That was a dream. I got up in the middle of the night and wrote it out whole; I don't think I embellished it much.

Inevitably now there's an essay I need to write. I have a weekly music column. But there's always an essay hanging over my head, usually through Wendy. It's good for me, because it's a struggle. I'm wired for poetry. Sometimes my poetic structures creep into my prose, probably more often than I suspect.

You skip around chronologically. You achieve an interesting combination of informality and exacting scholarship, all in lucid prose. I think your informality allows you to go places someone more rigid might not.

Well, in that I'm fortunate I never went to graduate school. I would never have considered getting an MFA. That existed when I was a youth, but I found the idea so disgusting, it never was a possibility. I did consider getting an MA in medieval literature, but I would have had a terrible time of it. I remember, even as a student, teachers scolded me for not sticking to the subject. I was being silly. I can't remember exactly: they said it's a mistake to be playful or flip when you're writing about a serious subject. More to the point, I had to teach myself to write an essay. My essays are of several different kinds. But if I wanted to write an essay, let's say about our neighbor Christopher Middleton, whose work I've had a high regard for all these years, I'd have to provide a pretty straight, sustained argument. It's not a place for my personality to enter in.

Out of respect for him.

And out of respect for the form I'm writing in. So what I have now is a pile of prose very different in tone. But that's all right, too; different subjects require different treatments.

Do reviewing and criticism play a crucial role in contemporary poetry, or is it basically parasitic?

I think the number one problem, which has now attained tragic proportions, is the want of responsible criticism and venues for that criticism.

When you say "responsible," I think of Lowell criticizing 77 Dream Songs despite his friendship for Berryman and knowledge that the review would anger, perhaps devastate, him.

They're a couple of messy guys. Jarrell was the critic of that generation. And Jarrell has his pros and cons, but he's someone a poet should read. I tried—and this was quixotic in the most extreme sense—when I first began making these visits a few years ago, to have my students read I. A. Richards' *Principles of Lit-*

erary Criticism. I don't think that was the best idea in the world. But I wanted them, even just for discussing each other's work, to have a notion—*a* notion, among other notions—of a disinterested approach to the discussion of a poem. But in the larger scheme of things, the level of what literary criticism of poetry now exists in America is a disaster. It's either academic and theoretical, *shtoopid* journalistic, irresponsibly partisan, or a combination of all of the above.

I discussed this with Jorie Graham when I visited at Iowa; she was friendly to the notion. She's very good about these things. There should be a formal course in criticism which people in creative writing programs should take. It would be useful to have MFA students discuss contemporary authors and write critical essays about them, poring over their work, making arguments, and considering different models and standards. I can't but see how that would be useful. Now, would it improve their own work? I don't know; it certainly wouldn't hurt it.

It would prompt them to read others' work.

Yes, it would prompt them to read others' work. And that's always useful. People aren't reading, particularly the people in these courses. And now you have this disaster: a large proportion of the readers of poetry now are creative writing students who have no background, whose idea of a traditional poet is Sylvia Plath.

Who can't scan. Not that Plath couldn't scan; the standard poetry-writing student today does not know how to scan a poem.

That's very important, what you just said. Plath—whatever you may think of her, whatever I may think of her, and my feelings are mixed—could very well scan a line and had read a great deal. She was technically very astute, deft, knowledgeable. Students running around with Sylvia Plath books, yelling at Ted Hughes or whatever, have no idea what she's about, what traditions she comes out of. Again, it's this cult of personality. So I think it would be good to have people do a little reading, and writing, and thinking.

I get the impression from some of your essays that you think we're still digesting modernism and that what one might call the po-mo hoopla of the last several decades is premature.

Absolutely. We haven't digested the events from 1905 to 1917 or 1921. It was an extraordinary rush of experimentation and discovery. There's this notion that one continues to make discoveries, revelation after revelation. And I think we may have exhausted many of the possibilities for the opening up of form and for randomness, for the aleatory. It might well be time to synthesize what we've come to understand and to continue blending that with the traditional literatures. That blend will create new forms. But this lust for the new—there is no avant-garde any more. The avant-garde is exhausted. It can be silly or naughty. It can get sillier or naughtier—no, it can't get naughtier. Perhaps it can't get sillier.

Is that something the avant-garde brought upon itself by marketing itself?

It's built into the avant-garde's notion of itself and game plan: self-obsolescence. There's a tremendous fear of emotional content among the avant-garde now, and I see it also among my students, a curious emotional disengagement.

They're fearful of it at the same time that they're often writing egocentric, emotional work? Or they're not doing the latter?

Half of them are doing that and half are trying to write like John Ashbery. And they're not as clever as John. They have a big problem with engaging emotional content. And then what I see with someone like Ann Lauterbach, who's ferociously smart and an interesting poet—in her last book, she tries to engage this in a very dramatic and brutal confessional poem.

You're talking about On a Stair's "N/est"?

Yes. I don't know if it works or not. It works in parts. But I thought it was very interesting and rather brave.

Some of your poems, like some of Lauterbach's, are spare of punctuation. At what point, during the composition of a poem, do you decide to leave most punctuation out?

I don't make clear decisions at the top. The feel of the poem as it's coming out pretty much determines that. If I want more flow or a sense of indeterminacy, I suppose, or to enhance the possibility of relationships between a word at the end of one line and the words that begin the next—if punctuation will impede some of those possibilities, I'll omit it. If the nature of the poem involves very clear stage instructions for how it should be read, I'll punctuate it.

Do you think poets have a responsibility to make their work accessible?

I'm usually surprised when somebody tells me they don't "get" what I'm doing. It just seems so plain. There are so many people leaving conventional meaning, such as it is, behind—fracturing syntax and meaning far more than I, leaving things much more indeterminate than I ever do—that I feel like I'm as simple as a piece of apple pie. But then I find that even some rather sophisticated readers, people who have followed my work for some time, don't know what the hell I'm talking about. And, yes, that does concern me … because that wasn't my intention. And then I have to figure out, *Well, how can I get it across without sacrificing some of the ambiguity I wanted to inhere in there.* So I think things can be difficult, but I don't think they should be difficult or impenetrable just as a gesture toward confounding bourgeois expectations.

So you do sometimes seek ambiguity, but you want the reader to be able to discern that it's an intentional ambiguity with which she will have to sit pretty, as opposed to something that's there to bewilder or alienate the reader.

I would like the reader to have faith that I'm not there to simply confound her, that if it's difficult, she can work through it and it will probably disclose its meaning one way or another.

Why do you think weather is so pervasive in your poetry?

Among the earliest kinds of poetry I read were Chinese and Japanese poetry, particularly the translations of Kenneth Rexroth. And in Japanese poetry, especially in the haiku, there's always an allusion to, or mention of, weather. Certain words or images or things denote a particular time of year. By setting up that kind of backdrop, you can go all kinds of places. It roots a reader in a particular mood, with a set of associations. And then you can go all over the bloody place.

And apart from that, the weather interests me, particularly weather in the city and the contrast between made things and macadam things, telephone poles, power lines, and trees. The most interesting thing, sitting here, is the spectacle of trees newly in leaf against I-35 and the trucks of I-35 and the billboards at sunset. That is the spectacle here on Robinson Avenue in Texas. And if I wrote about it, I suspect that would be in it. That's beautiful to me, much more beautiful than walking in the woods.

Because of the contrast?

Yeah. I've always loved that ... and being able to write about it in places like San Francisco or Montreal, Alaska, New York, Iowa. Everywhere you go there's weather. And there are cars and power lines and airplanes. I'm very interested in airplanes flying above, too. That's what one sees. It's very busy out there. I'm looking out that window through the slats of the Venetian blind to the trees, the leaves and branches, trembling there in the breeze. But peripherally I'm seeing the movement of cars, and I'm hearing them. There's also a soundtrack to my experience of nature. There are always cars or airplanes or shouts. There's always counterpoint. But I do, in spite of what some people giggle about, pay attention and enjoy nature. I'm just much more interested in it when it's against a backdrop or in the context of a town or city.

What's the role of humor in your work?

Well, that's a very complicated question. I'm sometimes referred to as a humorous poet, or a humorist, which I deeply dislike. The term marginalizes and trivializes what my work is about. But I refuse to jettison humor in order that I might be considered a more important writer because I think that would be like leaving the color green or red out of one's palette. I naturally ironize. My parents' humor, which is very good, is ironic.

Which is not to say sarcastic?

At its lower end it's sarcastic. And sarcasm and vitriol have their place, even in poetry. I encourage that because people are far too polite and prissy in their work now. I think too many people are afraid of humor and the risk of not being taken seriously. They have every right to be wary. But I don't give a damn. I can be as morose as I want, or as funny as I want, or as nasty as I want, or as romantic ... and enjoy myself. Certainly, I see some things in a playful way, some in an ironical way. It's something I'm aware of, and it's a risk I take. But I take it in good humor.

CHRISTINE HUME AND LAURA SOLOMON

Christine Hume's first book, *Musca Domestica*, won the Barnard New Women Poets Prize and was published by Beacon in 2000. Her second book, *Alaskaphrenia*, won the Green Rose Prize and was published by New Issues Press in 2004. She teaches at Eastern Michigan University. Laura Solomon's first book, *Bivouac*, was published by Slope Editions in 2002. She is poetry editor of *Castagraf*. This conversation was conducted via email in October 2001 and picked up again in May 2004. Solomon's text is in italics.

The proem to Musca Domestica, *"True and Obscure Definitions of 'Fly,' Domestic and Otherwise," christens your book with a flurry of fly verbiage pulled from the* OED *and is the first of many such compositions. It seems that collage works as both mode and motif for a lot of* Musca Domestica, *would you agree?*

Absolutely. I wanted the proem to announce the fly as a figure that collects and redistributes fragments; the fly is a vector and pollinator, as well as a trickster and talisman. So it seemed necessary to begin with the fly as a collage artist, spinning out several selves in order to override or break a bounded idea of self. The word possesses a voracious semantic appetite. With that poem I wanted to propel a more searching examination of flyness, one that extends thinking about conjunctions ("junk") and connotations ("nota") of language. Ultimately "True and Obscure ..." means to unfix and undermine the book title's classifying impulse. I love the elegant music of the words *Musca Domestica* — the Latin binomial for housefly; I love the way its sound syncopates with the thing it names and contains echoes of a domestic "muse" and "music." As much as I'm enthralled with the specificity and sonic slipperiness of the title, I didn't want readers to come to the work taking it too literally. You can't read this fly like you can read Hughes's crow, for instance, as a mythological character. Though I've thought of the fly as a dark counterpoint to the traditional lyric bird — Poe's raven, Keats' nightingale, Olson's kingfisher, Hopkins' windhover, etc. — I wasn't at all interested in creating anything so visible or representational with it. With flies, you see their motion more than their form. The proem also sets up motion and speed as issues central to the fly — again, counterpoints to the traditional "timeless" lyric. Lyn Hejinian points out that language is never in a state of rest, that language engenders a profound restlessness — I wanted the fly to become a ghost of that agitation, to create the story of the experience of linguistic adventure that goes off erratically, intrepidly, questingly. And such a rush would be at least partially entangled in sound. The fly may be a ghost, but an audible one, clanking about in the attic.

What I find especially interesting here is that sound plays such a vital role in your poems and that sound is itself a sort of sculptured motion. How instrumental is sound to your creative process? Do you find it a diving board spurring the poem on, or does it function more subtly?

The initial fly in my bonnet, a certain insistent rhythm and sound, often kicks the poem into being, but it also helps it to build its own order, its me-ter-making argument. I try to keep the sound going, to see how many sounds can keep it going and opening up to possibilities beyond my first impulses. Into the alchemy of slippage, cryptography, transumption, metalepsis, rhyme, echo — incarnational phrases that bring together sounds (and their ideas) that have been longing to be together. And resonate mistake. When you draw energy from error, mistakes become revitalizing. They can make cracks that hint at whole new vistas. (But like point mutations in genetics, mistakes can let in the future or repeat the past. Perhaps in poetry they can do both at once; in any case, I don't use most of the mistakes I make, but I'm always on the lookout for operative accidents.) Letting the sound and rhythm of language have its way excites a magic that leads the poem into "things counter, original, spare, strange" (Hopkins). Because there's no tabula rasa in language — every word has a past, it has many faces, and traces and futures — I tend to delight (perhaps too much) in its resonances.

You mentioned the fly as a figure capable of breaking "a bounded idea of self." It seems that echo works for you in a similar respect.

I'm fascinated by the differences in repetition, replication, and reproduction, and in the questions those ideas trigger about identity. No, let me start another way. In the Echo-Narcissus myth (from Ovid), the echo is exact but partial; even then, the context shift ruffles the surface of meaning. Echo is literally broken up by the listener's jilting response to her response — her physical self is absorbed into woods and her miming voice becomes a mockery to Narcissus. Echo shows that iteration can explode a category from within, and that the world has an inherent capacity to interrogate itself. I guess that external voice is a good antidote to the potential dangers of narcissism and hermeticism in poetry. It allows poems to acknowledge a world outside. Early on in the process of putting my book together, I considered titling it *Echolocation*—the process bats use to locate objects. It enables them to fly in the dark and get a bead on flying food. They emit ultrasonic sound, then read the echo reflected back to them. To me that's a fruitful way to think of poetry itself: how the world gets reflected back to us particularly and personally (and the writing of a poem might be compared to flying in the dark). This way, the poem can be a chamber of voices, both internal and external, one that keeps refracting and generating more questions. Keats talks about this (poems are "a thoroughfare for all thoughts"), but contemporary poetics have extended the practice in unforeseen and exciting ways. As a reader, I tend to think of poems as echo chambers for meaning in which multiple—but not indiscriminate—readings are actively invoked and one reading is not meant to displace the others.

Do you think that there is ever a point when such multiplicity turns cacophonous, or is this precisely the sort of unnerving, unsettling over-stimulation to which a poem should aspire?

The pressure from the marketplace is the most mundane obstacle a writer can face. I'd rather poetry disrupt received models of clarity and refinement; I'd rather risk the label "obscure" and take a risk; I'd rather awkwardness, misrecognition, dislocation, uncanniness trump comfortability and secure "understanding." What means, of the infinite number of ways, should a poet employ to make the poem "resist intelligence almost successfully?" Of course the whistles and lights of linguistic pinball are nothing to aspire to, but formal and lexical complexities don't automatically cancel out emotional heft. I'm stunned that people still seem to cling to the notion that narrative, plain-style poetry—where voice is attached to the baggage of transparency, presence, and claims to identity representations—is more "authentic," more "emotionally available" than other styles of poetry. It diminishes the very unmanageability of emotion itself, and it's blind to the fact that emotion is just as shaped by culture, just as culturally manufactured, as so-called rational thought. Why do you think such ideas are so strongly resisted?

There seems a pervasive supposition that language is utilitarian, a means to an end—and that end is the intentional communication of some pre-existing idea. I think this is rooted in a more fundamental prejudice that what separates humans from animals is rationality, and by extension, our "use" of language. I find both these notions simplistic. I'd say instead that it is the ability to reason and then to reject that reason that distinguishes us—essentially our chaotic imaginative energy, both destructive and creative. If poetry is anything it is charged, unruly, bendable language, language that extends (hopefully) far beyond rational use into some other, more willful element. Stevens says that often poems have "imaginative or emotional meanings," and that such poems "may communicate nothing at all to people who are open only to rational meanings." Mere sense-making seems a machinated, uninspired act for a poet to engage in—as does mere nonsense making. The poem should be an arena where sense and non-sense, rational and irrational, collide, where one gets the feeling of "words doing as they want to do and as they have to do," as Gertrude Stein put it. Of course, to actively experience language beyond rational referentiality, one has to be open to the experience and assume a more creative (though less authoritative) role. Until one realizes language is more than a conduit between two points, I'm afraid one is doomed to a rather banal experience of it. Do you think this sort of attitude or caste of expectations is indicative of the way we generally teach poetry at the introductory levels?

The academy is expert at polarizing—look at what they've done to "creative" and "critical" disciplines in English departments. The dichotomies that currently structure university systems—between reading and writing, between linguistic and social structures, between the known and the unknown, between instrumental and playful uses of language, between fiction and poetry, between left and right literary movements—makes for rigid thinking in the classroom. The myth behind the scene is that all our thinking can be reduced to the Apollonian/Dionysian model. A simplified, clichéd rationalism (one that's merely antonymic to irrationalism) has infected the academy. Its breed of either/or logic is a rut we've thought ourselves into thanks, perhaps, to the righteousness engendered by the Enlightenment legacy via analytic philosophy. It seems to captivate us because of the passivity it endorses. Most students' experience of language, especially as they encounter it in school, is as a vehicle for factual ("prosaic") information or a prescribed ("poetic") emotive vomit; utilitarian or blandly therapeutic. Neither mode acknowledges the power of language to transform thinking and feeling or commingle the rational and irrational. The academy wants the world in camps: Is Beckett's book indeterminate or realistic? A very strange opposition if you believe that the indeterminate is realistic, not Realism, but true to one's experience in and of the "real" world. Reading that expects a high level of readerly interaction and a trust in the process of reading, a willingness to listen to the way language sounds without "irritable reaching after" meaning and an openness to discovering dimensions beyond conventional boundaries, this kind of reading requires an active patience and curiosity that our culture discourages. The culture's compulsive tendency to favor the anesthetic and predigested, to comfort the comfortable, and to regard difficulty and pain as problems themselves shrugs off art that doesn't choose the well-trodden path—platitude, reified nostalgia, orthodox sentimentality, prefab rebellion. One essential quality of a good intro to poetry class is to show students more ways of reading. You show them that they are capable of flexibility in their approaches to the act of reading and they will learn from that which they don't initially understand. This relates to what you were saying about readers assuming a more creative role: complex surfaces frustrate normal reading habits and force a more intuitive, more active approach on the reader. I'm interested in letting students in on the pleasure of the writerly text. I don't mean that experience to be an academic exercise but rather, a revelation, a profound aesthetic experience, a regenerating experience, a political experience.

The idea that art has nothing to do with politics is a damaging construction. I recently heard someone talking on NPR about how in the wake of the terrorist attacks in NYC and DC, no one wants to go to art galleries because art seems sadly frivolous (reiterating what we all heard Billy fucking Collins say on the same station). This pervasive attitude masks the deep political and moral possibilities available to us in art that aren't offered to us by the media. What, if not art, might jolt us out of our thuggish habits? To shun art (and any dissenting voice or vision) out of the activity of patriotism diminishes the moral health of our country. Poetry, when not restricted in its scope to a merely rhetorical figuration of the world, is capable of extending human experience into the realm of consciousness and imagination. It can lead us out of passing disregard—a willing distractedness that seems to have the country by its nape.

Shelley defends poetry on this very basis, arguing against the position that gifted men should apply themselves to sciences, including the pseudo-science of political theory, and quit writing poetry. The imagination, he says (to paraphrase), is the origin of all morality, and without art to refresh us, and particularly poetry, as to refresh our very language, a society may slip further down the dire straits of tunnel vision. Since the terrorist attacks, I think many of us find ourselves reevaluating what we do. I know it's affected my own relationship to writing, has cemented a lot of previously held convictions while displacing others. I'm no longer comfortable with glibness. However, I do feel all the more devoted to poetry and an excruciating need, as my friend Paul Killebrew likes to say, "to do good work." It's easy to become nihilistic, jaded, cynical and thus complacent. These are some of the demons we've got to confront in poetry, and fiction as well.

Yes, it's a jolt to the whole shebang, one that has sparked complex reevaluations. And if certain poetry seems decadent and callow in light of national crisis, so be it.

On another note, how do you think the MFA culture and book prize infrastructure play into this atmosphere? I have mixed feelings about both. Both seem to encourage careerism and nepotism. Yet MFA programs afford the possibility of community for a poet and actual time to write and grow, while prizes seem often the only door within which one may wedge a foot. Still, it's disturbing to see some of the work that emerges—often safe and formulaic even in its "experimentalism"—and worse, the oily, corporate-style back-scratching going on between presses, prizes, and departments.

The most affecting and lasting part of both my MFA and PhD programs is easy to sum up in your word "community." Most of the closest friends I have I made in these programs; I can't imagine my life without the intellectual exchange and aesthetic provocations, the honesty and support of these relationships. At the same time, there is, you are right, a growing expectation that MFA programs should be pre-professional and commercially relevant. The academy in general is going the way of business, and that's not good news for the arts. Now we are looking at the flip side of poetry's entanglement with politics.

Your book won the Barnard New Women Poets Prize. What was that experience like for you?

As I'm sure I've told anyone who's talked to me for more than five minutes in the past year, I had a bleak first publishing adventure. I'm thrilled to have won such a prestigious prize and especially to have my manuscript chosen by Heather McHugh. Once the thing got handed off to Beacon, however, it was nothing but a series of disappointments and frustrations. Many small and large changes that I made on the copy-edited version were ignored: a prose poem is lineated where the manuscript margins ended; another poem is crammed onto one small page when the manuscript version is more than two full pages, and so on. I think most poets would agree—to varying degrees—that the materiality of the work is an important, intrinsic part of the work. Yet my editor repeatedly discouraged me from making any suggestions very early on in the process. You work to create a kind of theater on the page, and you expect that basic philosophy to be respected by the publishers. The book is by no means finished when the manuscript's complete; there are loads of aesthetic decisions to make, ones I believe the author should have some say in. My editor had different ideas: she didn't want dialogue; she told me that I needed to "let go," "stop micromanaging," and leave book production to the professionals. You have to understand: Beacon is under contract to publish the prize winner, yet they have no part in the selection of the manuscript. Because of the structure of the contest system, publishers inevitably must sign on with authors whose work they might not be enthusiastic about; it's potentially a very unsavory situation for all parties.

So it's a little uncanny that we are revisiting and expanding upon this discussion again at a time of national horror—after the invasions of Afghanistan and Iraq, and in the weeks following a deluge of photographs depicting some of our more appalling deeds in that area of the world, in the weeks following the beheading of Nicholas Berg—it seems this time however that national horror is focused (at least partially) on our own "thuggish habits." On a similar note, last weekend I attended a lecture by Marjorie Perloff regarding her new book, The Vienna Paradox, a memoir of sorts which also critically examines the costs of high culture. During her lecture she censured as precarious what she sees as an existing and growing segregation between intellectuals and the government, citing as a history lesson the failure of the Jewish intelligentsia in Austria to address escalating anti-Semitism just prior to World War II. It's unclear to me whether or not she pins this failure upon the Jewish intelligentsia's being too caught up in kultur, but that seemed to me the implication. I'm just beginning the book, but from the tone of her lecture I gathered that she was suggesting a more active political role on the part of artists and intellectuals—not simply to be assumed through artistic or scholarly means—but one that would require artists and intellectuals to infiltrate the systems that be. There is much of me, the realist in me, that would agree with her, and yet the anarchist in me, the monk in me, the idealist in me, and thus the poet in me, all insist that to enter that structure is to maintain it and that one should not compromise or assist by virtue of participation, even at the lowest level, governments in committing their crimes. At the same time, you'd have to beat me away from the polls in November. The question of political participation and the degree to which one should involve oneself has been pretty central to American artists from the get-go. I'm wondering where you stand currently on these issues and how events of the last three years have shaped your stance.

Yet you are in the structure because you use language, and language is an inherited culture and structure of thought and feeling. As a poet you do what you can to derail your habitualized trains of thought, and to awaken others to the discoveries that explore language as a reciprocal mechanism that permeates our relationships to the world. Poetry itself exists at a linguistic crisis point, evolving, as Stevens says, from a series of conflicts between the denotative and the connotative forces in words; poets exploit that half-latent unreason endemic to all ordinary language. Poetry especially encourages us to pay attention at the local level; reading and writing can contribute to and confront how we engage with community. This might seem an evasive or ephemeral response, but I think being an artist is a necessary political act that is easily ridden with guilt by product-happy people. The feeling of inauthenticity under much lyric activity, and a pervasive anxiety at the supposed halo of narcissistic leisure involved in "creative writing" turns on the idea of quantitative mastery and capital production. So much of the task of writing poetry means dwelling in dilemma and crisis, grappling with a trial-and-error method (Beckett's "Fail again. Fail better.") that it may not seem like the most efficient way to live one's life; those are attitudes that are recalcitrant in our culture and difficult not to absorb or internalize at some level.

The idea that one has the choice to be in or outside the system implies a kind of privilege; many folks don't have that freedom or access; many were born with it in their pocket and so enacting the rejection of it might be a bit naïve. I don't think anyone should get entangled in the base logic of all or nothing. You know there's nothing worse than a fallen utopianist. I haven't read Perloff's new book, but I think that the idea you suggest, to take action as a prescriptive measure is a good one. Paying attention is crucial. Poetry's attention to language and structure provides an exemplary model for local political participation and active speculation. Everyone got her leftist badge on after 9/11, but what kinds of local activities/activisms might she have been involved in prior to this cataclysm? There's something terrifying in the compassion and commitment (one not necessarily fueled by outrage) it takes to help on a local level—to volunteer at a food bank or a literacy program or a Big Sister program. Here's a way we might escape the bitterness of a crippling realization of political limits that require deeply ironic detachment or frustration.

I am in agreement with you that to be an artist at all is a political act or at least is chock full of political implication, particularly in a democratic nation, where, to a certain extent, all choices become politicized since each helps compose the

*nation's discourse, a discourse which in turn is supposed to determine the actual
course of the nation. I think that's part of the reason I found Perloff's comparison
between Austrian and American intellectual/artistic political non-engagement
to be situationally more of a contrast; and, after reading the book, it seems to me
Perloff is definitely contrasting the situations more than she is comparing them.
I guess what disturbs me, however, about the omni-politicization we experience
is that by focusing our attention on the political aspects of any given choice or
encounter we may in the process lose sight of more immediate obligations toward
one another which depend less upon political ideas or initiative than upon in-
nate responses such as sympathy, pity, compassion, mercy, and, above all, love,
or as Simone Weil explains it, upon our recognition of another's suffering. The
political seems to pay court to these feelings (and to other less noble ones) by
flattening them out, by implementing rational plans of action that allow one to
detach one's self from another human being's condition. I think this may be why
some artists wish not to avoid but to move beyond the political level of things
toward something more quintessential. For an American artist, how possible do
you think that kind of transcendence is?*

Your own poetry (at least *Bivouac*) steeps its inquiries in the overtly political
and suggests a fluidity between compassion and politic ingenuity, and is an
excellent example of work that exceeds the programmatically political by ada-
mantly ballasting empathy against ironic impulses. You are in good company:
Claudia Rankine, Rae Armantrout, Andrew Joron, Tim Liu, Tracie Morris
(for example) all have invented admirable approaches to radical political
poetry while never getting lazy about compassion. Or relying on a recogniz-
able formal fundamentalism; that is, they don't insist on the conservation of
an ideologically coded mode. It is precisely what is beyond the parameters
of prescription, the stockade of tradition (even or especially an avant-garde)
that liberates us to write poetry. In the poetry world, however, politics and
community building can take on a grotesquely myopic view. Poets magnify
their own petty grievances about the "industry," gossip about other poets, list
their own reading and breakfast ingestions with vague prolix commentary, and
self-promote on blogs by the hundreds. If this makes poets sharper and more
community-minded for the meaningful exchanges, fine. Surely, we all have
our mythologies, but the self-conscious historicizing you see all over even the
best of blogs seems horrifyingly cynical about art-making impulses. And artistic
orthodoxies at the heart of many of these "communities" are no different from
any other kind of orthodoxy—based on exclusion of the uncertified and the
impure. If a universal audience for poetry no longer makes sense, does that

necessitate cult-like communities, all festering in their own self-regard? What I'm saying is that an artist's life might be held as accountable as her product for ethics and imaginative integrity. For instance, many people claim Marjorie Perloff is a Republican, but I've personally found no real evidence for that. If it's true, does it discredit her as an advocate of an artistic left? What's your take on or experience with the interactions of small-scale poethics with large scale poliethics?

With regard to the first question, I'd say no. Perloff's too complicated and too thoughtful of a mind to get my blackball on her criticism for that alone, rumor or not. Somehow I find it inconceivable, though, that she would ever vote for someone so inarticulate as George W. Bush. Whether or not it's true, I think such a stance points to other strange-bedfellow politics of poetry at large. There's certainly conservatism to be found in much supposed avant-gardism, for example. And then there is, of course, the oddity of pursuing at all an art so ancient as poetry—something which may seem to many as a conservative or reactionary pursuit. Obviously, writing poetry or literary criticism doesn't make one an "aesthetic fundamentalist"—that's not what I'm saying—rather, I'm saying that I'm sure there are people out there who would argue that it does. To respond to the second question I'll have to reveal some serious former naïvete. When poetry took over my life, I was surrounded by some really wonderful people who were writing poetry too, and deep down I believed that I would never again encounter pettiness so long as I stuck with other poets. Okay, so I was mistaken. At this point, I have encountered more than my fair share of megalomaniacs, misogynists, and poseurs to disprove my hypothesis. Poets share the same shortcomings as other people and unfortunately have an unusual capacity for meanness of a certain sort—vanity. However, I think the feeling I had that "all will now be different" was not mere simpleness on my part but an indication of poetry's power to transform a life, beyond its meanness, if only for a moment.

Considering all that we've discussed so far, I'd like to take the opportunity to shift gears and begin discussing your new book, Alaskaphrenia. *After I posed the last question, I kept thinking about something Bin Ramke says of it on the back cover, that your poetry is, "like Alaska, American and not." Was this American-and-not aspect of Alaska part of its allure for you as a source of meditation?*

I wasn't interested in the state *per se*, just the idea of the place as it is embedded in our national mythology, as an imaginative retaining space and frontier. I tried to think about the poetic line in the book as a kind of shifting frontier, and the poems themselves as speculating on, among other things, the American promise of renewal and self-invention. Our national fantasy of Alaska's limitless vertiginous vastness and freedom has historically informed the dynamics of individual and collective self-definition. Its fictive emptiness ("In the United States there is more space where nobody is than where anybody is," says Stein) has always been read as an invitation to produce still more fictions, still more possibilities for transformation. If, as Alaska allows us to believe, identity exists as self-invention, one's identification and explanation of the self might always be in flux—just as Alaska is in flux, existing as a place of multiple possibilities, formed around one's attention to the messages arriving from "outside" (outside ourselves, but also more literally what Alaskans call the lower 48). So the real state does seem to hold a physical and psychic place for all disgruntled and down-trodden citizens who don't want to abandon their country altogether, but want to remove themselves from it in some part. If America were a brain and its map broken into phrenological assignments, Alaska would be the place of invention, imagination, and love-of-danger-and-the-unknown. That said, the book envisions Alaska as a mental space; it internalizes its paradoxes and stereotypes, and I hope makes a case for the reality of one's imagined life. The site of the book is an optical illusion, a Fata Morgana, where the peaks of the Alaskan Range appear to be floating in midair or an inverted crystal island. The term Fata Morgana takes its name from the Italian fable about the magic undersea palace of Morgan le Fay. From the lower 48, Alaska might just be an apparition, a projection, a propagandistic ruse. It's not on any map, as Melville says; true places never are. Of course this explanation is a bit of propaganda and a bit of a disturbing illusion itself.

Perhaps so, but throughout the book you also reference the real with regard to Alaska—its variable climate and periods of daylight, for example—environmental effects which would surely disorient and reorient the minds of most real-life visitors. There's certainly a case for making the connections you mention. In metaphorical terms, there seem indeed different sorts of dangers and rewards respectively for the daytripper who tours, the explorer who investigates, and the local who inhabits with regard to the imagination. I noticed several of the poems employing an imperative voice—"Do's and Don'ts About Fur" comes to mind—which seem to offer advice for surviving these "states." How inhabitable versus how inhospitable of a place is the imagination for different kinds of travelers, yourself included? Is it possible for one to become a local resident with or without going mad?

One of Pessoa's alter egos says that the best way to travel is to feel. Building on that, to travel is to follow with your imagination, to transform. Imagination collaborates with perception, and sets a community of moods in dialogue with empirical probabilities; when these conditions are extreme, one often reaches for a guidebook. Of course the authors of guidebooks have often inhabited a place so thoroughly, experienced it so severely, that they have been forever changed by that place, and could never go back to write the book that they would have needed to read, if such a book could even exist. Hell, every travelogue is someone else's home movie. Instructions, maps, advice, litanies of caveats offer a sense of expectation, which becomes part of the actual experience, not necessarily a master-narrative onto which one's experience is grafted, but a more fluid interchange and alchemical complication. This is not the fantasy of the elite. Wait, are you calling me crazy?

No, not at all. After I'd alluded to the possibility of a "local who inhabits," I began thinking that one could never really become familiar with the imagination, given its nature, so that really there could only be frequent visitors, so to speak, ex-pats perhaps, but never really locals, unsurprised by their environs, for whom everything is familiar. How could one ever become familiar with a town which upon every new day rearranges itself entirely? If the imagination is conceived as a place, it seems such a place would encompass all places, both real and imagined. So no I'm not saying you're crazy. If you are, I must be too. Back to the instructions, maps, and so forth—in those instances within the poems, looking back at the poems now, can you speculate upon for whom some of those caveats and such were originally intended, for yourself, for readers, etc.? Were you ever conscientiously creating an ars poetica by which a reader would learn how to read your work?

Imperatives weave themselves through the whole book as reorchestrations of received advice found in travelogues and psychology manuals. The shopworn retrofitted to a different purpose and attitude hopefully calls attention to caesuras, oppositions, assumptions, and rhetorics that they inhabit or force us to inhabit. The form plays straight-man to the content in some cases; in other cases there is a more urgent calling out for help and security. I wanted to use vast peregrinations of inquiry, and found non-fiction forms useful for structuring the unknown and stimulating a feeling of uncanniness, and of remembrance and oblivion merging in a place of origins. As for audience, almost no answer seems even momentarily accurate, but the closest I can get is this: I write for a self that foregrounds the books and people I've loved most ardently and the aspects of those texts and folks that I've been lucky (sometimes unlucky) enough to be haunted by. In doing so I try to let the language-object lead that self into a wiser, heartier acre. I have the sense that language works to assert itself in more and more expansive, inventive ways. If I'm intuitive enough, I can create a place (not a representation of a place) in and of itself, characterized and composed completely with language. The pieces that are most explicitly instructional are no different, and nothing in the book was written as an *ars poetica*. Why do you ask?

I ask because I see within your poems lines or language which, when taken alone or within the context of a given poem, transmit multiple signals at multiple strata, one of those levels being self-reflexive. In a single poem, the self-reflexive tends to abdicate to other registers, but I think when reading between the poems, a discourse (not dissimilar to the one we're engaged in presently) emerges about what it is to write, what it is to read—I think ars poetica *is probably the wrong term for what I'm talking about here since that term implies something less faceted, a sort of definitive claim about poetry which I don't think you're making. Obviously between the poems there occur all sorts of discussions and conversations, about what it is to think, imagine, feel, be alive, be alone or with another, to name just a few. As a writer though, I guess my radar's particularly prone to picking up those writerly signals I mentioned, since out of all of those conundrums of living and feeling, the conundrum of what/how/why one writes always waves its hand at me above the crowd as it is this conundrum through which I try to deal with all of the others. Of course, one sees what one wants to see, but I do think one of the great strengths of* Alaskaphrenia, *and all of your work that I've read, is that it makes room for different kinds of readers to assemble their own sandcastles within and between the poems. For me, the book's first poem "Comprehension Questions," with its not entirely tongue-in-cheek relationship between the title and the questions that follow, commences that discussion of writing/reading. I'm particularly drawn to the line "What dark authority lurks among the unpruned spruce?"—to its sonorous beauty, but also to its implications with regard to poetry. What's so exciting to me about the poem is that it invites "close reading" even as it discredits comprehension in any ultimate sense. As I continued to read the book, I carried with me that initial impression and was quick to eye other lines and moments that seemed part of that discussion. I assumed that much of this was occurring spontaneously since the poems tend to accelerate on sound (and thus seem to be written quickly) but still wondered how aware or unconscious you might have been of the emergence of such a dialogue. Am I correct to assume poems individually were written quickly? They don't feel heavily revised.*

The poems weren't written quickly, but many move fast. I wrote the book between January 1999 and August 2002, during which time I lived in Provincetown, Denver, Chicago, Taos, Bloomington (IL), and Ann Arbor, so Alaska became my home of sorts, absorbing the actual settings and movements of my life. Movement in poems comes doubly—the headlong rush of emotion, the kinetic lickety-split of associations, logics, and time frames—an accrual of elastic, electric presents/presences. There's a current suspicion of speed—the culture of scanning or skimming instead of reading and glib or linear poems that take the punch line as their signature move—in favor of delay and digression. But horizontal movement—and the dialogic or polyvalent—doesn't need to come at the expense of acceleration. We should expect poetry to do the impossible and so be capable of both velocity and full experience. To be fast is to intoxicate and to move. (My mother warned me about fast boys; later I became sexually attracted to the cold, probably because of my fear of it.) Speed flings us into ecstasy—we forget our heft and force our attention on the immediate sensation—it allows a "freak" thought to get out of hand. It quickens thoughtful connections and collapses time and space in such a way that cartographic failure frees us momentarily from our historically determined selves. The actual experience of speed attends to absence—leaving—and presence—arriving—at the same time; as with writers like Beckett and Stein you get amazing momentum in the service of ultimate stillness, also an illusion of movement in enduring stillness. In someone like Tracie Morris, an amphetamine rhythm allows for sonic puns, almost-heard words and such, expanding the subliminal and scholarly impact, punching holes in the "about"ness of the poem.

Your mentioning Morris's "almost-heard words" makes me think of some of Vic Chesnutt's best work. Of course, it's a different sort of challenge writing for the page alone where the reader herself must be relied upon to sing those subtexts. Your poems are fortunately highly scored I think. The musical and tonal cues are there. Still, do you ever wish more poetry books came with CDs? Is that something you've considered? I think about my first time reading Ted Berrigan's Sonnets—I was kind of underwhelmed. Then, about a year later, I heard a recording of them and the poems completely transformed. His voice attached itself to them and now they are among my favorite poems. Anyway, recording does seem a viable option nowadays considering how cheaply CDs can be made, though some writers might be hesitant about creating a competition between the two media.

Yes to all that—using technology and musical influence to renovate the poetry reading, letting initial judgment of work be transformed by performance, wishing more poets collaborated with composers or musicians or used their own talents (and the cheap, easy software available) to make recordings. The institution of the poetry reading is both wonderful and woeful; that it has an iffy reputation is no secret. Anyone who has sat through a mumbly let's-get-this-over-with recitation, a cloying sing-songy delivery, a pompous pontification, a histrionic performance, a rambling preamble about the experience that led to the idea that led to the digression that led to the revelation that led to the poem—what George Orwell called "a grisly thing"—feels at least some hesitation before going out to hear a poet, especially someone you've loved on the page, for the first time. Lots of poets cut their writerly teeth on awkward or painful verbal talents, and so the reading might not be their most shining milieu. Exceptions to this are many, though, and there's really nothing quite like a stunning "straight" reading. Last April I fell unrelentingly smitten with Jeff Clark at a poetry reading—I already knew that he writes kick-ass poems, but his voice right there on the spot, without any apparent ceremony or artifice, ensorcelled me.

Likewise, poets who break out of the cage of academic or slam conventions, giving the audience a more fully engrossing and enlarging experience, inspire. Lots of this stuff is on the web, and I wish there were even more of it and more cross-over artists who deal in sound like Janet Cardiff and Vito Acconci as well as sound poets like Cris Cheek and Christian Bök, and collaborative recordings like Matthew Rohrer and Joshua Beckman's. I teach a class in "Sound/Poetry" and am amazed at my students' stellar syncretic concoctions in this field, and I am also recording my own pieces, an impulse triggered by frustration with the programmatic nature of my own poetry readings and their crazy demands on listeners. My recordings, mostly collaborations with composers and other poets, are pretty basic—I try to play with words as physical objects, and to convey effects unavailable to conventional poetic structures and contexts not immediately accessible to the listener upon one hearing. Poets who don't write from a performance-based aesthetic usually stir up an "endlessly flexible language" (Toni Morrison) that invites and bears re-readings; if I'm hearing a complex poem for the first time, I'm fading in and out of its best presence. That of course has its own compelling merits, and perhaps is just a prelude to actually reading it myself with the poet's voice in mind. I'm just saying that audiences of poetry readings usually have little preparation for being absorbed in the temporality of a poem, and there's no need to stick with the given formula.

By letting sound captivate the audience on its own preverbal terms, you can create a fascinating suspension between referentiality and nonreferentiality, text and textuality, inscription and reinscription in ways not yet anticipated. In the movie *Ghost Dog*, Jarmusch gives us best friends who don't speak or understand the same language, yet there is a deep abiding comprehension and recognition in their exchanges. At a poetry reading, I think hearing extra-music, rhythms, and voices makes people more comfortable with trusting their listening trip, and chewing on—enjoying—the more abstract communicative aspects of music itself. It also can take the podium out of the picture—so an acoustic carnival or spell of rhythm and language might manifest. Your mother is a conductor, right? How do you think music and that immediate specific saturation in your mother's music and her knowledge of music have informed your own writing?

You might be in for a long answer! I'll just say a couple of things for brevity's sake. For me, mother, music, and language have been intrinsically connected for as long as I can remember. (My father too, I should mention, was/is a musician; he plays the saxophone. My extended family too—almost everyone plays an instrument, some by ear, and all of them can sing harmonically.) At three, my mother began teaching me to read and to write and also to play the piano, that is, to read music; so these two systems of communication coincided from the beginning and overlapped in my head, I think. I could see early on that music could create a narrative, for instance, without a single lyric accompanying it. Later I could see the inverse in poetry, that simply through the sounds of words, through a well-placed break, through a certain meter, one could capture and describe feeling as intuitively as could one through music proper. As a young girl, my favorite books at the library were almost always biographies of composers—Chopin, Beethoven, Mozart, Schumann—and I always dreamed of composing but could never break from my classical training enough to hear unwritten music. I had learned in such a way that I was doomed to be a reader rather than a writer of music. Of course, now when I write poetry I do indulge that aspect of myself and often think of myself in that way, as a composer of music, or at least as an arranger of it. Sometimes I think instead of citing poems as "by" so-and-so, it should read "arranged by" so-and-so. I would say that of my own work.

The second thing worth mentioning is with regard to my mother, who is a choral conductor, and so a conductor of voices. Besides being an arranger and/or composer, a poet to me is also a sort of conductor in two senses. The first sense would be as one who must keep the time, guide the dynamics, and conduct the various voices of the poem; of course, as the piece continues, the stronger the music, the more felt and in sync the voices are with one another, the less and less necessary becomes the conductor's managerial role. The voices have now a force of their own and need little guidance. The conductor then need only steer with a gentle hand and again becomes truly crucial only toward the end of the piece. The second way in which I think about the word "conductor" as synonym for "poet" has something to do with my father, who is a retired electrical engineer—the poet as a sort of channeler of electricity.

There's a poem of mine with a line that reads "think of the words of the poem as notes to the music" (please forgive me for being so obnoxious as to quote myself, for I do have a point), and the primary thing I was thinking of then, when I wrote it, was that the poem must be played; otherwise the words are as meaningless as notes of a score that may have well been read on the page but which have never been intoned by human beings who, each within himself, carry the capacity for deep feeling. The musical notes achieve their full meaning only when played. When one sits down to read a poem, the act should be similar to sitting down at the piano to play Bach. One has to interpret, not in the analytical sense—a player piano could do that—but in the intuitive sense and with the utmost sensitivity, as one plays. For a moment, one is, one must be Bach, however one imagines him to be. For me, without that transmigration there can be no music, no poetry, only a lifeless system of signs without significance.

I fear I've gotten a little carried away here. Looking back over this interview, I feel as though we've pushed upon all sorts of buttons. I think we might well end here with some final questions. I would like to know the obvious—what are you working on presently? And a more complicated question: is it possible to remain skeptical of a pure Platonic Poem and to believe in it at the same time? In other words, how romantic and how anti-romantic do you consider your vision of poetry to be?

That's a complicated set of questions, and because I'm in a simple mood, I'm going to comb their verbal wilds sideways. One obvious thing is that my reading aesthetic is much vaster than my own practice as a writer, and I love reading poems that I'd be skeptical of if I had actually written them. I'm not interested in writing poems that use the hook and ladder, tack and bait that are *de rigueur* in mass culture, yet I am probably involved in a tension between product and process. I want my own poems to be enactments of experiences, and to speculate on the back and forth of self and world and will and imagination. I want bewilderment, struggle, and mazy error; I want physicality in language which means both assertive presence and vulnerability. I also want to craft that mess without tidying it up, concocting a poetry that bears the burden of mystery and participates in it. I feel compelled to present a fine-tuned—even "efficient" with all its capitalistic folly—fine-turned composition that isn't against meaning but for new articulations of meaning and undistillable performances of it, gut, mind, nerves and all. I want to present something better than myself and also to surprise myself in recognition. These are all essential but impossibly difficult tasks that come through laborious experimentations and revision, calibrations, endless mundane and artistic diversions. The conflict between desire for unhampered, unmediated access to the world and desire for containment and coherence excites an energy for me, and to separate these impulses would be like trying to sever the lightning from its flash. Nietzsche's idea of "grammatical seduction," and its signature as-ifness, means that our language is always ready to fall into entrapment. But we must do what we can to keep it alive and moving, to take pleasure in it while registering the complaint, inquiring into the implications, and shifting the linguistic traffic or inventing a new current through which and by which to move. For instance, to return to your response, in music, sampling is an interrogation of meaning and context (renewal by repurposing). DJ Spooky's new book might be addressing a poetry community when he uses Emerson to bolster his argument for the era of the sample, and cautions against too much citation, not enough synthesis: "Who speaks through you? Sound creates a way of thinking about these issues [of citation and originality] in a way that the visual and the narrative flow into that rupture in the system of seduction."

Ed Dorn

Ed Dorn was born in April 1929, in Villa Grove, Illinois. He published nearly 20 books of poetry, including *Gunslinger* (1968-1975), *Captain Jack's Last Chaps* (1983), and *Chemo Sabe* (1997), as well as a novel, *By the Sound* (1971), collections of essays such as *The Shoshoneans* (1966) and *Way West* (1993), and numerous books of Spanish language translations with Gordon Brotherston. Briefly educated at the University of Illinois, his studies were corrected by Charles Olson at Black Mountain College. A railroad man and itinerant lumberjack, Dorn taught at the University of Idaho (1961-1965), the University of Essex, England (1965-1970), the University of Chicago (1970-1971), Kent State (1973-1974), and the University of Colorado at Boulder (1977-1999). He died of pancreatic cancer in December 1999, and is buried in Boulder, Colorado. This interview was conducted by poet and critic Peter Michelson on April 7, 1999, at Dorn's home in Denver. Wanting to follow up on his interview with Dorn the previous summer but aware of Dorn's failing health, Matthew Cooperman asked Michelson to act as interlocutor in the interview process. Although intended to expand upon Cooperman's earlier interview with Dorn (in *Salt*), this interview also records a long-time friendship, Dorn and Michelson having taught in the English Department at the University of Colorado since the 1970s. The interview appeared in Volume 20, Numbers 2 and 3 of *Verse*.

Since this comes from various quarters, let's start with Matt's question about documentation, about "journalistic poetry." How was Gunslinger *an effort to construct a political poetry, to document the strange media carnival that was initiated by Watergate?*

It was a very conscious literal hour and daily comment on what was going on as it unfolded, all through Watergate, through the Vietnam War, through everything that happened from 1968 to 1975 pretty much. But there was nothing quite engineered about it. It didn't necessarily show up that way in the text. I mean, it wasn't meant to be overt and obvious, but you know any reading of the poem will show that if you've got the smarts, and there's no secret about the time it was written in. That's when I began to seriously use — instead of talking about my own personal objections to the behavior of this so-called society — to actually use events as part of the play. This guy Elmborg, I like his title for that reason [James K. Elmborg, *A Pageant of Its Time*].

It is like a masque, actually.

Very much like a masque.

Then insofar as Gunslinger *is documenting Watergate in the way that you just described, and there is that* Abhorrences *connection, that bridge, what about* Gunslinger's *"prophecy," as Matt puts it, "of the developments in Clinton and Lewinskygate" and the impeachment and that whole panorama, that whole masque of its own?*

Right. And since that's a current question, I mean a current events question, how does that relate to the continuity of American policy in Clinton's regime?

You want me to say that?

Well, I just did. The events leading up to Clinton's impeachment, and the cast of characters and the story itself, all produced one important fact, which everybody should have known in the first place: that this public deceived itself that it could think as a body, which it hasn't done certainly since the turn of the century. It's been deprogrammed in its knowledge of history. And it has no means or mechanism by which to think, but the polls kept telling everybody that they were thinking. And nobody's questioned where the polls came from, or whether the polls were real or not. But it said the American people approved of Clinton precisely because of his immorality and we should all get on with it. This was largely Hollywood-driven, which is sex-crazed, and violence-driven—in other words, totally aligned with the White House. Bill and Ken Starr are cut from opposite ends of the same piece of peckerwood. Starr's from San Antonio and Bill is San Archy. The San Antonio guy was an arch fundamentalist, hard-assed, religious Puritan, and Bill is a libertarian, but they're both peckerwood culture all the way. They're both Southerners. This country has been in the hands of Southerners ever since the Civil War, and it will remain in the hands of Southerners. We should be bombing the South instead of Serbia now.

It has been noted that foreign policy now consists of the following and the following only: we don't like you, we're going to bomb you. If you try to defend yourself, we're going to reduce your country to rubble, and then if you survive, we're going to try you as a war criminal at The Hague. Period.

Nothing else. That's it. That's the principle and the details in one spoonful. That's the medicine. Clinton reduced leadership to where you couldn't even try him as a criminal.

He's not even a criminal.

He's not even a criminal. Which is not very much to prove, actually, in a country where the vast majority are criminals. I mean it's not all that interesting. So we dropped that. He's now declared himself to be proud of being impeached by a House of Representatives as dumb as this one. That's practically a quote. By the time anybody reads this, we'll be way down the line but, you know, reviewing the facts, I don't feel that there'll be any room for anybody to disagree with my estimate of the situation, and I certainly won't, and so that's how I feel about that. And did I predict this? I certainly did. The most disquieting aspect of the whole affair was the manipulation of public opinion polls that seemed to indicate the public could think. That's never even been tried before in the history of opinion sampling. It was a major triumph.

Now talk about the lines along which the prediction would go, because that's actually the interesting point, I mean not whether you predicted it or not.

Well, people who have been robbed of their history, who have no history, who have no moral base, who are the most programmable people who have ever lived in a single nation in the world, in the history of the world, a people who are interested only in shopping and who are only capable of shopping (we "ran out" of guided missiles in the present bombardment), and whose only product is shopping, are obviously going to be simple to program. For instance, just think of the duration required to teach them to hate the Serbs. It must have been a matter of hours. When Americans didn't know who the hell the Serbs were. Didn't know the Serbs were not a member of the Axis, that the Serbs were the only lonely bulwark against the fascists in WWII and, after, in the Balkans. I mean, that alone tells you the whole story practically. Was there ever a population made of such putty? I can't think of one.

Now, wait, let me interrupt there because that isn't quite right.

Who's being interviewed here?

You've got to correct yourself here.

How?

Because remember they were broadcasting Voice of America, or whatever it was, to the Serbs. It's not the Serb people that we're attacking, notwithstanding the bombs are falling on the Serbian people.

They're bombing them, anyway.

You follow what I'm talking about? What about that cynicism, that they would expect to float such a blatant prevarication?

Well, I don't see the difference here between the two campaigns against socialism, and Bill should be alert to this since he's claiming this big IQ. I don't see the difference here between Vietnam and Serbia. Now this time it's the West against the East. We're bombing the Orthodox. Now they're the Gooks. The people engineering this are Romans. The very word "orthodox" is like waving a red flag in their eyes. Actually, this started with Diocletian. Constantine broke the Church and actually removed it, and it was the Romans who became dissolute by not saying, "Sure. Constantinople is the greatest civilization and that's where the Church should be headed." And the Orthodox considers that Islam is apostate. And then Orthodox is orthodox; and anything that's not Orthodox is unorthodox. Frankly, myself I'm Orthodox. But anyway what's happening here is that when the wall came down, who was invited to be part of NATO? Catholic nations. The exclusion of the Orthodox was overt and very pointed in the case of Serbia.

What do you mean when you say you're Orthodox?

I'm saying that I think the Church should have gone to Constantinople, as Constantine so directed and wished. And I'm saying that I belong to the Orthodox Church; I've joined. And the reason I joined the Church is because I saw that anything the Western world so hates has got to be right.

Are you telling me you're giving up your Protestantism?

Well, I was raised a Methodist, but I'm going to die Orthodox. I need a faith. I'm a faithful man, myself, and orthodoxy is for me. I can bring a lot to orthodoxy. I am a child of the Enlightenment, which the Orthodox missed. I am, you know, a culturally useful person.

So when you're talking orthodoxy here, you're talking like a strict historical orthodoxy, that is, Eastern Orthodox?

I'm saying the Greeks, who are suffering a big attack by the West on their church and on their culture—a continuation of the Roman war against them. NATO is nothing if not Roman.

Right, right. Greek Orthodox, which is also Russian Orthodox.

Yeah, which is patriarchal. You know, there's a saying: when a Russian goes to Greece, he's not going abroad. This is not a cultural war we're having here. This is not about culture; it's about religion. This is a religious war.

Oh, for God's sake!

Wow!

All right. Matt wants to talk more about Gunslinger, *specifically something of its exploration of appearance and reality, the "inside real and the out sidereal," something of the political climate. Or more accurately, the philosophical climate that allowed for that commentary. I mean the big philosophers of the time were fascists—Heidegger, Wittgenstein.*

Appearance and reality is a kind of reference. It's a reference to Whitehead, who used it, and based his philosophy pretty much on it, and it interested Olson obviously a lot more than it did me. None of that stuff is important to me, really. But if it gets the reader to actually react by considering the difference between appearance and reality, so be it. In that sense it has a moral function or an ameliorative function. Most of the references to Heidegger, and the puns like Hi Digger and so on perhaps operate that way as well. For instance, at that time, historically, it's true, and a lot of people would know this, there was a revival of certain kinds of seventeenth century dissenting movements, and the Diggers were one of many, actually. Communitarians. That historical memory hadn't been entirely lost in the late '60s. And the fascists, the other pole. That's why the '60s loved them. *Gunslinger* has its roots in the '60s and its exfoliations in the '70s. And people knew about that. I mean, a few people did, and they led the rest of some other people to behave in those ways. And that was a good thing. But all of that kind of content in *Gunslinger* is meant to be intellectually altruistic. I think a lot of people who discussed this poem found a lot more profundity in these things than is actually there. It's an intellectual flight of the times, a recombining of certain phrases that were current. Its manner seeks to preserve the record. And it's not all that complicated and it's not all that difficult. And neither were the times. A simple-minded war on a very small country. I've always been for a rather literalist reading of that poem.

So I was able to write the essay by just staying literal ("Edward Dorn: Inside the Outskirts," Sagetrieb 15.3).

Yes, and I think there's enough story there to support a literal reading.

Yeah. In effect, I think in "Inside the Outskirts" I quoted you as, at various times, downplaying the philosophical frames of reference. Nonetheless, they are there, and they do, as you've just said, provide a kind of documentation of what was in the air at a certain time in the cultural panorama. When one talks about a historical poem, which obviously would include philosophy, whatever would go with the sweep of history is central. I think this goes to the heart of one of Matt's questions: what is your sense of what contemporary poetry can do? You know, when Olson says, "All right, now, with Projective Verse, poetry can carry more freight than any time since the Renaissance …" You remember what I'm talking about? What does that freight need to be?

Well, I think one of the great functions of that essay, its "projection," is the fact that it opened out the field of the business of the poem into literally every corner of life that exists and there is nothing, there is no form that the poem cannot now be able to bear. There's nothing you can't plausibly say in a poem. I mean, all we need is the poem, actually. And I've treated it in that essayistic sense. Any function that any other piece of writing has can be borne by the poem. It's just a matter of the writer's nerve to feel and to think and to actually behave that way. There is a tendency for people to say "poem," and think a certain way. I've noticed this over the years, partly with students, but with mature poets also, any kind of poet, actually. The idea is that somehow there's a certain kind of restriction imposed on something by being a poem. I feel that that's not true, that's not true in any sense. And in fact it's completely counterproductive and unreal to think of the poem that way. And I think it's spawned a lot of timid poetry. Why is this? It's not because the poet's timid necessarily, but because the poet refuses to see how, in fact, what Olson is saying, applies. I think in "Projective Verse" the overwhelming attention on breath and the kind of secrets implied in how you breathe, and how you actually do the poem, have been way exaggerated. And for me that was never the useful part of the essay because I don't think anybody does that. I think you can write a poem without breathing at all, if you practice underwater or something. I mean, you could do it, and it'd be just as good a poem, or it could be an even more interesting poem. The breath has gotten way over-emphasized.

So what you really mean is, I'll call it for lack of a better term, the intellectual capacity and mobility of a poem. And Olson just opened it up totally.

He threw open the gates of poetry to include the world and himself. Every one of its aspects. There is literally nothing that the poem cannot now contain.

Your work engenders a particularly interesting exploration of form. How has the question of form been, in Matt's phrase, "a necessary point of departure?"

Since form is 100% of what you see and a direct application of what the poet feels, form is in everything an announcement and expression of reality. Form is always an extension of everything. But to the question. I am actually an experimentalist. I was the first to make an extensive use of the footnote in the poem in the modern way in *Hello La Jolla*. I mean La Jolla itself, by virtue of its geographical location and function within the naval establishment, is a footnote.

It's true. In modern poetry … Jesus, what an idea. Where did you get that idea?

That idea was forced by the circumstance of the poem—San Diego is the corner pocket on an irrelevant pool table. And with *Languedoc Variorum*, as *Languedoc Around the Clock* is now called. (*Languedoc Around the Clock* actually was a title suggested by Jeremy Pryne at one point because that was his sense. But I don't think he had much faith in my ability to tackle his domain, so he was trying to relieve the situation in front in some way.) But anyway, I finally did land on this method. I wanted a poem that would be multi-cultural and multi-ethnic, and I just thought the only way to trash these ideas, actually, which certainly needed to be done and which is still, as far as I'm concerned, one of the main reasons for doing the poem, is to actually mimic the serious scholarly procedure of a variorum edition, and I think the heretics deserve at least that. You know, a kind of multiple commentary. And I had been interested in the stock market report at the bottom of the Turner network, that's where that comes from, the Nasdaq—everybody would know that. And then, of course, Naz being the Nazarene, the Nazz. That was a kind of Lord Buckley reference to Nazdak. And then the subtext. There's the famous charge of the theorists that everything's got subtext and everybody's lying anyway, so that worked out, just sort of found its own place floating at the bottom. In a true variorum, you've got all the historical commentary of people who have read the text through the ages, from, well, whenever Shakespeare scholarship began in the late seventeenth century and then went through the eighteenth century and the nineteenth century. That's what the variorum's about. So I found that part of the form to be a ready dumping ground for any kind of off-the-wall ideas I happened to have about what was also happening in the present, concurrent with the text, which was at the top, and ran across the top like in a variorum. I'm still doing this at this date. The poems are a fairly serious attack on how people who have questioned authority have been treated throughout the ages. This is an important and legitimate subject for poetry.

What we call poetry now may or may not be metered, and if it falls into meter once in a while, it could be by accident, it could be by intention, or it could be by instinct. I mean there's just no way now to use poetry unless it's constantly searching within itself for a new way to be read. And in fact that's what poetry is to me now. I can't understand how people who write poetry aren't constantly or incessantly searching for new manners of approach to the poem, because that's about what we can do now. I don't know of anything else that can be done with it. I mean sure, you can rhyme and you can think in rhyme, but rhyme that comes in the middle of the line is more interesting now than a rhyme that comes at the end, and that's a consequence actually of the reader having been worn out by several hundred years of rhyme coming at the end. We have no control over that. That just happened. That happened before we got here. But that doesn't mean that rhyme is not useful. I was trying to explore ways in which you could place rhyme in various positions in a line, as in "The Cycle," which is referred to here. You can call this experimental or not. Experimental in our time has largely come to mean incomprehensible, and I certainly don't have any truck with that. I'm very suspicious of any language that is not fairly immediately comprehendible. I don't have much patience at all with just sounds. I never have. I don't object to having some people do that, and I can be amused about as long by that as I can by a *poeme concret*, but that's not very long. And I don't myself indulge in any of that kind of stuff. I think that the poem should be pitched at as intellectual a level as you're capable of. Because if it's not, then you shouldn't be doing it. That's what exploration and experimentation *are* to me. That's the only kind that I would have any respect for.

What you say refers back to your earlier comment about what Olson was doing in his essay, and that he opened it up in ways that his own particular intelligence could explore. And what occurs to me, as you're talking, is how breath, really, for you was not a particularly interesting aspect of that essay, but for Olson I suspect breath was imperative because you can hear him taking these breaths and taking off.

Well, for one thing he had a lot of trouble breathing. He was an extremely heavy Camel smoker. And he had emphysema. I think the medical aspects of that essay would be worth exploring for somebody. And they could do this by listening to the tapes. It's one of the aspects of that essay that hasn't been touched on and for obvious reasons, but it should be. And, you know, when we're just about to drain the tobacco companies of capital, it could be an interesting question. There's a PhD subject.

But actually the other aspect of that is pretty interesting—that Olson is in a way a lot broader, because any given intelligence brings what it's capable of to the notion of "projective verse," and adapts it and just says "look, this is an open field, let's run."

I agree with that completely. All I'm saying in fact is that he gave me my license.

Right, right. And any license also imposes the notion that you know what the rules are by which that license is functional.

You have to qualify for the license.

Okay, let's see. The heretical is the topic here, and the term Matt hits upon is that you have the "sense of a secular heretic," and "what is your sense of heresy in the context of your own poetic mission?" I mean, you do that, you take up the whole notion of the antagonistic, both historically and culturally.

Well, in one sense this is not true, but in another sense it is quite true. I think that poets who collude with the government should be shot. And I think heretics are the only responsible citizens and heresy is the only responsible position, as well I've said many times. I don't consider myself a heretic in any important sense. I mean, the leading heretic now is Slobodan Milosevic.

Oh, that's interesting.

And he's being treated like a heretic.

I got into *Languedoc Variorum* really through my teenage experience with going through the rites of the ritual hero, Jacques de Molay, who was flayed by the church and was set up as a heretic because Innocent III—I think it was Innocent III; Innocent, that's very, very funny. At least the Huns had a sense of their own importance. They'd be like so-and-so the Momentous. That's cool, you know. But Innocent? Anyway, deeming someone a heretic was an excuse for seizing the property of the Knights of the Temple, the Knights Templar, and so Jacques de Molay was singled out. He was tortured hideously, and finally he was flayed; this is while alive, of course—that was the ultimate treatment of the heretic. And he was drawn and quartered, and his body was utterly taken care of. Jacques de Molay wasn't the only knight to be tortured; he just suffered the most spectacular and sensational torture. And death through torture: very, very slow. That's why the stations in the Masonic temple are so developed. You wear robes and you memorize your parts and you re-enact, because this is tantamount to or parallel in some strange way. I don't think it was intended by the Church, but it is the suffering of Christ that's evoked here very strongly, at least in my mind. That's the propaganda of the Western Church, and the ultimate goal of its centrality of power. And that's why, in fact, they couldn't stand the realism of orthodoxy. And that's why they had to stay behind in Rome, to make the biggest empire that ever was, the most successful empire, which is still actually largely intact. You have to know a lot about the Austro-Hungarian Empire to understand this current heresy, and the consequences for the Serb people, who are heretics now en masse.

Anyway, what I'm talking about is essentially a high school experience, which didn't come back to me until two or three years ago when I started reliving vividly the experience of when I was 16-18 years old. I was always rather doubtful about, well, virtually everything, because I grew up in a milieu which encouraged a lot of doubt if you wanted to survive with anything intact at all, but still I could see the point and meaning of the Jacques de Molay story. So I interposed a lifetime of learning and experience when I went to Languedoc in 1992. I used to go out after work, at the University of Montpelier (Paul

Valery's university) where I did my exchange, and just wander around, and the idea just presented itself. I mean these little towns, the people, the density of the Crusade history. When the Holy Army returned to southern France, these were the most experienced military men in Europe at that time, and there was nothing for them to do. All they knew how to do was fight. They were expert marauders and wasters, and they had their practice against a really tough enemy. I mean Saladin had valiant and experienced soldiers. These were professional armies going against each other. This is not kidding around. This is not death at a distance. This wasn't a cowardly, you know, B2 bombing. This was looking your man in the eye. This was real.

The heretic is always this guy with a horrible first name, like Slobodan. We don't even understand that. And we can pinpoint him with radar and laser shit. We'll write on him with lasers, but we won't ever face him. Never will we do that. We'll get rid of our heretics now at a distance. It was a Greek who pointed out that the arrow, in fact, was a dishonorable way to wage war. And that was the first projectile. And now it's the same thing. I mean, the SAM missile. These cruder things that they've got against our more sophisticated things are just arrows, really, when it comes down to it. And it all shares the same burden of dishonor in war.

So when I started doing the poem, there was a serious collision going on, a serious experimentation. I was impelled to do this from extremely early experience and passion. But in the meantime I became extremely loaded with other attitudes and opinions and information that, of course, you wouldn't have dreamed of in the DeMolay Hall. I mean, it wasn't part of the ritual. You just learned what that ritual was. And it prepared you for the bigger and greater ritual of the Masonic. I never became a Mason. Actually, most of the boys in my DeMolay chapter, most of their fathers were Masons. My father might have been a Mason, but I never knew my father. He was a railroader, and a lot of railroaders were Masons, especially conductors and the runners of trains. My father conducted a train. He was a rear-end conductor. He was the boss of the train. This is the age of steam. And later a little bit of diesel. But I don't know about that. My stepfather was never a Mason. He was a poor day-laborer on a farm, and the Masons in my town came from the skilled crafts population, and the merchants' part of the merchant culture. You had to have a certain status and rank. I imagine that the guy who lived in this house was probably a Mason. He could have been a plumber or something like that. But skilled crafts and guilds. You know the subtext of *Languedoc Variorum* covers a lot of what I'm talking about, and it's a rushy kind of information pattern.

So as a kid, for whatever reason, you were led into DeMolay, and suddenly confronted with this paradigm …

… a medieval paradigm, absolutely right. That's true, that's what it was. It's a play. You learn your part. You get a part and you do the same thing every time.

Fantastic. Back to the masque. And it's still with you, obviously.

Oh, yeah. We'd go to other towns and do our little variation on it, and they would come and visit us. Because there were these little towns around.

You mean, there were whole little provinces?

Yeah, and the drama, this little Passion Play. The Passion of Jacques de Molay. And he was singled out. I don't know exactly why he was singled out to the extent that he was. I just don't have that in my mind at the moment. But it's an interesting story. It was part of the campaign. Suddenly somebody pointed out to Innocent III how rich these Knights had become in land and money and commerce. And so he seized it. But in order to seize it he had to fabricate their heresy. Well, flash forward; it's not a very big jump to see that we are fabricating the heresy of Slobodan at the moment. Not all the world agrees with this Maine poet we have as Secretary of Defense, Mr. William Cohen. And I'm ashamed to say that I'm a poet because he's a poet. I find that really disgusting, actually. But still that's what poetry has become. It's become a helpless ruse that anybody wants. Poetry is the biggest whore now living, the biggest most pervasive whore now in practice. No doubt about it. And I mean multi-culturalism, the whole bloody works right up to the Secretary of Defense, dispatching our warships against the new heretic. This is part of the motivation of the poem.

But it's quite specific in that DeMolay was distinctly, at least I remember it as distinctly Protestant, distinctly anti-clerical …

Well, he became Protestant in the sense that the Masons were Protestant, but there were secret Masonic chapters in Rome at that time. And of course Jacques de Molay was Catholic, like everybody was. I mean this was before …

… as Pierre in War and Peace.

Indeed.

And you then playing out the DeMolay thing in the Midwest. Something that, incidentally, I never played out because it was never a factor in my life, so that's quite interesting; that in a small town possibly you're more likely to encounter medievalism as such.

Well, in my town you have to throw in the added factor that there was very little to do. I mean, you'd do virtually anything to have something to do. And that would've been the initial motive.

Perhaps that connects with another question. Matt's interest here is in the local, what one calls the local, its particular activity and complication today.

Well, I happen to know for a fact that Olson—because you know I was his student in that sense and he talked a lot about this—Olson was probably the greatest actual D. H. Lawrence fan ever. Just a true fan really, and he made everybody around him a Lawrence fan, too, because he spoke so eloquently and enthusiastically about him and the whole Lawrence canon. I think he picked up most of his enthusiasm for the significance of the local from D. H. Lawrence, because Lawrence has written essays about it, and I don't.

I never saw anything that would constitute an actual definition of a direct relationship between the local effects and what you did with it in writing. And I never felt that I ever knew what the connection was. I think it's important to be interested in the proximity of things, but that's not really what they're talking about. You can pick up the spirit of things that are close by and so forth. I ended up thinking of the local as just what captured my attention, really, what was close to me, and so that's why my poetry and my system of poetry could be described as a dumping ground for everything that I feel and think at any moment. The local to me is immediate experience, because you're affected by where you are, obviously.

Now, here's an interesting thing that seems to me pertinent, so I'll throw it in and you see what you think. Traditionally the Local would be subordinated to the Universal, and so what is it about that particular counterpoint that results, in terms of modern poetry, that gives the Local a priority over that old favorite, the Universal, which is still invoked by a certain segment of the academic community? That is, those people who talk about beauty as a universal, which in a sense flies in the face of what the modernists thought, and presumably Olson thought, what's their prerogative?

You know Olson followed Pound back into it in that sense. Pound was a great reactionary and was actually trying to restore a classical viewpoint. And I think Lawrence, in a sense, was parallel in his own way, in his kind of Nottinghamshire difference from Pound. They weren't characters who would be expected to get along. But they were contemporaries in a very real way. Both Lawrence and Pound took their intellectual cues from Thomas Hardy, who was the literary giant of their youth. If you follow Lawrence, to have a true local, you have to have gods of the local. You can't have monotheism; it does not tolerate the local. Monotheism is centrality of power and total control, and that's Rome. It sets up institutions to enforce this. Rome has created the most loathsome of institutions known to mankind, the priesthood, to enforce and to torture and to see, in fact, that the local didn't gain ascendancy without permission. Conversely, the Greeks were way too local, way too loose for the Romans. They set up little altars wherever they felt the spirit. And they had many gods. Theologically, they were a generous people. That's the diametric opposite of Rome, which is very, very selfish. You don't get to set up your own little god spot. You don't get to do anything like that. We're just talking about the disgusting habits of monotheism for lusting after control and dominance and bullying; it's a bullying theology. Definitely. I mean its whole strength is intolerance. That's why E.M. Cioran has interested me so much in the past few years. He was the last of the true cynics. I mean a real cynic in the philosophical sense, not just in attitude, which is what most people mean by cynics. And he had the best translator now working from French into English, which is Richard Howard. Those translations of Cioran are absolutely beautiful. It's just great reading. This was pretty lucky for Cioran, actually. I don't know that he would have had a chance if it hadn't been for the fortuitousness of Richard Howard's interest. Well, there's that. And then my natural affinity with cynicism in the philosophical sense as well, which really does believe that the only way to deal with an impossible problem is to laugh it away. I mean, only laughter can turn it to rags. You mentioned this in your essay …

Indeed.

I think that's at the heart of the cynic system actually. It's the ultimate desperation.

The ultimate weapon of the heretic.

That's right. And that's why the heretic gets flayed. The heretic also gets flayed because the heretic believes more than anybody else. You have to believe to suffer that much. In that sense, Jesus Christ was the numero uno heretic.

So when you talk about orthodoxy in your subscription to Orthodoxy, you sort of transform the sociology of that into a historical context rather than into a contemporary context. Am I making sense?

Yes, you are. I mean you get this out of Gibbon. The schism in the Church started with Diocletian and ended with Constantine, which is a period of, I would guess 150-200 years, maybe not that much. And the Orthodox kept up its tradition; they had the patriarchy. They got rid of the tiara and all of those effects, and they didn't have a priesthood set up to torture and to mount inquisitions and to physically and intellectually torture the subject. So comparatively, intolerance was not—which leads to religious wars—was not big in their canon. I mean any religion is intolerant finally. The Romans were intolerant of monotheism because they thought it was a cheap bloody trick. And that's why they suffered so many Christians to be eaten by lions in those arenas. Because they enjoyed that; the Christians to the lions was the literal joke. They said, "Let them eat those assholes." You know who wants one god? This is a reduction in aesthetic interest that produces a major kind of culture. And yet they put up with them for a long time before the persecutions. I mean the Christians went around, these seedy little people went around telling the Romans they were full of shit for having so many gods and how they were sinners and were going to be damned. Pretty pushy people. And somebody has got to resist. The Romans got lazy and that was that. Now? I don't know. But I don't think anybody has to belabor why somebody should be interested in Cioran. He's just one of the greatest writers of the century, and he's one of the greatest philosophers of the century, and he's a resistance. I mean philosophers don't count for anything now, do they? They're not even consulted on the abortion question, for instance. So Cioran's accomplishment is magnificent. If philosophers were the keepers of morality? There's nothing to keep now. It's a little difficult to understand how they just don't count for anything, really. I mean, poets are better off than that.

MARTÍN ESPADA

Martín Espada was born in Brooklyn, New York in 1957. He received a B.A. in history from the University of Wisconsin at Madison as well as a law degree from Northeastern University and held various jobs before becoming a tenant lawyer in the Boston area. He has published seven collections of poetry, including *Alabanza: New and Selected Poems 1982-2002* (W.W. Norton, 2003), *Imagine the Angels of Bread* (W.W. Norton, 1996), which won the American Book Award and was a finalist for the National Book Critics Circle Award, and *Rebellion is the Circle of a Lover's Hands* (Curbstone Press, 1990), which won the Paterson Poetry Prize and the PEN/Revson Award. He edited *Poetry Like Bread: Poets of the Political Imagination* (Curbstone Press, 1994) and co-translated *The Blood That Keeps Singing: Selected Poems of Clemente Soto Vélez* (Curbstone Press, 1991). His collection of essays, *Zapata's Disciple* (South End Press), appeared in 1998. He currently teaches literature and creative writing at the University of Massachusetts at Amherst. Brian Henry conducted this interview in Espada's office in Bartlett Hall on May 1, 1997. The interview appeared in Volume 15, Numbers 1 and 2 of *Verse*.

Because of your Puerto Rican heritage and bilingual background, the issue of language for you acquires an urgency unlike that in the work of most poets. How does bilingualism enter and influence your work?

Bilingualism enters into my work in a number of ways. First of all, I want to point out that bilingualism enters my work as subject, that I frequently write about language politics, that I frequently write about the fear which the majority seems to have for the minority tongue, or tongues, and that I write about incidents which have come to my attention in terms of language discrimination. So in that way bilingualism is subject in my poetry.

Bilingualism certainly appears as form in my poetry as well, in the sense that I utilize code-switching, going back and forth between the languages for effect, whether that effect is drama, irony, emphasis, a sense of authenticity. That was especially true of my earlier work. I do that somewhat less now, but it still goes on. Bilingualism also enters my work in the sense of translation, because I have one book which has been entirely translated into Spanish. And there are other individual poems in other collections which have been translated into

Spanish, and that has been quite a blessing for me because it enables me to take my work into settings where no one speaks a word of English. And I can do a reading in Spanish for an adult literacy program or an ESL program.

Finally, bilingualism influences my writing even when I'm working solely in English, because there is a flavor of Spanish in my English. For example, I am highly unlikely to use contractions; rather I will find myself using prepositions in English even though the option is available. Spanish does not have contractions: you look at the Spanish language, and everywhere you look you see those prepositions instead.

I have noticed your use of Spanish words or phrases in poems diminishing over the course of your career, but Rebellion is the Circle of a Lover's Hands *is a bilingual edition, entirely translated into Spanish by you and Camilo Pérez-Bustillo. How does the translation process work between you and Pérez-Bustillo? Is it a case of the translator working on his own and showing you the finished product, or is it more of a symbiotic relationship?*

It's symbiotic. First of all, it is true that the presence of Spanish within the English-structured poem has been diminishing. Paradoxically, my Spanish has been improving. Maturation in general has produced a maturation in my use of Spanish as well. Certainly, if you look at the poems that have been translated, you will see a pattern. First of all, one of the reasons why I do less code-switching in my poems now is because I think about the poem as existing in English and then in Spanish.

So you write expecting to be translated?

Hoping to be translated, yes. It's enormously difficult work, very time-consuming, and very precise. It requires a sort of surgical skill in two languages in order to render a good translation. As far as my relationship with Camilo Pérez-Bustillo is concerned, it works more or less like this: he's a very dear friend, very dear *compañero*, who can climb inside my head probably better than anyone, who understands the nuances of what I'm saying and understands the social and political issues I'm grappling with as well as anyone. So I have great trust for him. What characteristically will happen is that the two of us will sit down and we will bat the translation back and forth. Camilo is one of those phenomenally multilingual people. He also speaks French fluently.

Is he a poet himself?

He is an essayist, of course a translator, and a lawyer. He is currently a professor of communications at the University of Monterrey, Mexico City campus. And in fact, he's had some political problems there because he appeared on a government enemies list due to his human rights work. He has worked as a legal representative for a union of striking bus drivers in Mexico City. The leadership of that union was imprisoned a couple of years ago, and Camilo helped to get them adopted as prisoners of conscience by Amnesty International in London. And he's also had some dealings with the Zapatistas in Chiapas; he led a National Lawyer's Guild trip into Chiapas. Occasionally I hear from him that he may try to get out of Mexico. But for the time being that's where he lives with his wife and their three children.

So he believes in taking literature into the social realm as well.

Absolutely. We both come at it from the same place. We sit down with a poem, and sometimes we start from scratch and sometimes he shows up with a sheet of yellow legal paper with some scrawl on it, and we begin hammering away. And we do look at every word and weigh every word very carefully. The dynamic works well because Camilo is a veritable walking dictionary of the Spanish language; he understands nuance very well. At the same time, I am there to help render it from translatese into poetry.

Do you feel qualified to write poems in Spanish?

I sometimes fool around with it, and, as I said before, I've written poems bilingually with the code-switching.

Do you think in Spanish?

Sometimes, yes. If I'm in Puerto Rico and have been there for a couple of days, I'm thinking in Spanish, and it may even be hard for me to figure out what to say in English. It takes a little time for the bilingual mind to make that three-point turn, but once you've made it, you certainly end up thinking in the other language.

Mind you, my experience with the Spanish language, although I was born and raised in Brooklyn, is quite varied. I have traveled in Latin America—not only Puerto Rico, but also Mexico and Nicaragua. I have worked extensively in the community; for example, I was the supervisor of a Spanish-language legal clinic in Chelsea, Massachusetts, outside of Boston, and that required using the language on a daily basis. I have done radio in Spanish, I have done lectures and workshops in Spanish, and in fact I've even done court interpretation in Spanish, all of which required a great deal of work on myself. However, in matters of literary translation, I realized that the poet can be his own worst enemy, because the natural tendency is to insist on the most literal possible translation of your own work. When you go from English into Spanish, what you gain is music, the music of the Spanish language.

That music is also present in your poems in English.

Yes, there's a seed of it to begin with. What you lose, however, is a shade of meaning. Spanish is an older language than English; there are, simply, fewer words. So there are times when you have chosen a word in English and you go to translate it into Spanish and you can't really find the equivalent because there aren't enough words to reflect the nuance that you're looking for.

Or a Spanish word has to do more work.

Sure. In a way, there are a lot more ambiguities in Spanish because there are many Spanish words that are pulling double and triple duty, that mean two or three things that are totally different from one another, and so you need the context to determine what the meaning is. All of that can be quite maddening for a poet who simply wants the poem to exist in as close a form as possible to the original, and realistically that's not going to happen in many cases. So you need someone there to give you some distance, you need someone there to give you a sense of proportion, or a sense of perspective, to say "No, if you really want to convey this image, you cannot use the cognate in this case, you cannot translate it literally; what you must do is use this idiomatic expression or this phrase, which will convey much better the flavor, the spirit, of what you're saying." And that's what Camilo provides to me. He's always very, very precise when it comes to those issues.

You also have worked with Camilo on translating a book by Clemente Soto Vélez, the great Puerto Rican poet. Has translating Soto Vélez helped your own poetry?

I think that translating Clemente Soto Vélez was a great help in a variety of ways. First of all, Clemente Soto Vélez is not only a great Puerto Rican poet with a political history, he's also a surrealist. So it forced me to work quite a bit harder in order to have the linguistic competence necessary to translate very complex, difficult, and at times confusing work. It was useful for me to climb inside his mind and wander around there for a while. This is someone who, at first, was a great influence for me ethically. I thought that his example was a stellar example to follow—someone who was political, who was a poet, who went to prison for what he believed in, who never gave up, who was a mentor to countless writers and artists and other people.

In a sonnet dedicated to him, Jack Agüeros says, "He was so tall that he towered over himself, and his mouth / was so big that he spat whole Spanish diction-aries." His presence must have been huge.

Yes, vast, enormous, incalculable really. At first, I believed that his influence on me was limited to the ethical. However, what I found out subsequent to translating his poems is that he was having an aesthetic influence as well, in the sense that some of my poems became distinctly more surreal.

Like "Hands Without Irons Become Dragonflies," which is dedicated to him.

That elegy deliberately dips into surreal imagery in order to reflect its influence and inspiration: Clemente Soto Vélez. But even in other poems, I was able to suddenly indulge in the fantastic, I was able to expand the borders of my imagination in ways I had not thought possible.

You mentioned that you were born and raised in Brooklyn. How did growing up in Brooklyn affect your poetry?

There are two ways to answer that question. Brooklyn has certainly been subject for me as well, the people of Brooklyn. I grew up in a working class housing project called the Linden projects, and I frequently return to that experience as subject matter for poetry. That experience oriented me to certain themes which have stayed with me throughout my life as a writer, whether it's concerned with the working class or concerned with the Puerto Rican community, concerned with the black community or concerned with the inner city. All of those things spring from the experience of living in Brooklyn. But Brooklyn also dearly influenced the way I perceive the world. It influenced my character, it influenced what you might call a certain pugnaciousness, which develops inevitably in urban settings such as that, where you tend to see things in terms of struggle and conflict.

And you don't look away.

And you can't walk away from a fight because if you do, you get hit in the back of the head. So certainly all of those things made a big difference in terms of who I became as a poet and a person.

What was the literary environment of your childhood like? Did you read poetry outside of school as a child or adolescent?

No. Poetry was not part of my life growing up. Neither one of my parents is college-educated, although both are literate. During my early years, my father worked for an electrical contracting company at a step below electrician. He hated that work, so he endeavored to maneuver his way out of it. His salvation was, in fact, that he became a political leader in the Puerto Rican community in New York during the 1960s and eventually was paid for that activity. His literacy was really focused on reading books of history, politics, and so forth. That's what he was interested in, so that's what I read, and I ended up with a B.A. in history.

But I was an English major for about ten minutes. I went to the University of Maryland for my first year, and up to this point I had not begun to read poetry. I had written poetry since the age of 15, but I started writing poetry before I began to read it. I started using certain literary devices before I knew they had names. I didn't know what a metaphor was, or a simile, or alliteration, or assonance, and yet these are things I relied upon instinctively in poetry. Poetry was not provided for me in high school. The closest I can remember, and this goes way back, was an experience where I had to listen to the lyrics of light opera, and I was forced by a grim-faced English teacher to read aloud those lyrics. I remember chanting something from the Mikado like "They never would be missed, they never would be missed" and absolutely despising it.

Shortly after that, I remember writing my first poem, which also came out of a school setting. During one semester, I actually failed English. I was a totally marginalized student. I also failed typing, I failed gym—how do you fail gym? I was really the bottom feeder in that environment. But we had a rather creative teacher who gave a group of us young thugs an assignment in class, to keep us from throttling each other. The assignment was to reproduce a copy of *The New Yorker* magazine, and he handed us *The New Yorker*, which we had never seen, and told us to make our own. So we passed it from hand to hand, and it came to the first guy, who opened it up to the movie reviews, looked at it and said "Oh, movies. I've seen movies." He became our film critic. When it got to me, the only thing left was a poem, and I was very perturbed. I had to write a poem; that became my assignment. I was quite concerned and thought "Oh no, a poem," but I didn't want to fail English again, so I sat down and began writing. It was raining that day, so I wrote a poem about rain. I don't have the poem anymore, I don't remember anything about it except for one line: "tiny silver hammers pounding the earth." I had made a metaphor without knowing what it was. I would find out eventually and then go strutting down the hallway quite taken with myself. But that was the genesis of it, and I kept writing. Even in that setting, we weren't reading poetry, but our teacher was introducing us to various off-beat ways of looking at what could be called poetry He showed us a Simon and Garfunkel song and said "See, this is really poetry." But it wasn't a matter of reading poetry.

There were no books of poetry in my house when I was growing up. When I went to the University of Maryland, I had been writing for a couple of years, but with no support. It's not that people were unwilling to support me, but they didn't know how to support me. I went to Maryland and took two courses in my freshman year—creative writing and poetics—with the idea that I would eventually become an English major. Both were miserable experiences for me. This was 1977, I was 20 years old, and I had the canon pointed at me. I got Ezra Pounded. In the poetics course, I was exposed to the canon in its most conservative manifestation—not that we shouldn't know the canon, not that we can't gain something from knowing the canon, but we also have to recognize that the canon is constantly mutating, expanding, growing.

By the canon, do you mean what we generally consider the modernist poets— Pound, Eliot, Stevens, Yeats, et al?

Et al. Yes. The fact that I was not presented with any sort of alternative at that time was very disturbing. Langston Hughes was not mentioned in this course. I brought in Allen Ginsberg, whom I had found on my own, and was seriously discouraged from pursuing Ginsberg, but I did anyway.

And this was 21 years after "Howl."

Yes, so you can imagine. Whitman was not part of this course.

One would have a difficult time finding the influence of high modernists in your poetry. In fact, your poetry has more in common with a poet like Whitman than with the modernist poets. When you encountered Whitman, did he make poetry seem attractive to you?

Absolutely. I had to come to these poets on my own; they were not part of any formal education, and it was not part of any background at home. I came to these poets because I was hungry for this poetry, and so I had to trace the lineage backwards—I began with Ginsberg and worked back to Whitman, I began with Neruda and worked back to Whitman. But even before I could reach that point, I had to reach this apogee of frustration, where I dropped out of school. Not only was it a problem for me to be in the poetics course, but the creative writing course was likewise disastrous. I was referred to as hostile and aggressive by the professor because of the nature of my verse. I began to internalize these lessons, dropped out of school, and was essentially on my way to becoming a professional dishwasher, when a friend of mine, Luis Garden Acosta, gave me a book—*Latin American Revolutionary Poetry*, an anthology from Monthly Review Press edited by Roberto Márquez. And it was bilingual. Luis, who was a friend of the family for many years and a political protégé of my father's, handed me the book and said "You are going to be a poet." He was aware that I had been writing poetry, that I had dropped out of college and had stopped writing. So his words were deliberately designed to give me a jump start and it worked. I opened the book and found Ernesto Cardenal, the great poet-priest of Nicaragua, and his poem "Zero Hour," which is about the Samoza dynasty of the twentieth century in that country and the Sandinista resistance to that dynasty going all the way back to the 1930s. I saw next to that poems by Nicholas Güillen, the great Cuban poet of negritude, and next to that poems by Pedro Pietri, who was speaking about the New York Puerto Rican experience. Obviously I had something in common with that perspective, and I began to realize that I was part of a history, that I was part of a tradition. What reading that anthology meant to me was that I was no longer a literary amnesiac, which was the beginning of a certain self-respect and self-confidence, which were necessary prerequisites for sitting down and writing poetry. I began to write again and have been writing ever since.

One can see the influence of Neruda, particularly his determination to make the ordinary extraordinary, everywhere in your poems. What about Neruda—there are so many Nerudas—attracts you? Is it a particular Neruda, or is it the fact that he did so many different things in his life and in the poems?

I think Neruda is the most influential poet in my life, and I have come to realize that I don't know him nearly as well as I should, even after teaching a course on Neruda three times. I have begun to immerse myself in his life and work, and realized its vastness, realized that I have only begun to explore this poet. What I have also realized is that there are certain Nerudas I appreciate more than others, as anyone does, but that I can benefit from learning to appreciate other Nerudas I don't appreciate as much as perhaps I should.

I can see you gravitating more toward "Canto General" than toward Twenty Love Poems and a Song of Despair *or* 100 Love Sonnets ...

Yes, "Canto General," "The Heights of Macchu Picchu," the historical epics, the sweeping political poems seem to be the primary attraction for someone like me. Or "Spain in the Heart," the poems about the Spanish Civil War.

But I can also see how Residence on Earth, *say, perhaps via a poet such as Soto Vélez, could intrigue you and push you into new territory.*

Sure, this is what I mean by broadening my appreciation of Neruda. Now I can move beyond an appreciation of the historical epics or the political poems to also appreciate the surrealist verse, some of which I find enormously compelling, especially the *Residencia* poems that deal with death. I also find myself appreciating the odes, their clarity and ingenuity—the fact that Neruda has proved in his odes the proposition that, yes, you can write poetry about anything. I would like to be able to do that.

The ode to the artichoke.

Sure, the artichoke. That's his contribution to the literature of ugly food. But that's quite an achievement. Sometimes people dismiss the odes as trivial, and that really means that they've engaged only in a superficial reading of the odes.

I think the fact that Neruda could write love poems as a teenager, love poems as an old man, "Canto General," the odes, poems like those in Winter Garden—*that sweeping range, that vastness—sets an incredible example for any poet in any language.*

Neruda's example has also taught me the essential need to grow and change. Too often we see poets who know one trick, and they do the trick very well, but that's all they do, and they tend to repeat themselves. Neruda teaches that, in fact, it's essential for the poet to change and grow, to make leaps and take chances.

When you read poetry now, do you prefer poetry in Spanish or poetry in English, or do you read whatever seems appealing at the moment?

I am indeed part of a field. I am in the field of Latino poetry, which means that I have to keep up, and so I read Latino poetry when I have the opportunity. Certainly, it is a relatively small field, so I am personally familiar with most of the participants. I am very interested of course in keeping up with that work, so if Leroy Quintana comes out with another book, I get it and I read it. Usually I get it from Leroy Quintana. Likewise, when Gary Soto comes out with a new book, I'm probably going to get it. So those are the books that I tend to read, because those are the ones that land on my desk, from people I know who are in my field—besides, they're free books.

I am also doing what I can to expand my horizons all the time, and I will often read a poet who has relatively little in common with me on the surface precisely for that reason: I'm trying to broaden my perspective. I often try to go back and re-educate myself in terms of what I consider to be essential works, so lately I've been reading Whitman again. And I'm finding here a voice that speaks to me from the 1850s about the very same issues that matter so deeply to me today, as a poet and as a person. But there are all these poets who are coming to my attention, people that I've done a reading with, people that I see at a conference somewhere. To be an active participant in that community of poets means that this is how you discover new writers and new books. Remember that I worked for years as a lawyer, and during that time I was not able to keep up in the same way, so I have some catching up to do.

Robert Creeley and Amiri Baraka have written forewords to two of your books. I think that makes an interesting pair. Do you see any similarities among you,

Creeley, and Baraka as poets?

Robert Creeley is an extraordinarily sensitive and open-minded individual who is not simply looking to approve poets who write like him. I'm not sure if I can articulate a connection between my poetry and his poetry, but I can certainly articulate a connection between me and him. This is a very generous individual who is one of the first poets who ever mentored me in any way. I've come to truly appreciate his poetry over the years. Baraka and I clearly have more things in common on the surface. Politically we're at the same end of the spectrum, obviously his aesthetic is somewhat different from mine. He is one of the most brilliant performers of poetry I have ever seen and I aspire someday to be half that good. With Baraka and Creeley, it's not a case of wanting to turn out a cookie-cutter version of themselves. They are willing to sponsor younger poets for the sake of that unique voice, whatever it may be.

Delivering your poems to an audience other than by the written word seems crucial to you personally and poetically. When you envision your typical reader, what kind of person do you see?

I have given the question of audience a great deal of thought over the years and realized that ultimately my audience is anyone who will read or listen to my poetry. So in that sense I begin with a vision of my audience which is as inclusive as possible. Sometimes I view my audience as a series of concentric circles. The circle closest to me is of course the circle of people who are closest to my own experience and the experience reflected in the poems: Puerto Ricans from New York. Maybe there's another circle around that which might be Latino, and another circle around that which might be working class, and another which might be African-American, another which might be urban, and another which might simply be the left because of the political nature of the poems, and another circle around that which might be lovers of language, lovers of poetry. My audience is drawn from all of those sources.

Now in terms of a so-called nontraditional audience, which, by the way, is the most traditional audience of all for poetry, I make every effort to reach that audience. Why? Poets like me are subjected to censorship on a regular basis. Usually it's tacit censorship—the censorship of omission. We're usually not privy to the dynamics of censorship, but there's a pattern of exclusion which even today predominates with respect to both political poets and Latino poets, and I clearly belong to both categories. Once in a while the veil is lifted and you can see behind it. I recently had an experience with National Public Radio, where they asked me to write a poem for National Poetry Month. I wrote the poem, and then they refused to air it explicitly because of its political content, because it was about Mumia Abu Jamal, the black journalist who was wrongly convicted of killing a police officer in Philadelphia. NPR has a history with Mumia Abu Jamal—they refused to air his radio commentaries a few years ago—and they did not want, as they put it, to return to this subject in this way. So they were very open about the fact that they were censoring the poem due to its political content. The veil was lifted. Most of the time the veil is not lifted and we instead hear euphemisms or we hear silence. There's a way in which I constantly have to be concerned with making an end-run around these obstacles to my audience, and I have to take the words directly to the people who should hear them. I also believe this is important not only for me, but for poetry, which is in danger of becoming extinct unless it reaches out to people beyond the campus and the coffee house. It has to become relevant to the lives of people on a daily basis, and it can be if the effort is made. There is now an organized movement to bring poetry to these so-called nontraditional settings. There are all kinds of programs to bring poetry into prisons, hospitals, migrant labor camps, to bring poetry into ESL programs, adult literacy programs, community centers, to bring poetry into all sorts of places where it's never been before. I participate in those programs on a regular basis. I even did a reading in February at a boxing gym, in Willimantic, Connecticut, formerly known as Thread City, because that's where the thread mills were. A number of Puerto Ricans migrated to Thread City to work in those mills. Now the mills are closed and many of the young men are unemployed and they seek solace in the local boxing gym. So I did a reading as part of the Windham Area Poetry Project at the Windham Boxing Club. I came in, and the boxers broke training, sat down, and listened to me read for about half an hour. I read between two punching bags, and as I was reading, a number of these young men, who ranged in age from 10 to 20 and who were about two-thirds Puerto Rican, began to wrap their hands with gauze in what can best be described as a meditative activity, because at the same time they were wrapping their hands they were listening intently. I have a couple of boxing poems, so I read those, but I also read poems about their experience, whether it's working-class, Puerto Rican, or what have you. And that was something to which they could relate, so they sat and listened. If poetry can go into a boxing gym, it can go anywhere.

That you can take poetry into that kind of environment and that NPR rejected your poem due to its political content shows that poetry can have an impact.

Absolutely. Poetry is dangerous.

Creating change, whether that change is social, political, or personal, seems important to your poetry. Have any of your poems ever had a real-life impact other than on an individual level?

Yes, I wrote a poem called "The New Bathroom Policy at English High School," which was written in response to a case at Lynn English High School on the north shore outside Boston. At the time I was working for META (Multicultural Education, Training and Advocacy) as an attorney. We were representing the Hispanic Parent Advisory Council, which is the organization of Latino parents with children in the bilingual educational system in the city of Lynn. One of those parents called and asked us to come up to Lynn because Spanish had just been banned at lunch time. We went up there and took care of the problem; we had a hearing, and scared the principal, and they reversed the policy. Then I wrote the poem, which is essentially a parody of that situation. A few years later I did a reading in Connecticut, and afterwards a young Puerto Rican man came up to me, introduced himself as Wilson, and told me that he worked as the manager of a nursing unit at a hospital in Hartford (Hartford, mind you, is about one-third Puerto Rican). The hospital where he worked recently inaugurated a policy forbidding patients from speaking Spanish, because the doctors couldn't understand them; the notion of hiring some Spanish-speaking doctors had not occurred to the administration. Wilson took "The New Bathroom Policy at English High School" into a meeting of administrators and raised the issue of the new language policy and then read the poem. He told me they were so embarrassed that they changed the policy on the spot. There is one concrete example of how one of my poems found a home somewhere else and made some small difference.

Your previous occupations are more diverse and interesting than those of most poets, and they often form the subjects of your poems and affect the logic of your narrators. What about these jobs, from tenant lawyer to primate lab attendant to bouncer, compels you to write about them?

Well, I've had a colorful life. The jobs I've held appeal to me as the subject matter for poetry first of all because they make good stories, and it's my impulse as a storyteller that often determines what I choose to write about. Certainly, if telling tales about being a bouncer makes sense when you're sitting with friends, maybe it would make a poem, too.

I embrace the genre of work poetry in general. Work poetry tells us a great deal about our lives in this particular economic system, it reveals certain contradictions or shortcomings of capitalism, it is a way of documenting exploitation and resistance to exploitation, and it reveals something fundamental about the human psyche, even beyond the question of a particular economic system.

If you take a look at the sorts of jobs I'm writing about, you will find the poems very often reflect a working class kind of experience, or perhaps so-called unskilled labor, which I think has always been a cruel term. If you're working in a job where, let's say, you're a janitor and you're only seen for what your hands can clean up, your mind is dismissed, and once your mind is dismissed you become invisible. People therefore will say or do just about anything right in front of you, because you're not there, and that's wonderful if you happen to be a poet, because poets are spies.

Some of your poems address the life of migrant workers, which is a subject that few poets write about, with the exception of someone like Gary Soto. Do you feel an obligation to call attention to the often-invisible or the often-ignored?

First of all, there is a genre of farm worker poetry, written by people who in some instances were farm workers themselves at some point in their lives. Gary Soto is best known for that kind of poetry, but Tino Villanueva also has written that kind of poetry, and there are others as well. Diana Garcia, for example, has written of that migrant farm worker experience. In the Chicano literary world, this is a fairly significant subject. I don't know if anyone besides myself has written poems about Puerto Rican migrant farm workers, who tend to populate the northeastern states. But I have written those poems, not from the experience of being a farm worker, but a farm worker advocate. I worked as an intern for the Migrant Legal Action Program; and realizing that I spoke Spanish, they sent me into the fields and labor camps of Maryland and Delaware to do outreach in the Spanish language among farm workers and explain their legal rights. Do we need to put this into poetry? Of course we do. What did William Carlos Williams say about poetry? That men die every day for lack of what is found there. The way I understand that statement is that poetry is part of a larger tapestry of awareness, where we become gradually more and more cognizant of the lives of those people half in shadow, and that includes of course migrant farm workers, who live in conditions that most of us would not tolerate for our pets. Yet they do the work that provides food for us. It is still to this day a shocking scenario in this country, almost forty years after the famous Edward R. Murrow documentary "Harvest of Shame," where some of these conditions were first revealed. We're obliged to speak of these lives, and I do think of myself as an advocate in the poetry, speaking on behalf of those who don't have an opportunity to be heard, not that they couldn't be heard quite well given the chance, not that they couldn't speak for themselves, but they don't get the chance to speak for themselves. How could I know what I know and not tell what I know?

Authority figures, especially those with clubs or guns, but also policy makers, are often the villains of your poems. You're obviously working to subvert the current power structures and to call our attention to the various abuses of power in our governmental, military, and educational organizations. How can a poem stand against an unjust law, or against a machine gun for that matter? You mentioned how it can change a policy, but are you trying to pick up that vein of resistance in Latin American poets such as Cardenal, Soto Vélez, and Neruda, to call attention to practices that might not be as overtly brutal as the ones those poets wrote against but are still oppressive?

In 1949, my father, Frank Espada, was arrested for not going to the back of the bus in Biloxi, Mississippi. He spent a week in jail. How can one person, who refuses to go to the back of the bus in the segregated South, make a difference? Well, it's 1997, and the South is no longer subject to legal segregation, and people who are dark-skinned—black or Latino, like my father—are no longer required to sit in the back of the bus. How did that happen? Because of my father in 1949, because of Rosa Parks a few years later, because of all the people who refused to sit in the back of the bus and all the people who supported them, because of the Montgomery bus boycott, because of Martin Luther King, but also because of the nameless thousands who sacrificed so that things could be changed. And each one of them made a small contribution, as my father did.

So a poem is also a small contribution?

I see a poem as part of a much bigger puzzle, as one more gesture, one more moment in a much larger movement for things to change.

The spirit of resistance indeed seems strong in your poems. How does music factor into that? In "Trumpets from the Islands of Their Eviction" for example, the music, which "swarms into the barrio / of a refugee's imagination," is all that stands against the "predatory squad cars." You incorporate various types of music—salsa, jazz, gospel—into your poems. Are you striving for a sort of mimesis, or does music become a force of resistance?

Music is one of those essential products of the spirit that demonstrates irrefutably our humanity in the face of inhumanity. In a poem like "Trumpets from the Islands of Their Eviction," music is being used directly as a metaphor for resistance, as a metaphor for cultural identity, and the strength of that cultural identity in turn enables us to have the self-assurance necessary for self-defense in a hostile society. But more broadly than that, I feel that music as a signifier in the poems represents a defiant assertion of humanity. From my earliest books to my most recent book, it represents something unconquerable about human beings, and the circumstances in which people sing certainly bear out that sense. If you've ever listened to a recording of a chain gang singing, you know that people can make art out of anything.

Creeley wrote that you are "a poet of great communal power," and up to this point you've mostly discussed the communal aspects of your poetry. But Creeley also referred to you as "the voice of intensive isolation." How do you reconcile the tension between the public and the private? And how does identity—not only your personal identity, but your racial identity—enter that dynamic?

To a certain degree, I don't fret too much about the distinction between public and private, between personal and political, because I've found that those distinctions become very blurry in my case. I do realize that I'm moving, especially in my most recent book, towards a more intimate poetry—addressed to my wife, son, father, friends—but a poetry that's willing to take certain kinds of risks that perhaps it didn't take several years ago. I'm aware of trying to become more fully evolved, more fully developed as a poet, which means exploring areas that in the past have been left in the dark. For me that means doing more exploration of the private and the personal.

Another recent development in your poetry is a new type of lyricism. From book to book, your poetry has become more powerful and more verbally daring. In Imagine the Angels of Bread, *you experiment—and I would say experiment successfully—with a type of lyricism that is absent in your earlier poetry. Poems such as "Sleeping on the Bus," "Imagine the Angels of Bread," "The Prisoners of Saint Lawrence," and "Hands Without Irons Become Dragonflies" register at a different pitch than most of your other poems. What attracts you to that diction, which seems oracular if not biblical? And do you think you'll return to it in future poems?*

Well, certainly I'm still young as a poet: I'm 39 years old. And I am aware of my own growing pains, of the need to grow more, which means taking chances and experimenting with pitch, as you put it, experimenting with variations in voice. As far as the prophetic voice, or the biblical voice, that is something I see in the works of Whitman, Neruda, Ginsberg, Cardenal; and by using a term like "prophetic voice" I am not claiming for myself the ability to divine the future, but at the same time, I would point out that most of us attempt prophecy at one time or another. All of us attempt to act as prophets in some small way, to figure out what's going to happen next. So as a poet that's all I'm trying to do when I engage in that prophetic voice. I'm also doing what I can in those sorts of poems to broaden my vision as much as possible, to see the world as big as I can see it, because I think there is something I have to say on that scale.

MEDBH McGUCKIAN

Medbh McGuckian was born in 1950 in Belfast, where she lives with her family. Her recent books include *Selected Poems*, *Shelmalier*, and *Had I a Thousand Lives*, all published by Gallery Press in Ireland and Wake Forest University Press in the United States. Among the many prizes her poetry has won are the British National Poetry Competition, the Cheltenham Award, the Rooney Prize, and the American Ireland Fund Literary Award. She has been Writer-in-Residence at Queen's University, Belfast, and Visiting Fellow at the University of California, Berkeley. Vona Groarke conducted this interview in January 1999, in McGuckian's office at the Institute of Irish Studies, Belfast, and it appeared in Volume 16, Number 2 of *Verse*.

Can you tell me something about how you write: do you have a set time and place for writing, do you have favorite writing conditions?

It does involve a lot of preparation and reading and thinking, but when I do actually get to write, I would always write at the same desk, between about 8 and 10pm or between 10 and 12am, depending.

Do you know what you're going to write before you sit down?

No. Hardly ever. And if I do start with an idea, I usually change it.

Can you write with noise around you?

I can, yes. I have written while minding three kids, with my daughter Emer's arms around my neck, though I don't know what it would be like with anybody else's arms around my neck! Generally, I find the domestic situation vital. If they're all out, or if any of them are away, I find it very artificial, and this can get in the way too.

Do you go through periods when you do not write at all?

If I stop writing poetry, I think this can be a good thing. Then I would write a lot of letters and that eases it up. Or I would maybe write a bit of prose, perhaps a review, and that can help too. I think that because of all the reading that I do to get to the poem, when I actually get to it, it's a big relief. The act of writing is very short in comparison with the thinking and collecting that goes into it.

Do you think a lot about a poem's shape before you ever write a word down?

Yes. Well, I would give myself a rest from the last poem, or from the last book, or from the last idea. For example, at the minute, I'm … well I'm not fed up with the 1798 Rebellion—in fact, I think I've only just skimmed the surface of the '98 Rebellion, but it really depends on what book I come across. Right now, I've been looking for the *Life of Michael Dwyer*, because he's the one person I couldn't get hold of last year, and I've suddenly got it, so now I'm just reading and loving that. Of course, I know that I'll write poems out of it, but for now I'm just enjoying reading the book.

Is there a usual starting point for a poem for you? Will it start off with an image, or an idea, or a sound …?

It starts off with a word, and the words just seem to cling together, they kind of mate and multiply. If I thought "now, I am going to write a heroic poem about so-and-so," deliberately, obviously I would have certain biases. I couldn't make Michael Dwyer into a villain, although many people might want me to, but I couldn't. Or I couldn't be cynical about it. I think that a lot of other male poets who have been writing about 1798 just wouldn't be able to make heroes in the same way that I still am able to, or still need to—maybe there's a flaw in me, a weakness.

So if you were going to write a poem about Michael Dwyer, would you base it on a particular event, or would you take some aspect of his character? How would you approach writing a poem about an historical figure like him?

I think it would probably be the same as my approach to say, Father Murphy, in the poems about him in *Shelmalier*. I try to find the most striking image, the most vivid aspect, which in his case was the idea that the rebels used his charred chasuble, which he would have worn during funeral masses (you don't see them so much now, but as a child, I remember them), as a standard. I find that fascinating, and I used that to symbolize what he was—a different, strange, unique creature. That image would have held for me all of our conflicting attitudes about a militant priest. So I look for a motif that holds the meaning of the person in a very deep way—it's lovely when you find that, and you have to. You can't find that out of your own imagination, but your imagination can recognize it. I worry a lot about whether I'm original or not, in so far as these kind of poems require you to find something out there that meets something inside your head. I do feel that even though the image isn't mine, I make it mine by working it into my poem. I don't own it, but because I use it doesn't mean that someone else can't, or that it doesn't still belong in history.

So you colonize the image?

Yes, I suppose so!

Do you write quickly?

In the end, I do. I leave it overnight before I type it up. I write it out, and if in the morning, it's still alright, I might read it and say "goodness" or else see immediately what's wrong with it.

But they don't tend to stretch over weeks or months?

No. Just only ever overnight.

You have many extraordinary and striking poem titles. Are these starting points, or do you lay them afterwards on the finished poem?

I always lay them down afterwards, although sometimes I might have a title to start with. This happened once when I was away with Carol Rumens, in Poland. We were just talking, and then she said, "sometimes you feel like killing the muse," and I thought that would be a brilliant title, so for weeks I was going around with this "Killing the Muse" title, and I ended up writing the poem and pinning the title onto it, but that would be rare. Usually, it's the other way round.

Many of the poems in your Selected Poems *had been revised and edited since their original publication. "Minus 18 Street," for example, was republished "minus" one whole stanza. Do you have any misgivings about changing poems that were written, in some cases, more than ten years ago?*

The *Selected* was done by Peter Fallon and Dillon Johnston, and I was so glad to get that *Selected* out, I would have accepted any changes they would have suggested! That book was a big hurdle with me. It was supposed to happen ten years before, and that was the reason I left Oxford Poets, for whom I had done my own Selected. This book was based on that, and I think they made a good job of it.

Do you look back on your early poems with affection, or with horror, or both?

I look back on my early self with a certain amount of horror, but with affection as well! Those early poems were not made in the way that I make poems now—as in reading a book, and basing poems on it. They would be poems based on memory and on experiences, like having babies, that I would be nostalgic about now. So I'm fond of them, but I would also be very critical of them.

Have you a favorite?

I'm drawn to the one about my grandmother, because it's the only poem I've written about her.

Various poets have been cited as influences on your work, including Marianne Moore, Yeats, Keats, and the Russians, Mandelstam and Tsvetaeva. Do you acknowledge these influences, and can you tell me about any other formative poems or poets?

I tend to avoid poetry most of the time. There's very few poems or poets that I like—I know it's terrible, isn't it? But Marianne Moore would never have done much for me. I think as an Irish poet living here, I feel more in common with people writing in other languages translated into English. I feel more in tune with them than with people who write straight in English.

Is that to do with an attitude to the English language you're using having been translated, in a way, through the Irish language?

I think it's that whatever it is the translator has to do to get, say, Mandelstam into English, I have to do that too. There's some journey I have to make that they also have to make, that someone like Simon Armitage or Ted Hughes, who have a natural hold on the language, just don't have to make. I don't feel I have any right to the language. I feel like I'm a boulder in a field, and I feel like I'm lost in it.

Is this not an advantage at times?

Yes, it can be. I had a letter from a guy in India who is an Indian native, but who writes in English, although it is not his main language. He wrote that it was a good place for him to put his emotions, while he used his native language for workaday business and family affairs. I can understand this. The poetic language that you use is a very formal thing, and I feel that when I'm sitting down to use that language, I'm not using the language of speech, the speech that I use with the children. I use different words, very differently. So it is like a separate language, a specialized jargon. You are certainly looking for words which you would never use normally.

Do you use a thesaurus to find these words?

No, never, unless I might have to check the meaning of words, when I would use a dictionary, but the words I'm checking are never in the dictionary! I think I'm going to have to spend the rest of my life writing a poetic dictionary!

How do you respond to criticism? Do you read reviews of your books—what part does criticism play, if any, in your response to the poems you have written?

I like to read reviews, when they are sent by the publisher—I wouldn't go in search of them. I find it particularly educational for me to read when someone has difficulty with my work. Elizabeth Lowry's approach (in her essay in *Metre* 4) is wonderfully cross-examining and testing, she really cares about poetry. Hers is the most positive negative response, not reaction, I have had, and I am relieved by it and grateful for it.

Has criticism ever encouraged you to change something you've written?

Yes. I read something the other day where they said I used the word "the" a lot, too much, and so I'm very aware of that now! But I think that critics often try to fit you into an agenda, to label you in a way that's very narrowing to you. For example, I got a book recently—a survey of British poetry—which had a Chapter heading "Northern Irish and Black British poetry." I find the mindset there so weird. So when I looked to see where I was in this awful chapter—was I black or British or Northern Irish?—I wasn't in there at all, because I was in the chapter on "Feminist Poets," which seems extraordinary to me, as I've never seen myself as that at all. I've never been a full advocate of women without men—I've always seen men as being central or necessary in the lives of women. But then that's a very trite oversimplification of feminism they had fallen into.

The fourth poem of your recent collection, Shelmalier, *contains the phrase "a melanic / sky anastomoses." This vocabulary might be seen as symptomatic of more complex and challenging difficulties in your poetry. Do you see your poetry as difficult, or do you, like most poets do, see your own work as almost painfully simple?*

No. I think it's very hard. I do have a mathematical kind of mind—I like Greek and Latin words. A word like "melanic" I find amazing—there are so many roots in there, and yet it has an actual, concrete, and very exact meaning. English doesn't have an awful lot of those very exact words. But there's a lot of humor in putting together words like that. Very often, I would have to undo all the weaving of the poem if it's one I've forgotten about, to find out what it really means at the time.

But the poems are difficult. My life has been—well living here has been—pretty unliveable. So you wouldn't expect the poetry to be anything else but awkward. Also, there's the whole idea that you were hounded on two sides, by first of all the people you were trying to write for, and then by the people you were trying to get to publish you, and there was no way these two points could meet. You were currying favor with the powers that be, and trying to get a message through from a totally unimportant, depressed, and deprived world. What I would say would mean nothing to them, but it would also mean nothing to these people. So I would have to have some kind of register that each end would be able to, in some way, relate to. I don't know if it's getting any easier or not, with the cease-fire. They were rioting again last night, and as soon as you hear the riots again, you begin to draw in your horns again, and think, well now I can't write that. I can't actually dedicate this poem to Michael Dwyer. I have to pretend it's somebody else, because it could annoy people, or stir people up.

Your poetry might be said to work outside the tyranny of logical comprehension.

You accumulate words and images in the way of abstract rather than narrative art. A collection like On Ballycastle Beach, *for example, seems to be not concerned with being understood in any traditional way. How would you like your poems to be either read or understood?*

I don't care so much about being understood now, but I want to give pleasure. I know I am dealing with very ugly material, and a very ugly world, but I am always concerned with trying to take out of that what is most uplifting. So with Father Murphy, I'm not going to dwell on the fact that he was boiled to death in a tar barrel. I'd rather dwell on the black and silver chasuble, and try to get the beauty of that, of the human dignity or human assertion contained in that image. I got a letter the other day which said, "I read the first verse of that poem over and over again—I didn't understand it at all, but I thought it was beautiful," and that seems like a wonderful response to me. Some girl once said to me that a poem had saved her life. I believe strongly that poetry shouldn't be underestimated—its effect can be very, very powerful. And yet poems are so small: I wonder sometimes how something so small as a poem can even begin to understand something so huge as somebody else's life. But poetry helps me to understand my life anyway: it helps me to clarify a lot of very complex attitudes and positions and meanings.

Several motifs recur in your work, for example, furniture, rooms and clothes (especially skirts!). Yet your poetry does not seem at all domestic. What is the significance of these points of reference?

I suppose those things are very consoling and real and they tie you down. I always like, for example, naming things, or using them as detail for texture. I think they mean more than they actually say. For example, I was writing a small poem about the Nativity for next year (getting in early!) and in it, I talk about Christ as "the third window." Now that comes out of an Irish belief or superstition that three windows in a house represented the Trinity. In that sense, in Ireland and in Irish culture anyway, none of those things is totally without meaning or purpose.

And they're sort of sexy too. I think clothes are very sensual, and even rooms can be external expressions of something very intimate. You know the line about "the woman making curtains blossom"? That's very sexy, I think.

Does color work in the same way?

I use color to give density, though it can be very symbolic and political, and at times, very weighty, especially here, where green and orange have such resonance, where blue is religion and white is purity, etc. I think it goes back to Catholicism and the fact that all these colors had a special significance in the masses when you were growing up, and that still lingers with you. But I'm using color less and less now. I don't want to overdo it, especially after *Captain Lavender*!

Are you interested in visual art. Does it influence your work?

I love reading about art. I can't draw or paint or play an instrument, but I can't help thinking that all art is one, and it's just such a privilege to be able to read about other artists, and, of course, you can use things that you pick up about them in your own work. I think because of where I live being such an arid society, I don't meet many real artists and I don't have any real contact with that world, so reading about art is very necessary to me.

At the moment, I'm reading about the American artist, Joseph Cornell. His work is all boxes—he never actually made anything; he cut out pieces of images from newspapers and magazines and put them into the boxes. In those boxes are his whole psyche and his whole being. His works are love poems. There's one of a ballet dancer that he was in love with. He cut out bits of her shoes and of her outfits and made collages of them. I find that works very like poetry and that helps me to think and to see other possibilities and fresh ideas.

You have written, though not often, in traditional forms, especially the sonnet. How do you view form—do you see it as being in any way a gender issue, as Eavan Boland, for example, might?

Well, Ciaran Carson's last two books were all sonnets. I admire his use of it, and I admire the expertise of it, but I would get very tired of the sonnet. I have written in it, and I do try to write in rhyme whenever it feels right, but I think that to stretch and pull and twist what you're saying to try to get a rhyme, just to make your work look as if it's ordered and clear, just seems to me to be not a very musical thing to do. I like every so often having echoes run throughout a poem. I wrote something last week that had a lot of "ing" words in it—spring, sing, thing, a lot of present participles ending in "ing." So those sounds came dripping through the poem, making a nice music in it. But if they happen, they happen. I wouldn't twitch the thought deliberately to get sounds. It usually happens, if it happens, of its own accord. When I'm working on a poem, I would usually circle the words that sound similar, and I would try to make echoes with these.

You mentioned Ciaran Carson there. You once said that you didn't think you would have been a poet had you lived anywhere but Belfast. But Belfast is not a recognizable presence in your poetry in the same way that it is in Carson's, for example. How important is living in Belfast to your work, and how does this importance express itself?

Or not living in Belfast, as the case may be. I think one lives here in a very suspended way. You're in the world, but you're not of it. It is that kind of place. It's like being in an iron lung. It's like Manchester, but it's not like Manchester because some people don't want it to be. It's a very unreal place. When I go to the north Antrim coast, I like to say that Ballycastle is in the Republic, which it isn't (maybe the French Republic!). But it's like a place in the past—it's like going back 200 years. I drift between these two places. I get to the point where I want out of here—I suppose people do in any city, but particularly in Belfast, which is such a dangerous and cruel and dark and sinister and miserable hole, there's just so much suffering around you all the time. It is very painful to live here, and you get so you need all that pain to keep you aware of how very privileged you are. I could see myself leaving here, though I would always feel myself as having a root in Ballycastle, but I don't know where else I could go.

Does being the only woman in a "group" of contemporary Northern poets that includes Heaney, Longley, Carson, Muldoon, and Mahon matter to you?

Well, I don't see that I am the only woman, because there's Joan Newmann, who was in that group, and there are a lot of new women writers springing up here now, there are women getting first books out—Moira Donaldson and Jean Bleakney and Ann Zell. Some of these women are older than me and that helps. But for a while, I did feel very isolated amongst that group you've listed, and at the same time, I felt that what I wrote had to meet with their approval. I would have wanted their good opinion. I would have been very aware of their work, and if any of them brought a new book out, I'd be sitting in a cold room, poring over it, seeing what could I nick out of it! I think I would have been happier if people like Eiléan and Eavan were from the North, but the main thing was, I had Nuala, and I now have friends like Paula Meehan and

Rita Ann, and there were a lot of Galway women who, by coming through, really helped a lot. But I think there's too much of this "Northern" thing. I walked into a room the other night and heard myself being introduced as "the distinguished Ulster poet," and I thought, well I would rather be *anything* but a distinguished Ulster poet!

Are friendships with other poets important to you?

Oh yes. I had also hoped that one day I would be "important" enough to be friendly with Ted Hughes. Obviously that's out of the question now (or maybe not). It's nice to relate to other poets, but on the other hand, it can be a bit gossipy. Certainly, when I've written a poem, it's lovely to have someone to send it to, and I do always have, which I value a lot.

You are translating, with Eiléan Ní Chuilleanáin, new poems by Nuala Ní Dhomhnáill. Do you enjoy the process of translating?

I wouldn't say I enjoy it. I think it's too sad to be translating from Irish—I just feel such a loss and such a gap. And yet it's a chore that's so educational, and I like to keep in touch with whatever ghost of a language there might be, but I always get very depressed doing it. It's lovely to be translating Nuala, whose poems are full of life, like a beautiful, living creature, but then you wonder if you are destroying it by imposing a foreign language on it, and that's something I worry about a lot.

Why did you leave Oxford University Press for The Gallery Press? Was it in any way a political decision, and were you surprised when Oxford Poets recently folded?

It was political in a sense—a kind of "My passport's green" statement. But I was taken up because I had won the British National Poetry Competition in 1979, and all through the '80s I was almost like a kind of mascot, I felt. I wasn't really saying what it was I wanted to say, and I was being published under false flags. I was very grateful to Oxford Poetry for giving me that chance and allowing me to develop, but I think at a certain point, I couldn't develop any more with them. I wasn't surprised when they folded. I always was aware that they had very limited resources, and that it was a sideline for them, whereas with Gallery Press, it's their main business, and I think that makes a difference.

Did writing about your father in your recent collections lead you towards the historical, public subject matter of Shelmalier? *Is there a line, do you think, that takes you from personal to social or political history?*

When my father died, it released a lot of subconscious, repressed things that I had kept under wraps and that he had kept under wraps. When his life was finished, I was able to see more clearly the tragedy of his life as an Irish tragedy and as an aspect of the continuity right through from 1798 to now. I felt I owed it to my past and to him to study our history, and I'm glad I did, even though it was absolutely harrowing. It probably was a way of mourning for him.

Shelmalier *is concerned with history made and in the making. Yet it is not historically grounded: its references and presences are more suggested than specific. Can you say something about its approach to historical subject matter?*

Most of the poems were written before I started getting interested in the rebellion, because some of them were, in fact, quite old. But I put them together because they seemed to connect up. I felt my father was a victim, and that I wasn't going to be a victim. My father was never allowed to say anything or do anything, and this is even more true of my mother, whose life is a kind of living death, and it's up to me to try to understand why this is so, and where the paralysis came from. I called it *Shelmalier* because of the Wexford connection.

It's important to remember that even though the North has been so horrific over the past forty or fifty years—it's just been one awful thing after another—that people then had worse horrors. I've just read about a handicapped person who would not give information, so the soldiers just shot him to pieces, literally. That kind of connection between people who have witnessed other people around them being blown to pieces in their midst is there. Part of what poetry does is make these kinds of connections. It can't stop the horror, and it can't undo it, and it can't prevent it happening again—it doesn't have the power to redeem—but it can, at least, be a kind of witness.

So even though you did a lot of historical research towards the book, it's not necessarily a book about 1798?

It is and it isn't. Reading about the Rebellion was just such an eye-opener. Last year, I went to Auschwitz, and for some reason, those two things came together—the experience of absolute horror, and survival of it. I know that I had been protected from all that deliberately because people did shelter their children, particularly here. I know that if I had known all that, I would have been a lot angrier or more aware at a much earlier age, and maybe I'm glad that I didn't.

My approach to history was not to treat it as an academic or a dead thing. I wanted to write love poems. The reason why I've been interested in Michael Dwyer is that I feel that it's a big release for me to be able to relate to Protestant males from the North, non-Catholic men who actually died for Ireland, and although he was Catholic and from the South, he was part of the same movement.

Do you see yourself as a political poet?

No. I'm too frightened to be. I would hope no one would see me as a political poet. I think I had a duty to deal with our history and to try to make something of it, but I think it would be very narrowing. When Tom Paulin brought out a whole book of political poems, I though it was just so boring. I would like to think instead that I am a patriotic poet in the Yeatsian tradition, but that's a different and more challenging thing altogether.

REGINALD SHEPHERD

Born in 1963 and raised in tenements and housing projects in the Bronx, Reginald Shepherd has published four books of poetry, all with the University of Pittsburgh Press — *Some Are Drowning* (1994), winner of the 1993 AWP Award Series in Poetry; *Angel, Interrupted* (1996), a finalist for the Lambda Literary Award; *Wrong* (1999); and *Otherhood* (2003). He is the recipient of a 1993 "Discovery"/ *The Nation* Award, the 1994 George Kent Prize from *Poetry*, an Amy Lowell Poetry Traveling Scholarship, and grants from the NEA, the Illinois Arts Council, and the Constance Saltonstall Foundation, among other awards and honors. His poems have appeared in numerous magazines as well as in four editions of *The Best American Poetry*. He holds MFA degrees from Brown University and the University of Iowa, and he currently teaches at the University of West Florida. This interview was conducted by Christopher Hennessy in August 2003, and first appeared in Volume 20, Numbers 2 and 3 of *Verse*.

Many of the poems in Otherhood *keep me pleasantly stunned, even off-balance, after multiple readings. In so doing they remind me of one of your beliefs — that poetry is about more than a search for "meaning," that it's about finding pleasure through language. I think many poets and critics, including myself, from time to time forget about "pleasure."*

When I started writing poetry as a teenager, what attracted me was the richness of the language, the foregrounding of what language can do and the worlds that language can create — as opposed to language reflecting the world. Though there's been a definite revival of interest in the poem as an aesthetic artifact, as we've seen in different ways with both avant-garde poetry and neo-formalism, the poetry world is still dominated by what's been called the aesthetic of transparency, writers purveying little vignettes or moving anecdotes about some public image of themselves, often with an epiphany at the end. There's still a real neglect of the idea that a poem can be something, rather than just be about something.

In the "death of poetry" articles that seem so perennially popular, there's a consensus that people don't read poetry because it's too hard and too elitist. I've always thought the opposite, that most poetry isn't hard enough, in the sense that it's not interesting or engaging enough. It doesn't hold the attention — you read it once or twice and you've used it up. That engagement I look for and too often miss is a kind of pleasure — in the words, the rhythms, the palpable texture of the poem. It's the opposite of boredom.

I think poetry has to be able to give pleasure before it's understood; that's why you want to understand it. Whether my poems are always immediately graspable in terms of subject matter, I've always wanted to give the reader something, in terms of language, imagery, rhythm, etc., to have the poem be a sensual experience for the reader. There are certainly many poets whose work I've loved without "understanding." I read "The Love Song of J. Alfred Prufrock" in the ninth grade and it had a huge impact on me, but I'd say I didn't understand at least two-thirds of it. It was frustrating to me, because I was a smart kid, and I was used to understanding things [laughs]. But it also had this power over me, and I wanted to figure out why, so my lack of understanding drew me into the poem.

Over the years, you've moved away from a more narrative, more personal style. Can you talk about what happens to a poetics during that shift?

In some ways my compositional method has changed. I used to more or less write a poem from start to finish. Obviously, I would revise, often heavily, but I would sit down and have some notion in my head, and though it would always be tied to a phrase, a line, an image, I would have an idea of what kind of poem I was going to write and what it was going to be about. I'm much less likely now to start a poem knowing or thinking that I know what direction I'd like it to take. For the past several years, writing has been much more a process of accretion. Most of the poems in *Otherhood* and most of the poems I've written since then have been the result of collecting materials. I carry around little notebooks or pieces of paper all the time, always writing down phrases, images, things I've read or misread, heard or misheard, street signs, all kinds of things. And I've noticed, just as if you write down your dreams all the time, then you remember them more, that when you're constantly noticing things, more things come to you. To a large extent, the way I write poems these days is by accumulating a critical mass of things that seem to relate to one another in some way. Writing a poem is my way of figuring out how they go together.

I think I see that at work. At times, your poetry breaks into brief lists of things, of names, nomenclature — usually esoteric, always musical. I'm thinking of moments like the final, moving lines of the poem about Hyacinth, "Apollo on

What the Boy Gave":

> And where he was
> this leafless stalk (bluebell,
> tulip, torch lily, trillium:
> snowdrop, Solomon's
> seal) I break to take for my own,
> black at the core of blossoming
>
> (a bell shaped nodding flower,
> usually solitary)

Is naming for you connected to incantation? Casting a spell through the music of naming things?

I like that phrase, "the music of naming things." I'm obsessed with names. Part of it has to do with an ambivalence in my work between this Platonic—or even Adamic—impulse to give things their names and make the names stick and a realization that names are always arbitrary, that a thing will never be its name and a name will never equal the thing. There's a tension between nominalism and realism, between the will to have each individual entity be absolutely distinct and the will to label and categorize them. We have all these things that we call "leaf," for example, but each is irreducibly distinct. There's the desire to be able to say, "leaf, that's what all those things are," to name a thing and therefore to know it, to take hold of it (the double sense of the words "grasp" and "apprehend"). But there's also the knowledge of the gap between the word and its sense, between language and its referent. The lists of names I use are very specific, which is my way of combining the impulses of incantation and accuracy. For example, in the Daphne poem ["Apollo Steps in Daphne's Footprints"] and in the Hyacinth poem, the lists are specifically plants that are all botanically related. I want to make lyric out of fact, you might say.

I did notice in Otherhood *a desire to encompass the world, elements of the world, and by the world I mean that which one could observe, rather than what one might feel in an interior sense.*

In one sense, I've been interested in the transition from the "I" to the "eye." And not just in jettisoning one in favor of the other but in exploring their interactions, mapping the ways that the personal "I" is not just a singular unit, but a product and a nexus of its context, including very prominently the physical world of which it's a part while simultaneously standing apart from that world. There's much to explore in the quite literal analogy between the things out of which the world is made and the things, the words and phrases, out of which the poem is made. I think of *Otherhood* and *Wrong* as making those kinds of analogies. In part, that's also why those books are syntactically looser. I've always had a strong interest in syntax as a means of bringing things into relationship with one another, of organizing the poem, organizing the world the poem is creating. With *Wrong*, and in particular with *Otherhood*, I wanted to let go syntactically, to allow the poem's materials to float more freely, letting the elements find their own relations with less of a sense of my imposing those relations on them. I wanted to give more autonomy both to the words and to the world.

Speaking of syntax, the last two books work deftly with linguistic—and structural, for that matter—fragmentation, brokenness. Your notes tell us that the poem "Justice: An Ode" is actually composed entirely of phrases from the Book of Job, for example. Here we have all these fragments, and the lyric muscle is still strong throughout the book. Can you talk about how to sing among fragments?

I like the idea of singing out of fragments. Those fragments are all we have to sing out of, and unlike a lot of poets who consider themselves avant-garde, I have no interest in giving up song. In my earlier work, I wanted at least to try to make a whole song of those fragments, whereas in *Otherhood* I was more interested in a broken lyric, in letting the fragments be fragments, in letting things be broken and still sing. I wanted to know if they could still sing, even in that broken state. To misquote Frost, I've always wanted to know what can be made of a ruined thing. In a way, I've always been aiming at what a poem in my first book calls "the difficult music."

Just as I was interested in letting go syntactically, letting go of the controlling "I" that organizes everything, I was also interested in letting go of the will to make everything cohere. I wanted to see what pieces of wholeness would not only survive but emerge out of wreckage and fragmentation. Your formulation of singing out of brokenness is a very apt description of what I was trying to do.

In Wrong, *you end one poem simply, "there is no moon unless you say there is" ["Seven Little Songs About the Moon"]. A page later you write, "I'm a cup you can / drink me from" ["Motive"]. I don't see similar lines or sentiments in*

Otherhood—there's very little "you." First, why the shift? Second, are there risks to the poet when he speaks to that "you?" Conversely, are there pleasures?

The "you" has changed form in various ways through the course of my poems and did sort of drop out of *Otherhood,* or maybe the "you" was exiled from that book. I felt that I'd done what I could do with that figure. Recently the "you" has come back, but in a different form, as a real person, which may have something to do with the fact that I've been in a relationship for the past several years. The "you" in my first two books was more than anything a doppelgänger or a double.

That reminds me of Ashbery.

Ashbery does have a poem entitled "My Erotic Double," and many of my earlier poems were about or addressed to that double. That particular "you" was a kind of imago, an ideal image of the self. And that was very tied to the "you" as an object of desire. I think desire is always in part about what one wants to be as well as what one wants to have. The "you" in those poems was very much a projection of the man I wanted to be. Certainly, in terms of, say, Jacques Lacan's psychoanalytical theory, we're all striving toward this integral selfhood that we never really achieve. But very acutely for me as a black gay man who grew up in poverty, that ideal always felt particularly out of reach.

My first book was full of poems about imaginary love affairs, and I began to realize that this was an evasion of things I really wanted to address. I had this vocabulary—not just in the sense of diction, but a set of images, topoi, and tropes—that I could fit all kinds of material into, but which also distorted and constricted that material, and I began to get frustrated with its limitations. I also realized this absent other was in large part my own dead mother, that my love poems were trying to speak to an utterly inaccessible figure who had abandoned me by dying, but whose loss was too raw and immense for me to address directly. For years my mother floated as a kind of ghost through my poems, present only as a conspicuous absence, the empty center around which the poems revolved. So many of my lost lover poems were really about losing her: I never had a lover, never had anyone else to lose.

In *Some Are Drowning,* the "you" was almost always absent. The "I" was safely enclosed in its own lyric suffering, and the "you" didn't present any interference. In *Angel, Interrupted,* I was much more interested in the "you" being a person who might possibly have interests of his own, who might present some resistance to the "I." As Bidart writes, "If it resists me, I know it's real." I wanted the "you," the "he," to have more opportunity to resist me, to resist being made into a poem.

Here are a few of my favorite lines of yours: "death-dealing Eros / extinguishes the torch / and I am disappearance" ["The Practice of Goodbye"]. In "Blue One Lake," you write that Eros is "an appetite in place of self" and "When I use him up / there will be more." I get the feeling from your work as a whole that when you sit down to write about desire, love, lust, you—the poet, but also the man—bristle at a coming conflict.

Eros is not my friend—or at least hasn't been. Things have changed a bit since I've been in a relationship. The "you" has come back to my poems as a companion, not just an inaccessible ideal or a psychic antagonist. But in my experience, emotion is often dangerous. It tends to overwhelm the self, to break the self down, to destroy the self's defenses, and Eros is the most powerful of emotions.

Desire has been a reminder of what I don't have and what I can't be. And this again is not merely personal: Lacan describes desire as an activity within a lack, and for that matter so does Plato. Desire, want, lack—they're all synonyms, they're all about what's missing, what's not there, what we don't have. Desire tries to satisfy a lack, to fill an emptiness, and by definition it can never be satisfied, because there's never something we don't lack, never something we don't have or can't be. On the one hand, Eros has been a strong engine of my poems, a rich source of material and of energy; on the other hand it's also been a trap. That goes back to Shakespeare's sonnet "Th'expense of spirit in a waste of shame," and beyond that, to Sappho's "He seems like a god, the man who sits beside you." There's the sense of being overwhelmed and cracked open, suffering painful ecstasies. There's a long tradition in poetry of desire as something that raises you up but also smashes you into pieces.

Of course, you write about the Greek myth of Daphne and Apollo, where desire leads to tragedy. Is that one of the draws of Greek myth, that link?

I think it's part of a larger sense of Greek myth as a realm in which power, beauty, and force are all indissoluble.

You once said it was the "presence of glory and catastrophe." I liked that.

That would pretty much sum it up. That classical sense of the world has always corresponded much more to my experience than the Judeo-Christian sense. Classical myth presents a world not ruled by ethics or morality, right or wrong, but by power, and by the linkage between power and beauty. That also corresponds to my sense of one's relationship to the object of desire. He seems to be the repository of all this power and all this beauty ... and then there's little me. In Greek mythology the attention of the gods is always disastrous. Whom the gods will destroy, they first love. In the Daphne poem and in that Hyacinth poem, I was interested in what it would be like to be on the other side of that dynamic. Most of my mythological poems have been written from the victim's point of view, but in those poems I was interested in the god's point of view. I was interested in the god as the victim also, as a victim of his own nature. The gods touch you and you're destroyed, but also everything the gods reach out for, that they want, they destroy, so they lose what they desire. The Apollo and Daphne story is a perfect example of that. Apollo falls in lust with Daphne, he pursues her, she turns into a tree, and he ends up with a consolation prize—the laurel crown. So, for all his desire what he basically gets is: poetry.

For you, I feel it's important to note that often you're not "re-telling" the myths but rather cracking them open to see what you can do in terms of poetic re-invention.

That's a perfect formulation of how I approach Greek myth. I don't see any point in simply retelling the myths—they're already there. I'm interested in re-experiencing them and having the reader re-experience them, and in looking at their undersides, as it were.

Which must have been what drew you to The Marriage of Cadmus and Harmony *[by Roberto Calasso, which much of* Otherhood *was drawn from], praised for getting back to the origins of myth.*

That book was very suggestive to me for writing the poems of *Otherhood*. It really does engage in excavation of the myths, looking at them from perspectives very different from the official versions. Also, the book really opens the myths up in terms of philosophical and sexual complications. Calasso restores a lot of the bowdlerized sexual content of the myths.

I also wanted to talk about, well, the beautiful boys. You've written poems about Hyacinth, Antinoüs, Endymion, and Narcissus, of course—all images of great beauty. And there are poems about Telemachus and Icarus, as well.

J.D. McClatchy once asked me, "Don't you write any poems that aren't about gods or fuckable boys?" [both laugh]

Well, there's a lot that the myths and the images offer a poet. The young and the beautiful—what do they all offer you as subjects, as a poet, though not necessarily a gay male poet?

At least in the way that I treat these figures, there is a dialectic of desire and identification, especially because so many of these beautiful boys were also victims, and really victims of their own beauty. So they embody this power but also this subjection to their own power, to the consequences of their own power, their own beauty. It's theirs but it's not theirs at all.

I would say there's also a certain sadistic element, to have control in the poem over these figures, these imagoes, who have control over me or the speaker. Often there's a boy who's me and whom I'd like to be, an ephebe. We're on that liminal threshold, the boundary between the full power of adult man and the helplessness of a child, a sense of helplessness which can be carried over in any number of ways into adulthood.

I know the term "gay poet" is worrisome for you. Poetry, you've said before, should "not [be] the means to an assertion of identity," with which I agree. But any identity puts its own pressures on the work. Can you talk about how your gay identity affects your writing? For example, do you give form to Eros differently as a gay man in any way? I'm actually much more interested in how identity pressures how we write, not what we write.

This is a dire generalization—having never been a heterosexual I can't speak personally for its accuracy [both laugh]—but having read a great deal of heterosexual literature about desire and love, and having known lots of heterosexual men, it seems to me that heterosexual love is very strongly based on duality, on the object of desire being one's complementary opposite, and on a fundamental, assumed level of inaccessibility. A heterosexual man can want a woman but obviously can never be a woman (nor does he want to be, usually), and that's part of what drives the difference engine of heterosexual desire. For gay men, there's both the difference and distance that drive desire and an identification with the object of desire. There's a mirroring between you and the object of desire, because you want to have him and want to be him. There's the pressure of trying to be or become what you want to have, which is obviously not a part of the heterosexual desire machine.

My poems are full of mirrorings and doubles—of persons, of images, of words and phrases—and that mirroring is always full of misreflections and misperceptions; it's always shot through with distortions. The mirror doesn't reflect true. Narcissus sees a clouded image of himself in the water and doesn't know who it is. He falls in love with a stranger who's himself and thus he makes himself into a stranger. All of these elements in my poems relate to a particular experience of Eros, a particular experience of my body in relation to other bodies, since after all the poem is a body, too.

In "Little Hands," you write, "The man becomes a boy eventually / (blank body a white page / where wishes write themselves)," and later, "Mere world, where every man's / the artist of himself, body / his medium, interference (an inference / at most)." The body and "the page," two ideas you provocatively link. Body, of course, is the site of desire, but it also produces "voice"—

That takes us back to the story of Apollo and Daphne: what Apollo gets out of his desire is another image of his desire, a poem called desire. The first set of lines you quoted is about the projection of desire onto the other, about turning the other into an object of desire, which also means turning the other into an object of one's will. It relates to Hegel's Master/Slave dialectic: the master seeks recognition, but because he's reduced the slave to an object, he can never get that recognition, even though the point was to force that recognition from the slave. But an object can't give that. Only another full subject can. On the more metaphorical level, there's a sense of writing desire on the body of the other person, that you'll then be able to read back to yourself, of making the other's body the embodiment of your own desires toward it.

Are there ways compositionally in which you see the page as a body? Do you carry the link that far where you see that white space as a body? (And I think it's important that we say "white" space.)

There are definitely quite a few analogies in my poems between white skin and the white page. There's a strong impulse in my work to inscribe my presence, my desire, onto that page and metaphorically onto that desired skin. There's a definite will to power there and, as I said earlier, even a sadistic element.

The words of the poem are like wounds with which I would like to scar that white skin, leave my indelible mark—to blemish that white with my dark, the black words, if that's not too over the top.

Timothy Liu notices a connection between body and text in his review of your first book, Some Are Drowning, *specifically the juxtaposition of the "white page" and the "white skin." I see you imagining the white page as the body of your poem, whereas I see other poets, perhaps, imagining the words of their poem as the body.*

I see the words as constituent elements of the body of the poem, which is the inscription of those black words onto the white page, giving features and a face to that blank space—or imposing them onto it. The literalization of the idea of a body of work, a body of words, is very evocative to me.

Let's talk about race, which is something that is crucial to your work but conversely something which you've emphasized that, along with your gay identity, doesn't define the poems. Throughout your books, "black" and "white" are used so frequently and in such purposeful ways that they come to function as tropes in and of themselves. I was especially struck by the lines that describe night as "any disposition / towards blackened white." When the predominant colors of your palette are black and white, it seems to me the work is subtly steeped in tension, opposition.

It's actually something that at a certain point I started consciously doing. I was interested in incorporating an inescapable racial consciousness in a way that wasn't simply thematic or narrative, and color imagery was a way to play that out. There were some cases in which I went back to poems and added colors, taking poems that were not "about race" and adding that undercurrent. That also corresponds to my own experience, which is not always so much about the constant consciousness of "this person is black, this person is white," but of undercurrents which you can't separate out of the tangled threads of identity and relationship.

Color as a perceptual phenomenon and as a set of symbolic categories has always fascinated me. Black and white are opposites as colors, but they also define one another and define the extremes of color, and each represents both the absence of all color and the combination of all colors. That's an ambiguity I find compelling.

Can you also talk about "the expectations placed on black writers to perform a recognizable version of blackness," as you once put it to me? How have you experienced this personally?

I think that there's a Balkanization of literature nowadays. You've got the black artists over here, the gay artists over here, the women artists over here. Only black people can write about black experience, only gay people can write about gay experience, etc. Conversely—it's not so clearly articulated—there's the implication that only black people want to or need to read about the black experience, etc. There's a reification and simplification of the idea of experience, the idea that there's a black experience, a gay experience, a women's experience. Lip service is paid to the idea of a diversity of black experience, say, of diversity within diversity, but the expectations are still quite narrow. I certainly don't identify with most of the versions of black experience or gay experience that I see, in the world or in literature. I especially look at the work of some black writers who've grown up in privilege but still feel compelled and entitled to write a kind of protest literature, and I see no commonality between their "black experience" and mine. There's nothing wrong with taking on "blackness" as a question in one's writing—though there's definitely something wrong with taking it as a fixed, settled thing, something that explains or accounts for people and their experience—but I'd like a wider range of choices. I'd like less of a sense of prescriptiveness, an approach you're expected to take, subject matters you're supposed to address, a voice you're meant to adopt.

What interests me in literature is to be able to experience things outside of my own life, to be able to explore other worlds, to be able to explore the world at large. Identity politics is a way of looking at literature that is directly opposed to what literature really has to offer, a combination of otherness and brotherhood, the opportunity to find the otherness in the familiar, to find the familiar in the other.

All my life, various people black and white have criticized me for being insufficiently or improperly black, because I didn't speak, walk, or write the correct way, the recognizably "black" way. And that's continued into my writing life: I'm often just not considered a black writer. I've been struck by the vehemence with which some people have responded to my insistence that poetry could and should be something other than the expression of a group identity, as if that were a betrayal of some notion of my race or my heritage. But writing shouldn't be reducible to those predefined terms.

Race is part of your work, sure, but it's subtle, it's threaded in your consciousness, which isn't enough for some, from the sound of it.

I don't try to avoid [blackness] or deny it. It's not the definition of my work anymore than it's the definition of my life, but obviously it's an important element. I do feel we live in a cultural environment in which people are really encouraged to think about themselves in terms of their recognizable identity positions, and they're really encouraged to fit themselves into a much more tidy mold than I think most people really can fit into, and to ignore or repress parts of themselves that don't fit into that.

You've said before that, growing up in the Bronx, poetry's otherness was "liberating"—"transformation, not representation." In retrospect—and literary theory aside—did you feel that desire for liberation, or escape, in any way shaped your view that a poem do something, not say something?

I would say so. Poetry certainly did something for me. I think the idea of poetry as a pastime or a social ornament never appealed to me, because that would never have done anything for me. TV was my pastime, listening to records was my pastime. But they didn't change anything. If I had had a more comfortable life, I probably never would have written poetry at all, actually [both laugh]. What I was looking for was something that had the power to change my world. Poetry, as I encountered it, as I imagined it, held out the possibility of being that something that could change things, that could change me. If art really is some kind of compensation for what we lack in our lives, it can only be so by providing something different from what we already have, not merely by reflecting those lives and those myriad lacks. It has to be something that can do something; it has to add something to the world that wasn't there before.

The poems deal in a uniquely wrecked/wracked language. I'm reminded of Daphne speaking in "Wicker Man Marginalia": "words break me / break from me," and later in the poem, "everything / is alive but me, my words / mere wounds." It's not just about the breaking of syntax or the wreckage of language, but there's this emotional distress behind it. What draws you to this? Does it help the poem "do something"?

On the formal level, it prevents the reader or the writer from taking the language and the words for granted, from just seeing through them to what's being said. It keeps the language alive, an active partner in the enterprise. Frankly, much of my writing life has been about trying to find ways around what I "have to say." Because I'm somewhat obsessive in my topics, I don't want to repeat myself, to be monotonous or boring. On a more personal level, my own experience has been very "wracked/wrecked," so that does go into my work—it's part of the material I work with and that works me.

I see throughout the later work this intellectual distress/joy response to language become an emotional response to it. Of course, language poets can play with language, but I've not really seen a reaction to language re-translated through the heart as you do it.

A lot of the dichotomy between mainstream poetry and experimental poetry has worked itself out in practice into a division between people who write about things and people who play with language. But for the poets who inspired me, people like Eliot and Yeats and Williams and Stevens, their struggles with words were struggles with the world. They were trying to find words that encounter the world on equal terms. Simply to reflect that world would have been an abdication of responsibility. To me, passion is essential to poetry. Passion is not just a passion for my lover or for botany or for history, but a passion for words, a passionate struggle to try to create something in words that would be "up to" the world, that would have the same kind of reality as the world. Which also means it's going to be as resistant to its creator as the world is. That passion, which I do find really lacking in a lot of contemporary poetry, is a passion of world and word. And yes, the struggle such passion entails is always both joyous and painful.

For me the key is that part of the distress is in your work in direct relation to language: "words break me / break from me." The experience works its way into the syntax.

The relationship of language and experience is somewhat paradoxical in my work. On the one hand, you can read that language as expressive or reflective of an experience. On the other hand, it's clearly far from the language that would normally be applied to that experience, from the language one would use in the midst of that experience. There's a dialectical relationship between a desire to create a language that is going to be able to encompass that experience and the will to create a language that's as far from that experience as possible. That distance is, in itself, a way to control, to shape that experience. But it's also a way to control oneself and one's own ideas about and intentions

toward experience. If the language of my poems were more directly reflec-
tive, it would be much less wracked/wrecked linguistically, and it would fit
much more into the general discourse of self-display and the manufacture
of personality (especially a suffering personality) seen on *The Jerry Springer
Show* and in countless memoirs. But the language doesn't participate in that
suffering. It transforms it, remaking it without in any way denying it. At least,
that's my hope.

Language can be a means of mastery—over experience on the one hand, but
also over expression itself. But at the same time language is always resistant
to that mastery. So the very thing that could give you this power—which I
think is always at least partly compensatory—also denies you that power. It's
saying, "No, actually the power is mine. At best you're only borrowing it." The
thing that allows you to speak also silences you, or at least determines how
you can speak, what you can speak. Eliot said that the poet must always be
suspicious of his language, but I believe that the language must be suspicious
of the poet, too. You come to language wanting it to do these things for you,
and certainly there are lots of things language can do for you, but language is
both ours and not ours at all. We think in words, we feel words inside us. But
it doesn't belong to us at all. It's both intimate and impersonal, this communal
thing that pre-exists us and will go on after us. Words assist us and resist us at
the same time.

Let's end where we began: the idea of "transparency" versus difficulty. In Boston
Review, you once took Harold Bloom and others to task over the "aesthetic of
transparency." As we wrap up, let me just play devil's advocate. Can even a poem
with a fairly graspable meaning be considered a "good poem," if it's rendered
in transformative language?

Harold Bloom fulminates against what he sees as the evil politicization of
literature, but in a lot of ways I don't see him as very different from the straw
man that he sets up, because both are interested in poetry as a means to some
other end, rather than as an experience in itself. By definition the article you
mentioned was polemical, so it was engaging in deliberate over-emphasis. If
the dominant thought is that meaning is the most important thing, I'm going
to argue against that. On the other hand, if someone says that the only thing
that matters is form or style, I'm going to argue against that. When I read
"experimental poets," I often see a more or less interesting set of formal and
rhetorical gestures, but I don't see them really writing anything, I don't feel

any sense of necessity or passion. For that matter, when I read James Merrill, I see an amazing degree of poetic skill that's deployed to write pretty much about nothing, except perhaps how nice it is to be rich. Many of Merrill's poems are the literary equivalents of sophisticated parlor games. Of course, Thomas Campion wrote gorgeous, perfect poems that are pretty much about nothing, songs about song, about loving to sing, to the extent that in "When to her lute Corinna sings," the speaker actually is the lute that his beloved plays, and she's pretty explicitly only there to inspire the song. Love is just the pretext. So it's a lot more complicated than a dichotomy between "writing about something" and "writing about nothing." In general, "meaning" is not as straightforward as we often think it is.

I do think that a poem needs a degree of complexity to hold the interest for more than a reading or two, but a poem doesn't need complicated surfaces to be complex. I certainly don't think that there's only way one to achieve complexity in terms of technique or style. The important thing is that the poem takes you out of your everyday mindset, breaks the molds of habit and routine—that the language takes hold of you and makes you listen, makes you see. That's what poems have been doing ever since people started chanting or murmuring to themselves.

AGHA SHAHID ALI

Before his death in December 2001, Agha Shahid Ali published four books of poetry in the United States—*Rooms Are Never Finished* (W.W. Norton, 2001), which was a finalist for the National Book Award; *The Country Without a Post Office* (W.W. Norton, 1997), which engages the ongoing troubles in his homeland, Kashmir; *A Nostalgist's Map of America* (W.W. Norton, 1991); and *The Half-Inch Himalayas* (Wesleyan University Press, 1987). *Call Me Ishmael Tonight: A Book of Ghazals* (W.W. Norton) appeared in 2003. Through critical essays and verse translations, many published in *The Rebel's Silhouette* (University of Massachusetts Press, 1991), Ali helped to introduce Urdu poet Faiz Ahmed Faiz to Western readers. *Ravishing DisUnities*, his edited volume of contemporary ghazals in English, appeared in 2000 from Wesleyan University Press. The recipient of Guggenheim and Ingram-Merrill fellowships, he taught in the creative writing programs at the University of Utah and the University of Massachusetts at Amherst. Lawrence Needham conducted this interview over several late-morning sessions during the summer of 1999, and the interview appeared in Volume 17, Numbers 2 and 3 / Volume 18, Number 1 of *Verse*.

Critics, I among them, have represented you as diasporic writer—at least as a writer on the move: Kashmir—Delhi—Pennsylvania—Arizona—New York—Massachusetts. Now you have arrived after all this movement; that is, you have achieved some critical and popular success here and abroad. How different are the reference points for your arrival—different, let's say, in India than in the States? I'm referring to the ways in which you have been, and are, framed/received ...

A roundabout answer: I grew up in Kashmir under the *active* influence of three major cultures—Western, Hindu, Muslim—the Western represented by English, spoken fluently in our home, where Shakespeare, Keats, Shelley, and Hardy were quoted. My grandmother, the first woman in the state of Kashmir to be formally educated—she died this past January (1999) at the age of 98—quoted these poets by heart, just like that. I went to Irish Catholic schools (nuns and fathers). I listened to Western classical and popular music and saw British and American films (not dubbed or sub-titled). This combination obviously suggests a certain class background. Then, naturally, there was Hinduism—its Kashmiri and Indian varieties. My closest friends were Hindus.

Hindu rituals, temples, festivals, music, and their presence in Bombay movies continue to influence me. And then there was the Muslim. I grew up in a Shiite Muslim home (my mother was Sunni). All these traditions were there, not in any self-conscious way, and they mingled and overlapped in marvelous ways. I carry this baggage lightly—it is not baggage. This background (crystallized for me here in America, a home now, where I came for graduate education and then stayed) has been tempered with or enhanced by "exile." Am I along the right track?

Well, you can take it this way, through the influences—

I am coming to the reception part. When I write a poem, I don't worry about these larger cultural matters. Two chapbooks appeared in India—one of them before I came here—and a group of readers seemed positive. Never caught up with the "Oh, I am writing in English, notice me" kind of self-consciousness, I wrote because I had to. When I picked up the pen, everything happened in English (it was not a choice). Some readers in India found a certain honesty in my work. In America, workshops gave me finer strategies of craft. For a long time I worked on my first full-length book, *The Half-Inch Himalayas*, and some people in India think it was published because of its "exotic" nature. But a long time went into shaping it into its final version. For several years, it had been rejected in earlier versions, and I'm glad because it was not quite there. When Wesleyan took it in December 1985 (it appeared in Spring 1987), it had that year already been a finalist in all the national competitions. Groups of anonymous judges were out of six hundred or so manuscripts taking it to the final two or three. In other words, it got accepted when it was aesthetically ready. The exotic background has neither helped nor hindered my reception in America. Those who respond to me include poets I respect as artists. After publication here, my work received attention in India, which has not entirely shed the colonial mentality: publication here or in England enables a better reception in India. Penguin India and Oxford University Press approached me, as did journals. Because English belongs to the "educated" elite, writers still get their validation from publication abroad, though of late, everything does not get automatic endorsement—a sign of health.

Some of the poems from your chapbooks were included in Half-Inch Himalayas *and thus were recognized by their presence there in a way they hadn't been.*

Absolutely. And then a few were included in *The Beloved Witness: Selected*

Poems (Penguin India, 1992). But the work has received attention now, both in America and in India. However, the colors of my second book, *A Nostalgist's Map of America*, are so localized that Indians have not quite responded to it though the Americans have responded very fully to the colors of Kashmir and India in my work. I am in some ways very much a kind of American poet now.

Though certainly, A Nostalgist's Map *also includes non-American elements, which many Indians could respond to. For example, "From Another Desert" employs the Arabic legend of Laila and Qais which should have all kinds of rich associations for many South Asians. But—and you can correct me—Half-Inch Himalayas, a better known work on both sides, also suffers from a similar critical inattention or partiality, in America, from those who focus on its "exotic" subject matter, in India, from those who concentrate on its "native" elements. Has the richness of your work been scanted, its combination of western and non-western elements—that tripartite mix you mentioned before—and, if so, how do you address the situation?*

In India I make my case by making one for all South Asian writers in English—that they all are privy to triple or more mixes, which they can exploit from within, using their situation to go deeper and further. For example, in Arun Kolatkar, Marathi and English come together, and his poetry in English (he writes in Marathi also) has the spirit of his Marathi background the way the spirit of Urdu weaves itself into my English. When Oxford University Press brought out *Twelve Modern Indian Poets*, the editor, Arvind Krishna Mehrotra quoted—in his Introduction—from a letter in which I had made a case for this arrangement of three cultures and how writers could go for it in a very big way. In that context I talked about Rushdie, who does it in prose, and I was gratified to see this passage quoted in an editorial in the *Times of India*. So people who read stuff in English have become aware to varying degrees of this tripartite arrangement, if you will. In America, among poets, I find more and more people responding to *A Nostalgist's Map* whereas *The Half-Inch*, it seems, wins consistent attention because it fits neatly into various boxes and is also more accessible to the lay-reader.

My sense of the American reception of A Nostalgist's Map *in terms of courses and anthologies, is that it addresses the multi-ethnic issue but it overlooks the ways in which you are an American poet, in the American tradition, or that you can be read that way. Whereas the poets probably do recuperate your work in that sense.*

Responses to my latest book, *The Country Without a Post Office*, have been enthusiastic. Its large subject-matter, the turmoil in Kashmir, accompanies my largest aesthetic canvas so far. I wanted to honor the cruel luck of being given as one's subject the destruction of one's home, of a way of life, by serving the language and not letting it become an aesthetic convenience. Poets have responded to it by seeing, in my work, a more dramatic development, which even I could not have foreseen. I mean when I look at *The Half-Inch* I can't foresee *A Nostalgist's Map*, and when at the latter I can't foresee *Country*. Hindsight can lead one to see the developments as maybe inevitable—that is, to see the continual presence of concerns now diluted, now refined, enhanced, whatever.

I realize your current work has received a warm critical reception, but it is very difficult work at levels of forms, of allusion, of trying to stitch together the complicated strands of a difficult subject. Are you concerned that you may lose a "popular" readership for the "fit audience, but few"? The other thing is—something we'll get to as an awkward segue to our next discussion—might readers be justified in seeing in your development as a writer a deepening post-colonial sensibility? I know you feel a bit uneasy with such terms ...

No, I get impatient unless I know what a critic means by *post-colonial* or *diasporic*—they can mean so many things. Often a term can mean its opposite as well. Just look at *Modern* or *Romantic*.

Well, I'll let you comment on what they might mean to you. Do you respond at all to being called a writer in exile, an expatriate writer, a cosmopolitan? Any or all these tags?

My one distinct advantage is my temperament. I believe in making the best of any situation and having a good time.

That doesn't sound like an exile to me.

No, it does not. When I came to the States and wrote the poems in *The Half-Inch*, I was a student and did not have the money to go back to Kashmir regularly—there was a four-year gap and a six-year gap. But now I go back every year, and that particular sense of loss is not there. So the exilic temperament of

The Half-Inch was not a youthful pose, for I was constantly missing my parents, my home, my friends, Kashmir, Delhi. Everything seemed terribly far away. Technically I am not an exile. No one kicked me out of anywhere. I am an expatriate, a voluntary condition. But now America is very much mine and so is the Subcontinent and I feel equally comfortable, though in different ways, in both places. Some years ago I gave a reading at Columbia University. Among the largely South Asian audience were people from non-literary disciplines as well. I was asked how come I had not lost my sense of India and seemed to be at such ease with both my American and Indian selves—something they had picked up from my poetry. I answered: Must it be an either/or situation? Figures such as Said, a real exile, and Rushdie have, by their examples, made duality attractive —something I arrived at on my own because of my temperament. Said is absolutely a Palestinian and absolutely an American; as a matter of fact, his being an American has allowed him to be even more Arabic. This century's vast migrations have created these realities, and the writer can turn them into a real advantage—not that I wish to downplay the negative side.

*In this regard, your writing might be said to exhibit, if not a progression, than at least a variety of stances. The thrust of the question is not at the experiential aspect of your condition but rather your particular stance in the poetry. I see your early work engaging the idea of exile while some of your later work—*A Nostalgist's Map *in particular—calls to mind the concept of nomadicism, of those multiple orientations necessary for survival in a contemporary situation that needs to be de-territorialized. You have to move around in your tent of words.*

Nomadic is a good term, one that should suggest a positive condition. Nomads take the desert for granted and do not question that they will set up their tents here and then a hundred miles away.

Well, what about cosmopolitan? *Are you comfortable with that term, which suggests a citizen of the world but, on the negative side, elitism, privilege, detachment?*

My condition was cosmopolitan from the word go—what I meant by three cultures. In our home poetry was quoted in English, Kashmiri, Persian, and Urdu. We listened to Indian as well as Western classical music (my introduction to the latter was Grieg's *Peer Gynt*) and jazz and Elvis and the Beatles. I listened to Arabic music, Carnatic music. We discussed Ghalib, Hafiz, Shakespeare, Faiz, Goethe, Thomas Mann. And world politics; the world was our domain.

I guess that combination is elitist. But what can I do about it? If I am, I am. But *detachment?*

The cosmopolitan who is above local politics, nationalisms, someone who can be "objective."

I don't like nationalism in its exclusionary modes. Isn't generosity a more enlightened kind of selfishness? If a genuine struggle in an "enemy" country has led to a generous vision, I would never put that country down. And I would put my country down if it, for example, abetted human rights abuses. So a certain cosmopolitanism should be welcomed, no matter where it comes from, if it leads to cultural and intellectual generosity. I am involved enough to want people to be more part of one another. And in this regard I do respond to the Marxist and Islamic models—even though they have not worked out—for it is good to view the world in terms of global communities (I don't mean globalization). I know many cosmopolitan people who welcome something good in an enemy country—let's say an advance in women's rights. But this belief in global communities in no way precludes self-determination, which is an assertion against someone else's oppressive nationalism backed by ruthless state power.

That gets us to The Country Without a Post Office. *If your earlier poems represent the stance of an exile, and the ones following the stance of the nomadic writer, these new poems could be considered diasporic in that it seems you are interested in* homelands, *real and imagined—that for you there was some sort of trial, the kind of struggle the diaspora was initially, in order to find your way back to—*

—way back to Kashmir?

I am not sure. What exactly were you looking for as you wrote these poems?

Let me use the present tense, as if I am right now writing *The Country.* The crisis in Kashmir is engaging me so very much that I am not forcing myself to write about it. If political poetry is good poetry, it's because politics is part of the way the poet feels (rather than merely understands), so much a part of his *imaginative* world that he expresses it through his art as passionately as he does his love for God or a lover. The subject must happen to the poem, not be forced upon it. I'm writing about Kashmir because it is constantly on my mind, and a lot has sharpened for me because of the struggle there. Questions such as "Will this be the last time I will go there?" haunt me. Before the struggle became dramatic, in 1990, I had spent the three previous summers there, taking for granted that I would be there every summer, that America is mine and Kashmir is mine. But that is no longer an easy proposition. Thus I am dealing with this immediate situation, not with some grand pattern. But because such struggles, legitimate as they are, can be hijacked by "elements," emphasize (not programmatically) Kashmir's pluralistic history. So some "willed" moments, such as "A History of Paisley," highlight Kashmir's Hindu traditions. But such "willed" moments also must stand aesthetic and imaginative demands.

The final tag I wish to consider is "post-colonial writer," someone who comes after colonialism and yet is marked by the problematic of colonialism. Kashmir itself is a case-in-point, its struggle for representation and self-determination marked by the after-effects of the Partition. Are you, as a post-colonial subject, still stuck within the colonial problematic, writing back or against representations that define both limits and possibilities?

Actually, I never get caught up with that issue as I am writing. After reading *Orientalism* and works that book has given rise to, I realize "Oh my, I am part of other scenarios." But when I wrote, for example, "The Dacca Gauzes," a poem that strikes a responsive chord among different persuasions—the entire spectrum, really, from the formalists to the free-versifiers, from the liberals to the conservatives—what engaged me there was a horrific act, sure, but only as it was passed down to us, thus becoming legend, and it became tied up with a ravishing imagery and family history and my grandmother(s). But I did not say I must represent what the British did. In prose it may work differently. I mean, one project of *Midnight's Children* is to question—self-consciously—the way history has been written. Dr. Aadam Aziz is not accidental (Forster's protagonist was a Dr. Aziz). Rushdie is writing against previous representations of India. What gets me going, however, is a phrase, an image.

But having said that—conscious or not—your poems have a continuity in discussing certain thematics, for example, dispersed tribes, countries without names or without post offices ...

But that is because I have always been moved by injustice, ever since I was a kid. I remember my parents discussing Lumumba, the Rosenbergs, Nazi atrocities. Events like the Armenian massacre bring out a rage in me. So inadvertently I may be doing some representing. But I don't *represent*, never offer *the* correct version of history.

You never do that, but to put it in a post-colonial context, yes, you are not speaking for the oppressed, for the subaltern, but you are gesturing in a direction, illuminating traces of other histories, which then can be taken in certain ways. I find this as being part of the "project," for you to underscore lost histories out there.

Yes, that's true. You see, critics respond to every book about India with "Now we have understood India—this is the book!" Would they say *"This* is the book about America"? But India, the Arabs, the Muslims—one always finds them being *explained. Midnight's Children* led to "a continent finds its voice" and that sort of nonsense. How could India, eight hundred million of whose people don't know English, find its voice through a novel in English? Perhaps a more sensible, though still problematic, response would have been: "India finds its own 'English' voice." I want people to respond to me as an individual poet trying like other poets to charge language to its utmost. So that is why I refuse—and even this refusal is not willed—to "represent" Kashmir or India or Islam.

Even when you situate yourself as an Indian writer, you place yourself in a "regional" way, as you do in Twelve Modern English Poets—*the Mehrotra anthology, where you identify yourself as a northern Indian Muslim, not as someone speaking for all of India.*

Absolutely. But as an individual inhabiting Urdu, the landscapes and histories of Kashmir, my parents, ancestors, and ...

So you really, really don't want to be the mouth of India?

Most certainly not. God, it would be too huge a mouth, hideous. I like my mouth as it is, and I like to lick a stamp or a cone.

Also—and this goes back to your letter that Mehrotra quotes where you reference Rushdie's chutnification of English to state your aim to biryanize *it, which is a writing back as well—there's the sense you are not just making English yours but expanding its possibilities. Comment?*

Rushdie opened up possibilities for Indian English with a certain bravado, and many writers realized it's all right not to follow the rules left behind by the British—of grammar or taste. In India certain people sound more British than the British, all that "Jolly good" and "Yes, Suh" sort of thing. So irritating. And then Rushdie comes along and breaks the rules (or reinvents them) with such expansiveness! The fiction writers in his wake owe everything to his wild take on local colors, the way he even relies on Bombay cinema. We need this energy in poetry also. Nissim Ezekiel has done those poems in "Indian English," but they lack the largeness to uncover possibilities. Because Indian English is not going away—for self-evident reasons—those who write in it can take elements from Marathi or Bengali or whatever and imbue English in surprising ways, not only to have a Rushdie sort of fun but for the sake of the sublime (thus *biryani*zation as opposed to *chutni*fication). Rushdie has some biryanizing moments (drops of blood from Aadam Aziz's nose turning into rubies on the prayer rug and the diamonds he brushes from his eyes). I want more such heady stuff in our poetry because it, in fear of certain excesses, has been confined to some minimalism. Indian English should become a medium for the sublime.

That should ease us into the next group of questions, and that has to do with another way you can transform the language—if you will—through translation. Talal Asad argues—and I'm loosely paraphrasing here—that the relevant task for the translator is not how best to grasp or comprehend a source text within the bounds of some target language, but rather to test the tolerances of that language, that is, his or her challenge is not to straitjacket the source text in traditional forms of English, in this case, but to unsettle its limitations and/or expand its horizons. So if you are translating Faiz, you should not try for equivalents but in some ways test the boundaries of English in order to create larger or more expansive forms.

Let me tell you how I approach translation, and if a larger inference can be made, fine. When I came to America, I found no one who knew Faiz, a poet whom my parents and I knew by heart. He was an incredible figure of conscience, jailed often, awarded the Lenin Prize (Nazim Hikmet, Pablo Neruda, and Mahmoud Darwish have all been recipients), denied entry into the U.S. under the McCarran-Walter Act. So when I came here, I saw poets did know of Hikmet, whom Faiz had translated into Urdu and knew in the Cold War camaraderie of left-wings poets such as Neruda. I thought it would be nice to get him known here. As I tackled the problem, I realized how stilted he had been made to sound in English. Victor Kiernan, the Marxist historian and the first to translate Faiz into English, has provided versions that, though helpful, are not poetry. Then I came across Merwin's versions of Ghalib and from all kinds of languages he does not know—Korean, Arabic, Persian, Turkish. What resonance he creates! I think Merwin became Merwinesque by translating—I can't imagine *The Lice* being written by a non-translator. So I started my translations, and it became a challenge: What could I do with English to bring out the aesthetic feel of the original? I found myself in an unusual situation—and that too is part of the post-colonial world: as a poet in English I have immense loyalties to that language, but I also know Urdu intimately. My inwardness with both languages from infancy allowed me finally to let each poem dictate its own agenda, with no theoretical inhibitions, the only question being how I could recreate Faiz in English. I heard the originals in my mind, those rhythms, their manner. Who can observe absolute fidelity? Some of my versions contain vivid departures in order, paradoxically, to create the spirit of the original. So regarding Talal Asad, I don't know if I've answered you.

No, that does answer the question, in that you talk about the cross-fertilization.

And some of the elements of Urdu, largely unconsciously, have got into my own poetry along with elements of other Indian cultures, and it is fascinating how imagery and certain turns of phrase—that are just not native to English—have got into my own poetry, which, I emphasize, is exclusively in English. And that, maybe, has been my modest attempt at the biryanization of English.

I know you have expressed dissatisfaction with one kind of translation—of the ghazal form—with how it's been done.

Yes, but that is not the translation of somebody's work. If you are translating Ghalib, for example, I can see the need for free verse. My dissatisfaction is with people who took the translations to say *This is the ghazal* (chiefly Adrienne Rich though James Harrison sets a similar example) and paid no attention, even in their explanations, to what makes the ghazal. Its magic depends substantially, if not entirely, on its formal property, and I have been showing to American poets why this is the form. I am glad to see many exclusive free-versifiers tempted to try this very shackling form. Rich and others, given the late sixties and early seventies, may have half-heard the matter. For their example is not even an imitation of an imitation—there is no sense of the original "idea," except that it contains autonomous couplets. By the way, John Hollander's

Rhyme's Reason contains the first real ghazal I know in English, and from it I realized it could be handled in English.

These days you are consciously working with a variety of poetic forms, other containers—which may not be the best way to put it—but you also seem to be experimenting with voice, moving away from the first person lyrical meditation characteristic of your earlier work and incorporating more dialogue and multiple voicing into your writing.

My first person singular has never been just me. My "I" always contains, well, at least some of the multitude. For example, the speaker in "The Previous Occupant" is thinking about not just his new flat but about the vanished in Chile. The "I" is not drawing attention simply to his own life but is interested in larger patterns.

You progressively have gone on to poems in which someone other than the I speaks, poems involving impersonation.

Yes. Absolutely. What about that?

Well, you have experimented with more than just metrics and stanzas. You seem to have extended yourself in other ways. And you've worked on prose poems ...

Prose poems, canzones, sonnets, sestinas, envelope stanzas, quatrains, pantoums, ghazals, sapphics, Anglo-Saxon verse, terza rima, and more. But I should add that when I was writing the poems in *The Half-Inch*, I was simultaneously doing impersonations, so to speak, such as "Eurydice" and "Medusa," which—like the poems in *A Walk*, also were written then—did not fit into the thematic structure of *The Half-Inch*. Many of them ended up fitting into *A Nostalgist's Map*.

So those poems do not demonstrate a linear progression in your craft?

Evolving concerns, I would say, and sometimes previous poems have fit better into a later book. My fingers were in several pies, you can say (this fits into my tripartite heritage). While writing the poems in *The Half-Inch*, I already was trying to deal with syllabics, sonnets, pentameters. I already was trying humorous poems and persona poems, and you will find those elements in *A Walk* and *A Nostalgist's Map*.

So it was a question of a tonal fit for the volume?

That too. Certain things have got more accentuated, but they all are in my earlier work even though they are not present in *The Half-Inch*. For example, I was writing the telephone poems and my Red Riding Hood poems alongside "Snowmen" and "The Dacca Gauzes," and no one would think the poems are by the same person. And if by the same person then not at the same time. Such is the mysterious business of temperaments.

Throughout A Nostalgist's Map, *there is a blend of seriousness and humor, sometimes in individual poems concerning grave matters—by "humor," I don't mean the laugh laugh variety, but rather wit and wry touches—and I see this even in* The Country, *sometimes in the elaboration of a conceit, and I wonder if this might not be a problem given the serious nature of the subject, that wit is something that …*

Why do you think it should be a problem?

To me it is not a problem, but to others it might be—the way you cleverly extend and elaborate the metaphor of the post office and the dead letter department, for example, when writing about the troubles in Kashmir. Might not such writing, however brilliant at times, detract from the subject at hand?

The subject at hand is mediated through imagination and artifice. A created reality becomes its own reality. *The Country Without a Post Office* arose from factual reality in that no mail was delivered in Kashmir when the troubles started. The wit, as such, saves it from easy polemical gestures, for the interest in art is constant there.

Yes, that makes a lot of sense. I was thinking about a poem in A Nostalgist's Map, *"In Search of Evanescence," which deals with AIDS and the death of a friend, but there is also buoyancy, a certain amount of camping, which I find marvelous.*

If because of the camping there are incidental witty moments but the under-lying seriousness comes through—more heartbreakingly, perhaps—then it is all to a good effect, I think. One has a way of feeling, yes, feeling the world. But I can't stand being serious too long. For example, in a panel discussion when anyone is going on and on with "In my life this" and "In my life that,"

I feel the need to say something flippant so people can lighten up. The sheer earnestness that governs panels is so irritating. Solemnity drives me nuts. Humor can keep one from being solemn.

Can you comment on what you were trying to achieve formally and tonally in The Country, *a moving but carefully crafted response to tragic events in Kashmir?*

You can fit my very conscious use of forms in that book wherever, but I was telling you about this at times asserted and at times hinted belief that free verse equals liberalism and forms some conservative agenda. Well, Merrill wrote in forms because it was part and parcel of his temperament. Theorizing came later. And within his handling of forms there was an encounter with immense turmoil through immense experimentation. He wasn't saving Western civilization though he was situating himself in the higher art of Western texts. Forms saved him from Western civilization, if I may be perverse about it.

You may be as perverse as you wish.

I would be surprised if Faiz ever agonized over why a poem was occurring in free verse and why in forms. He wrote all kinds of poems, even one (not very good) in English. I am sure he agonized with pleasure over every word as a real artist must. One has inherited great forms from the centuries. Only insecurity leads to such debates.

So it's not just for variety's sake, it's for local effect …

To try to keep the language alive. What will save us from Western civilization and the horrors of globalization? Humanity has this incredible need to cling to illusions imposed upon it by all kinds of hegemonies even when realities contradicting them are in its face!

In some ways this volume seems to be directed to a fit audience—it is dense and thickly allusive throughout.

When I first read *The Waste Land*, I didn't know what was going on. Poets, at least after a while, must lead their audiences. Why should everything be immediately accessible? In my canzone—the last poem in *The Country*—readers may not get the allusions, but the poem is accessible in terms of emotion and narrative. The reader should make some effort, as I do when a compelling poet is difficult. My hope is that a "difficult" poet like Derek Walcott emerges in the Subcontinent.

In a way you are doing something like that ...

Modestly. But I don't have that kind of talent. Perhaps my work and others' is laying the groundwork for a Walcott or Merrill to emerge.

Do you think there is the necessary supportive environment, let's say in India, for that to happen?

That doesn't matter. Even James Merrill had to create his own space til people paid real attention. Stick by your guns so they grant you some space, and then create more space and so on. The time is constantly readied for you because you have created the space, because you are ripe for that ready moment. Ripeness is all.

CLAUDIA RANKINE

Claudia Rankine was born in Kingston, Jamaica. Her first book, *Nothing in Nature is Private*, was published by Cleveland State in 1994. Her second and third books, *The End of the Alphabet* (1998) and *PLOT* (2001), were published by Grove Press. Her next book, *Don't Let Me Be Lonely*, was published by Graywolf Press in 2004. She teaches at the University of Houston. Katy Lederer conducted this interview via email between September and December 1999, and the interview appeared in Volume 18, Numbers 2 and 3 of *Verse*.

I thought we could start with the remarkable formal and thematic differences between your first book, Nothing in Nature is Private, *and your second,* The End of the Alphabet. *In his review of the second book in* Boston Review, *Calvin Bedient asks, "Whenever before has autobiography (or at least an autobiography-effect) been so elusive with respect to the gross facts of life, so unbound by any logic of linear narrative circumstance, yet so ferocious and refined an act of self-scrutiny?" This is certainly not anything one would say of the first book, which very clearly delineated any number of narrative events — love stories, a child's immigration from Jamaica and so forth. What prompted you to move into the more elusive, though arguably more emotionally intense, style of the second book?*

Very soon after receiving the published version of *Nothing in Nature is Private* I felt it did not represent my understanding of the world closely enough. It is terrible to feel you have failed yourself. Part of the problem with *Nothing in Nature is Private* is that the subject did not determine the form. It was a book written too much from the head and not enough from the pulse and nerve ends. In the end it was disappointing to me because the characters, race and gender, acted throughout rather than embodying the text. My intent had been to write poetry that explored the conflicting ambiguities and complexities comprising our notions of race and gender. Beginning with such a specific field allowed me to think my way through the poems to the extent that, in the end, the point of view began to typecast itself in a performance of blackness and immigration. The poems began to enact a pre-conceived condition. My own consciousness began to seem lost and at times inappropriate to the book's subject.

I read and admired Cal Bedient when I was a wee gal in college, so it was a great honor to have him understand my intentions for *The End of the Alphabet*. He absolutely realized that my desire was to revise what it meant to be "confessional" or autobiographical. It seemed to me one could access emotional content without its narrative frame. In any case I wanted to go as far as I could without the scaffolding of narrative.

Essentially, I was experimenting with the idea that emotion could generate language. I wanted to create a "languaged self" that was built up from her insides, from her pulse and breath. I wanted to enter her subjectivity in such a way that the resulting text was ultimately the experience of her fundamental humanity.

How did you go about accessing this fundamental humanity?

The challenge was how to subordinate the "story line" to its subject, and then, ultimately, to the subject's subjectivity. At the time it seemed to me that the experience of feeling can be more authentic than the activity of living. It was a challenge to make real a synthesis of thought and sensation leading to no real place, no destination. In the end I wanted to re-enact feelings as a process more real than the real, constantly in flux, in and out of focus.

The way I work now is concerned with approximating the process of experience that leads to feelings and thought. *PLOT* might be considered, given its commitment to narrative, a novel in verse.

I decided to expose the external trappings that create the deeply lyrical moments. Despite the fact that how one is touched or touches doesn't vary radically, I decided this time around to expose those moments in order to track how emotions in a lyric moment are born, and vary. It is the individual experience of experience that is human, it occurs to me. I used to believe that feelings were properly private. I thought of them as separate from one's daily activities. But if you let yourself feel what you are feeling in the world, it is interesting how much more precious the details of a life seem. Anyway, *PLOT* tries to bring the world back into the text.

If the idea previously was how to get away from pre-narrativized, preconceived identities, then how is one to figure the necessity of one's interior experience? How do you know which feelings are worth reporting to a reader?

On one level, as a reader or writer, it seems to me it is only necessary to realize that all this ground water is always mucking up the interior. However we are existing, we are also failing. That stuff, the garbled and the hypodermic, is shifting our interior experiences constantly. We are hardwired to concretize, pre-conceive, and narrate so that we can sleep at night, but reality exists in the synthesis of the seen and unseen. Paul Celan wrote, "I knew that anything that happened was more than an addition to the given ..." Subjectivity is the more that ends up being the true reality of any given text.

In your personal writing process, is the writing itself a representation of your interior experience at any given time? Or is it a processual tool through which you arrive at a self that is always in a state of flux?

It sounds like there is a right answer. I would have to put my ten dollars on "Processual tool." It seems related to God somehow. The term God really for me is a way of talking about time. I am convinced motion is God. The kinds of things that mark time, a dripping faucet, or the kinds of things that defy time, airplanes for example, rebound me. That and chairs. The shape of chairs never seems to change.

What you say about chairs seems to have something to do with form — that the form of the human body does not change, that it must then be in league with repetition and by extension, with constraint, conservatism, and, of course, mortality. Is imagination a place of rebellion against such constraint? Or is it, again, a more processual place in which the quotidian can take on new forms and meanings?

You are exactly right about that chair. It does indeed suggest we are in league with repetition. My interest in the sameness of bodily form and function is closely related to the idea that the quotidian governs. The body is caught in a series of repetitions that wears it down to its point of disorientation and erasure. At least that's the fear. If we look closely enough we can see the drip that creates its own groove so that the wearing down becomes maddeningly soothing. That shouldn't happen. Enter the drip, I say.

My own notions regarding the imagination are tied into the static of the quotidian. All imagination, I think, is in some sense mimetic. We can't completely get beyond (or over) ourselves and this world. Though we should, shouldn't we? I love writing that includes a feeling of feelings (a core sense of basic humility) that is capable of taking into account a knowledge (including its chaos) of thought. Close-up we all live and die similarly, but the intersection of feelings and thought separates each of us out, one at a time.

What you say about thought is fascinating. I would be curious to know more about what the relationship is between thought and its expression in language. As a title, The End of the Alphabet *seems to reference both the fixed nature of linguistic systems and the abolition or subversion of such systems. How do you conceive of the book's title?*

The End of the Alphabet (title and book) was initially conceived as an argument against narrative, confessional poetry that is based on the remembered stories and the unpleasant details of a particular life. Emotions are in a sense beyond thoughts because, though they might begin with a thought based in language, they are felt further. This has something to do with why we have such a hard time describing pain. Without really understanding, I wanted the title to suggest a space where words, which are absolutely necessary and fixed in some senses, are also caught up in a windstorm larger than themselves.

The stories of our lives are so similar and repetitive that it seems to me that the moment where we are able to intersect into another's consciousness happens when we are allowed into the process, the flux of feeling and thought. This movement has the particularity of fingerprints. The specific, event-controlled details of a life unconnected to the activity of the felt experience are of little interest to me because there are only so many variables and then of course this happened and then this happened. Finally, there we are, mad, betrayed, relieved, or sad. But how does that madness or that sadness play/say itself.

It strikes me—and this seems to be an issue in much contemporary poetry—that it would be very difficult to convey in writing this flux of feeling and thought. Indeed, that preconceived narrative is there in a sense because it is, literally, accessible. How do you deal with this problem of accessibility?

I know, because I have been told, some people find *The End of the Alphabet* to be something other than accessible. This, of course, was never my intention. I wanted only to distress the reading experience so that words were no longer markings to be skimmed over towards the close of an expected narrative. The idea was that a word, any word, would cast its layers of meaning toward an emotional field that was triggered by certain unexpected juxtapositions on the page. The reading experience then would be a journey into a process outside of the narrative plot-driven arc. In this sense I indeed wanted an end to thought as I encountered it in narrative poetry. An end to clarity, however, was never my intent. Always we were meant to come up, to arrive at another mode of expression, for it seemed to me that language could be turned toward rendering an atmosphere, a feeling of flux and desperation, which seems the point of autobiographical, confessional poetry anyway. You know what I mean, people talk a lot and what are they saying beyond, we are not as we "are living" ourselves to be.

Marjorie Welish

Poet, painter and art critic, Marjorie Welish is the author of numerous collections of poetry including *Word Group* (Coffee House Press, 2004), *Vocalizing Difference* (Paradigm Press, 2004), *The Annotated "Here"* (Coffee House Press, 2000), and *Casting Sequence* (University of Georgia Press, 1993), as well as a book of art criticism, *Signifying Art: Essays on Art After 1960* (Cambridge University Press, 1999). A book on her poetry and painting, *Of the Diagram: The Work of Marjorie Welish*, appeared from Slought Books in 2004. She was awarded a 2005 Judith E. Wilson Poetry Fellowship at Cambridge University. This interview was occasioned by Matthew Cooperman's attendance at a lecture at the Naropa Summer Writing Program in June 2001 and first appeared in *Web Conjunctions* in 2004.

In your lecture at Naropa, I found your critique of "transparent language" in rereading New York School poets very useful, particularly as it points to your own poetics. The careful allying of French structuralism and Russian formalism to the poetic activity of New York City in the 1970s and '80s—its interest in proceduralism, and its conscious response either with or against Language poetry—is revealing in its rendering of effects in Ashbery, Guest, Koch, etc. As a counter-reading to the perception of New York School poetry as emphasizing spontaneity and volubility, you set its poetics in a much more intentional debate with contemporary theory. Could you elaborate on this recasting of New York School poets, both for Ashbery and Co. and for second- and third-generation practitioners?

Free verse and the prose poem may have emerged in revolt against the formality inhabiting French language, but insofar as New York School poets write imitating the relaxed line that they have read they persuade us of their urbanity and their literariness. The declamatory headlong urgency adopted by Russian Futurist poetry for the sake of life lived in the present is also to be found transposed in New York School poetry with varying degrees of self-consciousness: think of O'Hara's "Mayakovsky" and the lines "who am I? If he / will just come back once" that open the poem; and the lines "what does he think / of that? I mean, what do I?" that close the poem. They create not so much a return to O'Hara himself as a formalist scheme representing that shift in subjectivity.

Much more could be said to demonstrate the supple ranging over literary styles and devices that the New York School evidently enjoy. As you have noted, the point of my talk on the metapoetic lyric is that the American avidity for structuralist literary criticism and theory in the 1960s has contributed to a recent subsequent rehabilitation of the New York School poetics whose romantic affiliation had caused it to fall into disrepute (a fall occurring in the 1970s when the realist and/or objectivist Language poetics staked its claim). Whereas once the New York School was consigned to the domain of utterance, now it is possible to credit these same poets with discourse.

How has your own work followed this critique, say, from the period of the late 1970s and Handwritten, *to your more recent work,* The Annotated "Here"?

An interestingly formulated question! My work has advanced not at all by tracking New York School poetry but by crossing paths with it as sophisticated practice, as a set of options comprehended by manifold modernity. Growing up in New York educates one very fast to the complexity of cosmopolitanism. So, interestingly enough, my work was following the critique prior to engaging with the practice. It is also true that my tendency to gravitate toward critical issues, like the problem of revision or the issue of translation, persists even as my poetics shifts to a conspicuous privileging of formal operations and codes.

I'm struck by the pictorial intelligence of your work. The fact that you are a painter and art critic makes that perhaps inevitable. And of course there is the ut pictura poesis *tradition to consider, but what is the relationship between poetry and painting in your creative life?*

They are languages. Poetry, painting, music, dance, and architecture may have their own internal histories and yet the so-called intrinsic concerns may at once prompt creative solutions to intractable or routine thought and at the same time remain a signifying practice. Many writers pay abiding attention to developments in other arts, and whether or not they compose and otherwise consider themselves active in the field, they benefit from "acquiring a second language."

In the United States, we who are active in more than one field are still considered peculiar, even though cultural history is studded with poet-diplomats, poet-mathematicians, and poet-doctors, not to mention poet-architects, poet-graphic designers, poet-musicians, and performance poets for whom hybrid practices are commonplace. These days the centrality of genre no longer obtains, as the literary spectrum interpolates variants and other forms of expression. Hybridity, however, is not the only mode of engagement for those of us in multiple disciplines who persist in investigating poetics as a form of thought. Fortunately, the cultural traditions in Europe, Asia, and Africa argue for the textual understanding of a discipline, and that example has had an effect here.

I suppose my question regards this notion of "benefit." As signifying practices, poetry and painting obviously function differently. But their activity seems closer than, say, writing and doctoring such that a certain hybridity may result, if not in the artifact then in the approach. As you've noted, your poetry and poetics foregrounds "formal operations and codes." From what I've seen of your painting, that seems a similar motivation. Your creative work appears thus of a piece; poetry and painting relate in their intrinsic constructivist concerns, and perhaps in their creative solutions. What impels your decision to paint one thing and write another? If poetry and painting are not so much conversational in your practice, then how are they—as extended projects—distinct?

Yes, both my poetry and painting share a purposeful display and deliberate play, to think through the potentiality of codes and operations. For this reason the constructivist style in my painting is less concerned to argue the commensurability of painting's physical materials and the actual world than it is to display and interrogate a structure of formal relations across a surface. Conceptual formalism is more conspicuously consistent in the painting, I suppose, even as literary theory has had a decisive influence in shaping the meaning of the open-work on difference-within-similarity. By post-structuralist means, certain differentiation is likened to forms of questioning—not mere variation—and this critical approach which is capable of analytic as well as speculative thought may also be the very instrumentality for arriving at significant differentiating conceptual frameworks. And presenting these! As with the painting, the poetry is dedicated to these processes of abstraction for conceptual ends. Like the painting, the poetry represents itself through language and the sign that is the poem, but is willfully experimental and is apt to entertain divergent cultural contents put through differing stylistic filters. What informs the decision to paint or write is a question about what necessitates the choice. Less binding than the choice to eat or to sleep, the necessity may nonetheless still be in which instrumentality and medium will better realize the idea, and for some ideas or concerns, we can conceive of multiple expressions if not always multiple solutions. Put this way, the arts do not really compete but crisscross in certain respects and run parallel in other respects. Ask Leonardo.

Why I ask this question is that I think of your work precisely as an extended project, and if it continues, book to book, the concerns would seem possible, book to painting. It's something, for instance, that I found extremely interesting looking at the Gerhard Richter retrospective this winter. He works in a variety of painterly modes, which on first glance might suggest a restless remaking of aesthetics. But he's been exploring these "stations" over and over again from different historical periods in his career. The late monumental abstract paintings mirror the early realist deformations; his squeegying of surface is one kind of a response to focus. He conceptualizes representation by prior artistic production within his own work, and, more importantly, in the history of art. Is this similar to your approach?

Richter is an interesting case of the European mentality in art, which realizes that a 40,000-year-old dialogue antecedes anything an artist living today might presume to do. And that through trade and through conquest culture is intrinsically displaced, ramified, and rhetorically vexed. Moreover, it has continually encountered singular and radically differing mentalities "within" its putatively European identity: some cultures having a talent for revolutionary thought and institutional experiment, others having a gift for profound inscription of given cultural ideas. (By way of archival mentality, the Argentine-American Osvaldo Romberg exemplifies this will-to-encyclopedia but with a much more pronounced conceptual artistic philosophy than Richter.) Richter's inherent belatedness relative to American and European modern art after World War II is a situation he recognized early on and tried to express and it is this belatedness that he inscribes through his signature style. Although his retrospective proves his early work to be far superior then his recent suave consolidation of manner, the "Atlas" is another matter entirely. These studies for works to be scaled up and finished contain his ideas at their best.

It is said that the modernist attitude recognizes the archive, assimilates its principle ideas, and dedicates itself to creatively antagonistic paradigms worthy of their predecessors. In America, an example of this set of values is Barnett Newman, who deliberately stopped painting until by writing position papers and by sketching he figured out what should be done after Cubism and Surrealism. But the postmodern Rauschenberg had modernist training early on to think against the grain. And Jasper Johns, a postmodern in his hybrid practice and in his archival mentality, nonetheless is like a modern as he moves from paradigm to paradigm, from conceptual framework to conceptual framework, which he studies intently. Johns is the crucial recent American figure in this will to deliberate conceptual representation planned in advance. My own work affiliates with his in some respects but more obviously with Mel Bochner's conceptual formalism.

Your response confirms a spatializing impulse I see in your poetry, your ability to use codes of representation and speech to evoke seemingly actual places or narratives, when all the while it is the place of language that is being "depicted." As such, what does language "see"? Or more precisely, how does your poetry "see"?

Do you mean "see" in a syncretic sense? Sometimes. Do you mean "see" in a formal or structural sense? Decidedly. Do you mean "see" in the sense of "apprehend or discern?" Each of these has given rise to distinct and compelling poetics.

The distinctions you raise, the simultaneity of "seeings," are exactly what I find compelling in your work. For instance in "At Table" (The Annotated "Here"), where the history of 'Still Life' painting appears as an Ur-text to be worried through the problem of subjectivity, and by the differing languages of poetry and painting: "the drift of place setting iterated as a landmark / of the new school / attaining to non-aligned subject-object relations." Or "Chronic Dreams" (The Annotated "Here"): "a function of x / foreshadows / 'of' with 'less' / in an impaired crossing / of arithmetic processes, / while a number greater / than a portfolio of bathers / destroyed // takes the product ..." The mixing of codes and structures is startling; a variable of origin "foreshadows" a mathematical process, which is the product of an artistic cliché "destroyed," all of it somehow seen or objectified by the distance of the quotative figure. It's as if, to offer the title of your New and Selected, the "here," which is a spatial condition, is being seen, being "annotated," by the variety of semiotic choices any moment may imply. The differences in operation between languages are suddenly there, and their similarities. It all works at lightning speed, conflating math and artistic process, the passing of time and the "chronic" imagination. And it ends in an ironic narrative that parses the "greater than/less than, close and far" the whole poem circles: "he gave / the tablet a spatial location in haste." It's a way of making language processes pictorial.

Experiencing the world through the codes of language interests me enormously, and it is indeed this mediated experience through writing, cultural coding, and literariness which informs my poetics and governs most poems. My poems investigate and organize words and sentences as such, yet also the rhetoric posed through propositions in asserting, denying, and questioning in conventions we have learned to call discourse—that domain Hayden White locates between poetry and logic. White's scheme differs from Foucault's and defends itself from the "absurd"—White's term for writing that delights in opacity and so makes itself unintelligible—Derrida who engages the divesting of the objective statement of its so-called neutrality. But as you have noted, poetry I write brings attention to the speculative gamut.

Even so, your own interest in how the idea of seeing may be said to evolve in my work prompts the following. Heard sounds of automobile tires in a delay of recall suggested a transposition to iteration of similarities in language, and this structured statements in an early poem ("Among Them All"). Saying something again and again to install a motor rhythm was not so much a motivating factor; revising a notion again and again to create a domain of translation *was* decidedly the cause of repetition in this poem. It's also true that visual occurrences as well as verbal ones have suggested poems; once commissioned to write an essay on pattern and decoration as women's art, I wrote against and across that assumption, both in the commissioned piece of art criticism and in a poem ("Wild Sleeve") which defamiliarizes patterning through a discursive style that substitutes verbal expression for visual depiction and through frames "Figure A" and "Figure B," by which point pattern that was once culturally calligraphic is habit. By way of our initial acquaintance, Michael Palmer noted this poem in *Conjunctions*. I have never asked Palmer why he respected "Wild Sleeve," but assume he recognized a shared analytical mind toward semiotic poetics; writing poems about writing itself, about language, its signs and its constitutive or grammatical rules, is a shared point of contact. Although nature and so sight readily become cultural sign in my early poems, the tactics for composing the poems lay in operating embedded rhetoric and embedded devices. Spatio-temporal events now ever more frequently prompt a pronounced structural content.

Is this a kind of post-mimetic commentary, a newly inscribed ekphrasis?

No, because the visual spatiality is a pretext for a linguistic or critical or cultural lyric (see "Pages of Illustration"). The poems comprising the new chapbook *Else, in Substance* were all written from a structural rather than a spatial logic.

Or, as I should say, from differing structural logics which manifest the composition. My teaching an immersion course in the poetry and poetics of Wallace Stevens occasioned "Thing Received Road," a cluster of poems written in response to Stevens' having written "place" where he might have written "found." To consider the idea and word from differing, more particularly visual, frames of reference was the question; from the physical to the semiotic and cultural (in which reference itself is the point) to the linguistic (for which listing phases and sentences simply is sufficient). The syllogistic beginning of Stevens' poem "Connoisseur of Chaos" provides a brilliant opening gambit for displaying discourse foreign to the lyric, and at the same time appropriating the discourse for poetic practice. In what sense is the cosmology encapsulated "about" space? More pronounced is the shift from the semantic to syntactic work on behalf of language.

Analogously, in variously discussing Barbara Guest during your Naropa lecture you suggest too much attention is paid to her "sensibility" and not enough to her poetics. Not surprisingly, this privileges the more experimental recent work, say Rocks on a Platter *or* Quill. *Do you see her work as an active synthesis of the more painterly qualities of early New York School work with the semiotically-driven work of Language poetry?*

Barbara Guest's recent poetry has shifted attention from the literariness that has always engaged the Russian device as much as the French musicality to an experimental language ever more daring. Although she would not want me to insist on this, from book to book she reconceives disjunctive, then conjunctive, poetics as though renovating symbolism through a pragmatics drawn from the domain of statements. So in her own way she has indeed subjected forms and formalism to semiotic consideration. The pragmatics of language one finds in Rosmarie Waldrop, Norma Cole, and very differently in Susan Howe, is Barbara Guest's prerogative as well.

As a postmodern poetics this seems poised on reception. If the debate in New York School poetics has changed from the primacy of the senses or sensibility, say, in the '60s, to the primacy of signification more recently, what is the meta-poetic object?

I am not sure that the discussion of New York School poetics has changed the debate so much as that the supervening structuralist and post-structuralist literatures have diffused the dialectical model whereby romantic is the "opposite" of modern and modernity. So far as I know I am alone in pointing out that endorsements and testimonials from formerly antagonistic poets on behalf of the New York School have come about owing to a cultural sea change in literary theory that allows the possibility of interpreting the New York School through a framework of literariness. My proposal to acknowledge the discursive, written strata of this poetry still considered somehow spontaneous speech was designed to prod the critical community to a long-overdue rereading of the literature in light of the innovative poetics of discourse. This rereading would imply considering matters other than imitating styles, at which New York School poets are so adept; and it would imply considering forms of expression other than the urbane collage of found sociolect taken from travelogues, corporate reports, and film noir. The sense of the poem as text—a text of interpretive strata that embodies a semiotic of reception—may certainly be demonstrated here. So may the roving and diffuse subjectivity which occasionally comments on itself and the conventions of the lyric poem with which its urbanity is at odds. Reading this poetics as second-order discourse that does wreak havoc on the lyric and on the mode and genre altogether needs to be acknowledged as compatible with, say, experimental transtextuality for which literary critic Gerard Genette has written a credible taxonomy.

In the narrow sense metapoetic statements are those movements towards self-critical commentary on mode, genre, and other poetic conventions, within the poem itself. Pushkin's *Eugene Onegin* accomplishes not only a novel in verse and an erudite informality through which the poet's authority to parody lyric conventions is made secure: Pushkin will intervene as author, writing, for instance, "I'm always glad to mark the difference between Onegin and myself," or "once more I'll have them quarrel" (drawing the reader's attention to the literary mechanism itself), or stopping the tale of romance for a digression on French-affected words in the Russian society of the day that he has obligingly included. So, with Pushkin's poem in mind, Lyn Hejinian's *Oxota* enjoys the same liberties of literariness, quite deliberately splicing associative free-verse lines that describe or narrate with their literary equivalent or, on occasion, with lines of second-order commentary. The substantive issue here is that in the 1960s poetics reflected an ever more ramified and yet increasingly theoretical literariness in the artifice we call a poem. The metapoetic markers are symptomatic of the semiotic registers being imported into the poetic message to redirect it to the receiver, the reader of the poem, concerning norms and horizons of expectations.

What, then, is the role of the world in the formation of the metapoetic? I'm think-
ing of the world referred/deferred in your work, but also subject *in the largest sense.*
Ron Silliman says it well: "The writer cannot organize her desires for writing
without some vision of the world toward which one hopes to work" ("Of Theory,
To Practice"). Or Rosmarie Waldrop: "To explore the nature of rain I opened
the door because inside the workings of language clear vision is impossible. You
think you see, but are only running your finger through pubic hair" ("Inserting
the Mirror"). Even in its contingency, its literariness, language is an application
to something seemingly true. Of course it depends if you're interested in the rain.
But how, in a theory-centered poetry, does the world objectify language?

Well-defined poetics offer models for poetry and for created (im)possible
worlds, some worlds philosophically possible even though inconceivable
to middle management. An instance of this would be Jacques Roubaud's
deploying a technical sort of philosophy to engender and objectify the very
inaccessibility of the dead to the living. Here language objectifies pluralities
of worlds. Another poetics may objectify a world through the verbal construct
analogous to spectacle that passes for social discourse, or may objectify the
critical distance embodied in poetry that would shun spectacle.

You've mentioned formal operations as a method of composition. If procedures
are a place to begin in recent work, how do they lead to a more programmatic
inquiry? That is, resisting the arbitrariness inherent in proceduralism necessitates
a more conscious manipulation of signs. Would you say this is a passing from
structure to function?

Although OULIPEAN engines have generated some of my poems, the men-
tality of the procedural approach as such allows a poetics that is generative of
constructing arbitrariness. Algorithms of all sorts have informed my poems,
as have rules, and as often as not I am apt to begin writing from a set of these
constraints. However, I do often proceed with a conceptual envelope in mind
within which much experimenting is apt to take place. In advance of writing
"Gravity," for instance, I had determined that through the continuity estab-
lished in the word "gray," a stylistic and cultural discontinuity from part to part
would reveal a cultural content by structuring scale. What I had not determined
were the specifics of that similarity and difference—the very words.

Else, in Substance (Paradigm Press, 1999) and *Begetting Textile* (Equipage,
2000) are chapbooks published independently yet now also included in *Word*

Group, the most recent full-length book of poems, and both of these were writ-ten under self-imposed constraints that nonetheless invited experimentation. Although I've mentioned *Else, in Substance,* I have yet to speak of specific tactics: one poem internalizes a branching structure; another utilizes questions from known riddles that combine with those from a driving manual through a scheme determined in advance; yet another poem makes conspicuous use of passages alternating between repetition and difference—repetition of instruc-tions (to propose a differentiating spectrum of identity within a single statement) and difference through imagistic mental events (to advance through associative leaps from statement to statement). *Begetting Textile* came about in the course of teaching the workshop version of "The Lyric Lately," and was prompted by my deciding to follow Mallarmé's parenthetical "as if" to this extent: that poems I would then write were to feature an anthology of conjunctive "as if"s and variants streaming along the left margin but open his parenthesis to alternative series along the right margin; within these fixed margins, the field would be freely improvised

The lecture you delivered at the Barnard Women's Poetry Conference in 1999, entitled "Where the Lyric Tradition Meets Language Poetry: Innovation in Contemporary American Poetry by Women," opens with: "Let us take the lyric to be non-imitative, verbal music. Let us take the language of reference in de-composition. Let us examine the residuum." The lecture focuses on Barbara Guest, but could you apply this revision of the lyric tradition—away from self-revelation and speech—to contemporary experimental women poets, American or otherwise? Besides Guest, whom do you admire?

After delivering that paper at Barnard, I remember meeting Rob Kaufman with whom I shared further thoughts on my proposal that Guest's is a critical poetry, and some months later Rob published an essay developing just that idea. To the difficulty that modern and postmodern poets share, add an ex-acting yet fearless experimental will that is, if anything, on the increase, and you will understand why her poetry is being discovered by poets who would otherwise not affiliate with Symbolist-derived poetics. Guest's poetics are much more radical than many of her generation, not to mention than many of her younger contemporaries. But readers attend to certain signifiers of overt aggression and confuse that with a radical poetics, so her work—decidedly aestheticized in some respects—went misread for ages. Experimental feminist poetics and theoretically significant experiments in poetry by women may not always generate the same lists of writers. Even so, two anthologies sampling experimental poetry by women are *Out from Everywhere*, edited by Maggie O'Sullivan, and *Moving Borders*, edited by Mary Margaret Sloan. With its "linguistically innovative" poetry by women in North America and the UK, *Out from Everywhere* should be the more widely known here.

Would you call yourself a lyric poet in this special sense of "decomposing … non-imitative verbal music"? How is the lyric tradition being remade by a privileging of the impersonal, the operational, the material, the written?

That is the crucial question, isn't it? There are several ways of framing the response. An answer that assumes a normative definition of the lyric poem will, itself, need to establish whether the European Romantic tradition sets the standard, even though it provides a misreading of that mode since classical times. But apart from legislating some starting point for the lyric poem, defining the approach through some model is at issue. The analytic model has since yielded to what some call the post-analytic approach in philosophy and spun out differing pragmatics applicable to poetry. Alternatively, if historical trajectories through use establish an answer, then another somewhat different response would result. Writers as well as readers have adopted analytical attitudes. Analytically informed lyrics might well be said to parallel analytical philosophy as some modern artists and writers understand it: assume essences, then suppress one necessary and sufficient term in order to intensify the definition. So by analogy a lyric poetry could become even more of "itself" if, say, the first person were eliminated in favor of intensifying the musical expressivity (a poetic word salad would then qualify).

Pragmatic models favor contingencies over necessities. Histories of use come into play to skew the logic where they do not displace it. Wittgenstein has had a determining role in this post-analytic philosophy in which language is opportunistically grabbing what it wants from culture (and/or the other way around). In any event, a theory of contingencies informs a poetics. The poetry can stress material aspects of language—parts of sentences, parts of words—extracted from the conventional sentence, to be dragged across the page and arranged for sound or displayed for graphics. Elevated are textual strategies and tactics enlisted "to work" the writing for a social critique of conventions or for an interpretive meditation through language—this, not the same as the formal and systematic methods of the OULIPO at play. Also at odds with the analytical model to which it is indebted are the rhetorical investigations given us now. Studying writing through philology has proved to Derrida that fusing linguistic dalliance and philosophical analysis is possible. At any rate, post-structuralism investigates the analytical assumptions with rhetorical tools that reveal expressive subjective contents, and this bent has given certain lyric poetry legitimation (as Lyotard would say).

Given this merging of literary theory with poetics, a lyric that interprets and translates or otherwise examines its own statements is not so imaginatively beyond reach. Whether the interpretive lyric gives sanction to inter-subjectivity (between persons) or reveals the cultural subjectivity of concepts once believed to be objective is discussed in postmodern literature. So if you are asking how I identify myself, it is as someone who has from the start advanced the lyric as a critical instrumentality: either through the interpretive approach in transla-tions-without-originals and in the series, or through the speculative rather than the sensuous mentality concerned to interrogate and circulate analytic signs. As I said recently to Carla Harryman, I am concerned to keep analytic, speculative, and pragmatic models in dialogue with one another.

What's next, in terms of poetry and painting?

An email correspondence with Carla, for one thing! Since the publication of *The Annotated "Here"* a conference on my writing and art occurred at the University of Pennsylvania, initiated by Jean-Michael Rabaté and organized by Aaron Levy for Slought Networks. As with the conference on the art of Osvaldo Romberg in 2001, a handsome publication of the proceedings has materialized, thanks to Slought Books and the many participants who made contributions in person or at a distance: Kenneth Baker, Norma Cole, Deborah Gans, Olivier Gourvil, Carla Harryman, Ronald Janssen, Matthew Jelacic, Aaron Levy, Joseph Masheck, Bob Perelman, Jean-Michael Rabaté, Osvaldo Romberg, Keith Tuma, Chris Tysh, and Thomas Zummer. *Of the Diagram: The Work of Marjorie Welish* appeared in December 2003. Writing poems, I continue to ask: with the lyric poem so identified with early modernity, what role may it play under changed theoretical paradigms? An ongoing concern yet also an ongoing pretext to put the lyric on notice, this issue is a useful irritant for writing by means of writing. Importing criticism into the lyric is the least of it: reconceiving the lyric as though it were a written not oral enterprise — a written enterprise with reading privileges! — allows for a very ambitious poet-ics. Meanwhile, I am entertaining ideas for an alternative poetics with its own pressing concerns.

I suppose I have a tendency to introduce an antithetical principle into a discipline. The paintings (often provoking the remark "But these are too difficult for my clients") have nonetheless thrived on their pursuit of conceptual formalism with an emphasis on structuralist and post-structuralist relations that demand to be read as much as seen and to keep querying difference-within-similarity from this conceptual vantage. So the abstractions are about matters other than pure visuality.

Anselm Berrigan and Marcella Durand

Anselm Berrigan is the author of *Integrity & Dramatic Life* (1998) and *Zero Star Hotel* (2002), both from Edge Books. He is the Artistic Director of the Poetry Project in New York. Marcella Durand is the author of *Western Capital Rhapsodies* (Faux Press, 2001) and several chapbooks, including *City of Ports* (Situations, 1999) and *The Anatomy of Oil* (Belladonna, 2004). She is currently the editor of the *Poetry Project Newsletter* and co-editor of an anthology of contemporary French poetry, forthcoming from Talisman House in 2006. Anselm Berrigan and Marcella Durand interviewed each other at Durand's apartment in New York on July 6, 2004. Berrigan's text is in italics.

So you're writing a lot of discrete poems lately, or a series?

No, I'm working on a long poem that isn't quite a series.

Do you have a form for it?

No.

I mean, do you have a form that is developing as it goes on?

Well, I've been trying to write longer lines. I feel that I should be able to write longer lines, that when writing a line there's this wall I come to that I would like to push past.

I ask about the form mainly because I have found that if you're doing a longer work and you have a form that's ready-made for you to enter into, it's a little easier to manage, actually, in terms of how much of a decision-making process you have. It's easier to keep the momentum going. If you've got one in a certain way, there's one less thing to worry about, because the form is fixed. When I wrote "Zero Star Hotel," I knew what the pages were going to look like, so I didn't have to worry too much about structure, other than understanding its contours. I still had to make decisions about where a line was going to break, but the structure was in place.

What is the structure of "Zero Star Hotel"?

It's six ten-line stanzas, or stanzaic units per page, in two columns.

And did you have a syllable count?

No, I had no syllable count, no particular stress count. That was done by ear, basically.

Did you have any words that you had to use over and over, such as the "roachies?"

No, the roachies kept appearing in the poem because they kept appearing in my room. So that was literally like nature entering the poem, if roaches in a hotel room get to count as nature.

So your form was somewhat shaped by the location in which the poem was written?

Yeah, well, I realized at a certain point that the stanzas—I've never been sure about saying stanzas or units, so I'm gonna compromise and say stanzaic units, which sounds really pompous—were like windows, and the hotel was four or five stories high. So the way the poem is laid out on the page—I was writing into my notebook, into the form—looked to me like the façade of a building, with each stanza as a window of the building. That worked for me because I could think of each page as having six different rooms, and that made it easier to manage having different things going on in each stanza, either subject-wise or emotionally or sonically.

So each stanzaic unit is like a glimpse into the poem. I do think that your work sometimes contains a highly experimental narrative in which characters reappear and disappear, such as the character Pig.

I worry about that sometimes, because I tend not to introduce these characters. They kind of show up and disappear and there's no real thread to when they will appear. There's a little bit of that in "Zero Star Hotel," because I was sharing a room with my brother and my cousin, so they were there in certain parts, just because they were in the room, like the roaches. They were not the roaches.

The roachies.

The roachies. But I never thought about those characters appearing as having anything to do with a kind of narrative, it's just something that happens. They're names, so they're words, and sometimes they stand for people and sometimes they just function as a word that's getting the poem from one place to the next.

I think probably your most mysterious characters are Dalziel and Stamper.

That's the poem "Recalled to Life" [from Zero Star Hotel] and that was written specifically out of erasing, reducing a bunch of pages from a crime novel by Reginald Hill, I think. I wanted just the names, but then suddenly I wanted the verbs. So that there would be a name and an attached action, and everything else would be a vacuum.

Do you think you've invented new forms, such as how Whitmanesque experiments are about finding more organic form? How do you think you're continuing that?

I think that "Zero Star Hotel" is the closest thing to an original form, or a breakthrough form, that I've come up with. There are poems that are written in two columns by Tom Raworth and that one by John Ashbery.

"Litany" in As We Know.

But I wasn't reading those. Those poems had no influence on the form. I think in that case I just found the structure and it worked. I haven't seen anything that's really like it, and the poems that I've seen that are in columns tend to be long streams of information, whereas in "Zero Star Hotel," the stanzas begin and end, and the sense doesn't necessarily travel either down or across the page. It does in some cases. But the idea was that they would all be fixed units in certain ways, so they could be removed from the poem and seem to be their own poems. At least, most of them. Otherwise, I tend to let the form take care of itself as it goes along. I've experimented with classical forms, and they tend to be interesting and useful, but nothing's come out that I would want to publish, although I've been getting interested in syllable counts in the last year. But that feels slightly different then, say, writing in ottava rima.

For me, syllable counts are about going back to what I've already written and finding the core count, and using that to shape the poem. I want to talk more about "Zero Star Hotel," but first I wanted to ask you about your use of heroic couplets in "Some Notes on My Programming." I don't think I've seen many poems of yours written in couplets.

No. There's that one and then I have this other poem.

And you know I love couplets, so I'm intrigued by this.

Well, what happened was—and this was a function of how I've happened to write in the last couple years—I don't seem to be able to sit down and open up my notebook and write a poem in one sitting, or get most of it in one sitting. Or even sketch out the frame of the poem, or a certain idea. I just start to write, and then stop at a certain point. It used to be that when I thought I had enough material for about five poems I would take what I had in my notebook and sit down and type it up. Now I don't know, meaning I can't see distinct poems in what I'm writing most of the time, so I wind up taking these sketches and lines and notes and just sitting down and typing them all up, without necessarily putting any space between them. I might type them as they appear on the page and then insert breaks and try to look at them individually. But in the case of "Some Notes on My Programming," all of the material in there was written while I was in France staying with my mother. I was writing every night, but there was nothing fixed about it to give me the sense that I was writing one thing one night and another thing another night. I didn't really know what it all was. So when I got back to New York, and really this was several months later, I typed it all up, and I made it into one big text block with no indentation. Just one big chunk of text, which is actually the kind of thing I hate to see for the most part, when it's published. There is some very good work written that way, but I have a really hard time reading it, I think, because it runs counter to what I tend to do. I needed a device to go through it and make breaks. The material was so all-over-the-place that it seemed like an arbitrary system, or a semi-arbitrary system would work. So I started counting syllables, because that imposes a structure that is essentially an arbitrary device, unless you are actually trying to write through heroic couplets, like Alexander Pope, and then you might bend your thought to it. But I wasn't trying to write into the couplets, as I already had the material, and it was an extremely unheroic poem, so having a fixed syllable count and turning that into heroic couplets, because it is a really interior poem and the psychology is all screwed up, made sense to me in a somewhat perverse way. It *gave me a way to get into it and figure out what I had, and it worked. Actually it is quite nice to read aloud. Because I'm consciously trying to get rid of a line between where one thought ends and another begins in that poem, having the artificial breaks imposed by the heroic couplets lends itself to reading the poem aloud. There are places where you can actually get a 14-syllable breath coming out of your mouth, and that gets really interesting to me. But enough about me, I have to ask you something now. Tell me about how you worked out the form for "The Anatomy of Oil," which is what—21 pages?*

No, it just seems that long. It's 12 pages. I always want to do things that other poets are doing that I have the idea that I can't do. And one of those things is indentation. Speaking of text blocks, I have the bad habit of writing entirely in text blocks. I kind of like the idea of an unadorned poem.

But you have line breaks in most of your poems.

Oh yeah, I have line breaks and I don't write prose poems. I do have a romantic fantasy of the poem standing by itself and maybe just clinging to the left margin in its own little space. And not giving much to the reader, but then I realized that's not very fair. My impulse is to hide it all away, hoping that the content will eventually emerge on its own.

Most of the poems in Western Capital Rhapsodies *are flush left.*

I just have trouble releasing from that place, because I'm afraid of pretentiousness or of having the form take over the content, or of pandering I suppose. But in "The Anatomy of Oil," it seemed that the density of the content based on geology was too overwhelming, and I also wanted to try to release from that left margin and give some lightness to this heavy, rocky, dense material. Since the poem is really almost about water—I mean, I don't want to have any imitative fallacy in there—but I still have doubts about that poem, whether it moves around too much. The last part is in quatrains. After all the looseness of the form before that, I'm not sure it's such a good idea to have it end in marching quatrains.

I know what you mean. It's a funny thing, that, because you don't really know how people respond to a form that's kind of changing as the poem goes on, especially in a longer poem like that. The space that you get from indenting off the left-hand margin is really hard to talk about, because handling that space is something your eye does. I read fast, and it's taken me a long time to slow down and read poetry and figure out what is happening within the spaces as they occur around lines in a poem that isn't just flush left. I don't know exactly how much time someone is going to take thinking about that while reading the kind of open field work in which you just hang a few words here and there, the way Philip Whalen often does. That's just clear visually, and you're supposed to travel across the page from line to line. But it's harder to tell with floating stanzas. I don't think I'm saying this very accurately.

But Whalen was so good at accepting the void of the page. For me it's space that I have to fill up as quickly as possible, with as much density as possible, and a block of text is the best way to wipe out that void. I have a very hard time living with that, these words just leaning out in the empty white page. I have to overwhelm.

I got really interested in having those kind of shifting indentations that you're talking about, but having them shift every single line, so that you get these poems that are kind of column-like poems, and the column is snaking down the page, like on a roadmap.

Well, some of your lines are like arcs.

Right, well that's actually the one that I was thinking of, "Postcard to Brett Evans." In that poem I double-spaced the line and I felt like I was cheating, because I didn't have so many words on the page. You can't show that to the reader. I think the best way to describe the poem is that it sidewinds down the page, like the snake traveling across the desert.

It takes a lot of discipline to get away from the text block/flush left thing. I admire Whalen and Creeley, and Joanne Kyger, or even French writers who are able to deal with that void of the white page. For me, especially with the compressed time and space that I write in, I just want to spew it out. Kristin Prevallet has this idea of writing as a form of elegy that moves towards an object or a person that is lost, filling up that space. I wanted to ask you what you thought of that, especially in regards to "Zero Star Hotel."

I have to think about that for a second. I'm still sort of interested in the idea that a poem called "The Anatomy of Oil" is mostly about water. The title of that poem in and of itself is kind of fascinating. One associates anatomy with something that is alive—that is or was a living being that had an anatomy. I'm thinking of cross-sections of a human body, so when you talk about oil, it's this black, liquidy substance that is basically made out of bodies.

It is a cross-section definitely, but I also wanted anatomy not just to be about oil itself, but all of the processes involved with oil as well. Historical, political, simultaneously operating on a human and a geological scale. I'm very interested in scale in that poem.

So oil as a concept could have a broader anatomy than just isolating the idea of oil as a substance. It's one of those titles that really works because every thing in the poem can immediately refer back to the title and be given another angle. But it's different for your work too somehow, in some way that I can't explain very well. Something about "The Anatomy of Oil" as opposed to "Machine into Water," or particularly in "City of Ports," where you're dealing with the anatomy of a city. There, you're really dealing with structure on the level of pipes, tubes, concrete, and architecture. Those poems are really grounded, but don't have a great deal of direct self-reference. "The Anatomy of Oil" suggests something that could be more abstract, but the poem itself has a little bit more of an experiential base on the surface than some of your other work. You're trying to get at an extremely broad political subject without actually writing a polemic, and you do, and you're doing it without a fixed (i.e., unchanging) form.

Not only do I not have a fixed form, but then I do have a fixed form march in at the end.

But that's a little different. You can have a form be part of a field of changes, like Proteus. And you, Marcella, are squeezing the poem, which is continually changing shape, until you are told what you need to be told. So having it end with a few quatrains feels perfectly natural to me.

Well that is kind of an essential question for "innovative" poets. How do you find a form? You and I both studied Augustan poets, and one of the key things for the Augustan poets was matching their forms to the sound, to the image, to the content, all leading to a beautiful, shining, smooth delivery. I think you and I are both concerned about how these things come together, but on an innovative level. We're not writing sonnets—well, we are—but how do you find this?

First off, you say the word "innovative" with quotes around it …

Yeah.

… but that term has become extremely self-defeating for poetry.

Oh really? Are you shying away from the word "experimental"?

These words just become such general terms, given how many poets there are who are interesting, and who are making interesting shapes. I realize that one might be thinking about the difference between a certain kind of poetry that's represented in The New Yorker, *or something like that, as opposed to "innovative" work. The thing that bothers me the most these days is reading poetry that is essentially prosaic without any intention towards crossing genres. If a poem looks like it could be put back into a paragraph without there being any difference as to whether it is prose or poetry except that it has line breaks, that's really just thought handled in sentences. The thing about the Augustans that was interesting to me was that I wound up having a lot of sympathy for John Dryden. Not politically, but you have this situation where the Augustans had to deal with Milton, who just came through and completely changed the terms for poets writing in the English language. So what do you do when you have that weight on you? We don't really have that weight on our heads, because, for one thing—*

We're trying to have that kind of weight on our heads.

Maybe it would be nice, I don't know. But Whitman doesn't create that kind of weight because his spirit was so open to anything going down. And I feel that way about Dickinson too, though in a quite different way, one that has to do with a more distinct feeling towards how the mind works. I sympathized with Dryden because he seemed to be developing the heroic couplet as a way to get to that smooth, shiny poem, but he wasn't good enough to do it, in that he'd have an extra syllable or beat lying around, and he couldn't quite get his sentiment contained so precisely in the form. It's this classic case of being this person who develops this form and Pope comes along and perfects it and is just a machine within it, with these poems that are like jackhammers. But I wound up getting interested in Dryden because there seemed to be real limits to what he was capable of doing, and he worked within those limits quite reasonably. There's a poem of his that's an elegy that in a way is a great example of a collaged poem, with

elements coming out of Horace and Virgil, and is obviously pieced together. The
professor at Brooklyn College referred to it as a mosaic, which is just another
word for putting pieces together.

I'm interested in when you said—you didn't quite say it this way—something
about poetry having a certain integrity as an art in itself, that I have felt has
been kind of lost lately. There are things that only poetry can do and people
are not quite respecting that. Instead they may be bringing it closer to prose
or to an essay. I was wondering what you thought about that. I'm interested
in all of the things that poetry can do that no other art can do and that don't
seem to be analyzed or discussed at present. For instance, on the sub-poetics
listserv, when we discuss politics I never feel like we're approaching the issues
as poets.

No, we're approaching politics as people with opinions. I think that underscores
how difficult it is to approach political subject matter as a poet, rather than
through poetry. I think one ostensibly wants to approach politics as a human
being. I think a lot of the more interesting cross-genre work is being done by writ-
ers like Renee Gladman and Pamela Lu, though I guess at this point Pamela's
considered more strictly a prose writer. But I read a bunch of her poems in the
mid-'90s when I was living in the Bay area, so I think of her as a poet as well as
a prose writer. I think that when you're handed an identity or set of identities
that appear really fixed, publicly, that working in a space where you can blur
the lines between genres a bit might be quite appealing, because it is a way of
unfixing things. If you want to tell a story, but you don't want it to have a plot
that follows a purely linear temporality, you want to move things around a little
bit, and have it begin in the middle, then combining elements of prose and
poetry would be quite useful because you can have the kind of leap in thought
from sentence to sentence, or line to line, that you might have in a poem, but
you have a very flexible narrative. That's just one example.

But what about the "pure" poetic experience? Or like you said with "Zero Star
Hotel," being able to build this form? Or respecting language as language.
How primary do you think that should be?

I think that's dependent on each individual. I like how certain writers mix genres,
but it's not something I'm interested in for myself. It could become something I
get interested in. It's tricky for me, as I'm interested in what certain writers do,
no matter what they do, but I dislike the fetishization of prose poetry that's been

going on in recent years. I think that something being pushed by the forces of your life is more likely to take you to an interesting form than just putting one on and not doing much but wearing it. I'd rather see it get sort of torn up along the way than be so clean all the time, but I'm probably being a little too general, alas. What do you think a pure poetic experience is in writing?

There are some poems I read and I think, "Okay, this is going really well. I don't quite know what's going to happen next." There are certain words and concepts being played with in really interesting ways, and then all of a sudden there's a line that ties it back to a certain thing that is happening outside the world of the poem and I feel disappointed. Lately, in reading a lot of Ashbery's work, I've been thinking that his work is so interesting because it gives in completely to the language that it operates in without trying to tie it to something external of the poem. But also in thinking about politics and poetry—how much do you tether the poem to things external of itself? How much do you go beyond the internal reality of the poem? I guess I feel the poem has a certain integrity and I have to sacrifice my beliefs or feelings or whatever to the language that the poem is asking for.

That's a more interesting way of thinking about experimental or innovative poetry to me than saying an innovative poem is one that has big, elliptical spikes coming out of it, or is something that looks like a language poem.

If I have to be a conservative Republican to make a poem work, I kind of think I would do that—well, maybe not. I like to ask questions. A poem is a true experimental ground for me. I take these questions that I have in the real world and present them to the poem-god and the poem-god will let me explore these different things. What does it mean to be in a country that has this huge desert and started a war in another country that also has a huge desert? What does that mean? I don't know. So I'll present it to the poem-god.

I feel like my mind is the desert in my case, and language is something I get outside of myself to help me reckon with personal information, the blurry line between internal and external, and thousands of other mysteries. It has all these attachments to other instances in life that I'm not necessarily going to be able to shake it away from, or I'm not even certain I would want to shake it away from. In the last few years, I've been feeling more and more like my mind is blank when I write and that I'm reaching for language to combine it with something that is, that you could just call feeling, and what's happened in my life that's brought me to this moment. There's this other kind of energy that's being harnessed. That's why I get lost thinking about what innovation is or what experiment is. Mark Strand is not going to go around calling himself an innovative poet, he's not going to identify himself that way. Somebody like, say, Leslie Scalapino would be more likely to identify herself as an experimental writer. I don't mean to speak for others, but just knowing a little bit about them, about how they pitch their work publicly. It's not like I'm trying to say that these ways of approaching poetry and writing don't exist, I just can't locate myself within that kind of field. I know if I do something like I did in this poem, "The Autobiography of Donald Rumsfeld," where I'm running words through a poem in order to create strange word combinations, i.e., using a find-and-replace command on a computer to replace the word "in" with the word "drool," that that is a kind of experiment. And it happens in such a way that any instance of the letter "i" and the letter "n" being next to each other gets replaced by drool, so "interview" becomes "droolterview." But in terms of identifying with the broader definition, I can't really do it. I just know it's harder for me to do that, because I can't stand the restriction that seems inherent to doing so.

I think the lines have blurred. Before, the lines were pretty clearly drawn.

It also comes down to the poet and the work.

Some people might say that's the cult of the individual. I don't think we know enough about individuality to say why one person can take some rules for writing and do something spectacular with them, while another person takes the same exact rules and writes crummy poetry.

It's a similar dynamic to the poet today who is very young and using experimental techniques or what seem like experimental forms as a kind of training ground, as opposed to somebody who's doing the same thing with classical forms. There's a range of types of writing available now to anybody, really, if they can figure out how to get there, or get taken there. Where you can say, okay, I'm going to write sestinas and sonnets and villanelles ...

And pantoums ...

And pantoums, and I'm going to do this for a certain amount of time until I figure out something about how to use forms. The same person could say, I'm going to do erasures, I'm going to invent words, I'm going to wreck my grammar and sense of metaphor and I'm going to use that as a training ground to figure out something else about how to use form.

When I went to college I was not taught anything about forms, but I was reaching for form. At the time, it was regarded as weird and experimental to actually put your poem into a form, instead of having this free-form, personal narrative story.

That's part of the doom of professional poetry.

I read *The Waste Land* and wrote this whole cut-and-paste thing where one stanza was one situation and the other was another and everyone was like, huh? And I wanted them to figure it out, figure out that I did this weird thing, that I used this form. They just said you don't make sense. That was really difficult, so I can understand the rage. But then that rage carries over into "It's not avant-garde enough, you have to stick to this avant-garde formula."

There are all these tribes. It's one thing to talk about these things amongst writers. It's another thing to talk about them in terms of institutions and institutional power. Whether you're talking about a university or magazine, or an organization like the Poetry Project, there's a kind of essential conservatism. It's about telling you how to do things "right." A place like the Poetry Project might seem a little more benign, but at the same time there's a history and a way of reading the history that attaches itself to you by implying that you should be open to the kind of work associated with the New York School, say, and an approach to personal experience that's just as exclusive in some ways as any other institutional approach to poetry, such as that of the Iowa Writers' Workshop at its most pedantic level. And we both know writers who come from Iowa who are interesting, so it's not fair to draw the characterization broadly (in either case). There need to be some collective efforts to do certain things, like get a press going or get a reading series going or really get certain kinds of discussions going, but it takes poets to write poems. Collaborations are great, but actually I don't give a shit about collaboration because I want to write my own poems. I don't want anybody else getting in there and fucking it up. I'd rather fuck it up myself and sign my name to it and live with the consequences.

JOHN YAU

John Yau was born in Lynn, Massachusetts in 1950, shortly after his parents fled Shanghai. He received a B.A. from Bard College, where he studied with Robert Kelly, and an MFA from Brooklyn College, where he studied with John Ashbery. He has taught at Emerson College, Brown University, and the University of California at Berkeley, and the Maryland Institute College of Art. He is currently a professor of Critical Studies at Mason Gross School of the Arts, Rutgers University. Yau is the author of numerous books of poetry, fiction, and criticism, and his collaborations with artists have been exhibited in galleries and museums in North America and Europe. He and the artist Eve Aschheim live with their daughter in Manhattan. This interview was conducted by Matthew Rohrer in Yau's apartment on October 21, 2001.

I wondered if you could start by telling me about why you came to New York. You came here after college?

No, I came here in 1974, '75, just as the World Trade Center was being finished. And I came here primarily because I wanted to see a lot of art. And I had been in Boston for two years, I was recovering from a car accident. And as soon as I felt better and I was able to walk around fairly easily, I decided to move to New York. It was really just so that I could look at a lot of contemporary art.

Obviously art has been a big part of not just your writing, but your life. How did you get interested in it? Was that at Bard?

When I was at Bard College I met a number of contemporary painters who were on the faculty, and I started coming to New York with them in the late '60s, and even before then I was looking at art. I was interested in Surrealism, surrealist paintings, when I was in high school and I was trying to find out about it so I just looked at whatever I could find. And I went to the Museum of Fine Arts in Boston and I went to the galleries that were in Boston, and I looked at art there and at the Fogg art museum and at the museums connected to Harvard. So basically starting around 13. And that was probably because my parents knew a painter, a modern abstract painter, when I was six or seven, so I grew up looking at art, going to this man's house. He talked about Franz Kline when I was eight or nine, and the abstract expressionists. And I also went to weekend art classes for children. So I grew up in a situation where art was highly valued.

How did your parents meet this person? Were they involved in art also?

No, he was Chinese and somehow ... they met because I knew his son. His son was maybe a year older than me so we went to school and met, and then I went to his house, and I told my parents about his parents and they met and they actually became better friends ... I mean, this boy and I weren't really friends that long.

Did you ever consider studying art in college?

No. I don't know why. I was always attracted to writing. Probably the other thing I did besides go to museums a lot — my mother took me to lots of museums as a child — was read. I was just one of those nerdy children that read a lot. And my father bought me lots of books, and I just read all the time and went to the museum. Sort of an atypical childhood.

And then you went to Bard ...

No, I went to Boston University first. I transferred in '69, and that's when I met these painters and started going to New York.

And you were studying writing then? Or English?

English literature. I went to Bard primarily because I knew that Robert Kelly taught there, and I wanted to study with him. I'd read his poems probably when I was 18, and I liked them and I'd read this anthology that he'd co-edited, and it made me think that this would be a good place to go to school.

What was he like?

He was great. He was imposing. At that point he weighed more than he does now. He was a huge man. I think he must have weighed, like, 300 pounds, he had a long beard, and smoked Camels incessantly. He had a deep voice and I think all the students were in awe of his erudition. He just seemed to be able to quote something from the German, and then the Latin, etcetera, etcetera, and he just seemed to know certain poets who were kind of mythical figures even at that point, like Louis Zukofsky, or Charles Olson, or Robert Duncan—he knew their work and what their work was about on some level that us smart 19-year-olds didn't know. He could also talk about Thomas Wyatt or Edmund Spenser, he was kind of an amazing man in touch with lots and lots of different things. So in a way he was just inspiring as a poet. He was also the first poet I met close up. I'd gone to a lot of anti-war poetry readings in Boston, you know, so I'd heard Robert Bly, Denise Levertov, people like that, and Galway Kinnell. Robert Kelly just seemed a different kind of poet. Mysterious, in a way, in what he was interested in. He was interested in the occult, gnosticism, all these things—things that had a particular appeal to me.

So at that age, what writers did you most identify with? Was it the Black Mountain School, like Olson? A lot of your early work shares an affinity with early New York School writing. When did you find out about that?

Well, when I went to Bard I read Robert Kelly. But also in this anthology I encountered the work of John Ashbery, and Frank O'Hara, so I started reading all those people around the same time. At Bard I continued to do that, as well as read poets like Robert Bly or Kinnell, so I read everybody. I was almost indiscriminate in my reading at 18 and 19, largely because I wanted to find out everything for myself. Somebody would say, "oh, don't read that poet," and I would immediately go out and read that poet. So I never trusted what my teachers told me. I mean, Kelly was not particularly programmatic, he made suggestions of who to read, but he never made suggestions of who not to read. But there were other teachers at Bard, English teachers, who would say, "oh you should read this and not that," and there was a kind of war going on—well, not war, that's too extreme a word—between those teachers who taught T.S. Eliot and Robert Frost, and those teachers like Kelly who taught Ezra Pound and William Carlos Williams.

It's funny to think about that now, because you can take a class where you study all four of them.

So then you understood, in 1969, already you understood that there were different groups of poets, and different traditions, and that you had to find your own way through it. So I would study T.S. Eliot with the teacher who taught T.S. Eliot and then the teacher who taught Robert Frost, I would study with that teacher. And the teacher who taught Williams and Zukofsky ... and what I didn't realize then was that there are people in the academy who believe that, you know, it's really Eliot and Frost, maybe Williams a little bit but really not, who represent one thing and they ignored Olson and Duncan. But I saw them all as equal. It's not like the classes were graded, like this was an A class and this was a B class—these are the lit classes, study what you want. So in that sense, I knew there was an antagonism but I didn't know there was a hierarchy. It made no sense to me. You have to remember I came from Boston, so by the time I left Boston I was really thoroughly involved in, or had read, all the people around Robert Lowell. Sylvia Plath, Anne Sexton, Robert Lowell. Along with Berryman. I read those people, and then at the same time I became interested partly through a magazine like *Kayak* in American Surrealism, like Robert Bly and James Tate. And so that was like my engagement—I was reading the surrealists connected to *Kayak*, the confessional poets, Olson, Duncan, Creeley, the Black Mountain Poets, and then the formalist Eliot, Frost. All of it. Probably the person I liked most at that point was Jack Spicer. I really liked him, and I liked Kelly a lot, and then I started getting really obsessed with John Ashbery probably around 18 or 19. At that point none of my classmates read him.

That was, what, 1969? What Ashbery books were out then?

Tennis Court Oath was out by then, *Double Dream of Spring* came out by 1970, *Rivers and Mountains* was out by then, and *Some Trees*. The poem that came out before *Double Dream of Spring*—Black Sparrow published a poem called "Fragment," a long 500-line poem, somewhere I have it. I remember getting it, partly I think at that point I read whatever Black Sparrow published because it published Robert Kelly and other poets, so I read "Fragment" and I remember reading it and going back and reading "Europe" in Robert Kelly's anthology and I was completely perplexed by this. I couldn't make heads nor tails out of "Europe" or out of "Fragment" and nobody at the school ... I guess I didn't really talk to Kelly, but none of my teachers could make heads nor tails out of it either. So I got really intrigued by this and I went off and got every book of his I could. And then at that point I also realized that he was writing about contemporary art. And O'Hara was dead but he had written about contemporary art, so then that fed into my own interest in contemporary art and I became aware that there were these groups of poets who didn't teach, who made their living seemingly by writing about art, and that intrigued me because I wanted to be a poet that didn't teach.

What do you think it is about art and writing that has been so mutually beneficial for so many writers?

I think art's exciting. There's a sort of built in excitement around it. Partially because it has a public life: gallery exhibitions, museums. There's money involved in the art world, and "money is a kind of poetry" says Wallace Stevens and there's certainly that. And then there's a kind of sense of ambition among artists that seems grand. The ambition of, say, when you're a teenager, Jackson Pollock seems like a grand ambition. And you didn't necessarily find that counterpart so easily in the poetry world.

It's sort of like poetry's rich uncle?

Yeah, well I thought that art had a kind of grand ambition that poetry didn't seem to have … maybe I was also reacting to the literary aspect of poetry. Maybe what I really liked and what I then started to find out about French Surrealism was a kind of activism, or public aspect, and there's something about that that intrigued me, and also what I liked about art initially was just its scale, its size, its excitement, its immediacy. Poetry you read in books — I didn't know that much about the poetry reading world. I'd gone to a few anti-war readings, but that seemed to me something else. I was just interested in art, it seemed less reducible. I mean, in Robert Frost you have a kind of narrative behind the so-called narrative that's supposed to be moralistic or allegorical, even in some of Eliot there's that — earlier Eliot like "The Waste Land," it had a grand scheme. And I distrusted that immediately. What I liked about painting was that it was not reducible. You couldn't say what the scheme was behind a Jackson Pollock, you couldn't say what the scheme was behind a Franz Kline. It didn't seem reducible to a narrative. It just hit you in the face. I thought, "gee, I wonder if poetry can do that?" So I got really interested in that, and then I really wanted to know more about it. I read a lot of art magazines at that point as a kid — *Art Forum*, which was dense and theoretical, *Art in America* … all of them. I read that more than I read anything else except poetry.

Some of your work feels indebted to the OULIPO ethos, and it almost seems like a sort of literary enactment of art. Something that is what it is. Is art where you got it from?

Probably. You wanted to make the poem stand on its own in a way that a painting can stand on its own. You know, we mythologize Pollock, but you don't have to know about Franz Kline's life to see his paintings. I guess in a way I began to distrust early on the poems of confessional poets because it seemed so dependent on the poet's life. And I didn't think these paintings were so dependent on the painter's life and that really interested me as well. So there were a lot of different things going on. But I definitely feel like painting, abstract painting in particular, made me think about how to get writing to move toward abstraction, or what Zukofsky called "music." I did read Gertrude Stein, but I came at it through painting rather than through Gertrude Stein.

Do you see in your own work that the early poems are more New York School or Black Mountain School influenced, while the later poems are more indebted to the spirit of OULIPO?

Some of them are more OULIPO-driven, they have rules …

I'm thinking of that one where every word has to have a certain vowel. A program.

I definitely have done that off and on. I don't do it strictly, I do it off and on, and it's definitely influenced by painting.

It seems like it's got the same impulse behind it.

I read Perec, I read Harry Mathews. I knew Harry Mathews and met him in the early '8os. I liked his work a lot and thought about his work a lot. We talked about different methods that the writers were using.

There's a real pleasure in these programmatic poems, it's like a game played out to a crazy extreme. But I also have the feeling that among certain circles—certainly the people who were teaching you Eliot—that that is somehow a suspicious poetic technique. But the ironic thing is that it wouldn't be if you gave yourself the rule that it all had to be in iambic pentameter. That's somehow different to them. But it seems to me it's all a program.

Language is a set of rules. And I guess OULIPO just calls attention to it by making a new set of rules within the set of rules that we already accept as a given. And I think that really intrigued me. Just as, you know, with a painter, it may be that you accept a certain set of rules. A painting is a flat surface, and it's sort of accepted by a lot of painters. And therefore they try to figure out how to deal with this flat surface. And I always was intrigued that they just accepted this given, or that they tried to fight against this given but they also accepted it. There was this notion, I guess, when I was in college, and I think it still persists among some people, that poetry is an expression of freedom. That somehow there's no given. And I thought, "but there *is* a given." Why don't we call attention to it. The given is language, first of all, so there are these rules. And then we agree that language functions in a certain way so that we can understand each other, but built within that are all sorts of sentimental codes, codes of authenticity, codes of certain kinds of emotion. And I guess in a way, I'm against that. Not that I'm against it, but I question it. So I wanted to find another way to write so that whatever was given, maybe I decided in advance what was given, and see what I could do with it. So I'd work with a limited vocabulary, like seven words or five words, and I'd keep trying to rearrange them, recompose them. That's not really different from, say, Mondrian working with red, yellow, blue, black, and white. And working with only verticals and horizontals. Yet to me his paintings are both incredibly sensual, expressive in some way, they're all sorts of things. And the emotion of them is not so easily reducible to a kind of code. I distrust the codes.

You also write a lot of prose poems and short stories. It seems that in a lot of cases your prose poems are longer than what America accepts as the prose poem, and some of your stories are short enough that the line seems to blur between them. Do you think of them as different?

I guess I do think of them as different, but I'm not sure how. Partly through reading lots of European writers, you know, from Robert Walser to Francis Ponge to Marguerite Duras, I realized that writing—and also my interest in certain kinds of art, like Bruce Nauman, Jasper Johns—that writing shouldn't have to fit into a genre. I liked something that you couldn't really categorize. I was interested in that kind of writing, how I could do it. Yeah, I write "prose poems" but I don't know what a prose poem is. And also there's the example of John Ashbery's *Three Poems*, which are all in prose, which I read when it came out in 1972, and I was completely bamboozled by that book. I thought, "Wow, look at this." To me, also what intrigued me about his work in *Three Poems*, "Europe," and "Fragments," was that it was clear that this man had a grand ambition as a poet, and that instantly attracted me to it.

I think there's also a sort of a dig in the title Three Poems, *forcing you to accept them as poems.*

Right. The same way Stella says "this is a painting" and it's a metal thing on the wall with different parts and everyone says "no it's a relief" but he says "no this is a painting." Or Duchamp saying "this is a sculpture" or "this is art," and it's a bicycle wheel mounted on a stool. It's literally the naming of it that makes you have to accept it. And if you say "no, it's not art," then you're falling back on some traditional notion of what art is, just as if you say "no, that's not a poem," you're falling back on a traditional notion of what a poem is.

I'm in total agreement with you, but could you explain what you think are the perils of that kind of reductionist thinking?

Well, it's like you're seeking a certain kind of security when you're looking at art, or you're seeking a certain kind of security when you're reading a poem, so you want to know in advance what it is you're encountering, and you want to go by your previous experience. But art and poetry try to get beyond that, and go into new territory, new experiences in a way. So why rely on an old standard? It's also the same with music. John Cage—listening to John Cage, it has no harmony, and you're thinking, "what is this that I'm listening to?" It's "noise." Robert Kelly as a teacher really opened my eyes to that possibility. If it wasn't familiar, then you should be interested. And I thought "Wow, what is he getting at?" In a way he really opened the door to being more willing to listen or to look at or to read things that you didn't know what you were encountering, and you had no previous measure by which to understand what it was. And I think in a way, he was totally helpful in that. Kind of central, actually, to my life. In the '6os he introduced me to the work of Jackson MacLow, for instance, and *The Naming of the Presidents*, and that was just an eye-opening experience, a mind-opening experience.

Tell me about your publishing history.

Robert Kelly talked to a man named Gil Williams who ran a press in Binghamton, New York named Bellevue Press, and Gil Williams did these little letterpress chapbooks, and wrote me a letter and asked me if I'd give him poems. I think I was 24, just out of school.

Were you in New York then?

I was in Boston.

Kelly had told him about you?

Yeah, so he wrote me a letter and I sent him some poems and that became my first chapbook, *Crossing Canal Street*. And that came out about two years after I'd given him the poems. By then I'd moved to New York. I heard John Ashbery read at Columbia and he said he was teaching at Brooklyn College. I had no idea that he was teaching, somehow I think I thought he was still in France. He said he was teaching and so I applied to school. I had no intention of getting an MFA, I had no idea what I was going to do, but an MFA was the furthest thing from my mind.

But you had to enroll to take classes with him ...

Right. And it was a city school, so it was very cheap. I think it was $1500 a semester, and I could actually get together the money to pay for it. So then I got accepted there, and I was writing poems and David Lehman, who I think also taught there, I don't know for how long, asked to see some of my poems and he published my next chapbook, *The Reading of an Ever-Changing Tale*. And then what happened? After that John got Stanley Moss at Sheep Meadow Press to look at my work, and he published a book of mine, *Sometimes*. Rosemary Waldrop wrote me a letter and said she'd read my poems somewhere and was interested, so that became *Broken Off By the Music*.

When Sometimes *came out, that must have been pretty big for you.*

No ... What do you mean by big?

Well, obviously you weren't on the cover of Time *Magazine, especially with that picture on the back of it. Wait—did you really have that picture on there because you didn't want to get any teaching offers from the Midwest?*

Yeah.

But when Sometimes *came out ... Sheep Meadow has a certain cachet. When it came out did that get you attention?*

No. Actually, it was kind of interesting. I had that book come out and I had the book from Burning Deck come out, and actually I had a little book of prose pieces from a small press in Brooklyn called Release Press called *The Sleepless Night of Eugene Delacroix*—all three came out within a year. And as far as I could tell nothing happened. I didn't get asked to read anywhere, nobody sent me requests to publish my poems. I felt kind of invisible. And I just thought maybe that was the way it was. But I also think it was because at that point I didn't really fit in. I wasn't really connected. By then I felt like I was somewhat disconnected to the New York School, and at the same time I wasn't connected to the Language poets, who were kind of around the same age as I was. I wasn't really connected to anybody. I got some letters from the Asian-American poets on the West coast, and then they decided they didn't like my work, so I felt disconnected from them. And then in a way the disconnection became useful, actually. Because then I decided maybe it was better not to belong to any group. Not to be connected to any scene. And so I kind of just stayed on my own.

Do you think it was that, for the different groups you just mentioned, you weren't extreme enough for them? That for the Language poets you weren't purely "musical" enough for them? And for the New York School you weren't, I don't know ...

Confessional. "I do this/I do that." Well, in a way I didn't accept their ideology. The Asian-Americans, or the poets associated with the New York School, or the Language poets, each had a kind of overt or covert ideology and I didn't really accept any of them. So in a way it made sense that I didn't connect with them. I felt like at that point I was still trying to figure out what is the extreme limit of what poetry can do, what kind of writing could I do, so I accepted that I wasn't that connected. In a way it was also depressing. But I felt, well, I like what I'm doing. So why should I change?

It still seems today as if there's a gulf between two camps—the more lyrical and then the more experimental, the self-described "avant-garde," and there's very little middle ground.

What I really like among younger poets today ... there're two things I find really interesting, two things I'm aware of. One is I know more younger poets than I know poets of my own generation. I don't have deep friendships with that many poets of my generation. I know them, we're friends, but I wouldn't say we're close friends. I know poets far older than me like Creeley, Barbara Guest, that I feel much closer to. There's one poet who's somewhat near my age, a little older than me, who certainly started publishing earlier than me: David Shapiro. And then I know many poets younger than me. And what I'm really interested in is that the poets of the younger generation don't seem to want to fit in. They don't want to necessarily connect to a group or an ideology. They're really trying to make themselves up as they go along. And that, I think, is really exciting. It makes poetry, to my mind, right now very exciting. You can't say, "oh, he's a blah blah" or "she's a blah blah blah."

Right. Like Lisa Jarnot's Ring of Fire. *I don't know, I just sort of expected it to be a certain kind of extreme experimental thing, but it's all over the place, it's really great. There are moments of real lyrical beauty, and prosy narrative bits, and experimental stuff.*

Yeah, I think it's wonderful that people aren't just accepting the ideologies. They're trying to figure out their own identity, whatever that is. They're trying to make it up as they go along. Not their identity as a poet, but the identity of their work.

Do you think that you're less close to poets of your own generation because that was less of a concern for poets then?

They were just trying to find their own space and I socially or politically or ideologically didn't connect to a whole lot of people. And then I spent most of my time being in the art world. I didn't want to be part of all the poetry scenes that were going on, I just dropped out of that. I guess in a way I did want to go my own way, and I had no idea what that way was, I had no idea. Not that I didn't want to fit in, I knew that I couldn't fit in. Let's put it that way. On some level it has to do with my own autobiography, or maybe I'm using my autobiography as a metaphor. But my father was half-English and half-Chinese so he never fit in, and in a way my parents raised me that way. And the idea of fitting in wasn't an option in their life.

So you weren't raised in a traditional Chinese-American family.

No, not at all. The furthest thing from it. Even though my parents spoke Chinese, they spoke a certain dialect, and they would point out that it was a dialect that almost nobody else spoke in America, because they were from Shanghai and most Chinese in America at that time were from Canton. So of course they couldn't fit in. They thought of most Chinese in America as the country mice. And they were sophisticates from the city. They were interested in bringing me to concerts, and art. At the same time they weren't part of the educated Chinese class that taught in universities so they didn't meet people like that. They came to America in 1949, really trying to make a living. So they didn't fit in in any way, and they kind of made that a value, like fitting in is bad. And in a way I probably fell for their line. "Oh, okay, you have to be idiosyncratic, you have to be individualized." And of course this is America, which places a big premium on being individualized. And then you realize when you get involved in art or poetry that maybe there's a big premium on individuality but it's a big premium as long as you fit in. You see movements in the art world, and lots of people belong to it and join it, and it's like they're all trying to find their little niche within the scene. And I found that uninteresting. Probably what I liked about the New York School was that you could put the work of Kenneth Koch, Barbara Guest, John Ashbery, and James Schuyler next to each other—and Frank O'Hara—it sure didn't look like a school to me. It looked like five people writing really differently from each other. And even among that five, I'd say only four of them really cared about art in a deep way. Or maybe that's too extreme. Only four of them seemed to have any involvement in the art world; Kenneth Koch taught at Columbia, the others seemed more involved with art, at least writing about it. I don't think Kenneth ever really wrote about it. So that totally intrigued me. Even Black Mountain—you can't confuse Olson and Duncan. Then the goal becomes, in a way, how do you make your work unmistakeable, so it doesn't look like, sound like, act like someone else's work. That seemed to me to be a reasonable thing to do. A reasonable goal in some way.

But in the meantime you have three books out and you still feel invisible. Is it looking back on it that it seems like that must have been really cool? Or is that imposed on it by the passage of time? Were the books just too new to get a lot of attention?

I think I was the first book that Sheep Meadow published. Or maybe the second. And then when he listed the books that he published, subsequently, on the backs of other books, he left mine off. So there's that. It was odd. Burning Deck was great. I liked being published by them, but I think the people who'd read Burning Deck books would not go out and buy a Sheep Meadow book. And then I had the book published by Release Press and people who read that wouldn't have read the other two. So I don't know who was out there, and maybe there was nobody out there who would want to read books published by all three.

Then when did the John Ashbery connection come up, with the National Poetry Series?

That was in '83.

What happened in between?

I started thinking more about writing about art, and I really wanted to try and survive that way, so I paid more and more attention to that.

What was your approach? Did you just pick something you liked and write about it? Or did you have an aesthetic that you wanted to promote?

No, I had no aesthetic. I felt like I was just an uneducated fool trying to learn about art by writing about it. Basically, I knew a few things I didn't want to do. I knew that there was a tradition among the New York School of writing about a certain kind of painter, or certain painters. And early on I decided I would find my own way, and I wouldn't write about these painters that had been written about by the older poets: Larry Rivers, etcetera. So I decided I wouldn't do that. That was one thing. Secondly, *Art in America* basically assigned me to go to a lot of shows and I could pick some, and for whatever reason *Art in America* didn't give me the cream of the crop. They gave me lesser-known artists. And eventually that's why I moved to *Art Forum*. But I also really wanted to find my own way, so I had no aesthetic. And it took me a long time to begin to even have an aesthetic, and I'm not sure I have one now. But I talked to a lot of artists, I met a lot of artists, I tried to write about them, I rejected ways that they'd been seen by others — well-known artists like Jasper Johns, or Warhol. I felt like I had to see them for myself.

You had the big book on Warhol with Ecco Press that got a lot of attention. Clearly a lot of things had been written on Warhol before. What was it that drew Ecco to that manuscript?

He asked me if I'd write about an artist. I was with Charles Simic, who was writing about Cornell, and we met Dan Halpern at a bar with Charlie, and Charlie said "oh, you should get John to write about somebody," and Dan said "Okay, who would you want to write about?" and I blurted it out: Andy Warhol. Because I had no desire at that time, I didn't think I wanted to write a book about Warhol. But I also thought I wanted to write a book about an artist I neither love nor hate, but whom I'm immensely curious about, and fascinated by, and see what happens. So basically when I said I wanted to write about Andy Warhol I was given my assignment. And if he took it, then I would do it. And he said "okay." And that was kind of a shock. I proceeded to think about Andy Warhol in a way I'd never thought about him. And that's how I came to write the book. It didn't get any attention. I mean, it did and it didn't. It had a secret life. People would write me letters, but it wasn't reviewed in the New York art magazines. There was not one art magazine that reviewed that book, which I found ... I mean, speaking of not fitting in, it kind of continued this trend. It was reviewed by somebody who has a syndicated column so that particular review appeared in like 40 newspapers and magazines, which was kind of strange because it was like I had been reviewed a lot by one guy.

Was it a positive review?

It was mixed. He really liked a lot of it, and he was really disturbed by it. If you read only the first half of the review you might not want to read the book, but if you persisted and read the second half of the review, you probably would want to read the book. But certain people who are important to me commented on the book and that meant a lot, that was enough. And they didn't put it out in paperback, which they probably should have. It was only in hardcover. And Ecco doesn't exactly advertise or anything. I mean, it sold out and then it went out of print.

Did it work out for you then, to make a living writing about art?

I lived as modestly as possible, but yeah, it did. I liked it. I liked it up to a point until I got upset because I was charging somebody a certain amount of money for a catalogue and she didn't want to pay me the amount that I wanted. And I hadn't been smart enough to work it all out in advance. And in the course of figuring out what they were offering me, what it would mean, I realized that I was writing 400 pages of criticism a year, and that by her standard I would make $26,000, which was less than what a cab driver got in New York City. And I felt like I contributed as much to the life of New York as a cab driver so that I should at least be as well-paid as a cab driver, and she did not seem to think so. And then I got kind of angry, actually, and I realized that the art world forces you to write about everybody in order to make a living, and I'd wanted to pick and choose, so I resisted that. I started to charge more money than other people, and I got in all sorts of trouble about that. From people who were not exactly hungry. But I decided that if I lived modestly—my major expense is books—that I would be all right. Eventually I got jobs teaching, but I never tried to get a permanent job teaching till '97.

Did the National Poetry Series book help with teaching jobs?

At that point, lots of people didn't like John Ashbery. He'd won all these prizes, they thought he was a charlatan. So the fact that he was supporting me became like, "well, if we can't attack Ashbery, let's just beat up this guy." So I got pretty intense negative reviews, which persisted for a long time in association with John. They'd never read my work. They just associated me with John and dismissed it. And I also didn't try to get published that much. From '83 to '88 I didn't publish another book. After 1983 nobody asked me for work. No magazines, nothing. At that point I felt that I had hit a kind of wall, I wanted to go somewhere else, and I didn't know what that meant. I guess in a way I was inspired by Ashbery in the sense that each book of his was very different from the one that came before it. I just wanted to change, so I didn't try to publish much from '83 to '88. I had met John Martin (of Black Sparrow) somewhere around '83 or '84 in California, and finally around '87 I realized I hadn't published a book, I had work piling up, I didn't know what was going on. And I wrote John Martin a letter and said, "I don't know if you remember me, but maybe you'd be interested in looking at my work." So I got back this letter basically saying "I've been waiting for you to send a manuscript ever since we met." Ay yi yi. So I sent him something and he published it, the *New & Selected*. I guess around that time I also just started writing a lot more. And he seemed to take what I gave him and make these books.

How would you describe that change? What do you think happened?

I think it was psychoanalysis, frankly. I think it was kind of letting go of a lot of things. And then also just finally absorbing what I'd been reading or sensing about other people—that you could just make yourself up as you went along. A lot of things happened around the time that the first Black Sparrow book came out. Both my parents die, I get divorced, a lot of people who'd been my friends for many years stop talking to me because the divorce was not pleasant or nice. And I kind of went off on my own, again, in a way. And then I started writing differently. I lived even more modestly than I did before, in a tiny one-room apartment. I managed to make some money writing about art, and I was writing whatever I wanted. I felt like no one would read it and it didn't matter. And suddenly it was kind of great to have no audience because you had no expectations. In a way, that's been part of what's been going on, the idea that there's no audience. I wasn't connected to any magazines really, by then I'd broken off what tenuous connection I had to *Sulfur*. And then there was that big hullabaloo because I wrote that critique of Eliot Weinberger, so in a way I cut myself off from other people at that point.

Even people you hadn't met yet.

Exactly. My ambition, my writing, I just started to change. I thought, "it doesn't matter what you write, no one's out there." Like Jack Spicer: "No one reads poetry." No one listens to poetry. I thought, "that's not a bad thing, that's a good thing." And then I also think around the same time, the early '90s, is probably when I started to become aware that there are younger writers that like my work, and that became really liberating. I don't know, when did we meet? '97?

No, earlier than that. 1995.

That was great for me, just meeting younger people who liked my work. It was more than a pleasant surprise. I thought, "There ARE people out there reading me. Ay yi yi." I had no idea. So I think that helped a lot in the sense of making me feel secure—not secure, but it gave me a sense of something. I don't know what.

I guess looking back on it, the relationship with John Martin is really key to that, because it was more or less impossible to find anything earlier than Radiant Silhouette unless you were really lucky at a used bookstore. But as someone younger, there was this sense that anything between those really cool, rough covers that Black Sparrow does is going to be a certain quality and a certain aesthetic. Certain people out there are automatically attracted to whatever Black Sparrow publishes.

I think he's great, and I'm really happy to have him as a publisher.

He seems to support you to an incredible degree. You've done, what, five books with him, or more?

Let's see: *Radiant Silhouette, Edificio Sayonara, Hawaiian Cowboys, My Symptoms, Forced Entries.* Five, and my sixth one is coming up.

And that's prose?

Yeah.

Now, tell me about the Penguin book coming up. You're not really leaving Black Sparrow, right?

Oh, I don't know. It's your fault. Some years ago somebody said to me, "Oh you should have a book out with Penguin," and I thought, "Yeah, that would be nice," but I'd have to send them a manuscript, which seemed to me something I would not want to do. So I just thought, "Maybe they'll call me up." So in a sense that's kind of what happened, right? You did call me up. It's because of you.

Well, I made sure they looked at it.

Right. I wouldn't have sent it to them if I hadn't met you. So there's a clear example of a younger poet helping an older poet.

But it's also something that you obviously welcome. Do you have any sense that it's going to be fundamentally different from a Black Sparrow book, or that it will be received in a different way?

It may be … the poetry world is like a world of ghettoes. Black Sparrow books are not particularly reviewed anywhere. That's just the way it is, they're not reviewed, people don't review them. They're not seen as part of a group, other than that you're associated with this particular publisher. Whereas I think that because of Penguin, Alice Notley or Ann Lauterbach get read by more people or read differently, or Anne Waldman, and that's great. I like those poets and thought I would feel great if I was associated with them. And then in a way I wanted to get that possibility of a wider audience. Like in the New York art world you sometimes change galleries because you feel like if you're with this particular gallery you only get the same people to look at your work. And I felt like Penguin will enable me to do that. And the other thing I liked about Penguin was that they didn't want me to leave Black Sparrow, they want me to publish with both of them. And I talked to John Martin and he said it was fine.

Going back to the art world, you've done some curating. How did that happen?

I began curating in the late '70s. I curated a bunch of little shows. Curating is like doing an anthology, or editing a book. It enables you to shape something—a way of looking or a way of seeing. And I thought that was something I'd like to do. And then eventually I did do a show in '96 at the Museum of

Contemporary Art in Los Angeles: Ed Moses, a West coast abstract painter. That was his first big show. And I loved it. I loved looking at work that closely, thinking about it, writing about it, it was all important to me.

So as curator you not only chose the work but wrote all the didactics and stuff like that?

Yeah. And I spent three years going to Los Angeles once a month, looking at paintings, going to different people's houses, talking to him, hanging out in the studio. It was a great experience. I hope to do that again. And there are certain artists whose work I'm trying to do that with. But again, I wasn't connected to any institution in a permanent way, but a kind of guest way. I kind of like that and I don't like it. I like it because you're just a guest, and I don't like it because once you're done you have to make another relationship with someone else.

What about your collaborations with artists? I know you've done a lot of those. How do you approach that differently?

Give and take. Actually, you asked me what changed in my work in the late '80s, and beyond psychoanalysis, it was beginning to collaborate with artists. Because you hang out with certain artists, like Archie Rand, and they're immensely impulsive. Archie and I did a collaboration, I think it was in the summer of '87, we were both teaching at Bard, and I said "Let's collaborate." I guess I was thinking of Frank O'Hara's collaborations with Norman Blum and Larry Rivers. I had no idea except to do it. And Archie said "Okay, I'll be up to your house this weekend. Let's do 1000 watercolors." When I asked him why a thousand, he said "Well, we want to get to where we don't know what we're doing." I was just kind of looking at him and he said "You know, you've got so many tricks in your head, I just want you to get through them as fast as possible, then you'll just be on your own." And in a way it made me think about writing completely differently. In a sense, if before I'd had some sense that I was writing a poem, suddenly I was thinking that there are no rules, you're just writing. And I think that's what also changed my writing in the late '80s, starting to collaborate with artists like Archie Rand or Norman Blum. And also you write on a computer, you write in a notebook, you write in a typewriter—all of it is precious and small, in a way. Then you go to somebody's studio and say okay, here's the paper, here are the materials, and you realize you can just use this stuff. So that was also a big deal. If this man says "Let's do a thousand watercolors over the weekend," you get another sense of writing. You write for maybe two hours at a time, suddenly you're hanging out with an artist and working for twelve hours, you have another sense of the space in which writing can take place, you have this other sense of materials. The other thing, at least with the watercolors I did with Archie, is you try to make the language happen as fast as the image. If the image is always fast and immediate in art, how do you make language as fast as the image you're looking at if they're on the same paper? So it made me pay attention to language and the line and words next to each other in another way. I wasn't theoretically thinking about it, I was actively thinking about it, thinking my way through it. That changed my writing a lot, I know it did. I realized almost as soon as I started doing it that I was doing things on the paper that I might not have done in a poem. And then I thought, "Well, that's interesting. Why is that? What does that mean?" So in a way, I wanted to do the thousand watercolors as much as Archie wanted to do them, because I wondered what would happen if I wrote a thousand lines.

So what did happen?

We worked over different weekends, we did them every day like a job. We did them eight or ten hours a day. We took coffee breaks together, we made lunch. Archie is a guy who seems to get by on about four hours of sleep a day, immensely energetic. So that's the opposite of OULIPO, right? If OULIPO is about strict rules, there's this other writing and in a way I would write lines and literally not know where they came from. I couldn't say, "Oh, I wrote that." Maybe my hand wrote it. But I don't know who else was writing it. So I began to realize that I'd given myself a kind of space in which to write—a mental space, or a language space. That's a direct influence of being involved with painting—it was just immediate. It made me want to collaborate more, and with different artists, because I thought, "All artists are different, all collaborations will therefore be different, I will learn something from each collaboration." I just always want to do more, I'm always asking people. You get over your own ego because you've got to work with someone else.

Do you ever work with Eve, or would that be too … incestuous?

We've tried it but it never worked out. So we haven't really done it. I think the way she works is just so different from the way I work that we haven't figured out how to collaborate.

You have several books translated into German. Would you say that you're big in Germany? Both you and Eve have spent a good amount of time there. Is it mostly art criticism, or have you had poetry translated, too?

I've had poetry translated into German. There are people interested in translating my fiction though it hasn't quite happened yet. But certainly people are interested. I definitely have some kind of career or reputation in Germany, but you don't really know what that means, you know? I have books published in Germany, and I have catalogues, and sometimes they're reviewed, but I don't really read German so I assume they're nice, but I don't really know to what degree I've been written about. And I'm interested in a lot of the art going on there.

Did you meet someone and it snowballed, or what?

Yeah, partly it was that. I met this German publisher and then Bill Barette and I went to Germany in the early '90s, and it did kind of snowball. I met various German artists and worked with them, I did a book with this guy Jurgen Partenheimer that was in a show at the Museum of Modern Art. He came to New York, and he told me what the name of the project was: Giant Wall. Giant Wall is a formation of stars that existed beyond the Milky Way, that couldn't be seen. He made me think about my writing, too. He said, "Your images, one can kind of see them." I sort of knew what he was getting at. "Maybe you can write poems in which the images disappear." And that was my assignment. So things like that where the artist had read my work in some particular way and then would offer some other possibility I thought was really great. And it always came out of a non-literary context. It wasn't another poet or a literary reviewer, and in a way I wasn't really talking to that many poets, and literary reviewers weren't reviewing me. So I thought maybe it was good that they weren't reviewing me, because it means they don't know what they're reading. I'll just keep going on my way.

You said something interesting earlier on, that when you were starting out, you wanted to be affiliated with art and with people who did not teach. Did something seem corrupt about teaching?

No, I didn't think I could teach. So I thought I didn't really want to be a teacher. I thought teaching was having a certain pedagogical intelligence which I didn't think I particularly possessed. I didn't have any faith in myself for being able to teach. And also I thought I wanted to live in the world. What I really liked about, say, the Beat poets as well as the New York School, two radically different sets of individuals, was that they lived in the world. I also liked Williams Carlos Williams and Wallace Stevens, who lived in the world insofar as they went to a job every day. And I really liked that. I wanted to just read what I wanted to read. I didn't want it to fit into anything at that point. I wanted to wander off and read whatever I read, go whatever way I wanted to go. I guess in a way now I've done that enough so that I can teach different courses. I also considered studying X-ray—I mean I seriously considered that I would write about art or I would become an X-ray technician. I thought that being an X-ray technician was a portable skill. They have X-ray machines all over the world. So I could go anywhere after I learned how to do this job. And I thought proofreading was a somewhat portable skill, at least in English-speaking countries, but even in other countries they may need that kind of skill.

Did the X-ray thing come out of your time in the hospital?

Yeah, I think that's it. I thought there were certain jobs that were decent-paying that you didn't have to take home with you psychologically, and that were portable. And I wanted to learn a portable skill that was also useful socially.

I wish someone had suggested that to me. I think a lot of people could really profit from thinking that way these days, especially people who come out of MFA programs. If some of them were X-ray technicians they'd actually be bringing home some money.

At a certain point in the early '80s, I decided I'd publish something in an art magazine every month for a year. I knew there were magazines that would take what I wrote. And I thought that if I did that for a year and nobody noticed, then it was time for me to look for other work. But if I got some jobs, or people asked if I'd write a catalog, then it would be worth trying to stick it out. So I set out to write something for *Arts Magazine*, and he said he'd take whatever I gave him. And then there was *Art in America*, I think I wrote something for *ARTnews*, and I approached other magazines. I just decided every month something of mine will appear, and if nobody notices, I'm out. And I started to get people calling me up. And I thought I guess I'll stick around.

Did it work? Did you have something come out every month for a year?

Yeah. And then also I think that changes. I know there are poets who say they can't write when they teach, they can only write in the summer time. Or they can't do this or they can't do that. I think that one of the reasons I like writing about art is that it made me realize you just have to sit down and write the poem, the way you sit down to write an essay. It was just writing, it was a job—not a bad job, kind of a wonderful job. But then you couldn't be precious about yourself. And I think that's been really useful. I think writing about art, as much time as it took, made me more productive. You think about John Ashbery, certainly he's written a lot of poems, and he wrote a lot of criticism. And I was aware of that. And also I think the thing I liked about John and Robert Kelly, who also writes a lot, is that they have written all kinds of work—fiction, essays, prose poems, it's practically indefinable, the range of what they've done. For me, both of them were pretty inspiring in that regard.

LISA JARNOT

Lisa Jarnot was born in Buffalo, New York, in 1967, and educated at SUNY Buffalo and Brown University. She has published several poetry collections, most recently *Black Dog Songs* (Flood Editions, 2003). Her other books are *Some Other Kind of Mission* (Burning Deck, 1996) and *Ring of Fire* (Zoland Books, 2001). She has edited two poetry magazines, *No Trees* and *Troubled Surfer*, and she co-edited *An Anthology of New (American) Poets* (Talisman House, 1998). *Robert Duncan: The ambassador from Venus* is forthcoming from the University of California Press. She lives in New York and is an assistant professor of English at Long Island University. Rod Smith conducted this interview by email in Spring 1999, and the interview appeared in Volume 16, Number 3 / Volume 17, Number 1 of *Verse*.

Are you a Buddhist?

I'm interested in Buddhism but I'm not a practicing Buddhist. I still have a lot of questions about the Western appropriation of Buddhist religious practice. A couple summers ago I was reading the Evans-Wentz books on Tibetan Buddhism—especially a book called *Tibetan Yoga and Secret Doctrines*, which deals partly with real transcendent states, heightened states of consciousness. I'm interested in that based on what we already know (or are supposed to know) about relativity theory—that our own daily consciousness of the time-space continuum is pretty lame. Tibetan Buddhism makes sense to me on some basic level because it deals with concepts of knowledge and awareness. I think that the same concepts exist in the practice of poetry. But Buddhism is more complex, because it also has to do with practicing generosity, and with hacking away at illusions and accepting change. So, those things don't seem like they can become integrated into one's being without some real desire to follow that specific path.

Does the weather affect your poetry?

Mostly the sun affects my poetry. I'm a fire sign (Sagittarius). The figure of Helios appeals to me.

Who is Lance? It struck me the other day that one might call Some Other Kind of Mission *an "occasional epic." Am I right about this? It seems, in a way, that it could have been any length, but the rhythms took over and made it long.*

I'm not sure anymore what qualifies as epic—a heroic story "at length"—but then what length? *Some Other Kind of Mission* was described somewhere as "mock epic," but the book wasn't meant to be derivative or "mock" in a casual way. Lance I think came from two sources. I'd been reading Jack Spicer's *Holy Grail* and also Malory's *Le Morte D'Arthur*. I really liked the Malory. There are a few sections in *Some Other Kind of Mission* that play off of that, especially the Earl section near the end—"There was an Earl hight Grip." And obviously, Lance gets reconfigured into one of the subtexts of *Some Other Kind of Mission*—the information of the book accumulated over a two-year period and there were figures from my own life who became characters in the story.

It wasn't clear to me when I began the project what length it would be. I began the book during February of 1993 as "12 poems for St. Valentine's Day." Those pieces later became the numbered sections (1-10) which were collage paragraphs of phrases taken from a Japanese dictionary. At some point after that, there were visual collages, then the section "diary of a rough trade angel." It was almost a year later, during January of 1994, that I wrote the long prose paragraph section which begins "Blood in my eyes followed by truck in motel." That whole prose section was something I originally thought of as a novel. When I realized that "the novel" was a part of the Valentine's Day poems, I started to put the pieces together into the "epic" narrative. There was a five-month period during which I folded the novel into the collage pieces (which were really the skeleton of the book). Toward the end of that process I wrote "marginalia," which was also a collage text—a closure of sorts—with lines taken partly from the notebooks I had kept during the year and a half I had been working on the book.

The project always felt like it had a life of its own. One of my favorite books of poetry is Robert Duncan's *The Opening of the Field*, which is very much a book-length project. It was composed with certain themes in mind, and Duncan stretched and exhausted those themes through the course of the book. I was always very much in awe of that. A little homage to Duncan comes into play in section four of *Some Other Kind of Mission*, which begins with the line "Against the sun," pulled from Duncan's "Often I am Permitted to Return to a Meadow."

The hero of Some Other Kind of Mission *seems more daily life than mythic — maybe the hero is the poem, just its existence and continuation. That's always the case but it seems your sources become sources of energy rather than subject matter. That's not quite right either ... it's some other kind of subject matter though, don't you think?*

I think immediately of this great line from Duncan about matter and energy where he says something like "blow us up with an atom bomb and you still have not destroyed our chemistry." One of the first essays on poetry I ever read was Garcia Lorca's essay on *duende*. *Duende* gets translated as "the dark sound" but that doesn't really capture what it is. Bob Dylan has probably had the biggest influence on the intonations of my work (in getting the sources to be sources of energy in addition to subject matter). There are certain basic resonances (like in Buddhism) that can be accented — that's what a mantra does: each syllable penetrates a different realm of existence. It's pretty evident in Dylan's work, particularly in concert, that there are held vowels; and the purpose of the intentional holds or holding patterns must be "to hit the pitch co-ordinate" (that's Duncan again). I hear that a lot in Dylan's work — where he finds the word, then begins to bend the vowel until it hits the pitch, until it rings.

The point is that before I had such a theory about Dylan's work, I very much wanted to imitate the *duende* (unexplainable pitch) in it. This would have been when I was about eighteen and was still lingering on some edge of trying to be a poet. Then at some point after that I read "Howl" and I saw that energy placed on a page (Moloch!) and realized that I could imitate it from that model, which I proceeded to do for about two and a half years. The work I wrote was terrible, but it was very useful — I imitated everything I came in contact with until it turned into a ground that my own work later grew out of.

When did it click? How was the experience of the writing different from the work you'd done before?

The first poems that were really my own were in a series called the *Fall of Orpheus* which I wrote around 1988. I don't think that there has ever been a real break or peak in the continuum of my poetry though. I do think that the experience of reading has changed my work at various moments in important ways. When I first read Paul Blackburn (around the time of the *Fall of Orpheus*) something changed dramatically for me. I began to locate myself in the poem in a different way—like in Ginsberg's idea of being candid. It must have been the "recklessness" of Blackburn's lyric (both in form and in content) that gave me the permission to experiment. Later when I moved to Providence and started the MFA program at Brown I had a similar experience. I met poets (Jennifer Moxley, Lee Ann Brown, Michael Harper, and Keith and Rosmarie Waldrop) who introduced me to a lot of work that shook up my writing. It was like taking multivitamins: I was reading Christopher Smart, Bernadette Mayer, Robert Hayden, Hannah Weiner, Donald Justice, and H.P. Lovecraft all at the same time. Maybe that's more like LSD than multivitamins …

If you were to start your autobiography today, what would the first sentence (or paragraph) be?

"I, Thucydides, an Athenian, wrote the history of the war waged by the Peloponnesians and the South."

Was Sea Lyrics *written after* Some Other Kind of Mission? *It has some Whitmanisms going, no?*

Sea Lyrics was written after *Some Other Kind of Mission*, though I drew it from information (memories) previous to *Some Other Kind of Mission*. I lived in California for three and a half years (from 1989 through 1992) and *Sea Lyrics* sorts out all of that. It has some Whitmanisms, but it also has some Ferlinghetti-isms ("I am waiting") in it. *Sea Lyrics* was very much a response to living in New York in two ways. Firstly, I had just enough distance on the terrain of California to start to understand how shell-shocked I had been by its culture (in a good way, for the most part). Secondly, I had moved to New York early in 1994 and found myself in the midst of a community of young people who had come into poetry primarily through Language writing, and that also seemed very foreign to me. I realized at readings that it was entirely shocking if someone used the word "I" in a poem, so I decided to run with that, to exhaust the "I" and to bounce it off of the particulars of Oakland and San Francisco.

What's most important?

Love. Like Allen Ginsberg says, "the weight of the world is love."

It's my impression that most people don't understand this. Do you share that impression? If so, why/what do you think it is?

Poets must understand it somewhat, or at least they have historically. I think of Robert Hayden's poem, "Those Winter Sundays." It always seemed like a beautiful definition of poetry—"love's austere and lonely office." And then I think of Pound as well: "What thou lov'st well shall not be reft from thee / What thou lov'st well is thy true heritage."

I suppose that in a basic sense love is not "the currency" of American politics right now—and in fact it runs counter to the currency. We have a system at work that continues to perpetuate hate—really out of an interest in global capitalism—but then we bomb people under the guise of helpfulness and there's a lot of rhetoric about love and "liberation" that comes out of the Reagan/Bush/Clinton administrations. When I interviewed David Henderson a couple years ago for the *Poetry Project Newsletter* he was saying that it's the responsibility of poets to bargain for a position in society based on what they know, because they know a lot. That certainly has stayed with me. David's thought was that if poets don't respond, no one will. It's like Duncan's idea: "Responsibility is to keep / the ability to respond."

MATTHEW ROHRER

Matthew Rohrer was born in 1970 in Ann Arbor, Michigan, and grew up in Oklahoma. He attended the University of Michigan and the Iowa Writers' Workshop. He then moved to New York, where among other jobs he worked as a poetry editor for Penguin and directed Poetry in Motion for the Poetry Society of America. His first book, *A Hummock in the Malookas*, was chosen by Mary Oliver for the 1994 National Poetry Series and published by W.W. Norton. Verse Press published his second and third books, *Satellite* and *A Green Light*, as well as a collaborative book with Joshua Beckman, *Nice Hat. Thanks*. Matthew Zapruder conducted this interview in late August 1999, at The Gate, a bar in Brooklyn, and the interview appeared in Volume 16, Number 3 / Volume 17, Number 1 of *Verse*.

The epigraph to Satellite *is a quote from one of Tomaž Šalamun's poems: "The worst imaginable kind of fascism would be / if the soul belonged only to the living, / and not to the dust and stones!" I remember the first time I read Šalamun I was completely struck by that exact phrase. In fact, it's one of the few scraps of poetry I know by heart. Whenever I have had to describe Šalamun to anyone, that's the line I pull out as being a central, epic kind of insight.*

It's his whole thing … it's his whole program condensed in four lines.

What attracted you to that line? Why did you want that as the epigraph?

I think what it says is that the world can be created through imagination—not the real world, but a real world to each reader and writer. That is incredibly important. It's hard to think about his work without thinking about his situation. He was writing from a communist, and post-totalitarian, situation, where the state tried its best to control the imagination, and I think it did a pretty good job. But in a larger sense these lines represent an idea that's not just political. I think it's about how the imagination is necessary, not even important but necessary.

What is necessary about imagination?

In Šalamun's poems, and I think in people generally, the imagination creates the world in which we live. The world you see—for instance, these brick and metal tables—is pretty boring, but what *is* interesting is that we are here, that we have a history between us and we have histories and hopes and all those other things. And weird dreams we had last night and we don't understand why we had them. That's what makes it interesting to be here, and if we try to take that stuff away then you just have simple metal. The dust and stones are just dust and stones. Pretty bleak.

What's also interesting about the quote is that it's not just saying the dust and stones are alive like other sentient things, it's saying they are more alive. In the poem there is this willful privileging of the imagination, a bringing up of the imagination not only to the level of real life, but way beyond it.

I think that is what I love about his work. That is what I was originally drawn to ... that he is able to make these bold, declarative statements: "I am God's strongbox," "I am a pumpkin baking on the roof of the world." These things are obviously not true, but he doesn't care about that. He's not saying them because he's an idiot and thinks they're literally true. He's saying them because the act of saying them makes a world in which they are true.

In the same way, when you write [in the poem "The Bridge"], "at night the bridge crawls into town to drink," you don't mean that as some kind of a metaphor ... you're not saying something else in a fancy way and representing it by that metaphor. I think there's something crucial about the act of boldness of refusing to treat "real life" as the foundation of what is important in your work. There is a whole imaginary world that takes precedence.

Which is the most liberating thing that happened to me as a poet ... and it happened while reading Šalamun. The poems I wrote before I read him were fanciful, yet totally rooted in the real world. When a poem was fanciful it eventually had to become ironic. Because I had this guilty sense that you can't really just say, "I am a pumpkin on the roof of the world." You can't just say that. You have to eventually second-guess yourself and let the audience know that you know that's not true, so they don't think you're stupid or naïve. And when I finally read Šalamun ...

When was that?

I was at Iowa getting my Master's Degree, people were talking about it ... so

I picked it up, the Ecco edition, and the first poem I read was "To Have a Friend." Again, there are millions of poems about the devil or the whole Faust thing, and usually whenever people write about the devil and death they are so moralistic and the characters in the poem are so transparently a symbol for something else.

I think that is a mistake people often make when they read poems, or someone like Kafka or Borges. They have this compulsion to read allegorically ... they have to see the imaginary actions in the poems or the stories as being allegories for real life. Which is wrong.

That is a really limited way to read. That really prevents you from enjoying so much.

Not only that, but it's flat out not what the author meant to do.

Exactly.

I was also just struck by how the epigraph from Satellite *in a way is so true for your first book.*

Yeah, I think it could have easily been there, too. It seems so much about what the first book was about: putting the attention on the dust and stones to show that they are in fact their own thing, and not symbols of anything.

I think this idea is immediately apparent to the people who read the book. Over and over in A Hummock in the Malookas *you animate the inanimate. What made you want to do that in your poems?*

At the time, I never really thought about it. I guess I thought that was what you did when you wrote, probably since everything I read as a kid did the same thing. I didn't grow up reading poetry at all. I read C.S. Lewis and Tolkien and the Polish science fiction author Stanislaw Lem. And all the Grimm Fairy Tales. I always understood, I think, that obviously there is no talking fork but really if you accept that and go with it you have these new possibilities that you don't get with just a fork sitting on a table. I never really thought about it in this way before, but I think this personification of the inanimate simply allows me to write poems. The only time it ever occurred to me not to do this was when I was at Iowa, and people said to me, "anthropomorphism is totally out, nobody does that anymore," which just made me do it more.

Did anyone in a position of authority take issue with that?

No, I think people just tried to warn me against doing it. Teachers at Iowa would say, "this is really uncool."

That was really good advice for your literary career.

I think I just decided then that there was nothing I could do about it at that point. I loved it. I loved doing it, it made me happy. So when they said not to anthropomorphize, it just made me think, you know what, I'm really going to give it to you now.

I think it is precisely that relentless focus on something absurd like this talking fork that makes it successful. You start to believe a fork can have feelings and it all becomes okay and you're not even laughing about it anymore. It takes a certain kind of courage to stick with the device enough so that it becomes something real and not something merely funny.

"Suspend your disbelief." My teachers had always said this to me and now I often feel like saying, "is no one hearing this anymore?" I think the only writing help I got that was useful at all was that one phrase. I mean, if you don't suspend your disbelief, you're not even going to believe Lowell. You're not even going to believe things that are incredibly true to the real.

Why do you think Šalamun might have asked you and Joshua Beckman and some other younger American poets to translate his poems?

He is incredibly pleased that we like him. I think he can't believe it. I think he is honestly touched. There are a group of people who love him, not that many of them in the big picture, but they are out there, all over the country. People really love him, mostly people of our generation. I think it is high time he became much more popular, and I think this new book he is coming out with, to be edited by Simic, will really help. And I think he likes our writing and sees some similarities.

Not unreasonably. What was it like to actually translate his poems?

I feel very self-conscious saying I "translated" them, because I don't speak a word of Slovenian. Actually, I do speak one word, pismo, which means letter. The reason I was able to do the translations at all is because Tomaž speaks such terrific English, and he gave me these poems in English that were pretty much there, just the prepositions were all wrong ... but that's the hardest part of English.

The hardest and most irrelevant part of English.

Exactly, the prepositions were off and some sort of things that could have been more poetic. So I went through and cleaned them up and then asked him which of a few different versions he liked the best. His English is so good that when he hears the right version he knows "Oh, yes that's better." For him, I think getting it down the first time was not that easy. But then for me it was just a matter of cleaning the poem up.

What do you think it is about Central or Eastern European poetry that is so attractive to some young American poets?

Part of it for me is very simple, it's because I have Croatian background. I met my great-grandmother when I was too young to remember, so there is always a sense that there was a whole part of my family in a whole culture completely unavailable to me; I feel like I never met them.

In a more general sense, I think many of us younger poets are drawn to a sort of weird hermeticism Eastern European poets had to use to say what they wanted to say. Tomaž got away with a lot more, and I think it was because he wasn't living in the worst possible place. Most of those poets had to go the long way around to say something true; out of all that trouble they came up with some really interesting ways to tell the truth quietly.

By making up these totally unreal worlds, these poems somehow resonate very deeply with our own sense of the world.

For them certain things in the poems had to be said because they were of political importance. And those things couldn't be said directly. For us, who knows why we feel that way ... maybe we need to create these worlds that aren't real, not to protect ourselves from people who are monitoring us, but because everything else is boring now. Everything has been said. Using their methods is a way to say something in a new way. A way to talk about a world that is not real.

This reminds me of how many American poets of the 1960s took the "surrealism" of Latin American poets like Vallejo and Paz, and used those methods for their own purposes. We use the methods of Eastern European poets for our own purposes, even though we are of course not in any kind of analogous political situation. In fact, we are in an opposite situation; totally free to do anything we want as long as we buy a lot of stuff. The similarity, I think, lies in the technique: the willful effort of establishing an imaginary world.

Maybe that's where the techniques of anthropomorphization and personification come from … those poets couldn't really use people as their characters, because once you start, then the question immediately arises of whether the character is for or against the party.

That's the problem with socialist realism … you end up with these boring cardboard characters who are either "for" things or "against" them … and it's even worse in poetry.

But if you are talking about dogs, or something not human, then you can say a lot about them and there isn't that instant political content.

Of course then the problem is you get accused of being decadent and not politically conscious. And maybe the irony of this whole situation is that these poets are being allegorical and we stupid ignorant Americans just don't know it.

That is probably not too far off. Maybe the meaty and boring and pedantic political allegories go way over our heads and we don't see them as boring … we just take them for what they are, literally, on the page. And let's face it, if we knew what they were talking about, a lot of the time it would probably be like Americans talking about cutting down a cherry tree.

Which might be a totally resonant metaphor for some Croatian; a nineteen-year-old Croatian poet might become exhilarated by the idea of chopping down a cherry tree and the blossoms falling.

But to us it would be a real hackneyed way to talk about George Washington.

So we should probably be glad that we don't understand a lot of the context of what they are saying.

Overall, in Central and Eastern European poetry there is the incredibly wide range of techniques, and I think mainly we are fortunate to be the first generation of poets that has had access to that world, through the gradual then sudden improvement of the political situation there, and subsequent flow of translations. When you said you had Croatian background, I immediately thought of Simic and his Serbian background, and could imagine you getting in some kind of totally arcane argument, since your ancestors would have been enemies.

Luckily I know nothing about it. I think if people knew less about their ancestors there would be fewer problems.

Do you get anxious when you get called a Surrealist poet? Does that bother you?

Yes, for a couple of reasons. First, because I have this very literal sense of what Surrealism means, that it was a historical period and a movement and that technically you can't be "surrealistic" unless you lived in France in the twenties and thirties. So I feel a little silly taking on that mantle. But also it's a way of putting a tag on me, and I think that there is obviously more going on in my poems than just that.

Than just what?

Than just what mainstream culture considers surrealist. Which is wacky, dreamlike, imaginary. And whatever else they think of when they think of a talking fork. But at the same time I obviously totally love all of that stuff. Benjamin Péret is amazing. And more importantly, all their work influenced everybody, even people who would never read Surrealist writings or think it was a legitimate project. The Surrealists freed up a whole realm of subject matter for people to talk about. We are all indebted to them in a big way.

In terms of technique maybe?

Technique and subject matter and the freedom.

I think it is inaccurate to say about your work that it is surrealistic. Your project is less extreme. Surrealism in its purest form had a lot to do with automatic writing, with the attempt to directly access and portray the workings of the subconscious as a super-real kind of world. I've seen James Tate get very annoyed when people call him a surrealist poet, I think for this reason. Because he's not.

It is inaccurate. I think most poets share some of the subject matter and the spirit of it, but to say James Tate is a surrealist poet is as inaccurate as saying Peter Richards is a Language poet, or, I don't know, that Larry Levis is a confessional poet. It takes only one aspect of the work.

I think there is an aspect of calling something surrealist that ghettoizes the entire activity of writing poetry into a drug-induced Pink Floyd album cover expression of weirdness.

This is probably the most odious thing that can happen, when something strange or impossible or unrealistic happens in a poem and it's called surrealistic or just wacky. Like when someone says, "what was this guy *on* when he wrote this?" I become speechless with rage. I'm not even talking about it being said about my work, I'm talking about that reaction to anything. I think that is such a hideous discounting of any act of the imagination. Certainly plenty of the works produced over the span of history have been influenced by drugs. But let's face it, there are a lot of people out there smoking marijuana and not very many of them are producing great work. It is not like marijuana makes you instantly an artist. It just seems like such an insidious way to undercut the contribution of the individual, to take away the fact that the artist's imagination alone is the contribution itself. I think this is a smaller version of a problem within the whole culture. Those of us who went to high school in America know it's not really that cool to stand out. It is really not that cool to have different ideas. The interesting thing about Surrealism and how all this comes together, is that I was actually made fun of by my high school psychology teacher in Oklahoma for using the word "surreal." She actually made fun of me in front of the class because I said something was surreal. Everyone in the class said WHAT? And so she said to me, could you explain to the class what that means? I just assumed everyone knew what it meant, I was sort of stumped, so I said, "Things that are surreal, that's when incongruous things are in juxtaposition." And the class roared with laughter, and she joined in and was pointing at me with a belly laugh.

That's weird.

I guess the reason was because I used the words "incongruous" and "juxta-position." What the fuck is up with a culture that finds that laughable? That is sort of a larger context for this tendency we were talking about before, to critique things by saying oh, you must have been stoned, or drunk, or that's just so surreal. It's pigeon-holing and just takes away the power and dignity of it.

I want to ask you about childhood because that's a big part of the poems, an idea to which you return again and again—not any kind of sentimentalized version of childhood, and not necessarily an accurate portrayal of your own actual childhood, but an idea of childhood.

It seems like a time when everything is an archetype. It's a time when you can say someone is a bad person. Like *Johnny is "bad."* You can't really say that as an adult now. It wouldn't be true. But when you're a kid there can be a bad person. Everything you perceive is some sort of archetype.

One of my favorite poems in the book is "History Lesson," a poem that seems to exhibit this quality of childhood as archetype.

Like many of the poems in A *Hummock in the Malookas,* that poem came from something I was told (in this case by my father) when I was a little kid. We lived on an army base in Fort Rucker, Alabama, and he was in the army. Obviously nothing like this happened. There were no spies in Fort Rucker, Alabama. I was trying to recreate a sense of what happened when you were young and you have this clear picture of what's going on but you know most of it is made up. It is all atmospheric … and so it is a poem about memory, about how much is made up and how much is relying on feeling and filling up the spaces with more feelings.

Do you think there is irony in your poems about childhood?

Yes. When you go back to write about childhood and archetypal things as an adult and you don't use irony, you exude a schmaltzy sentimentality. I think you have to look at it ironically, in the sense that you're sort of looking at an earlier version of yourself. Unfortunately, I think a lot of irony tends to be self-mockery.

You don't seem self-mocking in your poems to me. What interests me is that you write about childhood a lot, and it's not sappy, that is, idealized from the point of view of some lost innocence. It's also not ironic, mocking or nasty, from some smarter vantage point. How do you do that?

I can remember being a kid and feeling really sensitive to those stories I heard … I had this constantly running sub-narrative the whole time. I think every kid has this very elaborate cosmology and mysticism, and I try to remember that. Maybe it is because I try in the poems just to be there, and not to ever step back and do any moralizing.

I'm wondering how you see humor in your own poems. Do you worry about it at all or do you see it as a powerful thing or a generative force?

I always feel like if I am reading someone who has no humor in their work, I mistrust it a little. It could be really great, it could be very smart stuff, but I feel like when humor is very obviously not in the work it makes me suspicious about what the author thinks the job of the work is.

What do you think that humorless author thinks the purpose of the work is?

What I always assume is that they think their work is more serious than humor. And I feel that sometimes there is nothing more serious than humor. I feel like humor is almost always miscast as a filler, as comic relief. Humor can be the opposite of relief. It can be a humor that is painful. It can be humor that is obviously in the wrong place at the wrong time, that can give you a sense of dramatic irony. It can be gallows humor. Humor can teach you as much as overblown seriousness. Obviously there needs to be a real balance … if you have an entirely jokey poem you lose the effect, because it is eventually just a funny joke.

Do you feel like you're ever misunderstood as a poet that particular way? That the humorous aspect is overblown in your work or misunderstood?

My alleged editor at Norton said one of the reasons they eventually rejected the new book was because it wasn't grown-up enough. What I think she means by that is *correct* and *respectful*. And first of all I want to say thank God. I would never want the work to feel grown up. What's the point of being reverent about something?

On the other hand, what's the point of being blindly irreverent ...

Pure irreverence is equally ineffectual.

Didn't your ex-editor say you should get more of your life and family into the poems, more biographical material?

She recommended I read the latest Donald Hall book because it was very honest.

It sure is.

It is, certainly. It is very honest and it's a powerful book. But let's face it, no matter what you think about Donald Hall's writing, that sort of thing hasn't happened to me. Thank God. The other thing she said to me was that she got a sense from the poems that there was a love relationship.

Duh.

But she said she didn't know enough about the other person in the relationship, like: what does she think, what do you do together, and so on.

It's kind of crazy to want that sort of conflict in the poems ... I mean, thank God there isn't that kind of drama and tragedy in your relationship.

Shouldn't we all be thankful when that sort of thing doesn't happen?

I wanted to ask you about this rumor that you are dead, which seems to be false. Do you know how that started or why?

I think I now have an idea. After I introduced Šalamun at one of his readings, this guy came up to me afterwards, someone I had never met before, and he was really excited to meet me. He had this postcard and said, "I know this seems kind of funny, but this friend of mine that lives in California thinks you're dead ... can you just write her and sign your name?" I think probably why that happened was that on Amazon.com one of the only reviews of my book, written by hanjob@aol.com, mentions the fact that I used to be a punk rocker and now I'm dead. Although I like to think the reason is because nobody will publish my second book.

How long have you been trying?

Actively, two, three years. A lot of that time was with Norton under the assumption that if I worked it different ways it would happen.

Did you make changes to the manuscript based on what they said?

Yeah, and I have gone back and unchanged them all now.

What kind of changes did you make?

Oh, they were all "clarifying" things … attempts to respond to comments like, "be more specific" and "what do you mean?" I would sit down with my editor and we would look at a poem and she had written notes on it. We spent hours after work going over and over the poems. I guess I thought someone in her position, with her kind of power, wouldn't just do that for the fun of it. So I really thought they were taking it seriously. Her typical critiques would be a note that said HUH? at the bottom of a poem. Or my favorite, which was SO?

Do you remember what poem that was under?

No, but in effect it was under every poem. SO? I made a lot of changes that I'm not very proud of, but I'm actually very happy that I got to go back and unfix them. Because there were a lot of times she would say something needs to be a bit clearer, and it would already be a good poem. So I would add a line and resay something that I thought was obvious.

So in a way you feel you have had this brush with this demon …

Of literalism.

Do you think that plainness of speech is important in poetry?

No, I could probably name a lot of poets that aren't plain and it works for them. But for what I want to do I think it is. For instance, when you're trying to write a poem in which you are artificially back in a time, at an earlier age, and trying not to comment on it in the present, you can't be too flamboyant or it falls flat. The whole thing is to try to convince people that it's real. People aren't usually convinced that things are real when they are super-flowery. I am not ashamed to say that I loved Ernest Hemingway and always loved him when I was a kid. He doesn't sacrifice anything by being direct. Take the opening lines of A Farewell to Arms, the description of the troops marching and the dust settling on the leaves is incredibly vivid. Beautiful, lyrical and all of that in simple declarative sentences.

I think what makes Hemingway ultimately interesting is the quality of the language itself. It is the very assertion of that plainness.

It is weird because it is beautiful. Because when you listen to people really talk, all sorts of weird flowery clichés work their way into the speech that they are not even aware of. Hemingway's not trying to capture real human speech, he is going beyond that to something very spare ... nobody could speak like this. Somehow you believe it because it is so strangely elemental.

Again, the suspension of disbelief—whether or not we know we're suspending it—creates a truer and more interesting version of reality. I think you do that in your poems, too; you speak plainly to the point where it is surprising sometimes.

I always thought it would be interesting to see if you could write poetically in a way that was not poetic. Or maybe it's that I pretty much thought you could be just as cool as anybody else anywhere else and speak plainly. There is definitely a middle class pride to it.

Dara Wier

Dara Wier has published nine books of poetry, most recently *Reverse Rapture* (Verse Press, 2005), *Hat on a Pond* (Verse Press, 2001), and *Voyages in English* (Carnegie Mellon University Press, 2001). She teaches in the MFA program at the University of Massachusetts at Amherst. Matthew Zapruder conducted this interview in Wier's house in Amherst in November 2000, and subsequently over email. The interview appeared in Volume 20, Numbers 2 and 3 of *Verse*.

To me, one obvious thing about the poems from your new books, Voyages in English *and* Hat on a Pond, *is that the poems aren't divided into stanzas. You've moved from a book like* Blue for the Plough, *which is mostly in couplets, through the mixed forms of* Our Master Plan, *into pretty much exclusively blocks of text. Was that a conscious decision?*

Well, it was a tiny bit of one, but soon it didn't matter. In an earlier book, *The Book of Knowledge*, I'm consciously working with a whole lot of different kinds of stanza patterns and line shapes, almost as a side bar to trying to write. I made all sorts of rules about what I could and couldn't do. I made it so there was something to work with. I swear, doing all those stanzas in *The Book of Knowledge* sometimes made me out of my mind. It was so hard, to make it work out like I wanted to make it work.

Did you have a pretty good idea of what you wanted to have happen in the book, how the stanza patterns would relate to overall moods, or themes?

I had no idea. You give yourself a technical problem sometimes, not necessarily because you even know how it's integrated with what you're doing but because it's something you want to figure out. You want to see how this feels and what this seems like. And so I made a lot of decisions. I did that through that whole book, *The Book of Knowledge*, and then I drifted into doing couplets in *Blue for the Plough* from that. And then once I started doing the couplets they felt right.

And you wonder why that is.

It's too private, in a way, to say, but I had more confidence when I wrote *Blue for the Plough*, as a poet, and none in my life. But in writing, I felt as if that were the only place I had any. I had very volatile, difficult material, and I wanted something very, very unthreatening to be looking at me on the page and couplets were very peaceful things. You fool yourself, too, into thinking you're thinking very rationally when you are thinking through couplets. They look rational, but then they are really crazy too, you know. I became obsessed with them. Then in some of the earlier poems of the next book [*Our Master Plan*], I was trying to stop doing that. I didn't want to keep doing the same thing. And I wasn't being too successful for a while. I was kind of writing stuff I didn't care that much about for a little while, and then I hit a poem that I really loved, a poem called "Untitled."

I was just going to bring up "Untitled" because it does seem like a really big change from the previous poems.

That's the first one when I got excited again. I think a poem like that comes from doing all that earlier work, of getting a sense of what I feel about syntax and what I feel about words at different times. Sometimes I love Latinate words, because I love the idea that these pieces of words accrue, build together to make a bigger word, to try to explain something that's hard to explain. So these words aren't even real, they can come apart, and you can get inside of them and think many things through them. I love that about them. And I also know you can create a deadly poem by using just that kind of talk, right?

In your poems, especially in the new ones, I see that you often start using an image to explain something, then all of a sudden the thing you are using to compare — the image — zips off and becomes the subject of the poem and takes on a whole life of its own. It seems like you feel like it's okay to do that all the time in your poems now, and maybe now that's one of the things that generates the new poems, this process?

Oh, you mean writing, and then discovering something along the way. I'm discovering, I guess you would say … but I think any poet would say that.

I think most poets pay lip service to discovery, but not many really do it. I think maybe we should not underestimate how radical it is, to start out with one subject, start explaining it, and then have the thing you use to clarify or explain your original idea go off and become the new subject of the poem, over and over.

Okay, you want to write. That's what you want to do. You want to sit there and be writing. You want to be working on a poem. You want to be faced with the kind of things that might give you a chance to surprise yourself. By sheer what? Sometimes luck. Sometimes a good sense of being in the right place at the right time. Louis Pasteur said, "Chance favors the prepared mind." That's a good thing. And how you prepare is by doing a lot of dirty work, and a lot of work before the moment when you are amazed at what's going on, and excited.

Is it a question of confidence, too?

After you do it enough times, write enough poems, you realize that it is the fact of sitting down and doing it, of writing, that makes it possible for you to be there to get the really good thing next, instead of expecting that you're not going to get inspired.

If you only sit down when you are, you're not going to write very many poems.

Oh, that would be awful. I mean, that's one baby step up from only sitting down to write a poem when you are depressed. Of course, there's no way of knowing that you are going to do it or not. And I make mistakes. Sometimes I go off on a whole launch of something that's completely wasted and I know it in the end. And sometimes I'll maybe work on something and start getting an inkling and it's somewhere and oh, those four lines, now that's really something. Maybe tomorrow I'll start with that and go from there. And that tends to help. I don't think you can be an occasional writer and get too much satisfaction out of it. Because then when you get it, you really think it's just luck. You believe you were struck by lightning or whatever. I don't in any way mean that hard work alone is going to do it. But I think you've got to practice the craft, be in poetry, stay there.

So, I know for a while now you've been writing a lot of poems. After you got done with Our Master Plan *did you just keep going?*

Pretty much. For one thing, I didn't read as much as I had been. I always read a lot, but I sometimes would let a whole three, four days be just only reading and now I don't do that, I make sure I go back and forth between reading and writing. And my kids are getting older now, and they don't need nearly as much of the all-day attention they used to. They go off on their own and have adventuresome lives.

And all these things in your life, between teaching and being in a community of writers and having so much of your life centered around poetry, must help.

I think it does. But also I don't think you go around talking about it all the time. We were talking about the Van Gogh letters earlier. He's got a beautiful letter where he writes—and I guess he's living with his parents at this point and they've about had it with him—and he writes about how he wants to go live where there are other artists around. He says he has to be able to be with other people who are doing the work he wants to do—both as models, and as people who are sharing the same kinds of problems. So, I liked it when I got to that part of the letter. I thought, "Oh, that makes sense. That's what goes on here." That's what goes on. It's not a school for poets. Look at us. We're not freaks. We're human beings who have families and who don't, or do other things and have passionate interests in fishing, in politics, or whatever it is that people do. It's just good to realize you're not a freak. Or that we're all freaks.

It can make all the difference in the world for a lot of people.

And I felt like falling into the well of this, of poetry, has saved my life practically. Because I didn't know what I was going to do. I wouldn't have been good at very many things. I had no desire to do anything particularly, maybe become a pharmacist or something because my parents wanted me to.

They did?

Yeah, they had a friend who was a pharmacist and they thought it was a nice, useful, peaceful job.

So you're talking about when you were in college.

Like this was when you'd mix your own medicines.

With mortar and pestle and everything?

Yeah, that kind.

Sort of like borderline being a witch doctor.

Medicine man, drug dealer.

At what point did you make the decision that this was what you were going to do and this was how your life was going to be? Did you just do it because that was what happened?

I didn't ever make a decision about it. I always wrote poems from when I was a kid. I think I lived in a perfect spot to daydream your life away. Living on a river that borders on a place where, you know, ships from every part of the world come in every day, that's a good place to daydream. You go sit out there and think about, "Oh, I want to go where that boat went. I want to be able to see that world." So, I lived in an isolated, tiny place. I also had two languages spoken in the house I was growing up in. That helped. Made you not know what was going on half the time.

What do you mean?

French and English were both spoken. My grandparents spoke French, and all their siblings and relatives and everybody and their kids spoke English.

And your parents did too?

Yeah. And some French too, but they were losing it.

Did both sets of grandparents live with you all? How did that work?

I lived with my mother's parents, while my parents worked in the city.

And you lived in what town?

It's called Naomi. But it wasn't a town. It was a handful of houses and farms.

So you stayed with your mother's parents while your parents were living in New Orleans trying to make money.

Living in a place called Belle Chasse outside of New Orleans, making money. I saw them on weekends. I'd cry when they'd leave me, I'd cry when they picked me up. But they also spent a lot of time at my grandparents' because it's a little farm and everybody worked on the farm. And down there the weather makes farming practically year-round work, so everybody planted, weeded, did everything, then we took the stuff to the market in New Orleans and sold it. My dad was in college and working at odd jobs, and so I'd see the books and I'd watch my mother forcing him to study and read. So early on I got that too into my brain, as an idea, books.

And how did you start to write poems?

It was really hot, hot, hot there, so I would go into a cedar-lined closet, in the house, where there was a typewriter, where it was really cool, and I would pretend as if I were writing. I'd imitate what I thought a poem would be from having heard people read poems, or probably nursery rhymes, who knows what. I'd give anything to see those poems. They must be a scream. I mean I must have been really funny.

It was a romantic place to grow up in, so many different cultures in operation. Besides the obvious French one, there were a lot of what they called Bohemians, you know, a lot of Czechoslovakian people for some reason, I don't know why. I never knew exactly the history of it. And then all the African-American families. Same houses, same fields, same farms, doing the same stuff, so that was all kind of wonderful. My Dad's family lived in the city. So I got to have the city, too.

Then a radical thing happened when I was around thirteen. My parents moved and took me with them and we went to Baton Rouge, because my Dad got a job, and they put me in a school where the nuns all spoke Spanish instead of English. Thirteen is a serious age, not only to move, but to get taken away from the little fantasy land I had. And you know, you think ninety miles, which is about how far Baton Rouge is from New Orleans, would be nothing, but I was treated as if I couldn't even speak English. I must have had some strange accent or something. So that was kind of interesting. It made me kind of back off. But then I got this English teacher who started giving me books to read like Willa Cather's *Five Stories*, or something like that. And that's the first time I read something on my own, not exactly being told to study it …

Did you go to public school or did you stay with the nuns?

Stayed with the nuns.

Did you like the nuns or were they crazy?

I liked some of the nuns a lot.

Were they mean?

No. Actually they were all really, really smart, loved books, loved—they were great teachers.

Sounds like you had a pretty decent childhood, all things considered.

I think it was excellent. I felt lucky.

At the time did you feel lucky?

I kind of think so. It seemed real interesting. Everything about it seemed to have so much life in it. It wasn't boring. By the time I was in high school I had settled on the idea that I wanted to write, that I wanted to write poems. And I had a best friend in high school who wrote with me. We wrote back and forth to each other all day long in iambic pentameter. All day long. That would be beautiful to have. 'Cause we had stacks and stacks of notebooks. It was hilarious. Talk about being a big nerd. And I'm sure that was good for me, I mean, my ear. So I thought poetry was a natural thing. Then I had the rude awakening of going to college, where all of a sudden poetry was treated as this battleground or battlefield, where people were going to butt their heads up together and decide "what it really meant."

What year was this?

1967, at LSU.

That's kind of an interesting time to be showing up at college.

I know. There were demonstrations all the time. Demonstrations, vigils.

Did you get involved in any of that?

I went. But I always stood on the sidelines a little bit and watched. I was very sympathetic, I could be in spirit with what was going on, but I also always felt I wouldn't be good at joining any group. I don't think you are necessarily a good part of a thing like that unless you really say, "Okay, I'm committing—period, no matter what." I think maybe I have too many ambiguous feelings about too many things. If it was push come to shove, then yes, taking a real stand is one thing. And I'm grateful for people who are always pushing people in directions that they need to be paying attention to.

There's a part of me that makes fun of those demonstrations, but deep down I think they're good.

They are asking all the right questions, all the right questions. If nobody did that, then the other extreme would become more and more extreme. That's what I feel like I do at UMass a lot of the time. That's a little bit my role, to say, "No, poetry really can't be watered down and watered down and turned into nothing or we will lose it, and I don't want to lose it. We need it." That's okay, isn't it? If you let poetry be in the charge of people who aren't passionately staking their lives on it, I think it will disappear. Because you know what happens in colleges then happens in the high school, and then happens in the elementary schools. It all has a big effect.

Do you still write them on a manual typewriter?

Pretty much.

In a closet?

Sort of.

Do you get sick of typing them over and over again?

I always felt like that was a rule, if you can't stand to type your own poem one time, forget it. I don't do them that many times. I prefer to reject and edit in my head a lot before I commit anything to the page. When I'm having problems, when there's a transition, I'm going to tend to think about it before I retype it again.

So you don't end up having to retype it a hundred times.

Sometimes I type three times or get started and quit, and get started and quit.

Is there anything you want to say about the relationship of the titles to the poems?

Oh, I've always been a title collector. I remember I went through a horrible time, after finishing *Blue for the Plough*. I'd started working again, but I could never end a poem. I could write all day long and be blissfully interested in various things and I could not get out of a poem.

Why?

I think I had been writing myself into these corners that were so difficult and I hadn't yet figured out how to get out of them. I think I had to learn that a lot of the time the end doesn't come out of the poem that much. It's an addition, in a big way. And I didn't know where to go to even begin to look for the additions for a while. Finally I said, well, all right, let's just stop all this. We're not going to work like that this time … we're going to write the table of contents first.

Did you do that?

I did a whole table of contents with titles I loved.

When did you do this?

I did it probably about two years ago. Then I wrote a poem called "My Table of Contents," in which I tried to lace them, get them together, but that didn't work. But I had a lot of good titles lying around. And so occasionally I've used them, but then I've gotten more. You make them up as you go along.

Between books, do you generally have to go through some period of not writing, or not being able to write, before you move out into a new style?

I used to think very, very hard about making a book, and when I thought I'd done enough to make a book, I'd stop and get very interested in how to put the book together, just like you'd hang paintings in a gallery. So I think I probably thought too, oh, every book has got to be really different. I'd make a big effort to let some time pass, which would automatically make everything different, because your mind changes, you've looked at different things and you've heard different things. To me there's always a sense of a million possible things that can either be balanced or out of whack when you are writing. So I'd stop.

Deliberately.

Yeah. And then eventually I couldn't stand it any more and I'd start doing something. And that's not for long times, I'm talking like maybe three months … I don't think it's ever been more than that. But that doesn't mean it's easy to get started. You can be pretty messed up for a while.

That's a tough thing.

Since *All You Have in Common*, I've almost never stopped. But I have had interruptions of kids, and all kinds of things slow me down.

Is teaching one of those interruptions?

Oh, again, I think it's a great privilege. But I also get to teach some of the best poets around. I mean, I work with them … I don't feel like I'm teaching. I feel as though I'm in a community of other artists and I happen to be, at this point, one of the ones around who's got a little more experience than some of the other ones. But when I first started doing this I was twenty-four years old. More than half the students were older than me. And I probably thought I knew more then, you know what I mean? I feel like if I don't interfere and if I help people see that what they are doing is valuable, and maybe save them some time, then I'm doing something. If somebody is going off down what really looks like a blind alley, maybe they could go snoop around down there for a while but then run out and come back to a bigger place.

I think that's probably best, especially for graduate students, even though they might crave more direction.

I hope this doesn't sound too awful, but, in a way, half the time I don't think I'm teaching. It's not even teaching, it's getting to participate in a true conversation about pieces of writing that literally make my heart go crazy when I'm reading them, and make my mind feel more alive than it does almost any other time.

I feel sorry for kids and young readers trying to love poetry, and being scolded and forced into not being able to like it because it's used against them. Being told, "you don't get it, you don't get it." A teacher says, "Okay, I'm the teacher in this class, and I know exactly what John Clare has to say and I know what it means, but you don't know what it means, let me tell you what it means." Well that's wrong. You ought to just say, "I love listening to John Clare. He's who you're supposed to be listening to, not me." And that's your big job as a teacher. People get scars early on. It starts early.

Not too long ago I was talking to a poet who was feeling guilt and anxiety about spending time writing poetry ... thinking that's so privileged, and so you know, it's not really affecting anything. Part of me says, well, if that's what you think, then that's what you think, and that's fine. There's nothing wrong with it, that's a fine feeling to have. But if you're asking me to tell you if I agree with you or not, that poetry's not as important, I'm going to probably say, well if you're writing really beautiful poems, you're changing people's lives, by keeping their brains alert to not being treated the way you want people to stop being treated. You want people's brains to stay active, alert, flexible. And poetry does that. That's one of its purposes.

Where do you draw the line between that and the idea that poetry is primarily for the purpose of edifying people and making them think and act "correctly," helping them do the right thing and be good people and all that kind of stuff?

To me it's about having your brain used to doing the kinds of things that a poem helps it do. Or asks it to do. Or allows it to do, that's different from any other kind of activity practically. I think you've got to be careful about what you train your mind to do. Because you can narrow your mind, and narrow your mind, and narrow your mind, instead of making it be more amazingly flexible. There are a million things to read out there, from the very beginning all the way up to now. If you believe in that as something that makes your mind operate in ways it wouldn't do by itself, you're going to get to be part of that, too. You will think in those various ways. You will know why you loved a poem. You will really know why you loved a poem. Then when you are practicing and working, when you start seeing that you're doing something kind of getting into the right territory, you're shocked. You can't believe you got close to that.

Like, this poem, "The Grade School Angels" by Rafael Alberti ... this poster [from the Poetry in Motion project] has been sitting here on the table for about three months, and this morning Emily [Dara Wier's daughter] said to me, "You know I really love that poem." And she said, "I especially love the end and that the wondering stars are children who don't know arithmetic." And she said, "I really love it when it goes, that an eclipse of the moon confuses the flowers." And the reason she likes it is because it's been sitting here so long she's read it a hundred times. She reads it every day. And I think that's really a miracle.

Because I love this poem, I was going to put it somewhere else, out of the kitchen, because now that school's started we do a lot more in here, and she said, "Oh no, you can't put it away. You have to put it up there. Because then I can still read it." She was allowed to have an absolutely private meeting with this poem. Nobody told her to read it, nobody asked her to explain it, nobody did anything. She just lived with it. And let it do its thing. That's what it ought to be.

I wonder, since at this point you're writing so many poems, if you don't start to think of your work almost as one big poem, or at least like one big process that you are perpetrating on people a little bit?

I could think it would be kind of wonderful to be feeling as if I were working on a long, long poem, but I don't think I am right now. I'm doing them one at a time. But it would be great if I thought, this is all a piece and I'm staying here.

It has that effect.

Well, the first book or two, I was just terrified.

You mean in Blood, Hook & Eye.

I was terrified.

Why?

I didn't know anything. I knew I was stupid. I knew I didn't know anything. I was afraid. I thought, how dare you? What makes you think you ought to be doing this?

Does that in any way strike you as an aesthetic strength right now when you look back at the book? Do you think there's anything about that fear that made good poems?

Yes. I think that being so afraid was good. For instance, I had all these arbitrary rules, like no abstractions. I don't think there's an abstract word in the book. I don't think there's a generalization in the book. I didn't dare generalize about anything. I was thinking, who do you think you are? And it was probably limiting to make that kind of choice. But I think it was probably good in terms of learning about writing, and it made me believe in the true amazing quality of ways you can get words together to eke out a new kind of an image.

So if you can think back on it, what was it that made a poem then for you?

I would feel that the accumulation of the sounds of the language and the moods and the tones and the images had to amount to something. I mean I couldn't just be exercising language by itself.

Or merely telling an anecdote ...

You can kind of kill yourself by a kind of timidity, too, you know ... there's the kind of poem that goes, here's an image in the present that's resonant and kind of poetic in various kinds of ways, maybe like a white boat on a lawn. Say it's kind of suggestive. Then the poet says, oh, that makes me think of my Uncle Jack and how we used to go fishing together all the time, and he's dead now and that makes me really heartbroken. But he taught me this really important lesson. And the reverse of that is the same problem: here's this past thing, and that infuses the present with some kind of meaning. And those two methods are traditional ways to make poems. And they both amount to dead ends. And even worse things can happen: one can see a poet analyzing a poem as it unfolds in a self-conscious way that is deadening.

I don't get the feeling in your poems that you're primarily trying to express or explain something that's more important than the poem itself. That is, I don't feel that your purpose in writing is that you have some kind of idea you want to express, and that the poem exists primarily for that purpose, to express an idea, or a moral.

I love it when for some reason you see something of your own that you did and you go, "Wow! How did that happen? There's no way I could have written anything like that!" But it's terrifying, because you never know if you can repeat it.

It's so terrifying.

I'm fearful, so fearful. It's crazy. I'm one of the most fearful people in the world. And I think writing poetry probably has something to do with that. Because a poet's always looking off into empty space, and you can get kind of nervous.

TESSA RUMSEY

Tessa Rumsey's first book, *Assembling the Shepherd*, was published by the University of Georgia Press in 1999. Her second book, *The Return Message* (W. W. Norton, 2005), won the 2004 Barnard New Women Poets Prize. She lives in San Francisco. Heidi Lynn Staples conducted this interview via email in Spring 2001 and again in Spring 2004.

What is your writing schedule like?

My writing schedule changes depending on my other commitments. My preference is to have a stretch of relatively uninterrupted time during which I can throw myself into a poem or a group of poems. And I'm talking days here, not hours. A friend of mine can come home from work every night and write for 45 minutes. I've never been able to do that. I like to get lost, and it takes me a while to lose the relevant coordinates. As I mentioned earlier I also like to have time to lie on the bed and look at the ceiling, or lie on the floor in front of the heater. So I suppose that's the closest I come to a schedule: stare at the ceiling, write a little, lie down in front of the heater, write a little more.

Is there anything that helps you "lose the relevant coordinates"?

I pick a really good pop song, program my CD player to repeat, and slide on my headphones.

Do you revise? If so, toward what, how often, in what time frame?

I call my recent group of poems "bricks" because they're all fairly straightforward in shape—rectangular and compact. On a more fey note, I also like to think of them as Fabergé eggs. I'm fairly obsessed with the poem's detailing, and I like them to be intricate and restrained yet lavishly over the top. This requires, for a slightly flaky California girl like me, an inordinate number of revisions. I tighten, rework, and tinker incessantly. Thank god these poems are relatively short.

Assembling the Shepherd *is strongly thematic. At what point did you decide on the themes, and how did this realization impact your future writing and reading?*

I never consciously decided on a theme, or even multiple themes, for *Assembling the Shepherd*. If I had, I probably wouldn't have been able to write another poem! Predetermining subject matter too rigorously hasn't been a useful strategy for me. I would say, however, that after I had written about 20 poems from the collection I began to be aware of lingering "instigators" within poems I had already finished writing—holes that needed filling, questions that wanted exploring, images clamoring for more screen time—and these instigations were often what led me to new poems. So I am aware of threads—or rather vast obsessive nets—of themes within the book.

One theme that struck me right away is displacement. Did you move a lot growing up?

I was born in Stamford, Connecticut, and lived on a hippie artist commune called Harmony Ranch and in various geodesic domes for the first four years of my life. Allegedly as a toddler I was transfixed by the computer-generated sound and light installations that my parents' art collective, PULSA, installed in public spaces—I guess this was news at the time since the intensity of the installations made some adults throw up. My father was teaching art at Yale and in the early seventies was asked to teach at Cal Arts in Los Angeles and at Mills College in Oakland, California. After various cross-country commutes, he and my mother finally packed up the VW bus and we settled in the Haight Ashbury neighborhood of San Francisco, which was an extremely cool place to grow up. We had just missed the summers of love and the streets were filled with the lingering detritus and rancor of that movement. We bought grains and canned goods from a garage co-op run by militant White Panthers. Liquor-soaked panhandlers ruled the streets. Everything was going down, falling apart. I roamed the ruins wide-eyed and in heaven; my favorite mode of transportation was roller skates and ski-poles. My father left for a year to travel around India and Indonesia giving grants to musicians on behalf of a foundation. In 1976, my parents separated. I shuttled between their two homes, which were always in the Haight and within walking distance for my benefit, until my mother, stepfather, and baby sister Madeleine moved to England in 1986. My stepfather is French-Swiss but grew up in Southeastern England. So my shuttling now involved a transatlantic flight and adjusting to new time zones, which heralded the beginning of my tempestuous affair with insomnia. Meanwhile, I began to accompany my father on his regular sojourns into Nevada, which heralded the beginning of my tempestuous love affair with the desert. He has lived in an abandoned radar station outside Winnemucca and on an abandoned ranch near Gerlach, where I continue to spend a lot of time. In 1988, I went back east to attend Sarah Lawrence College in New York and then headed west to the University of Iowa Writers' Workshop. After that I moved home to San Francisco, to my old 'hood, and that's where I live today.

How did the workshop experience impact your writing?

The two years I spent at Iowa were invaluable. The place was pretty insane, and I spent half of my time participating in the madness and the other half holed up in my flat, working and watching various dramas unfold from the sidelines. My writing desk was literally crammed inside a second-story, window-lined turret, so when I wrote I felt as if I were looking down onto the people and architecture of Iowa City from a glass pod. It was completely bizarre. The first winter I spent in Iowa was the coldest on record in 80 years; the following summer brought the Great Flood of '93. It was all very biblical. One night I parked my Subaru station wagon outside George's bar and when I emerged at 2 a.m. not only was the street a rushing river, but my car was completely flooded. I only mention these extreme weather conditions because, growing up for the most part in San Francisco where a belt of fog is the closest we get to a "climatic situation," Iowa's weather had a huge impact on my writing. The workshop provided a stable, supportive environment in the midst of all the atmospheric tantrums, and this helped me to establish a writing practice that endured changes and unpredictabilities in my life. The writers I studied with at the workshop—Marvin Bell, Denis Johnson, Jorie Graham, James Galvin, Gerald Stern, Donald Revell, and Jane Miller—all helped me to develop an internal editorial process that would guide me once I was away from the workshop and writing poetry between time sheets and postal visits. They were all great writers and great teachers—the two aren't always synonymous—and also fun to be around. I tried to soak up as much of their mojo as possible.

In terms of poetry influences on your work, I think of Carolyn Forché, later Adrienne Rich, Jorie Graham ... What poets have most influenced you? What is the nature of this influence?

In addition to the three you mention, I'll list some others. In the interest of time and space, I'll just mention three from various eras of my so-called life.

My earliest influences were the anthology *Reflections on a Gift of Watermelon Pickle ... and other Modern Verse*, selections from which I memorized and performed on auditions for commercials, plays, and TV pilots (best role: a member of The Lollipop Guild in a Rocky Horror-style performance of *The Wizard of Oz* at the Roxie Theater in San Francisco c. 1978); C.S. Lewis's *The Chronicles of Narnia* which I related to because I, too, wished to escape through a wardrobe and eat never-ending Turkish Delight while discovering that God is, in fact, a lion; and T.S. Eliot's *Old Possum's Book of Practical Cats*, which I performed with an ensemble at A.C.T. (the American Conservatory Theater) in 1981 and thereby learned the invaluable word "ineffable." In high school, I got hooked on *e.e. cummings: Complete Poems 1904-1962*, which was wacky and liberating; Charles Bukowski's oeuvre, which introduced me to the sentimental; and anything by E.M. Forster, whose prose I still worship. In college, I was most influenced by the poets Tom Lux, Jean Valentine, and Mark Doty, all of whom were writing teachers of mine at Sarah Lawrence. While I was writing *Assembling the Shepherd*, I was haunted by Forrest Gander's book *Deeds of Utmost Kindness*, John Ashbery's double sestina near the end of *Flow Chart*, and Wallace Stevens' "Sea Surface Full of Clouds."

I'd like to return to the theme of displacement in your first book. Has travel been an influence?

I'll stick to islands. I had strange, revelatory, almost phantasmal experiences in Indonesia, where I lived with a family outside Ubud and studied Balinese dancing and mask carving. The father of my host family played in a local gamelan and I stayed up most nights drinking coffee and listening to him jam. That music completely rewired my brain, as did spending no fewer than two weeks learning isolated eye movements from my dance instructor. I've spent a lot of time on Kauai since the age of eight, and the island's ecology and local dialect has had a strong influence on my image bank and linguistic sensibility. My 1988 stay on the island of Lamu, off the coast of East Africa, introduced me to Islamic architecture, Muslim culture, and malaria. It also sparked my interest in Sufi poetry.

The collection is full of spiritual longing and desire.

My mother and father did their best to make me spiritually conscious without enforcing—or even suggesting—my participation in any kind of religious community. We never went to church or said grace at the table, yet both my mother and my father encouraged me to be curious about my own and others' spirituality. And I'm deeply appreciative of their technique because it allowed me to clear my own path.

What was that path?

I pursued information and experiences of a spiritual nature. I became a cultural interloper. I started attending a Jewish Community Center when I was seven and continued that inquiry until I started high school. The summer I turned 16 I traveled to France through a language-exchange program and the magnitude of the cathedrals I saw literally put the fear of God into me. The following summer I went back to Europe to backpack around with a friend and my refusal to visit any religious sites felt wonderfully defiant and gave me a new kind of confidence and energy. The next summer I lived with a very generous Kenyan family in Africa, and our discussions about their relationship to faith helped fuse my earlier responses of intrigue and horror into a kind of critical seeking that continues to evolve.

What part does poetry play in that evolution?

What excites me most about language systems is their reliance on change, chance, and transformation in order to survive. Though fixed by rules and games, languages thrive on user-based mutations and slang evolutions. In this respect, language is fabulously organic, utterly receptive to tweaking and prodding, and infinitely sexy in its allegiance to morphability. Such a responsive system is highly useful for approaching tasks that require a pledge to form alongside a vow to serendipity.

In your work, you seem to apply the spiritual/philosophical problem of dissolving the binary of subject and object to address political questions …

I think it's harder to kick someone's ass or kill them if you are truly conscious of the inevitable dissolve of self and other on a subatomic level.

Was writing a second manuscript [The Return Message] different from writing a first for you, and, if so, how?

Both manuscripts took me about the same amount of time to write (5-6 years). I suppose one difference in writing the second manuscript was that I had a first book to be in conversation with. Sometimes the conversation entailed ignoring *Assembling the Shepherd*, rejecting aspects of it, revising strategies, teasing the poems' tics. Other times it involved conjuring unfinished threads, pining for certain atmospheres, romanticizing perceived achievements. When I wrote my first manuscript, the conversation was with my influences. Writing the second manuscript became more self-referential.

Was the actual process for writing your second book the same or different from the one for Assembling the Shepherd?

It was very similar until I had a baby, and then it changed utterly.

In The Return Message, *did you make any conscious departures or conscious consistencies? Did you decide on a subject or themes and set out, or did you, as in the first manuscript, just keep writing and then decide at some point to stop?*

The title of the manuscript and the first poems were my points of departure and my guiding principle, in a way. Questions about longing and abandonment led to questions about construction and genesis, and the interplay between those themes became the impetus for the poems.

How do you know when you're done with a manuscript?

I don't think they're ever done, but at a certain point it seems like a good idea to begin the next one.

How did you approach the writing of a second book? In one poem you write, "—and what did the soul say, but 'know it better,' then in a fever, 'go deeper.'" Do you feel you did this in The Return Message? *If so, how?*

I tried to know it better and go deeper by staying on the surface as much as possible.

Some of the material in your poems seems traces of lived events outside the poems themselves—most obviously in The Return Message, *for example, "The Engagement," "Bridal," and "The Butterfly Room"—yet these same pieces are easily read on their own terms and in terms of the book's larger themes as well. How would you describe the way in which you use autobiography in your poetry?*

I think the most autobiographical element in *The Return Message* is the sequencing of the poems. They appear in the order in which I wrote them. I couldn't bear to reorganize them to conform to a different system or narrative other than that of time passing. Every other element of the poems is susceptible to revision, reimagination, and remembering, so in that sense I don't think of them as autobiographical at all. The act of writing a poem is an act of alchemy, but the order in which they are written is a clock I can't reprogram. So the book's table of contents feels more "personal" or "authentic" to me than the actual poems. Which ends up being a nice way to placate and contain those two kind of yucky elements.

Displacement continues to be a theme in your work, as does spiritual longing; and, in particular, the second book foregrounds a desire that seeks to depart not so much from a literal place as from a conception of the unified, stable, and solitary self and which seeks to embrace an understanding of an inter-dependent, contingent, and permeable being. Do you think poetry can facilitate or merely record this departure? If record, why? If facilitate, how?

Your question is much more interesting than any answer I could give! But what you're describing is what I look for in art: a dismantling of perceived systems and limits (whether it's in a chord change or in the way I read an exclamation point) so that a euphoric connectedness can occur, which may give way to new ways of thinking, hearing, seeing, acting. I live for those moments, and try my best to conjure them through my own art making.

Of course, this displacement is quite literally achieved in the experience of pregnancy, when you literally are, as you write "(Where one body begins, where the next body ends—)." You were pregnant during the writing of The Return Message—*would you say this experience informed the manuscript?*

I wasn't pregnant until "Interpreting the Mood of the World and Turning it Into Things that People Want," which ended in miscarriage. And then I wasn't pregnant again until "The Butterfly Room," which I started writing while pregnant and then finished once I gave birth. But the desire to have a child and to become a mother aches through the entire book.

What impact, if any, has becoming a mother had on your writing beyond this particular manuscript?

It changes all the time! That's what's so amazingly excellent. My daughter will be two in August [2004], so I'm still completely wrapped up and unwrapped by her daily existence. The writing and thinking and reading happen around her.

Throughout The Return Message, *you use periods to end-stop lines and, in the process, often interrupt full sentences, creating a point and counterpoint between end and continuation. With the book's themes of life, death, and perpetual transformation, those emphatically end-stopped/overflowing lines struck me as a profound example of form meeting content. I don't want to say too much, but read in conjunction with the epigraphs for* The Return Message, *this doubleness reminded me of something I read that discussed life as an example of a dissipative structure — a phenomenon which includes both stillness and motion. Could you say a little bit about what you were thinking and trying to accomplish with this formal choice, and any literary models that informed it?*

Yes, I think you've said it very well. I was attempting to instigate regeneration within the text through formal means. Thinking a lot about Mircea Eliade's *The Myth of the Eternal Return*. Listening to a lot of pop, the endless assembly line of hits. Remembering the first time I read Anne Carson's "The Life of Towns" in *Plainwater*, which completely reorganized my relationship to periods.

Also, you have introduced a lot of white space into The Return Message. *Could you say a little bit about what you were thinking and trying to accomplish with this formal choice, and any literary models that informed it?*

The white space was informed by my obsession with glass houses, with domestic structures that blur the distinction between indoor and outdoor living. I like the exchange between the dead materials of construction and the sexy rush of plants, trees, and photosynthesis that glass can facilitate. I also love the way certain architects have tried to simulate the organic in urban settings through surface sensory overabundance wrapped around airy, lofty interiors, such as Renzo Piano and Richard Rogers' Centre Pompidou in Paris. Or Rem Koolhaas' Villa Dall'Ava in St. Cloud. Or Christian de Portzamparc's LVMH Tower in Manhattan, which has a folded surface so smooth it reflects everything around it.

How do you see contradiction literally and figuratively manifesting itself in your work, and for the expression of what?

Maybe the impulse to contradict myself, and thus free myself and the reader from fixed meaning, gets expressed in the triptych of *Assembling the Shepherd* and the diptychs or "doublings" of *The Return Message*. I'm drawn to multiple versions, doppelgängers, and replicants to throw us off the scent of authenticity. Of authority. My challenge now is to try and do this in a single poem.

In The Return Message, *you explicitly address the "Beloved." In the context of your pregnancy (during which, as you so beautifully describe it, the "map for finding home unfolded timely as a flower"), I read the "Beloved" in your poems as the fetus and as the erotic principle that unfolds into all life; however, the allusion to the Sufi tradition also brought to mind Iraq—Sufi poetry originated in the area of the world now known as Iraq. You've mentioned already that you love Rumi's poetry. Because the allusion is so explicit, however, I'm curious what relationship, if any, exists for you consciously between these poems and your feelings about what's currently happening there.*

You know, it both amuses and creeps me out the way Rumi's poetry has been conscripted into America's self-help militia. I'm aware of my complicity in this cultural mining and so I try my best to engage with Sufi poetry on its own terms, and to not get scared away by all the Rumi calendars and Robert Bly books-on-tape falling from the shelves of integrative pharmacies. Navigating the dynamic of being an American—a Northern Californian!—who loves reading Rumi is practice for many more important cultural relationships. I'm doing my best to stay worthy.

The themes and formal choices in both of your books suggest a spiritual, philo-sophical practice with the aim of experiencing a crossing of cognitive boundar-ies—a breaking down of dualism—an opening up of limits. What limits, if any, exist in your own writing that you would like to approach and/or "demolish ... with tenderness"?

Everything! As soon as I use it, I abuse it and it's time to tear it down.

HAYDEN CARRUTH

Hayden Carruth's many books of poetry include *Collected Shorter Poems,*
1946-1991 (Copper Canyon Press, 1992), which won the National Book Critics
Circle Award, *Scrambled Eggs and Whiskey* (Copper Canyon Press, 1996),
which won the National Book Award, and *Doctor Jazz* (Copper Canyon Press,
2001). After many years of freelance reviewing and editing while farming in
Vermont, and a brief teaching career at Syracuse University, Carruth now
lives in Munnsville, New York. The following interview was conducted by Roy
Scheele in separate sessions on February 8 and 10, 1995, in Crete, Nebraska,
between appearances by Carruth at the University of Nebraska-Lincoln and
Doane College. The interview appeared in Volume 14, Number 2 of *Verse*.

It's been twenty-five years since your anthology of twentieth-century American
poetry, The Voice That Is Great Within Us, *first appeared. This has been a very*
successful anthology. How do you view it now?

Well, I like it still, as it is. I made some mistakes: there were one or two people
I left out, and one or two people I could have made wiser selections for, I think.
But in general, as it stands it's okay. It's very out-of-date, and in the latter part
of the book many of the poets younger than I am are represented only by their
earliest work, and it doesn't do them justice. There should be a new edition,
in which their selections are brought up to date. I once suggested that to Ban-
tam, but they weren't interested. The book is quite successful, it's selling quite
well, and they're happy with the way it is—they don't want to spend any more
money. So that's that. I do wish it had an index; that's the thing that people
complain about the most. In fact, there was one guy—in Detroit, I think it
was, some years back—who made up an index and sent it to me, and I sent
it to Bantam, but they wouldn't put it in. But Bantam was not to blame for
the fact that the anthology appeared originally without an index. When I was
putting it together I was told I could have an index if I'd sacrifice twenty pages
of poetry, and I was the one who decided the poetry was more important. In
fact, the editorial people at Bantam, Gregory Armstrong and Ted Solotaroff,
were very good to me. The idea for the anthology in the first place was theirs,
they treated me well, and I owe them a good deal.

The lack of an index is one difference from the previous generation of anthologies—the Little Treasuries *by Oscar Williams, for instance, where you had all that apparatus at the back. Some of it was quite useful.*

Yes, but I had a problem with Oscar Williams' anthologies, because he put too much of himself in, and also too much of his wife, Gene Derwood. One of the principles I had in mind when I made my anthology was that there would be as little of me as I could get away with. If I had a mentor it was Conrad Aiken, because his anthology of American poetry of the first half of the century I always felt was splendid, and I hoped to be able to do as well as he did. But I didn't read any anthologies while I was doing mine. I made myself reread everything by everybody, from Robert Frost on down. And I decided that some people who had been in prior anthologies, who were quite well-known, were really not all that good, so I left them out. And I caught some flak for that. But mostly people seem to like the anthology fairly well.

That's a gargantuan task, to reread everybody.

It took me four years of pretty steady work. I spent a lot of time going back and forth to the library at Dartmouth. They were kind enough to let me take out as many books as I wanted, so I'd go down there every couple of weeks and load up the back of the car with a couple hundred books and take them home and read them and then take them back and get another couple hundred. In the end, I exhausted that library, and I had to go down to Providence, where they have a collection of contemporary American poetry and drama, and work there for a few weeks. Gathering information for the notes was almost as big a job as making the selections of the poems. I wrote those notes with great care. I wanted to get as much information into as short a space as I possibly could, and with enough distinction between the notes to make people interested in them and want to read them—I felt that that was important. And I wanted them to be headnotes, not buried in the back of the book.

I want to jump back now to your student days, as an undergraduate at the University of North Carolina and a graduate student at the University of Chicago. Who was in school with you at North Carolina?

North Carolina back in the '30s, before the war, was a wonderful place in many respects. At that time it was still a very small campus; there were only 3,500-4,000 students. And there were some great teachers there, because the university was receptive to people who couldn't make it elsewhere because of their political views or whatnot. So we had some fine people. And there were some other writers there but I didn't know them. It's strange. Larry Ferlinghetti was there, but I can't recall that we ever met, and Ted Weiss, the editor of *The Quarterly Review of Literature*, was there. I do remember meeting him, but we never really became friends until later; we didn't have much to do with each other.

The people that I knew were mostly the people who were interested in journalism. I worked on the college daily, and I believe I learned more from doing that than I ever did in the classroom. It was very good for me. Some of those people have gone on to become quite successful. Lou Harris, the fellow that runs the poll, was a friend of mine there, and so was Dick Adler, who wrote *Pajama Game* and other Broadway musicals. My best friend was Sylvan Meyer, who became publisher and editor of a daily newspaper in Miami; he served on a Pulitzer committee and is quite distinguished. So it was a pretty lively group. And I myself thought that I would become a newspaperman, until I discovered that I simply couldn't. I was too shy to do a proper interview; I couldn't go out and gather the news the way you're supposed to. I tried it for a little bit, but then I quit.

And the University of Chicago—who was there?

Chicago was a wonderful place too when I was there right after the war because, in the first place, Robert Hutchins was the chancellor, and without any doubt he was the greatest university administrator there's ever been—at least since Erasmus. He just did so many fine things for that university, and one of the things he did was open it up to any European refugee scholar who needed a place to stay and work and make a little money. We had people like Jacques Maritain and Paul Tillich—a very distinguished faculty. And there was a very free and open atmosphere, and some great students were there—Saul Bellow, for example, and Paul Goodman. It was just a great place to be.

And of course it was a big city, with a lot of nice bookshops. I had never heard of T.S. Eliot before I went to Chicago in 1945-1946, but as soon as I got into the bookshops along 57th Street I was reading Eliot and Williams and Stevens and all the rest of them just as avidly as I could, and that's when I became truly serious about my own poetry. Then a couple of years later I became editor of *Poetry* magazine, and I enjoyed that a lot. It was a boost, you know, sitting in the same chair as Harriet Monroe and Zabel and all the rest of them. It was in a very small room with an old battered desk, and the walls all around behind me and up above my head just filled with back issues—the magazine had been going since 1912—and I could pluck one of those issues down and blow the dust off it and open it up and there would be a new poem by, say, Wallace Stevens. What more could you want? I loved that.

For many years you made a living largely by freelance reviewing and editing, and I recall your saying somewhere that as you look back on this period you marvel at having been able to do so. When exactly did this period begin?

Well, it began somewhat gradually. When I was living in Chicago and editing *Poetry* and working for the University of Chicago Press back in the late '40s and early '50s, I was doing quite a bit of reviewing, especially for places like *The Nation* and *The New Republic* and some of the local newspapers like the *Sun-Times*. Then I became sick and went in the hospital and didn't do anything for quite a long time …

That was in the mid-'50s?

Yes, I was out of circulation almost entirely for eight years, from '52 to '60. And then I began to move out again a little bit, and I got married again and moved up to Vermont and began trying to make a living as a hack writer and reviewer, and that lasted for 20 years—more than 20 years, I guess. Now I don't do very much of it at all. But it was tough. I was isolated. I couldn't make contact with people in New York who might have given me better assignments than I got, and there were plenty of times when I was living on the money from reviews that I did for the literary quarterlies and magazines like *The Nation*. They paid very little, and so we were poor. I supplemented all of that by raising all our own food and gathering our fuel and working on the farm. I was very busy and I did, truly, a lot of work during that period. When I look back at it now, I don't know how I did it.

I've read that you used to go out to mail something to meet a deadline just as the sun was coming up.

That's true, yes. I often worked all night, especially in the wintertime, and it would be six o'clock in the morning when I finished up. I used to work in a little shed—it was maybe fifty yards from the house—and I would go out and post my night's work in the mailbox by the side of the road, and then I would unwind by taking a little walk down the road with my dog. It was nice in the winter, because in the early morning it was likely to be clear, and there'd be a lot of stars, and my neighbor was always getting up at just about the same time, as he went to work then, and he would come by and we'd chat for a minute. I look back at all of that with nostalgia, which at the time would have seemed ridiculous to me.

You've spoken of the powerful body of literature that has come out of conditions of rural poverty, including writers as various as Robert Frost, Toni Morrison, and Cesare Pavese. Much of your own best work, I feel, comes from this period when you were living in the country in northern Vermont. What in your view is salutary about living and working in such circumstances?

Well, it's very difficult to generalize about these things. People are always trying to make broad sociological conclusions about artists and writers, and I think they mostly fail. Obviously, for some people it would be a disaster to have to lead the life that I lived. In my own case, I found the hardship and the hard work stimulating and challenging and something that I faced with a certain kind of pleasure. If I got through a really tough winter, when I burned fifteen cords of wood and the average temperature was ten below zero, I felt that I'd done something. And that was a good feeling for me. There wasn't much of that in my earlier life; I didn't have a sense of having accomplished anything. So living up in the north country and living in poverty were like a game in a way. Sometimes it was a very desperate game and I got fed up with it, but it helped.

Another thing, which I think is terribly important: I do not see how anybody can write poetry, or write anything, if the environment is simply literary and intellectual. I think you need other things in your life, and if your life is attached to a university or a cultural center of some kind, then you have to go out and seek it. In my case, it was forced on me; I didn't have any choice. I had to cut wood and work with the local farmers and learn how to repair machinery and do all that kind of thing. And much of my poetry was written as I was doing these other things. I would never compose a whole poem in my head because I didn't have that capacity, but I would compose lines and think of imagery and textures and moods, and then I would go home and get in my little shed and at four o'clock in the morning I'd put them down on paper.

In your long poem "Vermont" you say that "The Hill Wife" is one of a handful of Frost poems that you reread once a year, and that you wish you could have met her. What in particular do you admire about the poem, and about the woman herself?

Well, one of my principal topics, from adolescence on, has been my love of women and my sympathy for their plight. This is not a programmatic or ideological thing; I was thinking in these terms long before the neo-feminist movement began, and I can't altogether explain where it comes from. But it's there, in me and in my poems. The Hill Wife is a person I admire greatly for her fortitude, and her Vermont character, which is important to me, and I also sympathize with her: she's stubborn, she's dealing with hardship, and she's surviving, and I have a strong feeling about that—that's what people have to do in order to make their lives full and interesting, even though it's painful.

You've written a number of poems yourself about Vermont country people. Do you have a favorite character or two among them?

Not really. The people that I wrote about were the people whom I liked the best.

So they'd already undergone some selection before they got into the poems.

Yes, there were other people in the town where I lived that I could have written about and didn't, because I didn't feel the same sense of urgency about them. I suppose Johnny Dryden is the one that I feel closest to—I *was* closest to him, in a way, except for Marshall Washer. Marshall Washer—that's his real name—was my closest friend when I was there. Johnny Dryden's real name is something else. I did invent some of the things that I put in a poem about him, but not very much; most of the things that went into the poem were things that he told me or things that I observed over a period of twenty years of knowing him and talking to him. He was crazy, he was just nuts, but I have an affinity for crazy people. In fact, most of my best friends have been nuts in one way or another.

In order to write about a character like that, your experience and knowledge of the person has to deepen and settle over a considerable period of time, doesn't it?

It does. In my case, at any rate, I have to get to know the other person well enough so that I can *be* him or her. That's what I did with people like Johnny Dryden and Marvin McCabe and others: I just put myself aside. They were more interesting than I was to myself.

Do you think that might be the basic impulse behind a desire to write monologues or narratives—the momentary effacement of one's own personality, the sort of thing Eliot talks about?

I think it's true. It's a very deep impulse in some poets. As you look at poems by Eliot, for instance, or Browning, you can see that the poet is coming alive through the voice and attitude and personality of another person, and to me that has always been not only easy, in a sense, but necessary. I think it ties into the neurotic difficulties that I've had all my life. I've been inhibited and incapacitated by neurotic anxiety, which obviously is connected with a sense of low—what do they call it nowadays?—self-esteem. So I esteemed myself by writing about other people's lives, in other people's words, and that helped me.

Many of these country poems are monologues. What is it like for you to write a monologue? Is it more or less difficult than other long poems?

Well, the monologues—once I got started, once I got the poem in mind—were easy to write, and the reason is not what we've been talking about, personality and all that sort of thing. The reason is that every one of those monologues is also a narrative; there's something in there that appealed to me, and usually something that has at least some comic side to it. I'm a humorist, and though most people don't know that, or don't care if they do know, to me it's important. I love telling tall tales and exaggerating things. My grandfather was a professional comic writer, a friend of Mark Twain and John Kendrick Bangs and people like that, and I can remember him telling these terrible fibs, you know …

This was your mother's father?

No, my father's father. I was named after him; his name was Hayden Carruth too, and he published a number of books. He was a sort of Baron Munchhausen of the West. He wrote these stories about strange people in Wisconsin and Minnesota and Nebraska that were quite popular at one time, but I don't think anybody remembers him much today. But he *was* known. I can recall one time when I was about seven or eight years old, walking home from school in this little town where we lived, and I went into the dry goods store to buy some penny candy, and I heard my name. And I turned and looked at the woman who was standing at the counter talking to the store owner, and I realized that she was talking about my grandfather, not me—she didn't even know I existed. And I thought, "That's fame."

I don't see how anyone can miss the humor in your work, especially in the mono-logues. A moment ago you mentioned your love of tall tales, and one example that leaps to mind occurs in "Crow's Mark," where the speaker tells of a high wind out of the north that wraps the beam of his flashlight several times around a tree. Contrasting with this sort of exaggeration, and often existing side by side with it, is the literalness and understated humor of a lot of your characters. Isn't all this typical of New England speech?

I think so: it's in the speech. Some of the back country people I lived among all those years, especially the older people, were such wonderful story tell-ers. Almost always they told stories on themselves, you know, and they were very funny, very dry. I think all good humor has a dark, existential truth lying behind it. This is certainly true of Jewish humor, for instance. The country people up there in New England had the same quality, and I liked that and tended to try to imitate it. You can find it in Frost, you can find it in Robinson, you can find it in a lot of nineteenth-century American authors whom I read when I was a kid.

Is the humor of these country people one of the things that you found most at-tractive about them?

Oh, yeah. These people are all poor, they're all struggling, not only with pov-erty and sometimes illness but with a harsh climate and all that goes with it, which most people don't know about today in our civilization of controlled atmospheres and so on. But part of the way they get through it is by making a joke out of it, making it funny. There's a Vermont author whom I've been interested in for a long time—people outside Vermont scarcely know him—his name is Rowland Robinson. He lived in Ferrisburg and wrote during the latter part of the nineteenth century and the early part of the twentieth. He had a wonderful ear. He wrote in the local dialect and did it very, very well, and there's a lot of humor in his writings. They were not full-fledged fictions, mostly, they were just sketches, little episodes. But he did it very well. One of the things that people did in the old days was to get together on Saturday night in the local one-room schoolhouse and have readings from Robinson. They would listen to someone who was good at reading and doing dialects, and then they'd have some square dancing for a while, and then they'd get out the hard cider and get drunk. It was the way they got through. It was great!

Tell me about "November Jeans Song." I'm curious to know how that poem came about.

I can't recall exactly. I can recall in general because my life at the time when I wrote that poem had a good deal to do with working in the woods, and my jeans were always in terrible shape. And I was always broke and couldn't buy a new pair, and my wife was always trying to fix them up. I don't know, I felt exuberant, and I felt like writing a little jazzy poem, and that's what I did.

It's really a fun poem, I think—for instance, the way you break the line in that first verse paragraph:

> Hey, hey, daddio,
> Them old jeans is
>   Going to go!

I love to write, and sometimes even to speak, in the semiliterate language of the people with whom I was associated most of the time when I lived in the country. To me there's something more eloquent about the misuse of tenses and pronouns and so on than standard speech is capable of. I'm not sure why that is, but I think it has something to do with rhythm. When you catch the colloquial rhythm of a certain phrase or idiom, it's moving, it makes it go. And I've experimented with that in my poems in a number of different ways, and at the same time I've sort of set that kind of writing in the middle of more standard writing so that there's a contrast.

I suppose one classic example of that kind of thing would be what Twain achieves with the speech of Huck.

Yes, I think that's absolutely superb. Twain did it, and I don't know how many people today know how much he achieved when he did that, because the dialect writing in the nineteenth century before him had been very broad and almost grotesque in caricature, with a lot of orthographical fanciness and so forth. Twain was able to do it by suggestion, and by using rhythm and idiom, the spoken language. He had a wonderful ear.

"November Jeans Song" is just one of your many poems dealing with work, either as subject or background. In "Essay on Love" you speak of labor as "the only meaning." What did you mean by that?

Well, I think I know what I meant at the time. As I said, I was living in the country and I was poor and I worked very hard, all the time, as most people do who are living as I was. I'm not saying I worked any harder than anybody else; my wife worked just as hard as I did. But we were always working and it was prominent in our minds, and much of the work was done for other people, out of a sense of affection and obligation. Labor was the glue that held my family together and held the community together, and almost everything we did was, in one way or another, focused on some kind of work. And many of my poems are about that work, because I was doing it and because while I was doing it the poems would occur to me.

In connection with your many years of reviewing you told me the other day there were only a few essays that you had written to your own assignment, simply because you wanted to write them. You mentioned an essay on King Lear. *I'm wondering whether your long piece on Paul Goodman would be another.*

Yes. I had wanted to do that for a long time and hadn't been able to—I couldn't find time for it. And then one winter I got a residency at Yaddo for a couple of weeks, and I wrote the Goodman piece there.

It's a beautiful essay. You're a very articulate spokesman for Goodman's work.

Well, I would like to think his work was important. It's also very enjoyable to read. And yet most people don't seem to know anything about him nowadays.

It seems to me that we're in danger of losing track of a lot of good poets.

I think we are, and I suspect we always have been. Poets come and go, like anything else. Many of the poets whom I admired when I was young—poets who were a little bit older than I was—now have no readership at all, as far as I can see.

You've written a number of essays on Pound. My favorite is the short piece "On a Picture of Ezra Pound," where you talk about a photograph of Pound that you had on the wall of your shed. What has Pound's work meant to your own practice as a poet?

It has reinforced my sense of the music of poetry. I could have gotten by without Pound; I could have gotten by on Shakespeare or any one of a number of other poets whose lyric ear has been important to me. But Pound is just so musical, so exact in the placement of every phrase, every word. He could write anything. He wrote an awful lot of dumb stuff, and he wrote stuff that's offensive, everybody knows. But in the parts of his work that *work*—that are successful—he's just superb.

He's il miglior fabbro, *in Eliot's phrase.*

He is, he really is, and I think the best in our century in that respect, although there are some others I like a lot too. Conrad Aiken, for instance, is another poet from the past whom nobody pays any attention to nowadays. He had a wonderful ear and wrote some really fine lyric poems. People like that have influenced me. I think I would have been doing it anyway, because that's my natural bent, but these people reinforced me.

It seems to be your natural bent: from your earliest work there is a lyric note that is yours.

Well, I do believe that a good poem has to sound nice, and I've always taken care to achieve that, in many different ways.

In Fragments of Autobiography *you write, "A painter whom I particularly admire and whose work seems to me close to my own painting is Vlaminck, especially in his later paintings of French farms and villages." What qualities in Vlaminck's paintings make you feel a kinship with him?*

I like the feeling that he has for the land, for trees and roads and things like that. It reminds me of the part of New England where I lived, but more than that it reminds me of the way the people there *looked* at the land, and the way they used it—it's beautiful, but at the same time it's functional. I have not spent any time in the part of France where he lived, but I have lived for a while in the south of France, so I can see some similarities in his painting to the south.

But basically, I just like the way *he* is, as a presence in the world, looking at whatever he is seeing. It's firm and full and affectionate and functional and *individual*—he's his own man.

Is there some aspect of your poetry that you feel has been overlooked?

No, I can't say that. I don't really pay much attention to what people write about my poetry. Mostly people have been very kind to me; they like my work and they say so. I've had a couple of bad reviews. I got one *infuriating* review one time from a guy named Simon in New York—John Simon. He reviewed an early book of mine called *Journey to a Known Place*, which is included in my *Longer Poems*, and his review was one sentence: "The only journey this book should take is to the wastebasket." But mostly people have been kind to me, and generous. The only reason I take any interest at all in what people say in reviews is because sometimes they give me a slant on my work that I hadn't seen. And that's interesting, it's entertaining to me, the way somebody can have a perfectly legitimate response to something I've written which didn't even occur to me. That's the kind of review that has the greatest value to the poet. I don't think the poet is ever very much influenced in his work by what the reviewer says, but there are clarifications and different perspectives that the reviewer can give the poet. I did an awful lot of reviewing myself, and I sometimes had to review books that I knew were no good, and I had to say so. I disliked doing that. I much preferred to be able to review books that I liked and to recommend them wholeheartedly, and as I acquired a certain status as a reviewer I was able to do that—I was able to choose my own books instead of simply taking what editors sent me. I wanted my criticism to be positive and to be helpful, not to the writer but to the reading public. I did a lot of it, and for a long time nobody ever mentioned my poems; all they ever mentioned was my criticism, and I didn't like that. I felt that my poetry was more important than my prose, and I still do. I wished that people would pay some attention to my poetry, but for many years they didn't very much. Now it's beginning to change.

Decidedly it is. Is there anything you'd like to talk about as we come to the end of this interview?

Oh, I don't know. I'm about written out. I'm not doing much critical writing. I still would like to do another essay or two on Shakespeare, and I think I will. Most of the time I'm not writing much poetry either; I am content not to.

A trip like this, where everything is focused on me and my poetry, is refreshing and invigorating, and I meet nice people, and I'm in a part of the country that I haven't seen before, and it's good. But it's also terribly exhausting, and when I get home I just collapse—for weeks sometimes—before I can go out again. All this attention, being in the center of everything, and the focus—I don't think it's good for me, or for anybody, and I don't like to do it any more than I have to.

MIROSLAV HOLUB

Czech poet Miroslav Holub's books of poems in English include *Intensive Care: Selected and New Poems* (Oberlin College Press, 1996) and *The Rampage* (Faber, 1997). His essays on science, poetry, and other subjects are gathered in *The Dimension of the Present Moment* (Faber, 1990) and *Shedding Life* (Faber, 1997). Holub lived in Prague, where he was a research immunologist at the Academy of Sciences, until his death in 1998. Roy Scheele conducted this interview on October 29, 1996, at his home in Lincoln, Nebraska, where Holub stayed while making several appearances at nearby Doane College in Crete. Reference is made at the outset to Scheele's earlier interview with Holub, which appeared in the November/December 1992 issue of *Poets & Writers*. This interview appeared in Volume 15, Numbers 1 and 2 of *Verse*.

When we last talked, in the fall of 1991, Czechoslovakia was still intact. How has the subsequent breakup of the country into the Czech Republic and Slovakia affected Czech life and literature?

The split has had a minor effect on the Czech soul, so to speak. We lost something, maybe in the way a young person growing up loses something of his childhood. Maybe the whole state has become more mature than the previous republic was. In the area of culture, there has been an influx of Slovakian artists who fled the stern nationalistic measures of the Slovakian Ministry of Culture. We had a wave of Slovakian writers and filmmakers. The Slovakian producer Fero Fenic established many interesting TV and film programs, such as the series *100 Important Czechs Today*, and the excellent Slovakian political satire *Miroslav Markovic* was transferred from Bratislava to Prague television. Overall I would say that Czech culture may have gained something from the Slovakian temperament and sense of elegance. We still have common magazines, like *Mosty* [*Bridges*], which tries to keep some of the spirit of the former Czechoslovakia alive, and every decent Czech magazine publishes Slovakian writers, very frequently in Slovakian. Of course this means that each magazine has to have a special editor who has mastered Slovakian grammar.

In the earlier interview, you said that Czech literature had not yet come to reflect the change of situation from life under communism to life under the

Havel government. You observed that it continued to be "a literature of basic complaints." Is this still the case?

It is still the case, and obviously it will never reflect the change. If you looked at some typical articles and books from the time of the relaxation of the communist rule, say, from 1984 on, you couldn't tell them from what has been published since. The only difference would be that formerly forbidden names now began to appear in print. But there was not a basic change in the plaintive mood of the individual writer. On the contrary, the main characteristic of the literature of our very young writers today is a sort of amorphousness, not only in terms of the human perspective but also in terms of form. Many of them write something between a prose poem and an absurd short story. The only real change which one can register is that the dust—that is, the writers of lower quality, whose only merit was that they had been in exile or had written in dissent—is settling. More purely literary criteria are prevailing nowadays.

Are there emerging Czech writers whose work you feel is promising?

It would be unnatural if no new talent emerged. We have some young poets who may get their own voices someday, and we have a number of prose writers who are really very interesting, who are experimental and still readable. Of course sometimes experimental postmodernist writing is just a kind of literary hermeneutics, but there's a good young novelist from Brno, Jirí Kratochvil, whose situations are slightly Kafkaesque—not quite natural, sort of dreamlike, and yet still palatable to the normal reader.

I've recently begun to read in translation some of the novels of Bohumil Hrabal. I'm impressed by Hrabal's energy and restless wit. I wonder what you think of his work.

I think Hrabal represents the real mainstream of the Czech national character as reflected in literature. He is the sequel to all that is best in the work of Jaroslav Hasek, the author of *The Good Soldier Schweik.* Like Hasek, Hrabal can isolate and remember and consolidate little stories overheard in a pub or on the street. His attitude is extremely human. He himself is just a plain man, but he's well-read. He's definitely one of the major modern European writers. He's old now and just goes to his pub and feeds his cats and doesn't write very much anymore, but even his letters still reflect his inner intensity.

I take it you know him.

Yes, I've met him a couple of times. I was even in his famous cottage at Kersko, in the woods away from Prague, where he keeps his cats. He's a very nice man. But I am just the opposite of him. I am unable to sit in a pub and just drink beer after beer and chat with others: I am uneasy there.

What established Czech poets deserve to be better known here? Are there some who are being ignored by translators?

Well, somebody is always being ignored. Translation is a kind of discrimination, so you never get a full perspective of a nation's literature from the mirror of translation. The trouble is that the most interesting Czech literature cannot be properly translated. This is true of Hrabal, for instance, and especially of Hasek; it would take a master translator to bring across all the qualities of *The Good Soldier Schweik.* This is also true of the greatest Czech poets. The Nobel Prize-winning poet Jaroslav Seifert, for example, is very hard to translate into English because in the most representative period of his career he used very strict rhyme and meter, and in Czech the possibilities for rhyming are so much more abundant than those in English that it simply doesn't work. Of course Seifert can be translated in his late period, when he wrote free verse. Vladimír Holan, who was one of the greatest writers of the century, I would say, cannot really be translated into English. Maybe he does better in French or Italian, but in English it's never the same Holan; it's slightly changed. But Holan at least is represented in most English anthologies of European poetry. Another major figure is Karel Siktanc, who comes from the same group of poets as myself, those who write of everyday life. Siktanc developed into a sort of language poet. His playfulness and his mastery of the Czech language — coining words, using unusual inflections, and experimenting with the syntax — are extremely interesting but not always comprehensible, and his work pretty much lies beyond translation.

Oberlin College Press has just brought out your Intensive Care: Selected and New Poems, *and it's a very impressive achievement. What's next for you in the way of publication?*

Nobody believes this, of course, but I have the feeling that one shouldn't publish too frequently or too much. There are so many words around already! So sometimes I say to myself, "Well, let's wait a little bit," but usually there are other conditions which make the publisher want to accelerate a book's publication. My fear is that I will bring out books that are weaker, so what I try to do is bring out books which are, if not stronger, at least on the same level. I don't want to just go on. When I publish something, I want it to be really new. The Oberlin book is extremely well-done, but it's a sort of personal anthology. Next year I should have a new book of poems from Faber & Faber. My editor's feeling is that the new book is stronger than *Vanishing Lung Syndrome*; my own feeling is that it is slightly better. But of course the writer himself cannot judge that: others have to say.

I would like to do something new, something different. And so I fluctuate from longer poems, as in *Interferon* and *Vanishing Lung Syndrome*, to very short, condensed poems. My desire to write shorter poems is preconditioned by the literary situation at home, because the public which reads and buys poetry is slightly diminishing, and what can make poetry popular again is comprehensibility, not postmodernist hermeneutics. So I'm trying to be even more comprehensible, with just a few surrealist images—sometimes weird, perhaps, but basically comprehensible.

You've written prose poems. What attracts you to the form, as opposed to writing verse?

Just an instinct for change. I would hate to have a book of one hundred poems with the same structure. Therefore I insisted, in *Intensive Care*, that there should be some of my prose poems and all of my stage poems, which are just poems written as stage dialogues. I included these in the book only as an alternative to what one might call the "normal" poems.

Your stage poems are extremely interesting and work very well. Was it fun for you to write them?

It was great fun. And occasionally I get ideas for new kinds of poems. In the new Faber book there is a very mixed poem which is partly prose, partly statistical statement, and partly verse. It's called "Not-So-Brief Reflection on the Edict" and has to do with slavery in ancient Rome. Again, it's something different. I firmly believe that one of the greatest dangers for poetry as published in books is monotony.

As I continue to read your work, a quality that I appreciate more and more is its dry humor, which is a quality that many contemporary writers seem to lack. What is your view of the importance of humor in poetry?

I think humor is one of the principle aesthetic qualities. An aesthetic quality should join the writer and the reader; it is one of the bridges. And humor is the most solid of these bridges. When you see someone reading something that is deadly serious, even if it makes the greatest possible leap and uses the greatest metaphors, you notice that he doesn't react visibly. But with some things, the reader will smile, and the human smile within a poem is something very beautiful and reassuring for the author. Of course the same thing is true at readings. I've given many readings, so I already know the places where people will react with a smile, and I can judge an audience by its proneness to smile in the proper spots. I believe humor is inevitable today. And it's one of the positive sides of the Czech national character. Even the Czech postmodernist philosophers use lots of playful allusions and some humor, which, in the case of postmodernist philosophy, is a great relief.

Could you speak of the relation of your poetry to modern art?

I don't know, it may be the colors, it may be the playfulness of modern art. I used to give readings with slide projections between the poems, so I had to pick my favorites, and it was always Miro, Klee, Dali—

Magritte?

Oh, of course, Magritte, because for me every Magritte is a very clearly suggested poem. Anyway, I would always show these slides at my readings, and then, as always when I do anything too many times, it got boring for me, and so I stopped doing it. But I still have that collection of slides. When I was still showing them I would always include the Czech experimental artist Jiří Kolár, who was also an extremely interesting poet. He's presently living in Paris, though he frequently returns to Prague. He's stopped writing but he still makes collages. He will take a Renaissance portrait, say, and cut it into pieces which he pastes back together so that it looks like the portrait is in motion. He is one of the really innovative European artists.

Don't you find a correlation between modern abstract art and the sorts of things you see under the microscope in the laboratory?

Oh, constantly. You know, the statement "I do not understand modern art" has always seemed nonsensical to me; what a person usually means is that he simply doesn't like it. But once I had to stare into the microscope and find a pattern in the "nonsensical" background, I started to appreciate all kinds of geometrical abstraction and even abstract expressionism. I learned to appreciate this kind of modern art through science.

The cover of Intensive Care *has an illustration of figures from the workshop of Czech sculptor Olbram Zoubek. Could you tell me something about him?*

Well, of course one would like to have Czech art on a book of Czech poetry. Olbram Zoubek is an old friend of mine, and so I asked him if we could use one of his sculptures on the cover of *Intensive Care*. But then I thought, that would be sort of routine. His workshop is in a yard between two tall apartment buildings in Prague, with a few large trees overhead, and the immense number of statues there makes it look like a scene from a fairy tale. And it occurred to me that maybe that whole scene would have more intensity, would go better with the title of *Intensive Care*, than a photograph of a single figure. And then he produced this slide. At first we didn't notice that the slide shows not only the statues but Olbram Zoubek himself, pushing one of the statues toward the door of his workshop. That was a nice revelation.

Again, a touch of humor.

Yes, that's what I wanted. You know, for a long time I dreamt of having one of the excellent Czech cartoonists do the cover art for one of my books, and so for my first book after the long silence, from 1970-1982 [when Holub was not allowed by the Communist regime to publish his poetry], I thought I would use a cartoon by Miroslav Barták. The title of the book was *On the Contrary*, and the cartoon showed a man sitting on a table holding out a telephone to an open box of sardines, so that the sardines could have their say. My publishers thought it was too outspoken for an emerging, forbidden author, and they said, "No, we can't use this." But I still have the cartoon at home, and I hope to use it someday.

In your essay "Poetry and Science," you remark that the basis of any modern art is "exactly that which cannot be recorded by this art's specific means ... The basis of poetry is the unpronounceable, the basis of a picture is the unpaintable, the basis of music is the unplayable and the basis of drama is hidden beyond the action." Is this why so much modern literature alludes to its sister arts — to refer beyond itself to the larger question it faces, in common with the other arts, of the inadequacy of its means?

I think so. It's instinctive to try to reach for help in the other arts, and I'm always intrigued by any artistic activity which combines two media, such as poetry and music or art and music. At times they may be complementary. When you are listening to music in a concert hall, or even at home, you may just look around the room, at this corner or that crack in the wall, and that's a kind of illustration, so why not look at changing pictures or even just changing colors while you are listening?

It seems to me that you have a particularly rich resource because you not only allude to the other arts but also have constantly present your experiences as a scientist.

Yes, actually this started even before I became a practicing scientist. It started with the thought, "Why does poetry only include the invertebrates, the insects, the higher plants, a couple of stars, and a blue sky in its repertoire?" It's very limited, the visual world. So I always wanted to use other data from the world which would lie beyond the senses yet still be comprehensible in a human context. I simply realize in poetry an obligatory distrust of the human senses. Poetry is not only about using the senses and the sensitivity and the sensibility but also about using the plain human mind in the way a plain human being is using it anyway while crossing the street.

A number of poets today are putting their work, or some part of it, onto the Internet. What do you think of this?

We just had a conference on human communication in Prague, a big conference with some very interesting personalities from abroad taking part. And one of the issues discussed was that the Internet, provided there is free access, may represent a great danger for scientific communication. There is a lesser danger for art. But if one were to show scientific results, without a strict peer review, it could be a problem, because somebody might mistake it, especially if it were very intelligently done, for scientific information. And the same may be true for poetry, when unreviewed poems get in. The Internet is a fantastic medium for sharing hard facts, but poetry, if it is good poetry, is not hard facts, and neither are nascent scientific results. I've looked at my own pages on the Internet, and they are just haphazard. Somebody prints something about me and it gets in; it doesn't depend on me or on the medium where it was printed. So my own portrait on the Internet is distorted, in a way: I don't recognize myself. It's like trying to read my own poetry in a language I don't understand.

I'd like to finish with a brief summary on your part of how the writing of poems may have changed for you over the years.

I would compare it to the labor of Sisyphus. The hard thing, really, is to push the stone up the hill. At some point, the stone starts rolling down, and that's the motion that the poet has to control, the moment when he has to apply the brakes. With my earlier poems, my stone sometimes started rolling very easily. But nowadays I recognize this moment, and I drag my feet and brake as much as possible. I am much more critical of every line, every word. In my early work part of a poem might be successful, and part, I would have to say, just didn't work because the metaphors would start rolling downhill. But now I try to think of every component of the poem many times, sometimes even to the point of destroying the poem before it is finished. In my poem "The Moravian Castle," for instance, there is the image of a ten-point stag seeking its own head in the corridors of the castle. This image is a remnant from an earlier poem which I worked on for so long I destroyed it. The image is all that I saved from the earlier poem. The present poem only has eight lines but it took me about half a year to get it to come right. And that half a year must not show in the poem, which must be all of a piece and very fluent and quick. So that's the sort of thing I've learned: to try not to write poems quickly, but to write quick poems.

HEATHER RAMSDELL

Heather Ramsdell grew up in northeastern Massachusetts. She received a BFA in sculpture at Cooper Union in 1990 and later earned her MA from City College in New York City, where she studied with Ann Lauterbach. Her first full-length collection, *Lost Wax* (University of Illinois Press, 1998), was chosen by James Tate as a winner of the National Poetry Series. She currently works as a food researcher. This interview was conducted by Katy Lederer via email in September 1999 and appeared in Volume 16, Number 3 / Volume 17, Number 1 of *Verse*.

I want to begin with something you said about irony and wit in a conversation with Ann Lauterbach, which was published in a recent issue of murmur: *"I think irony disturbs the pretext more than wit. Irony undoes the pretext. And wit leaves everything more intact and adds a layer on top of it." I would be excited to hear more about your sense of what the "pretext" is.*

Well, I think what I meant by pretext was a shared understanding of the grounds that something rests on. I think I was talking about a more general sense of pretext and not strictly something that applies to poetry. An example is an assumed relation to reality that makes it possible to have an ordinary interchange with someone in a cab. I think the poetic sense is not so different from the mundane one, but the amount of shared material is more rarified, and often more disturbed.

Interesting. One thing that seemed to relate to the idea of "pretext"—poetic, or to be more generous, artistic pretext in particular—was something else you said in the Lauterbach conversation about style. Lauterbach asks you what's left if you take away the surface and you reply, "It has something to do with making marks on the world." In the context of your work—both the section I have here from "Vague Swimmers" and your book, Lost Wax—*this called to mind something Roland Barthes says in* Writing Degree Zero: *"Whatever its sophistication, style has always something crude about it: it is a form with no clear destination, the product of a thrust, not an intention, and, as it were, a vertical and lonely dimension of thought." So to go back to the idea of an "ordinary interchange with someone in a cab," is style in itself anti-social? Solitary? Is pretext then garrulous? Or am I being too simplistic …*

I am often confounded and a little bored by the idea of "style" even though Barthes, and many other writers I respect, aren't. The word has become fused in my mind with its least fortunate incarnation as cheesy pedantic formula. I think a lot of people who are starting to write are urged to "find their own style" and it has become a mythicized thing, like "The Right Stuff" producing a lot of styley work in its wake.

I'm not sure I really want to say that style is solitary and pretext is garrulous. But I think what you are trying to do is make a framework, and establish certain tent poles for the framework. Then we'll use the structure to talk about poetry or art. This, among other things, would be the pretext. Style would be something on top of that, to use the same metaphor, not exactly the fabric of the tent, but a certain quality of the tent that someone would recognize as they are walking by. The quality would place it, in time or in place, or in relation to other tents. I don't think that style can be recognized from the place of creating in the same way as it can from the place of spectating, or of analysis.

When you are writing, is style something you are thinking about?

I guess I would have to say that style isn't something I'm normally thinking about on a conscious level when I write. In this sense, I agree with Barthes that it's the product of "a thrust" and not of an "intention."

But maybe let me take this to a more straightforward level—the level at which I'm actually, as a fellow young poet who is living and working in a similar milieu as you are, recognizing your work. While reading Lost Wax, *I get a strong sense of solitude, but this is something that I wouldn't normally want to ask in an interview, because it seems too direct or too forward. But, let's try it: I want you to talk about solitude in your work.*

Oh, okay. I'm sorry to do this, it is unintellectual, but: What I did on my summer vacation—and for the last part of it I was completely by myself, in a little room with nothing in it but a bed and a desk, with no friends and nobody who could tolerate my abysmal French. And I had little chunks of free time—one or two hours a day, in which I could write, and I still found it incredibly hard to do, even though I had nothing to blame it on. This was great. It was the closest thing to being in the vacuum I have always dreamt of. So the struggle was with a great blankness, and the responsibility of what to put there, where so often it is with obstacles that I have flung into my path to prevent that struggle. To prevent the bareness of myself deciding over and over again to write poems. I am not exactly getting to the point yet, but I will. I think when you are trying to make something that wasn't there before, which for me requires a whole apparatus of horrible questions to be going on, it is intensely personal and strange and closed. This doesn't have to do specifically with the writing it produces, but with the process of making the thing.

I love the fact that the medium we are working in is the same thing we use to have interchanges in the cab, and to ask ourselves why we are undertaking the creation of this thing that wasn't there before. It gets very slick and hard to stand far enough away from to see any of it. It keeps a comfortable amount of occlusion in there, so that there is always something more to do, and there is always something sort of wrong that feeds the next thing. This is more bio-graphical than I would like it to be.

To pick up on what you say about there always being "something wrong" that feeds the next thing, or what I would take to mean that writing is a revisionary act—revising of oneself, history, narrative, music, image, whatever ... Maybe you can talk about these: From "Service of Pointing" in Lost Wax:

> could it be known in the lab what the result would be
> enough to leave without looking
> with bags with assistance with suicidal resolve
> in reflection's stead
> the water rocking/rotting clouds
> of, clouds of
> crowds
> of
>
> crows, a field, black,
> burning with crows

and from "Vague Swimmers":

> during the first few days the bird is prone to
> dehydrate. It cannot survive without insulation the
> parent and other hatchlings provide. Its fluid
> evaporates quickly through the skin becoming in a
> short span

husk, a leaf drawn

up and over the rooftop.

The images seem to me like "answers" to some question that the poems are asking.

If we could just figure out what the question is. I find it hard to talk about my own work intelligently, and without seeming to skirt the issue. Especially work that is fixed, that there is no way to change anymore. With writing that is still in progress there is a hopeful blurriness, there is room for an ideal and a sizeable area of the unknown to examine in this thing you are producing, and talking about it becomes part of that. But this also has to do with what I wrote before about working in the medium of language. To shift the approach to a poem from an analytical mode to a creative one rests on intentionality. These approaches strike me as being binary, though I have tried to defend this hunch before, and I was not altogether satisfied with what I came up with because of the problem of the poet regarding their own work. I think many poets experience this switching back and forth as a difficulty. As one of the fundamental difficulties of writing. There is always a criteria for making one decision instead of another, but there is always the fear that if you examine these criteria too much the poem slides away. I could say, looking at these excerpts, that I notice both move by means that some surrealist work uses. They both contain references to science; the first directly, and the second in tone, as well as to natural phenomena: birds, leaves, water. And both of them are located in a puzzle scenario that is essentially unsolvable in spite of the information and facts that are at hand. I did not think any of these things, of course, when I wrote these. I suppose I always want the poem to slide away, but not too far away.

What if the poem slid too far away? Where would it go? Where would you go?

It would not be engaging on enough levels. Reading it, you would not get enough out of it. Like listening to someone whose language you don't speak. The criteria for what is engageable enough is a matter of opinion or taste, and a person's poetics would determine those criteria. To go with the idea that writing is an act of revision, the poem that has slid too far away has lost contact with the thing being revised, and fails to evidence it. But certain poetics would not consider this to be a failing of the poem.

Huh. That's funny. The notion of a poem as evidence — or even more funny — a good poem as evidence. That seems really interesting to me. The idea of a failed poem, too, is interesting. Whether or not to keep working on a poem that seems like it's failing.

In your writing process, how do you deal with this sort of thing? Do you toss poems that slip away? Do you work them? I get the feeling from some of your work that you aggregate fragments on occasion. What's your process here?

I don't necessarily mean that a good poem is evidence. It's become sort of a taboo to even claim that a poem is good. All of these terms are scary to me because they seem to threaten the place of interpretation. But I'm not using these terms in the way that someone would state a fact. What I was getting at when I was talking about a poem evidencing the revisionary act is that if the product, which in this case is a finished poem, doesn't do that, it becomes an unsatisfyingly private activity in the way that listening to someone else's dream is less rich than thinking about your own. But the process question: It changes. I edit my poems heavily, wrecking most of them along the way. They often just get too bald, or too slick, or too elliptical, and they don't interest me anymore, so I take little pieces of them and put them in other poems. Like sourdough starter. I wrote all of "Bridge Segment" using small strips of paper that covered the entire floor of the basement in Queens, where I was writing then.

I keep a journal and periodically go through it and lift parts, normally very small parts that relate to each other in some way. Then I write things inside of these parts and around them, and I take out stuff, and put it back somewhere else, feeling miserable and anxious for most of the process. Often no words are left from what I started out with. Very rarely I will write a whole blob of text that can just stay as it is, which is nice.

You must also have that experience in writing. Kierkegaard wrote in *Fear and Trembling*, about faith not poetry: "It is supposed to be the most difficult feat for a ballet dancer to leap into a specific posture in such a way that he never once strains for the posture but in the very leap assumes the posture." The relief from self-consciousness is definitely welcome. More than once non-writer friends of mine have said that poetry seems like a religion to poets.

When you finally decide that a piece is actually finished, does it please you? Is it like a sort of penance? Or just a relief?

There is relief, though finishing is not actually an event. How do you decide when something is finished? And what is it that stopped you about the idea of a poem as evidence, and a poem that fails?

I didn't really want to stop with the evidence/failure thread, but I wanted to continue very much with the notion of faith in poetry—poetry as an expression of faith, thus the idea of "penance." One thing that's struck me so far about the way you've described your process is its asceticism. It sounds very disciplined to me. The way you describe your process seems more painful than the way I would describe mine, for instance. The words it's calling to mind: evidence, penance, asceticism, success, and failure—these all strike me as belonging to a discourse of discipline.

Yeah, of discipline or of a practice that resembles religious practice in certain ways—that it is ongoing, interpretive. I think I have to be careful about sounding too floaty and immersed in a kind of soft spirituality that I can't stand, though. Because poetry isn't a religion. And art has enough of its own paradigms that we don't really need to use religious ones in order to talk about it. There can't be poetry if there is no product, though to understand anything about it you have to extend beyond the product. I guess we are talking not about poems but about making poetry and what has to go on in order to be doing that. The notion of this endeavor in relation to faith seems a richer thing to explore than poetry as a religion.

Kierkegaard's attachment to the absurd in *Fear and Trembling* is interesting to me in this context. Writing poems in a culture that poetry fits into in a very minor way, because the culture at large doesn't value poetry, poets have to figure out how to exist simultaneously with two value systems that don't overlap. Practically, what that means is a variety of conflicts and experiences of alienation. And viewed from the one value system what has to go on in order to write is clearly a sacrifice—of money, or security, or oblivion, or happiness, or leisure or other "American Dream" components—that is inexplicable according to it. But these things are not all that necessary to the endeavor of poetry and some of them are destructive to it. I think it requires a faith in something that is unknowable. This is something that concerns me a lot. What you are calling ascetic and solitary may be a kind of absurd resolution of these conflicts into something that is immovable, or irreducible, or uninterpretable.

JOHN KINSELLA

John Kinsella was born in Perth, Western Australia, in 1963, and educated at the University of Western Australia. He is founding editor of the international poetry journal *Salt* and its imprint Salt Publishing. He has published many collections of poetry, including *Peripheral Light: Selected and New Poems* (W.W. Norton, 2003) and *Poems 1980-1994* (Fremantle Arts Centre Press/Bloodaxe, 1997/1998), as well as a book of prose fiction, *Genre* (FACP, 1997), a collection of stories, *Grappling Eros* (FACP, 1998), and an autobiography, *Auto* (Salt, 2001). He edited *Landbridge: Contemporary Australian Poetry* (FACP/Arc Publications, 1999) and is co-editing *The Salt Book of Contemporary American Poetry*. He lives in Cambridge (UK), where he is a Fellow at Cambridge University; Western Australia; and Gambier, Ohio, where he is Professor of English at Kenyon College. Brian Henry conducted this interview by email between October 1997 and May 1998. The interview appeared in Volume 15, Number 3 / Volume 16, Number 1 of *Verse*.

What does it mean for you to be an Australian poet in Cambridge? How has it affected your sense of yourself as a writer and your allegiances?

I first came to Cambridge because Jeremy Prynne was here. I was in England in the early nineties reading experimental (or maybe "linguistically innovative" is more appropriate) poetry. I was quite familiar with what was going on in American innovative poetry but knew comparatively little about that side of things here. And not only English poetry, but Scots, Welsh, and Irish poetry being written in English that stepped outside the usual lyrical-I format. Or lyrical eye for that matter. Of course, the reference point as far as innovation in the U.S. went was Language poetry; I was interested to see how much influence it had had here. I discovered Prynne's work in the Poetry Library in London. I was lucky enough to come across a librarian who was interested in such things—Simon Smith, who at the time was editing a saddle-stitched journal called *Grille*. Prynne was the discovery of a lifetime for me. This was the next step in a tradition of lyrical innovation first championed by Wordsworth and Coleridge in *Lyrical Ballads*. Of course, many avant-garde commentators would be horrified to see Prynne and Wordsworth linked in such a specific way, but I believe it to be the case. Prynne is the greatest of the late Modernists, though he'd deplore such a term as "greatest." I read Prynne through and against the pastoral tradition but as a poet who has displaced meaning to an extent which leads us to question the nature of our interpretive and translating machinery. His is a unique voice and one that has led to the "Cambridge School" of linguistically innovative verse. Prynne destabilizes the contemporary canon—he has not sold his soul to the devil of market fetishization. He generally publishes with very small presses, eschews public appearances, and avoids open discourse. The work does it. It is rich, subtle, and complex. He is the only poet other than Lyn Hejinian who, to my mind, has subverted lyrical intent yet retained a "lyricism." Theory meets utterance. This is poetry about the stuff of language. So, that's why I came here.

And then I met Rod Mengham, great poet and brilliant academic, who was then and is still editing the innovative imprint Equipage. We found that our interests were similar, and a dialogue began from that point. Each year there's a festival of innovative verse in Cambridge called the CCCP, or the Cambridge Conference of Contemporary Poetry. It is put together by Mengham, Peter Riley, and Ian Patterson. I was invited to read in 1994; it went particularly well and I was invited back in 1995 to give a paper and chair a panel. Tangentially my work was being followed by others here and a position emerged at Churchill College as a By-Fellow. Through that I have been teaching in the Commonwealth Literature paper, and recently have been appointed a Fellow of Churchill.

So to get back to your question: it has affected my position only insofar as it is a realization of predetermined goals, it is constantly evolving, and is as much to do with "internationalism" as being specifically Australian. Having said that, however, I subscribe to something I've termed "international regionalism"— that is, preserving the identity of place but opening avenues of communication between different "regions." Living in Cambridge doesn't delete my Australian identity but does allow me to place it in a more "universal" context. Cambridge is an island like Australia! A conceptual space. And like Australia, it's a pretty multicultural place and has a history of multiculturalism—though Erasmus hated it (as an aside!). My allegiances have always been to place—though in my case "place" is problematic because of the occupation of another people's land. I've always seen myself as an exile within my own landscape because of this. So I am no more or less comfortable living outside Australia—the same feeling of displacement follows me. It's having an interesting effect on my poetry—landscapes overlaid on each other: the fens running into South West Australian wetlands, forests, north-eastern deserts …

Do you think this feeling of displacement is a characteristic one for Australian poets, or for expatriates in general?

Depends which "Australian" poets. I daresay indigenous poets such as Lionel Fogarty and Lisa Bellear feel dispossession to be a displacement. That the white Anglo-Australian poet should feel displacement within Australia becomes extremely ironic in this context. Also, the fact that Australia is a multicultural nation means implicitly that a vast array of displacements occur, be it in the work of a poet like Pi O or Anna Couani or others. As a whole, an Australian poetics must be conscious of shifts in the demographic base. Consequently there cannot be, nor should we necessarily desire, an idiolectical base. In my mind, Australian poetry is increasingly an assimilation of negatives rather than a homogeneous, nationalistic certainty. Pluralism and guilt undo the collective Identity. I look to the development of an Asian Australian poetic voice, or voices. Obviously displacement is relevant to any expatriate. A poet like Peter Porter who has spent much of his life in London writes consistently about Australia—both his alienation from it and the duality of his identity. Nationalists have tried to exclude Porter from the Australian poetics, which is absurd—it informs almost everything he writes. Thing is though, it's not always in a direct or prescriptive way. It avoids jingoism. Porter is an Australian who has entered the discourse of other cultures, particularly the English. This places him in a unique position to make comparative observations. I find this thrilling. Porter is a great poet because this is melded with superb technique.

So would you consider Porter an "international regionalist"? Does he preserve the identity of place, or work against such an identity because of his long experience as an expatriate?

No, I wouldn't call Porter an international regionalist, because he is more concerned with observing tropes occurring in the actual dialogue between cultural spaces and geo-political zones. There is a process of externalization going on in his work. He extracts things. In my own work, I am still very much part of my expatriate space—I am much more of Australia than of the place I now inhabit. Sure, I am consciously working out of a "new" region, but there is still much collusion with the space of origin—in fact, this is really my project. And yes, Porter's long experience as an expatriate would seem reason enough for this, though I'd argue that it is also implicit in terms of his general aesthetic—which has been shaped by his experience but also comes out of something inherent. Not that I'm arguing for a kind of biologically determined way of seeing! Of course, even external observation works as sign-posting, as a form of preservation itself. And if one undoes the codes of the poetry, the original maps are there.

Would you apply your comments about the multiculturalism of Australia, and the displacements and dispossessions involved, not only to England but to the U.S.? Native Americans are the aboriginal peoples of the U.S., and writers of Asian background have attained increased visibility within the past decade, as have Latino writers. If all these writers are working from a feeling of displacement, do you think displacement has become a fundamental condition?

The U.S. is a really interesting case study in the generative aspects of displacement. You know, it has always struck me that Spanish poetry isn't considered to be part of the canon. Charles Bernstein has written some fascinating stuff on the idiolect and American poetry. In fact, I've recently collaborated with him in a dialogue and have written an article on this for a book he is editing; I've focused on the poetry of Lionel Fogarty, the Murri poet, in my considerations of hybridity, the idiolect, and displacement. The comparisons with the English-language poetry of Native Americans and First Nation peoples in the Canadian sense are there to be made, but this is often problematic. The struggle may be similar, the effects of the colonizing voice may be similar, and any other "postcolonial" signifiers, but it in many ways is futile to draw a comparative picture, and certainly a patronizing process. The conditions are unique, as every indigenous struggle is. Indigenous peoples may well work together in their struggle for rights and "justice" but this is a cooperative interaction, not an assimilation of situations. It's an important difference to qualify.

Multiculturalism is quite different from indigenous rights. In many ways it is the assimilative flipside, and because of this it is ineffective to read the two together, or indeed against each other. They are two specifics in the geo-political and cultural cauldron. The terms of negotiation are different. This recognized, common ground can be outlined and explored, inasmuch as common ground between the parent colonizing language and the indigenous language it hijacks, bankrupts, and eliminates can only be explored when the destructive nature of the interaction is qualified. For me, the most interesting poetry being written in the "English-speaking" world is coming out of indigenous and multicultural communities—anything that undoes the binary is positive and likely to produce something "new."

At the moment I'm working on a critical book on the "Pastoral." What fascinates me is the colonizing process that goes on in the occupation of the rural space by the urban cultural way of seeing. Do we read Robert Frost because he is "of the country" or because he makes the country available to "us" (i.e., products of urban sophistry, regardless of which space we live in)? Do we read Les Murray because he is the authentic voice of the country or because he defines some "country of the mind" against the "country of the mind" we inhabit? Is his target audience really the rustics of Boeotia or the urbanites of Athens? I'd say the latter!

Isn't it striking that it's only in recent years that the "Asian" voice, despite the proximity of Australia to Asia, has been allowed as part of Australian writing. In the ambient shelter of multiculturalism fine voices have been "allowed" to appear. Writers like Beth Yahp and Adam Aitken have not only "legitimized" the Asian voice, but are conscious of the way this legitimizing process works. They are working on a meta-level—entirely necessary given the condescensions that work within the nationalistic reading process. A really interesting poetry journal that has emerged in the last few years is *Tinfish*, which is edited by Susan Schultz in Hawaii. It publishes Pacific rim nations and is experimental in temperament. *Tinfish* is a kind of interactive space for a pluralistic English that doesn't appropriate, but doesn't play the game with excessive politeness.

The Western Australian landscape figures prominently in many of your poems. Would you describe what you call the "anti-pastoral" and its relationship to both the pastoral tradition and to your own poetry? Is the "anti-" a result of the landscape or of your poetic sensibility, or both?

"Landscape" dictates my poetic. Not "nature" per se, but rather the interaction (mostly in a negative sense) between humans and nature. To grow up in an environment that is steadily being denuded and altered is destined to make you "anti" almost everything. Especially when the logic of the interaction undermines even itself—clear more land to grow more food, land turns saline and no food can be grown on it; pour tons of chemicals onto crops to increase yields, chemicals poison the people who apply them, the people who consume them, and every other living thing in the vicinity. Doesn't make sense. Nothing idyllic in that. Not much for the city folk to learn from the simple, pure, and spiritual ways of the country. Pastoral as urban moral guidance construct starts to look a little leaky. But this is the tragedy of the human condition; and I have sympathy with the seemingly inevitable road to destruction, regardless of all good intent. I have little faith in Les' good husbandry, or Virgil's neat fields, or Theocritus' "authentic" shepherds. Nothing in the country (as elsewhere) is clear cut. Landscape has always been a political concept for me—again, dispossession, occupation, etc. The movement between the spatiality of landscape and the spatiality of language began early. And I was fascinated by the "translating" of nature (the ultimate other) into poetry. It seemed to me that song was the weapon used by humans to oppress place—to mimic the "spirit" of locale, to convince itself it was in tune. I've referred to "the vocal chords of scrub"—as if it sings for us (i.e. "Settler"/invader culture) and we sing back, and then sing it to each other (or appropriate Aboriginal "song" in order to legitimize our own). The home of the lyric: the lyric as rural propaganda! One other thing—within Australia, Western Australia exists as almost a separate entity. This has to do with "isolation" (from what, whom, and on what grounds?), the politics of late convict transportation and the kind of white settlement pattern it engendered, the goldrush (different in many ways from those in the East), size, and relative wealth. The Western Australian landscape is poetically (at least for me and also I think Randolph Stow) going to be different from the conceptual "Australia" we are fed in text and coffee-table books. There's a lot of desert between WA and the East Coast. The pastoral traditions of Australian verse don't fit the rural impetus of Western Australian poetry. Perth has never been the great urban power structure that Sydney and Melbourne have been. The "pastoral" requires such centers to flourish and define the "other" against. Western Australian poetry has been more rural celebration. In terms of Australian poetry my work *is* anti-pastoral; in WA terms it is rural with an ecological and anti-racist and anti-misogynist and so on angle, or angles. Thing is, even in the city (Perth) the bush has been available—there's not the separation (in the mind at least) between the urban and rural that would make the pastoral construct entirely functional.

Do you see a relationship between colonization and genre? In your book Genre, *you use the phrase "Common ground and neutral ground being reterritorialized, edited." Juxtaposing "reterritorialized" and "edited" implies a relationship between the two, particularly in their effects upon the two types of ground you mention.*

At the moment I'm completing my new novel *Post Colonial*. It is a book in which occupied space is edited over and over again as part of an independence struggle. National identity is synonymous with an "integrity" of language. The editing of this language so it subscribes to the colonizing tongue, or dominating language, is both a physical linguistic process and a conceptual one. *Genre* is a re-territorializing of linguistic and conceptual space. It is an internalized struggle within predetermined boundaries—i.e., each specific genre. The physical process of editing might transform a specific genre into another, or even undo it completely. The mixing of these identifiable forms and their processes immediately undoes them.

Genre *is* specific—its codes are what give it its marketability. As a work, *Genre* is consciously unmarketable. Still, what is unmarketable is quickly fetishized and made "valuable" in its uniqueness. It becomes a genre-commodity in its own right. I've been told *Genre* is of the genre of *Finnegan's Wake*—strikes me as strange, as the interconnectedness of words drives *Finnegan's Wake* while the interconnectedness of context drives *Genre*. In many ways, they are opposing texts. *Finnegan's Wake* has an integrity and defies the reader to reject its wholeness. *Genre* is complete and defies the reader to not read it as such. The reader becomes involved in an editing process as soon as s/he runs with it—there is a subconscious effort to dot the Is and cross the Ts—to make sense of it because there are elements of stories that "should" add up. It's what the eye expects. The body of text is about space. It is potentially a neutral space upon which we impose our own reading—and every reading is valid—but the text *is* manipulating the reader—the interconnectedness of territories, the fluidity of boundaries is working against a freedom of interpretation. The reader is reterritorializing almost without knowing it—it is familiar territory. The reader has always been there before. The book works with deception and artifice. Like editing. Who really wrote "that" book—editor or author? And author as editor? *Genre* integrates text from numerous sources. It doesn't recognize the agency of the author as "in the mix"; authorial integrity has been subverted. Edited. Reterritorialized. You've read this before. On a bus. At an airport. On an island in the Indian Ocean where they speak English and Cocos-Malay. Of course, there's a specific answer on a post-colonial level to your question. Colonization obviously produces genre—e.g. the Orientalist text, the convict text, the frontier text, etc.

You allude to the potentially (and actually) harmful effects of editing, especially how it relates to genre and space. I'm interested in the relationship between the presentation of your magazine Salt—*as an "international poetry journal"—and how you perceive your role as editor, particularly in conjunction with this edited/ reterritorialized dynamic. Do you consciously try to avoid a reterritorialization of space, text, genre in your work with* Salt? *Does this dynamic influence the outlook of the magazine?*

Salt is a field of potentials — in presentation, in meaning, culturally and so on. There are the individual texts and there is the collective whole. Each poem may be read singularly, of course, but it also can (and in reality will) be read against other work. Taking it as a whole we might assume some kind of cultural/social/political comment is being made. The editorial policy of *Salt* is eclectic — as long as a poem achieves what it sets out to do in its own terms it will find a place in *Salt* (space permitting — though we have a lot of it!). However, the way the magazine is collated is all-important to this overall impression. What I am seeking to do as editor is to create an interactive space — a gallery — in which text defines itself within a larger context. Experimental, or linguistically innovative, work plays against "traditional" pieces and so on. The editor becomes curator — even if an individual piece is finished it becomes something organic and without closure in the greater context of the book. Herein lie my difficulties with conflating cyberspace with the book, the codex, the page. And herein lies my general aesthetic.

In Genre *you write: " … with poetry, beyond inspiration and the intent to convey a stimulation, define a territory (whether for occupation or abandonment), all else is decoration. Of course, we in this capitalist-with-a-guilty-conscience society know that decoration, even beyond the implications of the word itself, is unnecessary … Decoration, in a sense, is all that which makes us human. Idealism is in fact decoration. It represents comfort. It does not harm. It may adorn the instruments of torture, but does not make them … Learning is decoration. Poems about themselves are supreme forms of decoration." Given the polyphonic texture of the book, I don't assume that every comment in* Genre *is your own, but how would the idea of the poem not as a completed thought but as a representation of the mind thinking compare with this notion of poem as decoration?*

You're right in not assimilating "ideas" in *Genre* with the author. How many authors constitute *Genre* after all? But, in this case, I do agree with the narrative voice. The point is, any utility in which profit is the motive — to gain something other than the fundamentals of survival — is decoration. And no, I don't buy the one, if you'll excuse the impoverished pun, about poetry being as necessary as food and water and other such pseudo-romantic rubbish. It is a device and it has a political, cultural, and personal agency. It is a decoration that expects a reaction. The process of writing has intent. Now, that doesn't mean that the poetic idea is decoration or, indeed, has intent. It may be fresh, spontaneous, and vital—it may have its own purpose and direction. Who is to say? But it's the process of transference that fetishizes it. The so-called spontaneous poem is the biggest con in history (I use the word not as cliché but selectively). Breton and his cronies had the best advertising-propaganda campaign of the twentieth century, for that's what the Surrealists were—a bunch of self-appointed advertising gurus riding on the coattails of Freud.

Much of your poetry seems "committed," in the sense that Adorno describes in his essay "Commitment," in which he writes, "The committed work of art debunks the work that wants nothing but to exist; it considers it a fetish, the idle pastime of those who would be happy to sleep through the deluge that threatens us ..." How does Adorno's view relate to your notion of the poem as "decoration that expects a reaction"?

Committed art is not prescriptive. The artist is not necessarily looking for a specific social, political, or cultural end result. Adorno says, "Instead, it works towards an attitude ..." There is an attitude I am implying exists, that my work might lend itself to, and that as author I am by definition complicit in, in the subjective sense. But only in the language of the "human" as, say, in Beckett (Adorno: "Beckett's *ecce homo* is what has become of human beings. They look mutely out from his sentences as though with eyes whose tears have dried up ..."); is this the non-dialectic, not historicized and commodified moment in time? Is this possible? If we look to the "pure" avant-garde, we'll find the decorative motif in different guises, replicating itself where the space is seemingly occupied by anti-meaning. The poet, no matter how innovative, has to recognize this.

The poet must question the relevance of "speaking"; Adorno quotes Pascal, "On ne doit plus dormir." The process of art rendering horror readable, absorbable, is simultaneously deplorable and inevitable, I feel. The offense to the victims is instrinsic to such art. The poet, through confronting the horror of language that allows (and thus indicates a priori knowledge of) the representation of horror, is recognizing the loss of voice of the victims. Narrative poetry with horror as its subject subscribes to the worst aspects of commitment. It necessarily becomes fetishized and commodified in itself. In my poem "The Benefaction" the tension between narrative and the voice/s of the victim/s becomes the displaced "lyrical I." This is where autonomous and committed art "meet." It doesn't necessarily mean the two can be hybridized, but the nature of capitalism is such that each is invested with the same potential for value in the marketplace.

"The Benefaction" is a poem moving through this conceptual space. Adorno's recognition of the colonization by "meaning" of autonomous art, the resulting "cultural twaddle," the unavailability of immunity in the non-committed, is the key to understanding my position here. "The Benefaction" is as much about the representation of intrusion, dispossession, and ultimately genocide, as it is about the process. The historical acceptance of responsibility (and its deplorable and disingenuous manifestation as "guilt"), the creation of a space for a literature of the oppressed, the rereading of "history," and so on, inform language usage in the poem. It is written in fourteen-line sections: the sonnet reaches down and controls the presentation of political and social concerns—its structure is indicative of its, and art's, failure in general in the expression of horror. Adorno says: "When even genocide becomes cultural property in committed literature, it becomes easier to continue complying with the culture that gave rise to the murder." The question becomes whether to remain silent or to commit and be appropriated. I have chosen to follow the path of engagement but with a poetry that incorporates a dialogue with the machinery of the colonizing culture. This is to do with "text," not "meaning."

In my poetry I isolate the decorative—I feel there's a kind of honesty in the "repetitive formulaic play" that allows me to explore its terms of reference in an apparently disconnected kind of way. But such exploration always reveals the potency of the decorative—it is a core language which backdrops the drama we accept as committed, and frames the autonomous construct that allows, as Adorno conveys, a story such as: "When an occupying German officer visited him in his studio and asked, standing before the 'Guernica,' 'Did you make that?,' Picasso is said to have responded, 'No, you did.' " It would be problematic not to add Adorno's comment: "Even autonomous works of art like the 'Guernica' are determinate negations of empirical reality; they destroy what destroys, what merely exists and as mere existence recapitulates the guilt endlessly." So, I guess, "The Benefaction" engages with issues of commitment and autonomy in the language of Adorno though rejects what in essence becomes a binary opposition (though he accepts coersion, movement, and corruption, the definitions remain intact). Decoration is the key—and exploring the different codes of identification inherent in speech and inherent in writing is always evident in my poetry, especially when the "colloquial" voice is being used. Because speech *cannot* be reproduced in text, text will always be decorative. There's no getting away from this. So I agree with Adorno only in part.

How do you generally view narrative, then? Do you see it as a viable strategy in

poetry today? Many of your poems employ some sort of narrative line while oth-
ers unsettle it or seem to discard it altogether. And Genre *repeatedly questions*
not only the efficacy, or adequacy, of narrative, but the possibility of narrative
to convey meaning or, in fact, a narrative. In a December 1997 article in The
Australian, *McKenzie Wark writes that* Genre *"has something of the flavor of the*
reading experience in the age of email." We don't think of email as a continuous
text, like a conventional novel or story or narrative poem.

Narrative is a device, an artifice, not a reality. It is the arrangement of events, or
possible events, into an interpretable pattern. Character is narrative's foil—by
creating verisimilitude it seeks to convince us either that this is the way things
are or might be, or that we share experience with that conveyed by the text.
Even in deconstructive narratives we are working within this particular binary.
I don't recognize the validity of narrative processes. They are a construct that
has more to do with social/cultural/political control than with the legitimacy
of "representation" or "observation." Narrative for me becomes a framework
upon which one can hang ethical and aesthetic debate. As it works towards
resolution it increases the value of its own decorative process. I use narrative in
poems and prose to show how disingenuous the author can be. For the author,
it *is*. And the reader it is. And all in between is contrivance. And both author
and reader are constructs of environment and inheritance. And this leaves us
going in circles. Exactly.

In my obviously narrative poems—those poems that have a "plot" and use
a "persona" to convey the story—the reader is likely to ask: why is the poet
telling me this? My narratives are fraught with ambiguity—and this is why.
They don't resolve themselves even if the story seems to have closure and
the poem concludes with a nice moral conclusion. The reader is always left
uncomfortable and dissatisfied. I learnt about the deceptions of narrative
technique from Frost.

What about Les Murray? How do you view his earlier poems, many of which
operate largely by narrative? Does narrative forward his sociopolitical and ethical
values? Murray's recent poems seem more lyric than narrative, more circular in
their logic. Do you think there has been a shift, however gradual, in his work?

Murray's prime concern is the morality of language as a thing in itself—I mean
language as a gift from God. Language as doing God's work. The responsibility
of the poet. And so on. His linguistic skills have been employed to create a

spiritual aesthetic; at least this is what he's attempting to convey to his readers. The poetic voice presents itself as authentic, legitimate, and paternal. As he's grown more skilled with his language usage, he's been able to dispense, when he's chosen to, with narrative structures which are, on the whole, vehicles for moral intent. His narratives have always only been "partial," however (fascinating early poem in this context is "Evening Alone at Bunyah"). What he retains from his narrative origins (bush ballads, etc) is the need for closure, or a full turning of the wheel. It will be interesting to see how the narrative voice works in his new verse novel *Fredy Neptune* and whether the narrative leads to a flattening of the usually heightened register of poetic language, a more prosaic effect. Murray's "Bunyah" is more of the mind than place — it is a pastoral construct that has become increasingly Georgic in its lesson-making. A guide to a moral life!

Which Australian poets do you feel your work has the most affinities with?

Historically? Well, Christopher Brennan, Kenneth Slessor, Judith Wright, Gwen Harwood, Michael Dransfield, and Randolph Stow. And of course the late John Forbes. Some have said they believed I had a strong link with the work of Francis Webb but this is only an external thing — our deployment of language is entirely different. So there's a kind of interest, if not influence, but there's no real affinity. In terms of poets writing now: Robert Adamson, Dorothy Hewett, Murray, and John Tranter. Other poets have had "peripheral" influences — people such as Vivian Smith (in terms of control), Vincent Buckley, Rosemary Dobson, and Chris Wallace-Crabbe have been there in a variety of ways. Fay Zwicky's wonderful long poem "Kaddish" had a profound effect on me when I first read it. Gig Ryan and my partner Tracy Ryan are poets I deeply respect and with whom I feel strong socio-cultural and political affinities and affiliations. I also find them interesting in their respective working methodologies and processes. In terms of experimentation, other than Tranter, most of my affinities are with poets outside Australia.

Could you name some of those and describe their importance to you?

Well, it's a wide-ranging "net." Aside from Prynne and Mengham, Drew Milne is another innovative poet based in Cambridge I feel an affinity with. Ian Hamilton Finlay is a visual-text "poet" with a rich and seemingly infinite oeuvre. Lyn Hejinian was one of my earliest "Language" influences, along with Charles Bernstein. John Ashbery consistently astonishes me. Susan Howe and

Barbara Guest fascinate me though are not entirely unproblematic, which, of course, can be quite invigorating. The Canadian poet Lisa Robertson's book *Debbie: an epic* is really impressive and I feel a distinct affinity with her radical pastoral project. Pierre Alferi, Urs Jaeggi, Anne Marie Albiach are just some of the dozens of European poets who interest me. Each undoes the centrality of language and ignites the possibility of "the word," of displaced syntax, or a grammar of the poetic. Each undoes the "lyrical I." Closer to home I think Michele Leggott in New Zealand is well worth reading.

Do you think the tendency to categorize poets, to lump them into schools or camps, is waning? You've written about the uselessness of grouping certain Australian poets that way, and I wonder if the younger generation's refusal to be categorized has had a larger impact.

Unfortunately, it's a tendency that will probably never fade entirely. People define themselves by working against what is already present. Not a little of the Oedipal thing here! What is refreshing is that the present "younger generation" has been caught up in the spirit of flexibility and investigation that comes with new media such as cyberspace and other technologically innovative territories. Of course, this generation will probably "grow" into division. Categories have always seemed to me things of political convenience—and are about imitation and even mimicry. And binary divisions such as that which formed in Australian poetry (between the formalists/traditionalists of the so-called Murray-Gray-Lehmann camp and the "Generation of '68" with Tranter, Forbes, and Adamson) are largely about the exclusion of other groups, such as feminist poetry, indigenous verse, etc.

Do you consider yourself a postlanguage poet?

Yes, I consider myself a hypermodernist, which is basically the same thing. I had a notion that I wanted to move between forms, that I wanted to write against genre, against style, against definition, to employ decoration as an alternative matrix of signifiers, long before I'd heard of Language poetry, or indeed anything beyond structuralism. In an environment of dispossession and occupation, hybridity is a knee-jerk reaction. To invert the hybridizing process and use it against itself seemed the only option. This might happen by social interpolation (putting oneself in the place of the dispossessed—expanding and extending the terms of reference) or by rejecting participation in the primary language—e.g., by subverting text. I would later become fascinated by the "opacity" of poetry (not in the New Critical sense but opacity as the rationality behind construct and the semantics of presentation) that allowed the author to convince him or herself that he or she (primarily "he") had control of a reader's response (and the "better" the author the better the control!) to a specific observation, or, if you like, set of data. Increasingly I've realized that the author has no more control than the reader wishes to apportion him or her. Interestingly, creative writing classes purport to teach the author how to control the presentation of subject matter but I feel more time should be spent on how a text might be read—i.e. not how to say it but how it might be read. But I've never had much faith in the teaching of writing.

How do you perceive the relationship between your critical work and your poetry? Although you have blended the two modes before, you don't make that strategy your primary focus, as language poets have done.

No, I don't systematically blend the two modes but I do find the question of separation and isolation problematic. Theory is a spatial zone for me. I move through it as I move through a physical landscape. I map it, not the terrain—those things in the terrain that might be threatening or useful, and those things that act as decoration and seemingly serve no purpose. Sometimes these are the aspects of such a landscape that prove most interesting. They have no agency outside themselves and resist the anthropomorphics that skulk in any expedition through such conceptual zones. Quiddity as an owl or a Norfolk pine tree! Mmmm. In a sense, however, all poetry is an engagement with theory. Problem comes with poets trying to convince the reader that they are saying something that works as theory and still functions as the "lyrical I" poem by making commentaries on what their poems are attempting to do, or perform, or say. Hopkins tried to convince himself that he knew what he was doing, but the poems will outlive the theoretical add-ons because they have created their own space. They don't need explaining—the theory is internalized. Makes for good poetry I think!

Is criticism a necrophiliac act? Is it so only if the lyric is dead?

Yes, this is often the case. But the lyric isn't dead—rumors of its death have been greatly exaggerated! It's just that we're recognizing that it's a political construct. Criticism can only move in the direction of dialogue. To engage with material you have to recognize its terms of reference and then work with or against it. The relevance of "external" observation is passing. The reader is winning out. And the reader has become the author. The costs of publishing are down, the internet has opened our eyes to thousands of new poets. Whether they are "good" or "bad" isn't recognized by the browsing machines, though I dare say this will come. But the expansiveness of the medium and the glut of choice will undermine such efforts at control and exclusion. The controls over what is considered good and why are breaking down, have been breaking down with every gain "democracy" makes. The critical faculty is being morphed into questions of reception. Poetry has always been about delaying the death of the ego. And if critics are failed poets, then the unholy alliance between the two is bound to come up with something interesting. So much for genre.

Your work seems to be becoming increasingly multilingual. What attracts you to introducing French, German, Italian, and Latin into your writing?

Well, I'm interested in the way language works across the board—it seems logical that I'd want to examine the structures and specifically the poetics of languages other than English (and specifically Australian English), my standard or primary tongue. And what's especially interesting to me about English is how it readily absorbs other languages and adopts them to its own ends. In this way there's a built-in resistance to colonization and extinction. This is what has made it such a dangerous language— how it easily "occupies" and "consumes" other languages. In a sense, I try to reverse the hybridizing process and reinvest English with the standard words from languages it has appropriated (and has to, in order to exist).

I'm surrounded by language—Tracy is translating French poetry consistently, and also has German, Italian, and bits and pieces of other languages as well. We share an interest in the workings of language generally. Many of my friends and collaborators have English as a second language—our interaction often happens (creatively that is) in a hermetic language we evolve to express the untranslatable. Poetry has always been about a dynamic equivalence re subject and object, between perception, speech, and text, so it follows that "translation" might be an embodiment of these issues.

Visual art seems to have affected your poetry. What about music?

Well, I come from a very musical family—my mother even put herself through university by teaching piano when I was a very small child—so it's always there. I don't think you can write poetry without some kind of musical consciousness. But in my musical tastes as in my visual arts and poetic tastes I'm eclectic. I'll listen to Einstuerzende Neubauten, Beethoven, Suzanne Vega, jazz, Ministry, and innovative "new" classical pieces all in one sitting. Jeremy Thurlowe, a music Fellow at Churchill, my Cambridge college, has been setting some of my poems to music and arranging them for voices. He recently won a New Music Award for his setting of "Black Suns" for contralto and organ. At the moment he's working on a selection from *Syzygy* and will shortly compose the score for the Cambridge production of my verse play "Crop Circles." Music occurs and appears in a variety of ways in my work. It's there as a specific theoretical language, but also structurally. The ecological structure I am increasingly using relies entirely on "song," and counterpoint is at the core of experimental works like *Syzygy* and "Skeleton weed/generative grammar." Early reviews of *Syzygy* described it as "improvised jazz," and in some ways there's a consciousness of this present through all my innovative work. The gap between language and music is an artificial one. Music, art, language—they can be all one and the same for me.

What in your life accounts for your prolificacy in the 1990s? You published three collections, one of them quite short, in the 1980s, but in this decade you already have published more than ten books. You must not sleep!

My decision not to publish for a sizeable chunk of the '80s was political. I was convinced that publication, in any forum, was just a process of commodification. I didn't want to participate in the market processes, if you like. What's interesting is that I'd always wanted to start a literary journal. In the early '80s I'd talked to David Brooks about the possibility, and was set to go with a mag called *Canti*. It fell by the wayside due to financial problems and this experience probably added to my skepticism. I actually went through a period of burning checks that were still filtering in from poems I'd published before my decision to become "silent." Of course, during this time, I was still writing furiously. It's always been something I've had to do. It started incredibly young, and it's at the core of most things I do. Anyway, for a variety of reasons I returned to publishing. There's an unusual story (true) about my mother submitting a manuscript to a publisher and their accepting it and me eventually coming around to the idea that it would be a good thing to do. That book was *Night Parrots*, and it was accepted in 1987 and came out in 1989. It was primarily written during that "silent" period. In 1990 I successfully started *Salt* magazine and have been involved in publishing in a variety of ways since then. Part of the resolution of my publishing crisis came through publishing other people's work. It helped me deal with placing my own work in the public arena. So the 1990s haven't necessarily been more prolific for me, but rather have been a time when I've been comfortable with the publishing process. And sleep? A couple of hours a night! Or so they say …

You seem to be uncommonly autobiographical in "On Entering Your Thirty-First Year," in which you write "the question is what to do (with) / this excess energy that seems to be / the signature—de rigueur—of the Age" and "as long as the lines keep writing themselves— / which they don't—you won't need pay // for therapy or attend glum AA meetings." Have energy and poetry—"the saturation of your art"—somehow saved you from something, a life that's "a catastrophe just waiting to happen" perhaps?

I've always been skeptical about "autobiographical" poetry. And poetry for me is largely a construct. Such a reading of a poem often says more about the reader's "autobiography" than it does about the writer's. That's not to say that those who know me well wouldn't be tempted to laugh on reading this—on my thirtieth birthday I may well have fitted the persona of this poem! It's largely having a go at myself. It's a poem that undoes the "seriousness" of the vocation. It was composed in a world in which "God" was out of reach, or maybe entirely hidden (via and a la Beckett … ?). And on a literal level it's having a go at the idea that a birthday is a time when we might be "legitimately" self-indulgent, our one day of the year and so on. The poem might be read through the models it consciously plays with and against, including those by Australian poets such as Porter and Tranter.

I suppose it's true that poetry has "saved" me in that it has focused a fairly obsessional personality. I tend not to do things by halves.

KATE FAGAN

Kate Fagan is a writer, editor, and musician. Her books of poetry include *The Long Moment* (Salt, 2002) and the chapbooks *return to a new physics* (Vagabond, 2000) and *Thought's Kilometre* (Tolling Elves, 2003), and her work appears in the anthology *Calyx: 30 Contemporary Australian Poets* (Paper Bark, 2000) edited by Michael Brennan and Peter Minter. Fagan is the editor of *How2*, an on-line journal of innovative contemporary and modernist writing and scholarship. She was born in 1973 and now lives in Newtown in Sydney's inner west. In 2002 she completed a doctoral thesis at the University of Sydney on Lyn Hejinian. This interview was conducted over email by Andrew Zawacki between May and July 2004.

Which arrives on the scene first in your poems, the eye or the ear? Do they compete with one another, or are they mutually supportive? One can't help but notice the phenomenological angles to your writing, but you're just as obviously attuned to the beautiful phrase, "erratic" music.

Almost every line of *The Long Moment* can be sourced to material phenomena. The book is a study of occurrence and poetic language, and an irresistible but unsteady compact between perception and description. As you say, my poems often explore ways that phenomenological encounters and (perceivable) states of objectivity might alter our sense of subjectivity and encourage us to adjust borders we have established for defining human consciousness. However we choose to interpret lyricism and its relation to our different senses, object-apprehension remains a base element of lyrical poetry—as do images themselves, as one scene of transaction between languages of description and objects of perception. Apprehension is probably a useful term to apply to my writing for several reasons. It suggests facing the material world, perhaps with a desire to encapsulate something of that in our expressions of experience. But it also implies uncertainty about what we are seeing and doubt about our capacity to contain things. To me this is not necessarily troubling. I feel comfortable with the idea that being in the world is both phenomenal *and* inexplicable in some way. This has not led me to seek transcendental answers, but rather helps attune my eye to an ethics of materiality.

I wouldn't exclude "the beautiful phrase" from phenomenological thinking. Although contemporary Western culture is led by sight, and visual elements play a dominant role in our construction of historical narratives, sound and touch are equally significant means of phenomenal apprehension. To some extent, text-based poetic cultures have come to depend for transmission on visual senses—the poem as read from the page, often in relative silence—and this reflects changes in poetry's technologies of circulation and social function. However, thinking about poetry in terms of composition can move us closer to dialogues between "eye and ear." I imagine perceptual and sonic elements of my poems might arrive haphazardly to different eyes and ears. Your reading of mutual support is probably closest to what happens during composition. On one hand, my writing is driven by images, and I mean this in a qualified way: my poems don't prioritize finessing the image as a point of arrival, so when I talk about images, I am speaking more about an inevitable aggregation-effect of description. On the other hand, when I am making the mental associations that literally produce specific arrangements of language in a poem—or simply balancing a line—the linkages are likely to be driven somehow by internal sonic patterning, even at the level of syllable or morpheme. Perhaps the "erratic music" you identify is made by a constant segue from eye to ear and back again. Or perhaps this movement of sense is about reciprocal presencing: at any moment within a poem, neither visual nor musical elements predominate.

Much of The Long Moment *is, architecturally, serial. Several of your sequences are organized within others, while your series tend at the same time to be quite formally different from each other. "Calendar" is nine prose poems, "return to a new physics" is 35 lyrics in relatively short stanzas, "Lighthouse series" is ten poems of exactly five tercets each, "Ecologue" is in eight sections of three quatrains apiece, the closing sequence "The waste of tongues" is seventeen ten-line poems, and so on. What is the drive behind writing in series, as opposed to writing in relatively discrete poems? And is the formal variety that you pursue across sequences meant to provide a sort of counterword, antiphon, or antidote to the interior consistency of a given series?*

One response could begin with the book's title. Uppermost in my thinking was a spatialized temporality, in which time and its movement are understood through the arrangement (and description) of events as they inhabit space, often in chancily patterned ways. A person exists in many time frames at once, which is only to say one series of occurrences can break off and resume on the far side of others, moving a person's consciousness *between* or *among* interrelated moments of being. Certain spatial cues involve us in states of temporal density that feel like "returns"—a powerful sense of location *déjà vu*, as though a whole timeframe or place has simply resumed. We often comprehend time in terms of comparative material duration, or the happenstance of things and events. Linear time is of course a very limited construct. These ideas provide some coordinates for the book's repeated exploration of serial forms.

We could also connect "the long moment" to a span of artistic attention. During the two years of writing *The Long Moment* I was working through an explicit set of material refrains, and wanted formal vehicles for extended meditative thinking. I was wondering how to produce ideas *as* actual poems, and seriality seemed to meet my desire. What began in "return to a new physics" as an exercise in perception and line became an exciting method for making more poems while creating rich meanings. The book became a series of series, or an elongated and momentary study of that poetic design and its infinite changes. You're right that interior consistency is broken across sequences by different exterior and formal provisions. This is partly due to diverse pressures materials themselves exerted on my choice to interact with, arrange, and write about them. Even though "Calendar" and "physics" both employ seriality, for example, their lineation alone suggests different requisites for dealing with divergent subjects and objects.

I don't think discrete qualities of single poems are absent from serial writing. Poems in series communicate in many permutations. But equally, the singular characteristics of each poem in a series become subject to intense scrutiny. Do elements work on their own objective terms or depend on relation for meaning? What is happening in spaces beyond imagined horizontal and vertical scales? These are old ideas—perhaps my early long poems are overly invested in them—and serial forms are just one way of staging dynamics of part and whole. There are mathematical differences between elements arranged in sequence or in series, and I like the chance kinship suggested by discrete seriality. Seriality also admits narrative in curious ways. I mean narrative in the sense of my earlier comments on duration, and mobile links between things that emphasize their spatial being. Serial poems do not pretend finitude. Their apparently arbitrary logic suggests that many more utterances could have emerged from that space, in that time, or in response to those human and earthly conditions.

There are at least three more reasons why I am attracted to serial forms. Their potentially prolific nature is a safety net against the possibility of never writing another poem—though the moment they start acting to constrain rather than provoke, they do a disservice to poetry. They encourage lengthy speculations upon worldly relations, and I am seduced at times by such perseverance for philosophical and spiritual reasons. They can also be extremely elegant.

The book's opening "Calendar" runs from April through December—what happened to the first three months of the year?

Events created the gap and I liked the resulting formal puzzle. I was writing about a particular set of circumstances that began in April. The whole poem was composed in one day the next December and given as an end-of-year gift, stitched together as a handmade book. So that's the short answer.

But less random elements were also involved, regarding a poetics of the piece. I had been playing with improvisatory effects of juxtaposing discrete ideas as sentences, influenced by some key directions of U.S. innovation in the late 1970s, and more recent work by Rosmarie Waldrop and Clark Coolidge. Unremarkably, the poem has many formal antecedents. I'm sure many writers have experienced a desire to react to a sheer mass of detail, knowing they are limited by temporal and spatial qualities of descriptive media, including pages, and with a precious and partly narcissistic sense of keeping history. Writing most of a year in a day is the structuring device that gives "Calendar" its tension and purpose. Such an impossible task is bound to produce an incomplete work that might have emerged differently through another lens of memory. Why are inventories destined to be inventions, actively fabricating while moving away from things they try to organize? What constitutes our cognizance of being, in perception and word? "Calendar" comments on these generic formal equations, knowing the unfeasibility of reconciling them.

By "missing" three months, "Calendar" avoids superimposing a neat resolution upon the problem of description. It formally imposes something else—a hiatus—which in turn lets other things proliferate: the vastness of worldly surrounds, and new contexts that prevent experiences from repeating, to echo Gertrude Stein. I was reading Lyn Hejinian closely during that year and think her "Rejection of Closure" makes a terrific argument for the artifice of both closure and open-ended forms: "[T]he work gives the impression that it begins and ends arbitrarily and not because there is a necessary point of origin or terminus, a first or last moment. The implication (correct) is that the words and the ideas … continue beyond the work." The absence of three months in "Calendar" is a *sotto voce* reminder that poetry's work is inconclusive, as is the world and our knowledge of it.

Your "Anti-landscape" sequence shares affinities with John Kinsella's "anti-pastoral" poems. What is the nature of this "anti-" impulse?

When I began writing and named the "Anti-landscape" series, I had not yet encountered John Kinsella's counter-pastoral work in any direct way. The concept may have lodged in my subconscious eye or ear, as you write. Poets are *samplers* in all senses of the word. *Exemplars*, where the word means "a parallel instance," and exemplifiers of historical minutiae—samplers of riffs from cultural discourse and samplers of each other's thinking. I am reminded, too, of samplers as stitched artifacts—those highly wrought, kitschy, framed aphorisms that constantly undercut their own plausibility and domestic environment.

I was reading and listening to *Kangaroo Virus* when composing the last of the anti-landscape works, "Ecologue." That poem or sequence of tides is a considered transposition of Kinsella's original series into and through an entirely different terrain. *Kangaroo Virus* is ambitious and intriguing in its ethical scope. It requests, perhaps covertly, that it be transmitted in some way *between* bodies and habitats in order to effect its ecological and political wager. It also demands, somewhat pathogenically (and I mean this in the sense of causing generative dis-ease), to be rewritten or *un*written. I find these ideas particularly apt when addressing the environment that situates "Ecologue" and all the anti-landscape poems. They are written about a single stretch of coastal beach below Sugarloaf Point Lighthouse, north of Myall Lakes in New South Wales. At the time I was also reading George Oppen's *The Materials*, which begins with an eclogue: "Pinpointing in the uproar / Of the living room // An assault / On the quiet continent."

There are important reasons why, in context of Australia's ongoing history of colonization, "landscape" can never be a neutral moniker or genre. Whether poetic or plastic, Australian landscape art is charged with the violently normalized absence of Indigenous peoples whom such "scapes" have erased from "land"—via claim and representation in and as *landscape*. As a non-Indigenous Australian poet I was dealing explicitly in "Anti-landscape" with this dilemma. How to write about and into a space embedded within colonization narratives, such as the entire "assaulted" Australian continent? What is the purpose of throwing more language at a place or living system when language has been a primary tool in robbing that place from and of its traditional owners? Stepping toward these questions requires a conscious admission of stories underlying even the most seemingly transparent utterances in colonized habitats. Lighthouses are fascinating scenes of mechanical evolution. Their glass magnifiers were sometimes ground below the earth to minimize flaws produced by atmospheric vibrations, and I find this physically awesome. Lighthouses have undoubtedly saved many lives at sea, but simultaneously, they are blazing signals of impossibility and illuminate the exact hazard of maritime navigation in an Australian context—i.e., vessels in the wrong place, or actively *out of place*. Many lighthouses are built close to middens, Indigenous shell-mounds marking significant and ceremonial sites of gathering. Describing these "landscapes" is a complex event that requires some basic and respectful acknowledgment, including the paradox of description itself as an experiential and constructive medium of encounter with habitats and their deeper histories.

Much later I learned of a work entitled "Seamless Antilandscape" by Leslie Scalapino. Her "seamless" points to an important part of your question. The hyphen in anti-landscape is a sign of dilemma. It literally keeps *anti* from *landscape*, thus anxiously rehearsing a separation it seeks to effect. My poems are *against landscape* in the sense of resisting ways landscape might be used to advance cultural repression. However, as Henri Bergson suggests in *Matter and Memory*, the hyphen is ineluctably a term of connection and linkage. It joins as it separates: "[it] is then the place of passage of the movements received and thrown back, a hyphen, a connecting link between the things which act upon me and the things upon which I act." As we write "against" landscape, we lean on it and are implicated by proximity. My "Anti-landscape" tries to unwrite itself across a sequence of poems that inhabit a similar perceptual and geographical site, while repeatedly questioning their own reason for existing. Ultimately, though, the poems realize what they resist by piling more words into the space and constituting another kind of landscape, albeit with careful intention and attention.

The Long Moment *is pervaded by a constant sense that the world is something fragile, too often taken for granted, and that other people are equally susceptible or vulnerable to damage, colonization, carelessness. Can you say something about the ethical impulse in your work? A deep concern for otherness, whether it's human alterity or the strange exterior of geography, informs a great deal of what you do.*

I think strangeness is a great starting point for an ethical poetics. *Strangeness* as a means of recognizing ways in which fear of difference is used daily to condition and compulsively "familiarize" our environments, thereby deeply limiting them; *strangeness* as a trope for facing the particular qualities of other people and places we encounter; and especially, *strangeness* as a method for seeing ourselves as others to other people, even while we assume the centrality of our own experience in organizing our knowledges of being. To follow my previous answer, it is undeniable that estrangement and displacement are formative to many Australian cultural experiences. It would feel ethically remiss to ignore those weathers, and the extent to which non-indigenous Australian cultures (including poetries) have been founded on attempts to familiarize and contain what seems utterly foreign. Our current political administration resolutely encourages this kind of severe domestication. In context of *The Long Moment*, I would again cite Lyn Hejinian as a useful source of thinking around the poetical task of estrangement. Her translation with Elena Balashova of Arkadii Dragomoschenko's *Xenia* is, in some ways, an exemplary act of self-estrangement as an address to cultural difference.

One extra thought: I hope my work doesn't imply something protective or patronizing in relation to "other people's vulnerability to carelessness." Nothing could be further from my intentions, and I am uncomfortable with the self-righteousness potentially invoked by that idea. To me, existence is founded on contradiction—in the constancies of change, for example, or people's everyday optimisms when facing the necessities of death. Without embracing inconsistency, ethical thinking would be virtually impossible. I am interested in my own capacities for change, and recognize damage and inconstancy with a kind of tenderness for human being—and I am almost entirely disinterested in an ethos of protectionism as it relates to other people's decisions. This is not founded in a "free will" philosophy, but rather tries to meet otherness in a spirit of respectful, non-authoritarian engagement.

There are hints of eroticism in The Long Moment. *What is the role of the body in your poems—or the role of bodies, plural?*

It is impossible not to give bodies starring roles in art of all kinds. I have always been compelled by the certainty and passionate unpredictability of links between bodies and language. I am also quietly stunned by gesture, and states of embodiment that seem utterly to exceed language or description. There is something exceptional and unwriteable about bodies, and that is part of our habitual want to place and displace them. But like anything material, bodies are everyday scripts. They are part of the ordinary substance from which poems are made, even while formed in writing.

"Bodies" in my work can manifest experiences that ground us on another side of language, or carry us through language and imprint our use of it, even as they find necessary limit (and articulation) in word. Or they touch on sensory scales and moments of feeling presence: "sharpening the tongue," "nothing incorporeal," "breathing through your throat," "disharmonic with sound." Bodies are electric sites of implication, difference, and power. They give and gain meaning in expression, sex, culture, contestation, viscerality, play. Desire—a kind of mobile longing to arrest the skin of mortality, in feeling, through identification with circumstance—is a state in which I live my entire relationship to life. There is desire in every poetic utterance I make. Desire to encounter the world, to experience, to feel engaged with and by and toward others, with other materials and beings and ideas. To me ideas *are* a state of desiring. Perhaps writing never exceeds desire, though it often excites it. Eroticism is different even as it shares terrain with desire; and while desire in my poems is often directed erotically, eros is not its only intention. Eroticism is a very important part of my experience in and through writing and being.

As a performing musician I have an immensely physical and hypersonic relationship to my poems when I read them aloud. This experience is embodied, desiring, sometimes erotic—and those corporeal charges also provide a pulse for my writing practice, regardless of any audience I might imagine for a work. Curiously, my sense of "audience" for my poetry is not always embodied. This is often different for music I write.

Can there be a disembodied poetic? While I have no clear answer, I admire various thinkers and writers who have trodden this path. I am not interested in a poetic that resorts to tedious clichés about the irreducibility of some bodily experiences, or gives aggressive significance to some bodily states and identifications by repressing others. If a disembodied poetic can estrange us from normalization of certain perfunctory responses to the cultural role of bodies, sexuality, eros and desire, then I'm all for it. Maybe re-embodiment follows.

The cover of The Long Moment *is a retro-reflective road sign on wood by Rosalie Gascoigne, titled "Hung Fire" (1995). How did you decide on that image?*

I am a huge admirer of Rosalie Gascoigne and her sculptural art. Her expansive, exacting use of found objects and discarded resources chimes with some way I see the world—its soluble order and purposeful superfluity. Gascoigne saw attunement among materials at levels I find profound, while admitting chance, scarring, and mis-seaming into her work. She recognized both the relative transience of human designs and the enduring grace of temporary invention. Without wanting to distort Gascoigne's intentions or make outrageous claims, I imagine a quiet conversation between Gascoigne's lyrical assemblages and *The Long Moment's* rendition of seriality through poetic language. I specifically wanted a black and red, non-photographic cover image for the book, and was thrilled Roslyn Oxley9 Gallery was happy for *Hung Fire* to appear in this context. I wish I could have asked Gascoigne directly for her permission.

What is your role with How2, *and what are your hopes for the on-line journal's contribution?*

I am editor-in-chief of *How2* magazine, which was founded in its print incarnation *HOW(ever)* by U.S. poet Kathleen Fraser in 1983. Late in the 1990s, Kathleen re-launched the project as *How2* while also establishing an electronic archive for back issues of both journals. Australian critic Ann Vickery assumed editorship of *How2* in 2000, having worked closely with a range of U.S. innovative poets during her doctoral thesis. She invited me to become managing editor that year, and in December 2002, I began as editor after completing my own doctorate. London-based writer Redell Olsen now works with me as managing editor and this has brought U.K. experimentalism into sharper, welcome focus across the journal. Our web designer Roberta Sims operates from Bucknell University, so our chief editorial team is transnational, which I find exciting and vital. We are assisted by an advisory board comprising writers and scholars who at various times have edited magazine features, or who coordinate sections on an ongoing basis, or were involved in *HOW(ever)* during the 1980s. The EAB moves across locations: Canada, Germany, Japan, the U.K., the U.S., Hawaii, Australia, New Zealand. For me, *How2's* capacity to reinvent and test the limits of writing community in response to new spaces and technologies is one of its most thrilling contributions.

While it's almost impossible to comment, my own hopes for *How2*'s contribution have been threefold. I have tried to strengthen the journal's international scope and profile, and make links among writing practices in ways that might explore a transcultural poetics. This helps open poetical histories and genealogies to kinds of spatial connectivity that exceed "nation" as an organizing principle. To me this is a basic extension of commitments to feminist poetical inquiry that shaped the journal's origins in the early 1980s, and that continue to enrich our progress. Thinking locally for a moment, this overall approach has allowed some exciting Australian innovations to enter dialogue with relevant work from different countries, resulting in events of contemporary poetical *xenia* that have been exciting and necessary. In addition, I have wanted communitarian principles to continue to guide the journal's direction—very much following the initial intentions of *HOW(ever)*. In context of an international on-line project, where pragmatic boundaries are sometimes hard to define and much gritty work is usually done by a couple of people, this is always challenging and rewarding. Lastly, I want to see *How2* reassessing its true role as an electronic publication. New media and digital technologies are having a profound impact upon poetry, and journals like *How2* are in a great position to track and respond to some of these changes.

Tell me a little more about what music you play and what kind of relation exists for you between writing poetry and performing songs.

I grew up in a family of singers and musicians who play roots-based acoustic folk music. My brother and I feel we had a charmed life as kids, and our performing history began when we were quite young. Music brought adventures and traveling experiences I now see were amazing. We wrote music and recorded it on a decrepit stereo for fun instead of watching television—we didn't have a TV until we were teenagers. By then it was too late and we were already folk singers, despite early flings with other genres (like wanting to be rock stars, obviously). I am haunted by acoustic music, quite happily, and love recent flights into shadowed and raw playing by superb writers like Gillian Welch and Will Oldham. While earthed in very old forms, their songs are utterly contemporary.

There's no doubt my immersion in traditional lyrics and melodies deeply affects my sense of poetic composition. Sometimes I am at a loss to describe the crossing, and some qualities of playing don't translate easily into words. The spatial-sonic textures of music have opened doors when I've been stuck in the studio of poetic improvisation. I get equally transfixed writing a song or a poem, and feel an accelerated perceptual pressure when doing either. If poetry is leading my senses, I often walk around and hear the world literally atomizing into phrases and words. If I'm inside a song everything becomes a soundtrack and the street falls into riffs. Lately I've felt these experiences to be much closer than I've imagined previously. When writing a song I usually begin from a melodic phrase that fits a lyric, and develop a story that works to the measure of the music, and vice versa. Neither element dominates. Other compositions are very different—inventing solely in music can free the unwriteable. When I first read Louis Zukofsky's integral "lower limit speech / upper limit music," the emotion of recognition was so strong I was staggered. "Being as such" in *The Long Moment* begins from that integral. I sometimes feel language is my work and music my breath.

What are you working on now?

I am working on a CD of songs for release in mid-2005 and will navigate two more issues of *How2* before passing on the editorship. I would eventually like my doctoral thesis on Lyn Hejinian to become a book. Meanwhile I'm slowly developing two poetry manuscripts, *Book of Hours for Narrative Lovers*, and an untitled collection of shorter lyrics, many addressing the necessities of invention in the face of impasse and human catastrophe. *Book of Hours* is a study of temporality and desire—a history of occurrence—that inhabits a strange zone where prose condenses or leaps into poetic line. It has become a kind of Steinian clearing site for my story-telling impulses. There's an element of fate in all these projects! They may jump ship and combine, or take more water than I can predict. I think my songs will probably float.

DON PATERSON

Don Paterson was born in Dundee, Scotland, in 1963 and moved to London in 1984, where he has worked as a musician and music teacher. He lived in Brighton and London, with a three-year period in Dundee as writer-in-residence at the University of Dundee, and moved to Edinburgh in 1998. His books of poetry include *Nil Nil* (Faber and Faber, 1995), *God's Gift to Women* (Faber and Faber, 1997), and *The White Lie: New and Selected Poetry* (Graywolf, 2001), as well as *The Eyes* (Faber and Faber, 1999), his translation of poems by Antonio Machado. He is poetry editor for Picador and co-editor, with Charles Simic, of the anthology *New British Poetry* (Graywolf, 2004). This interview with Lilias Fraser took place on March 12, 2000, in Edinburgh. A slightly longer version appeared in Volume 20, Numbers 2 and 3 of *Verse*.

If you were writing a blurb for yourself, what would you write?

Aw, Christ. Well, you wouldn't, and that's it. You shouldn't ever be in that position. You should try to avoid thinking about yourself at all; I think it's quite destructive. If you can caricature yourself in a paragraph, it's a form of self-censorship—you'll end up thinking, "Oh, that's the sort of poet I must be, these are the sorts of poems I must write." And you mustn't do that, you mustn't limit yourself in that way. And given your average artist's propensity to swither between total inferiority and total egomania, what would come out would be either something so humble it wouldn't be worth reading, "I'm no' very good, you know," or it would be, "Off he goes again, sailing into the uncharted waters of the imagination, the wind in what's left of his hair and the mind ablaze" kind of thing. That's why I'd never let a poet write their own blurb. And I'm a shit blurb writer, but at least I'm objective.

Do you get classed as a Scottish writer?

Some people do, but again I don't think it's important. The only reason for coming back to Scotland was so I could stop thinking about myself that way altogether. I was sick of being Scottish, and you're only ever Scottish in exile. I wanted to stop listening to myself speaking with a Scottish accent, and this is the only place you can do it—like your man eating lunch in the Eiffel Tower 'cos it was the only place in Paris he couldn't see it. My accent was steadily getting more and more affected anyway, in an effort to preserve these very fragile Dundonian tones, you know, it was coming out like Rab C. Nesbitt. And of course that happens to a lot of ex-pats; but I don't really think you can go on calling yourself a Scot if you have the opportunity to go home and you constantly spurn it. Exile should be an enforced condition, or you should call it something else.

Can you walk away from the collections that came out a while ago now? Can you think about them as if they're someone else's work?

Yes. If it wasn't for the poetry reading, I would never even think about them. You take a lot of parental pride in the thing, initially, and carry it about with you, but it's like a kid—eventually it grows up, and you think, "Well, you're on your own now." I don't feel attached to the books and always end up giving them away. It's not a kind of wanky gesture, "Oh, I can't *bear* having my work around me …" You know, I really don't care. I had a reading in Dundee a few days ago and ended up having to borrow books from the audience, because I had none at home, which is just stupid.

Do you recognize them as your offspring?

I do for a while, but again, it's like children: they come through you, not from you, and parental responsibilities are, actually, voluntary. It's the same with a book, you skelp its arse and you make sure it goes to a good school and you do your best for it, but after that …

What about the Machado book, was that a conscious shift or was it just the nature of writing in someone else's voice?

Partly that. I think one of the things about that kind of versioning is that it allows you to take on a voice that you wouldn't have had the confidence to project yourself: you should have done, but couldn't for whatever reason—confidence, cultural conditioning. There are poems in the Machado book that are nothing to do with Machado at all, but were just written out of that voice I was trying on; there's a couple of poems that were written at the time I was working on the versions, and I wouldn't have put them in any other book, so I just stuck them in that one—not really as a postmodern thing, saying, "These are apocrypha." As dishonest gestures go, it was quite an honest one. But it feeds back into your own stuff, and that's the most valuable lesson: that you remind yourself that there is an infinity of voices you could adopt if you chose to, but there's no such thing as your own voice, just an attachment to one—and you should never get used to it. It's not that I don't believe in the individual voice, it's just that I think you shouldn't make a personal, internal cult of it. Voice is something you can't avoid, for God's sake, not something you have to cultivate.

How did you come to work on Machado?

Penguin Spanish Poets, originally. I'd seen bits and pieces of Machado and thought, "That's really amazing, but it doesn't ..." Well, stuff like Robert Bly's Machado, which you're grateful for in the way a boat is grateful for the lighthouse. You think, well, at least one can't do any worse. And also it's nice to be working with a poet who you feel wouldn't object to your preferred modus operandi—in my case it was to start with a literal version of the poem and treat that as a first draft, then take it anywhere it wanted to go until it was a poem again. I feel sure Antonio would have agreed entirely with that, or at least not had a problem with it. All his work is unsigned.

Some of the poems in your other books make the reader feel dumped halfway through, or jilted at random points in the poem. That doesn't seem to happen in The Eyes.

No, it's a much more optimistic book from that point of view. I think what I was doing there was looking for some kind of constancy, looking for a form of address that I believed in sufficiently not to disrupt in that way. Partly that came about by my very cheerfully attenuated reading of Machado and his concerns. I worked on all the poems simultaneously because of not wanting the usual kind of productive discontinuity. I think it was a bit more self-confident, in a good way. You know, the poems in that book don't come out and do a wee turn for you, the way my other stuff often does, or tries to; the poems aren't so keen to impress. But I like that kind of poem too, I like poems that try to entertain. It's just a matter of trying to broaden the scope a bit.

The Machado doesn't seem to have the same sort of fantasy-scape as a lot of your other work. Is that the sort of landscape you write in all the time, or is that something you want to keep out of?

Well, that would be for other people to say. If that's the case, then that's the case, but the most important thing is that I mustn't think so, I mustn't feel seduced by it to the extent that I wouldn't want to leave it. You've always got to feel that you're extending the landscape somehow. The truth of course is that I'm probably not extending it very far; I'd be the last to know. The worst thing for me is feeling I'm writing the same poem twice, that's a big sin for me. It's like what I was saying about the working class poem, that's all I've got to say on the subject; if I returned to it I'd just be being sentimental.

Is sentimental that bad?

Oh, it's the enemy. It's the cancer of poetry, sentimentality. It's being in love with your own sensitivity as opposed to actually feeling anything. Ask that question to Kathleen Jamie, she'll send you away with a flea in your ear. But you wouldn't believe it, the number of people who prefer that kind of verse to the real stuff …

But it doesn't look as if you're simply slamming the door on that kind of emotion. You're not completely detached from sentiment.

No, sentiment is a different thing from sentimentalism, isn't it? No, I think you should write out of a feeling, at least initially, even if in the end it just ends up feeling stone cold because you've been working on it for a year and a half. By then it's only a form of words on a page, which is fine, it's the way I like working, but it has to start with something, absolutely, and that's the feeling that all the cold technique works to preserve. Sentiment's different. But sentimentalism is second-guessing what people might find moving, as opposed to what you think is moving yourself, or what might surprise yourself. The one thing you have, the only thing you can be true to, that you can ever possibly trust, is your own direct response to the world. And that can be very subtly perverted as soon as you start making a reductive sense of something, or start congratulating yourself on your own strength of feeling. It's the end.

In what way has working on Machado changed your own work?

I think the way it works is that it changes your imaginative environment, because you get sick of the reflection it gives you of yourself. So you then proceed on the assumption that your work will change as a result, because your work is responding as honestly as you possibly can to that environment. See, that's what I'm saying about how you don't have a voice. You're defined by circumstance: if you're in a dodgy relationship, the reflection you get from the other person comes to define what you think about yourself, and it circumscribes your actions, it limits your potential, censors your imagination. And it's the same thing if you start falling in love with your imaginative territory—you'll only ever get one reflection back.

Sounds like perfectionism ...

No, I don't think it's that. I think it's the opposite. It's a commitment to change. It's choosing the river and not the path—you can't step on it, ever, and even when you do it's changing. I think you lose if you don't change. And it's just easier to change if you're not seduced by your own voice.

Some of your earlier poems are very verbally extravagant.

I think there's a couple things going on there. One is that you want to stake out the territory, make it big, a various landscape, something you can colonize. And everyone wants to show off in their first book, unless they're a saint.

Why did you give God's Gift to Women *such a provocative title?*

Oh, just to draw attention to it. So people would go, "Who the hell does he think he is?" And then they'd read the title poem and realize their grave mistake. It came off and it didn't. Some of my colleagues seem to feel the title is a part of a book that must remain irony-free; they might be right. I notice Bill Herbert referred to me as "Modesty Don" in a bit of online correspondence recently, which was a bit hurtful. I assume, I hope, in reference to the foregoing. I mean it was a joke. And of course it wasn't a joke at all, it was about what men really do give women.

A lot of self-disgust was fueled by the Bosnia thing (like it ever needs any help), so there's that shadow behind it. I got terribly disillusioned with my gender, to the extent that I was appalled that I might bring more men into the world. Quite funny since I've managed two since then ... So there are these poems about misogyny, which try to find the line between our routine mundane misogynies and the rape camps, or those mythic cults in the 1001 *Nights* or whatever. A few folks, nearly all blokes, inevitably, thought the poems were misogynistic—at which point you just give up, really. But you can't spend your time subtitling for the thick, so there's always a risk, I guess.

Were those the ideas behind "Scale of Intensity"?

It was reacting to some of the war poetry that was going down at the time. I felt that the only poem I could write in response was one of brutal neutrality. Anything else was a lie. All that caricaturing of the Bosnian Serbs as innately evil men, another species—which of course is exactly what they did to their victims—I detest that sort of stuff, I think it's utterly reprehensible. The first thing you have to do when you see that sort of thing going down is admit your own complicity, just by virtue of belonging to the same species, and particularly the same gender. You should be thinking, "Jesus, that could've happened here, that could've been me—so what is it in me that I should eradicate, so that no set of circumstances could ever arise that could trigger that kind of behavior?" If you don't start from there, you're condemned to learn nothing.

I was thinking about "Imperial," why you put such a tight formal net on it.

I find it easier to write about more grim things the tighter the form is. I think that's part of the conceivably neurotic justification for doing that, but also I like the discontinuity of it. I mean, the two voices I hear in that poem are Norman Mailer and Emily Dickinson, hardly natural bedfellows. But I was reading a lot of Dickinson, and the form seemed valid, or at least to fit the conceit. I think things are more shocking when they're in tight form sometimes, because we tend to associate that with a feeling of predictability—you're lulled by the repetitions.

Do you remember at any point in your formal education having it hammered into you how you should read a poem?

Absolutely. All those definitive explanations. "When the poet says ____, what he really means is ____," and you'd think, "Well why the hell didn't he just say that then?" Which is the only sensible response. And I always think of Eliot talking to that woman after the reading and saying—I never get this right—"Madam, it means what it means; if I'd meant anything else I'd have said so just as obscurely." Which is as much as you can say, really; you've found the words that approximate what you're feeling as closely as you can possibly manage. That's it. Though it's asymptotic, so you're always aware of that little gap, the shortfall, and God, that kills you, because that means there's always something wrong with the poem. All that I can think of when I think back to poems is what's wrong with them.

But is that shortfall not the space that means other people can get different readings into it?

That's actually the best justification I've heard for it. Thanks, I'll steal it.

What about funny poems, then? You were talking about the temptation to make people laugh, getting the magic sound from the audience. Do you ever use humor?

Aye. Well, I might if it's not just a joke, if it's also the point. Again, it entertains, but that's only first base, and you have to think where you'll go from there. The values have been corrupted by the poetry reading. I don't care much, well not that much, what folk think of the poems—not arrogance, it's just that I can't do them any better than I've done them. But I want folk to like me. So when you're on stage, you're going, "Was that a bored silence or a very moved one? Shit, I can't tell. Hey—I'll read a funny poem!" But sometimes you wonder ... I don't think Machado cracked a joke in his life. That's interesting, because I was thinking about that in relationship to albums I like: I really love albums that are totally consistent, I love putting on an album of ballads because that's what I'm in the mood for, and if there's an up-tempo number on it, I'll skip over it. Yet the albums that I've made have all been insane in their variety, and that's what I don't like about them, they're just trying so hard to prevent the listener from falling asleep.

Is it the same in the poetry?

Yes, maybe. You can't work on the assumption that you're constantly flirting with boring the listener to death. The stuff I've been writing since the Machado has been far more serious, or at least less funny. I haven't been thinking about what anyone else might like. It's all after the event, this stuff, so it's a form of lies, you know that, don't you? All these conversations are an indulgence. I mean, that has to be the case if I was being truthful in what I was saying about distancing yourself from the work. So necessarily, any comment I make on it is going to be by definition unreliable, or at least just another opinion. I mean, that's the other thing, sometimes people will say, "You said five years ago, X," and you find you now think Y, and I don't see anything wrong with that at all, because you're a verb, not a noun. The work stays fixed, you change in your relationship to it. I don't think being consistent in your opinion is a virtue at all. I think what I'm proposing is just that your values change. I'm not saying you have to contradict yourself, destabilize everything; you have to be consistent at the time, rigorously so. But only at the time. It's part of a longer dialogue.

We've got this idea that poetry's got to be marginal. Do you think it ought to be?

Well, I think it's difficult, and it should be. I don't mean that quite like Eliot, but it should make you think, which takes a bit of time, and that might not be for everyone. It's got to be a bit hard, that's the whole point of the thing, so you read it more than once, so it can take you on a journey. Whatever you're talking about has got to be transformed at the end of the poem, and you're not going to do that if you're not on some kind of pilgrimage, some transforming process that the reader has to make with you. Poetry's as much a mode of reading as writing, an innate capacity we possess for reading significance into the world, which it may or may not possess, but poetry is where we meet, it invites that kind of signification, then rewards it. Totally interactive. It's such a creative thing to do, reading poetry.

So maybe it should be compulsory to have a stab at writing a poem before you take a poetry book home?

Oh no, definitely not. I think what we need is a program for teaching people how to read properly, which is a different thing entirely. All this technical stuff you have to keep as far away from the reader as possible, because it's completely irrelevant to them. All these invisible means are just that, the practitioner's business, and it destroys their innocent reading of the poem. I've said it umpteen times, but it's like when you go to the chemist: it doesn't make any difference if you know what's in the bottle—it'll either help your cough or it won't. You've got to teach that the poem isn't a search for meaning. If you want meaning read history, read philosophy, but poetry's not about meaning at all, at least not in the sense that they are. It's about connecting you back up to a primal feeling of unity, that's what you've got to teach people. It's finding equivalences between sound and meaning and space and time in a way that unifies the world again. Or at least is symbolic of a unity, but humans can feel symbols. And the whole thing about reading is that you are driving the poem, it's your poem to make of it what you will. And to insist on the necessity of the informed reading of a poem at the same time; if a poem were just something you could read anything into, there'd be no point in it.

KEVIN HART

Australian poet Kevin Hart was born in 1954 and grew up in London and Brisbane. His recent books of poetry include *Flame Tree: Selected Poems* (Paper Bark Press, 2002/ Bloodaxe Books, 2003) and *Wicked Heat* (Paper Bark Press, 1999), and have earned him the New South Wales and Victorian Premiers awards for poetry as well as the Christopher Brennan Award. He is also the author of *Samuel Johnson and the Culture of Property* (Cambridge University Press, 1999), *A.D. Hope* (Oxford University Press, 1993), and *The Trespass of the Sign: Deconstruction, Theology, and Philosophy* (Cambridge University Press, 1989/ Fordham University Press, 2000). He edited *The Oxford Book of Australian Religious Verse* (Oxford University Press, 1994) and has translated Giuseppe Ungaretti. Having been a professor in the Centre for Comparative Literature and Cultural Studies at Monash University in Melbourne for many years, he now teaches at the University of Notre Dame. This interview was conducted by Stephen Watson in 1999 in Kevin Hart's house.

Do you recall Robert Frost once saying that there are, in the end, only two basic meters in English: iambic and loose iambic? I remember this now because, although you clearly pull away from the iambic measure at various points in your poetry, that meter is, with whatever variations and substitutions, very much your home. You gravitate toward it so naturally and to such a degree that it's almost impossible imagining that you might stray very far from it in the future. Was it nevertheless a long process finding your feet (if you'll excuse the bad pun) in this meter? Or was it more or less instinctive?

I must have had a very strange time growing up in Queensland in the late 1960s and early '70s because when I started to write poems—I was fourteen—I also started to think about versification. It was more common elsewhere in the country to start to write poems and not think about versification. I remember reading a local magazine called *Endeavour* that featured a series of articles on prosody. It was roneoed like the avant-garde little magazines coming out of Melbourne and Sydney, but diametrically opposite to them in its tastes. I submitted a poem and received an acceptance letter in which the "cadence" of the poem was singled out for admiration. I had to look up the word. I was trying to write both metrically regular and free verse from the beginning, imitation Shelley followed by imitation Eliot. One afternoon I discovered

James McAuley's *A Primer of English Versification* in the school library, and I found it fascinating, partly I think because in those days I was very interested in mathematics. Thereafter, when I was reading poets at university, I paid attention to their metrical practices. Particularly Wordsworth: I marked up a good deal of *The Prelude*. Today when I'm teaching and pick up a book from my undergraduate years, I often find lines marked up to show how the accents and stresses are distributed. When I started to write blank verse in a more concerted way, particularly in *Peniel*, I went back and re-read Wordsworth.

A benign presence in my undergraduate studies was Alec Hope — not so much as a teacher but as a friend and mentor — and he had been a fierce apologist for accentual-syllabic verse. In my first year the English Department made available, in a slightly embarrassed way, a set of notes that Alec had written on how to scan a poem. Out of school, one of my favorite poets of the day was W.H. Auden, and wasn't it John Hollander who said that Auden had an almost moral sense of meter? So without a doubt I learnt a lot about meter in one way or another. But I feel that over the years the knowledge passed into my muscles and bones. Of course, like many others writing these days, there's a slight anapestic push in my use of iambics.

You've also experimented with syllabics.

Yes, a few poems that seem iambic are actually written to the count of syllables, not stresses. "Prague, 1968" is written in lines of alternating nine and eleven syllables. It gives a slightly disconcerting sense of moving toward and then away from an iambic tread, and I think that contributes to the uneasy mood of the poem. It is very difficult to write syllabic verse in English: the language is so heavily accented. If you choose a line of five or seven syllables, as Thom Gunn or Sylvia Plath do, you can set up an intriguing play between the qualitative and the quantitative. If you write in elaborate stanzaic patterns, like Marianne Moore, you can establish a tension between eye and ear, but that sort of thing seems rather abstract to me.

Of course your use of meter, and especially the dominance of the iambic measure in your work, is also a link with tradition — almost the entire tradition of English poetry. And yet in terms of its preoccupations, your work pulls away quite sharply — I would say even radically — from the English tradition. There's the line of wit in your earlier work — and doubtless in your later work as well. But you seem to me to be after something else. Your poetry, in significant respects, reminds me of what Charles Simic once said: "I'm in the business of translating what cannot be translated: being and its silence."

I know what Charlie has in mind, and part of me responds very strongly to that view of things. Yet I don't have the same sense of sheer, naked being that Charlie testifies to there. Sometimes silence is to be respected, and sometimes it is to be turned inside out. In my poems the horizon, shadows, and stones all talk. And they talk about their relations with people and God. So another part of me wants to respond to Charlie's line by quoting Eberhard Jüngel's expression: *eine Erfahrung mit der Erfahrung,* "an experience with experience." Every poem of any value is an experience with experience: it reconfigures past experience or brings about a new experience, while also giving a new charge, a new sense, to the category of experience itself. That happens for both reader and writer.

How have Australian critics responded to your poetry? From my first acquaintance with your work, I was quite certain that the distinctive note that your work struck, almost from the outset, was really quite foreign to Australian poetry—or, perhaps, the ways in which other Australian poets have registered similar kinds of concern.

When I was growing up in the late 1960s and early 1970s and writing my first poems, I subscribed to *Poetry Australia* and a couple of local little magazines. I'd flick through *Quadrant* in the Corinda Public Library, and I must have found *New Poetry* somewhere. Those were the days when poets divided along the lines of "nationalism" vs. "internationalism." Especially in Sydney, poets coded themselves as internationalists by rejecting English poetry and affirming American poetry, either what was written on the east coast or what was written on the west coast. It was all the roar of distant battle, though: I was a High School kid in Brisbane, reading as much about anarchism and communism as about our local poetry wars, and, in the beginning, I was more interested in mathematics than in poetry. Those poetry wars seemed very far away, but I could at least make out the shape of the passions.

In retrospect, I was perhaps alone in that the most important poets to me weren't talked about: central and eastern European poets, South Americans, some of the French and some Italians. I came across a few of these in the Red Book Shop in Elizabeth Arcade where I used to go to find out more about anarchism and Marxism. And I came across others in the Brisbane State Library because

I'd go there to do my homework. It was the one air-conditioned building in town where a teenager could go in order to escape the sticky heat outside. I read a little North American poetry there too, but must have got into dead ends. I remember opening a thick volume by Conrad Aiken and not getting far. I had fun with e.e. cummings. But those European and South American poets were the ones who really excited me.

I remember that when my second and third books came out I was reproached for writing so openly about the experience of faith. Some people said my poems were more European than Australian, and I was puzzled to hear that. I hadn't taken in how narrowly the adjective "Australian" was being used in those days. I was delighted to find that a woman in one of Helen Garner's short stories read *Your Shadow* so well; that person remains my favorite critic. It's a pity she doesn't exist. [Laughter.]

Once I started writing a doctoral dissertation I received a fair bit of stick for being an academic. I couldn't see why this was any better or any worse than working for the ABC, for a publishing house, or playing the Literature Board lottery. But I underestimated how deeply anti-intellectualism runs in Australia. Because I was studying philosophy, it was said that my poems were "academic."

It doesn't follow.

Well, I couldn't see it. I think it was only when my *New and Selected Poems* came out in 1994, by which time some of the passions of the '70s had died down, that people started to read those poems for what they are.

Helen Vendler once said that the primary function of criticism is to describe somebody's work in such a way that it can't be confused with anybody else's. I was wondering to what degree critics here have followed what I take to be the essential trajectory of your work. I suppose earlier, as you said, they might have claimed, "he's not Australian enough," "he's too academic," "what's all this Roman Catholic stuff." But it seems to me that your poetry has something quite distinctive in the context of Australian poetry — or anywhere else for that matter. You're much more the contemporary of someone like the French writer Philippe Jaccottet than perhaps any Australian poet. Have such things ever been mentioned in local criticism of your work?

David Campbell showed me a poem by Jaccottet after a very boozy lunch at "The Run" in 1974 or '75. I remember it well: it was "*Sur les pas de la lune,*" a very beautiful lyric, and one that was close to David's late style. But I don't think that Jaccottet's writing has ever been a part of the conversation here. Maybe only a dozen people in Australia would read Jaccottet, alas. I could probably name them; they're probably all friends. You're right: I think of Jaccottet as a contemporary, especially the author of *À la lumière d'hiver*. I feel close to him, as I do to several others: Yves Bonnefoy, Roberto Juarroz, Tomas Tranströmer, Eugenio Montale, and David himself. When critics "place" poets in reviews and articles here it tends to be done in terms of local polemics: "X is closer to Hope than to Forbes …"

Which is a meaningless distinction.

Well, meaningless to me, at any rate. Alec Hope is a wonderful poet, especially in *The Wandering Islands*, and we probably share all sorts of things. We're both drawn to the myth of Orpheus, although on very different levels. I'm not a satirist, as he is, and our erotics could hardly be confused. I admire some poems by John Forbes, but John was interested in popular culture in a way I'm not.

I assume, though, that this hasn't necessarily given you a sense of exacerbated personal isolation in Australia. Or has it? Or how has what you've just mentioned affected your sense of the situation of poetry generally?

I don't think it's affected me very much. I can feel not at home anywhere. [Laughter.] Whenever I write a poem, I switch off the world. But one cannot switch off language, and my language is surely marked by having lived for so long in Australia … A little isolation is not a bad thing, and because I have a job I enjoy I'm less caught up in the poetry world than I might otherwise have been. All that jockeying for an imaginary position!

Yes, an imaginary position in a non-existent kingdom.

Absolutely.

Speaking of other domains now, have you ever come across Czeslaw Milosz's Harvard lectures, The Witness of Poetry? *There, at a certain point, he writes of "the strange fate of the religious imagination in the 20th century"—a century singularly uncongenial to that type of imagination, like his, like yours, which, I take it, is naturally religious in its orientation, whether in its desire to sacramentalize or to detect the traces of the divine in our experience of the world.*

My academic training was in English and Philosophy, but I think I read Philosophy only because in those days it was almost impossible to study Theology unless you were in priestly formation. As a student, I gravitated to philosophical theology and, after I graduated, became deeply fascinated by some of the Christian mystics: the Pseudo-Dionysius, John of the Cross, Teresa of Ávila, Meister Eckhart, Julian of Norwich, Nicholas of Cusa … That was another education.

I didn't have a religious upbringing. On the contrary, I was raised as a lapsed Anglican. I converted to the Catholic faith in my early twenties. After I had done that, I discovered that I had been born Jewish. Now I'm married to a Jew, and we celebrate both rituals.

Your immediate context is obviously that of Australia; you are an Australian poet. But all of the evidence of your work suggests this is not at all the essential context.

On one level you are quite right: it doesn't seem to matter at all. But on another level I doubt that my poems would be as they are without those early years in Brisbane. What I take away from those years, though, is not a litany of fauna and flora but rather an experience of strangeness. It is something I tried to evoke in "Poem to the Sun," "Her Name," "The Voice of Brisbane," and a few others.

Is the place from which you truly start, then, that context which you allude to in your article on Tomas Tranströmer, "Experience and Transcendence," where you gloss Hölderlin's notion of our "double infidelity": "God has turned away from human beings, leaving us to experience his absence, and we have turned away from Him, no longer regarding this absence as significant"?

I think that something in Hölderlin's talk of the "double infidelity" takes us more deeply into our—for want of a better word—"spiritual" condition than Nietzsche's talk of God's death does. I don't think that we have entered an age of atheism or even agnosticism. It is a religious age, perhaps more so than the one in which Hölderlin lived, but it's an unsettled age, increasingly an age of individuals who might as well whisper to themselves, "I choose therefore I am." People don't want to be cued into a tradition, certainly not their own. They don't want to learn about what spiritual directors used to call "the path," they want to find a path that's right for them. It is personal, if not downright private. So you find people, especially younger people, going to Bali to "find themselves." They don't deny the sacred, but they think it must be elsewhere. Or they think that they have to be elsewhere in order to be receptive to it.

I would never say that God has turned away from us, but the mainstream churches have surely lost confidence in themselves and in their language. In Christianity, only the Catholics and Orthodox have retained a deep sense of the sacred, and it is a wonder that the Catholic Church let so much of that sense go in the revision of the liturgy in the late 1960s … I would never say that the poet occupies the place of the sacred. It would be more accurate to say that these days the sacred gives a little poetry to people who would not otherwise have much in their lives. I'm thinking of charismatic churches in the States and in Latin America … Besides, I'm wary about taking the sacred just by itself: unless the sacred is linked to a vision of the good, it can be put to dark ends.

I notice, though, that your poetry does not bear the imprint of someone like Milosz's concern about the plight of the religious imagination exiled in the land of modernity and assailed always by science and its corrosive effects on our capacity for belief.

I've never understood what people mean when they say science can erode faith. How could there be an abyss between truth and God? Science makes us wonder about nature, even when it explains nature to us. No scientist can, as scientist, speak about the resurrection because it is not the story of a revived corpse. It's the story of Jesus' passage into glory. An archaeologist could find the cave where Jesus was buried but could never find the place where eschatology and history intersect. Biblical criticism cannot stymie faith, although it can and should make any Christian reject easy, foolish, or complacent positions. I'd also say science helps to separate mystification from mystery. To find the truth in a rigorous scientific fashion is no diminishment of the mystery of things.

I'd agree with Milosz, though, were he talking about technology in Heidegger's sense of the word. Science tries to wake us up to beauty and truth, but technology all too often urges us go to sleep, especially under the sign of the media.

I would say that the central political issue of our times is the media, and it consists in the censorship of the complex. All faith—in God, in the polis, or in one another—can be damaged by the media. Why? Because the media makes us live in a world that is not a world; it is too narrow for even the most ordinary of human experiences to be unfolded with care.

How, then, would you define the specific terrain of your own concern?

I had to write a line or two about the writing of poetry for John Kinsella's anthology *Landbridge*. Perhaps I can quote it here: "Poetry is an experience of limits: it travels around the borderlines of what can be named and what must be left unnamed. It does not betray these borders: it respects their mystery and complexity. The best conductor of mystery is clarity. The true bearer of complexity is simplicity."

My sense is that by living thoughtfully, by dealing with one another and the world, we are pulled ever more deeply into something we cannot name. Saint Paul spoke of *epectasis*, a stretching out toward—what? We cannot say. Gregory of Nyssa had this in mind in *The Life of Moses* when he has God tell Moses that "the place with me is so great that the one running in it is never able to cease from his progress." I wouldn't say that we run free: we are always pulled this way and that because we are always in contexts that make demands on us. And there is also stillness to be valued.

Poetry, for me, always involves a response to mystery, even when it starts by considering ordinary things … I'm not sure, though, that I understand mystery to be sublime. To the extent that I do, I have to stand aside from the tradition that figures the sublime by way of obscurity, and I dislike that tradition which separates the beautiful from the sublime. I think Jean-Luc Nancy is right to remind us all that for Kant the sublime is that by which the beautiful touches us. Nancy is concerned in *Une pensée finie* with the nature of the limit, and he insists that there is nothing beyond the limit that gives us the feeling of the sublime. I won't dwell on this except to say that there is a limit that we keep brushing against in our daily living, a limit that seems to pass through ordinary events. One does not have to be a poet to sense this limit, although I suspect that a wealth of poetry is written as a response to it.

Does this link you to another French poet, Paul Éluard ("There is another reality, but it resides in this one") or, perhaps more pertinently, again, to his compatriot

Philippe Jaccottet? You may remember the latter once wrote of "the other world present perhaps in this one."

I'd say that any experience contains the possibility of being an experience of the divine. One thing I distrust in the expression "religious experience" is that it implies that there is a particular range of experience that is "religious." On the contrary, any experience can be charged with mystery.

In fact there are many signs in your work that you share some of the preoccupations of the French poets I've just remembered—but by no means only French poets. I'm thinking of those writers who have never quite relinquished their religious, though not necessarily Christian, presentiments—the hope of glimpsing or experiencing what the French call présence, *suddenly, if ephemerally, incarnated in the here and now. I remember a critic of French literature (I think it's John Taylor) speaking of Jaccottet's "attempt to commune with elusive spiritual mysteries situated nearly beyond the grasp of language, yet which, to his mind, permeate every element of our world."*

He could just as well be speaking of Yves Bonnefoy, whose entire project is to glimpse those moments of *la présence* and who finds them in the natural world about us. I greatly admire Bonnefoy—our greatest living poet, don't you think?—and I am deeply moved by his repudiation of gnosticism. I don't share his Neoplatonic vision of reality, however. He's a lot more Greek in his talk of "earth" and "light" than I could ever be.

A moment or two ago you quoted Jaccottet speaking of another world "present perhaps" in this one. I like the prudence of that qualification, but not because of any agnosticism on my part. My sense is that God does not present himself to human consciousness, does not offer himself as an object of theoretical contemplation. God might be present—that is a matter of faith—but he does not present himself to consciousness as created things do.

Jaccottet also speaks—it's in one of his reviews—of a landscape by Poussin which "ceases to be decor and becomes a presence." If this comes to mind now, it is because that, too, seems to describe the essential trajectory of many of your poems. It's entirely characteristic of you, it seems, to move from meteorological conditions to metaphysical needs …

The sort of event Jaccottet evokes is analyzed at length by Jean-Luc Marion in his *Étant donné*. It's what he calls *"le phénomène saturé,"* a phenomenon that exceeds the Kantian categories of the understanding. This phenomenon is saturated in intuitions rather than concepts. Gabriel Marcel talked about a saturated experience, but Marion's notion is his own and is quite brilliant. No one can foresee a saturated phenomenon, and it cannot even be seen: it dazzles us. I like Marion's idea that a saturated phenomenon is not so much an experience as *"une contre-expérience,"* a disconcerting awareness of what cannot be rendered as a theme or an object. And I am profoundly sympathetic to his idea that the saturated phenomenon is in no way an exceptional case.

I don't doubt that poetry comes as a response to saturated phenomena, though I wouldn't say that it responds only to phenomena. I'd also say that a poem is itself, in some respects, a saturated phenomenon, although not everything in a poem comes as a phenomenon. All this requires a lot of close talk. Had we world enough and time, I'd have to refine all this, and I'd offer some friendly disagreements with Marion. My sense of what he calls saturated phenomena is not one of bedazzlement, but of radiance. I know what Marion means when he talks of the counter-experience introducing disorder, but it also brings calm. And one wonders how the act of writing enters into all of this … I'd like to write about it all one day. I gather that Marion is writing a whole book on the saturated phenomenon, and perhaps that will give me an opportunity.

One of the things most often mentioned about you is that you are not only a poet but also a practicing Roman Catholic. How does your faith, your religion, manifest itself in your poetry?

Could I go back a few steps and approach this a bit obliquely? I grew up in the east end of London. It was a rough area. I was an excruciatingly shy child, and was thought to be very slow. I hated school, and stayed home every chance I could get. My teachers didn't think there was much point in me going on to secondary school. So my mother tried to have me apprenticed to the butcher in Ford Road, but he wasn't interested in having me. And my teachers were right: I failed the 11+. The examination paper was unintelligible to me.

A year or so after this happened my father was threatened with being made redundant, and after a worrying time the family immigrated to Brisbane. I still hated school and once again I slid to the bottom of the class. One morning, when I was ill in bed with some stomach bug, my mother came into my bedroom, stood near the door, and said very distinctly, "You are going to grow up into an idiot." She probably thought I was putting it on. I was very hurt. In my bitterness, I thought, "I do not trust you," and then I felt even more desolate. I realized that I had never really trusted the world around me. I had been trusting in an inner world, and years later I saw that that trust had sustained me. When I became a teenager, and experienced a violent turn to religion, it was easy to cease trusting in myself and to trust in God because—although it sounds strange now that I say it out loud—he was not visible, was not a part of the world in which I had grown up. I think my poems reach back to the inner world I cultivated, and slowly, over the next five to ten years, my inner and outer worlds adjusted to one another.

And that profound inner confidence as opposed to distrust in the outer world—it's manifest, I find, in the very tone of voice, the sensibility, which imbues your poetry. One of the effects of reading it—I remember contacting you about this—was to experience a serenity that one very seldom meets with. Your poetry is, in other words, a poetry of deep assurance. It strikes me as being confident in a way that goes far beyond the conventional meaning of that word—in fact, to the root meaning of that word.

There's also, in your poetry, an almost Wordsworthian emphasis on finding that which is healing and self-healing.

Writing a poem can help you find what needs to be healed; it can lead to "at-one-ment," as Geoffrey Hill says. But there's always a risk that you will end up picking at old sores.

All the things I've already indicated would seem to set you apart from much contemporary English-language poetry, particularly the sort that parades its own insouciance and is coolly, self-consciously ironic and parodic. In point of fact you're not primarily an ironist …

Writing poetry always involves an exposure to risk. You chance encountering feelings and thoughts that could change you. You chance becoming a slightly different person, precisely the one who will have written the poem in hand. In a sense, writing is experience. I think Walter Benjamin says just that about Julian Green, though if I'm not mistaken he's talking there about *das Erleb-nis*, and not *die Erfahrung*, the German noun for experience as a journey or a trial. Yet it is also possible to use poetry as a way of avoiding experience, of ironizing it out of existence. That's formalism, regardless of how the poem is put together.

There is more than one instance in the contemporary world of poets who are, in a sense, religious poets without religion (or the consolations of religion). Charles Wright springs to mind. And much has been made, perhaps understandably, of the strains and tensions involved in such a paradoxical, albeit quite common role for the poet as this millennial moment. But you are a religious poet with religion. Does this, to your mind, pose dilemmas for you as poet which are essentially different in kind to the dilemmas facing someone like Charles Wright?

A couple of years ago I wrote an essay on Charles Wright that I called "'*La Poesia è scala a Dio*.'" The line comes from Montale whom Wright has translated, though neither poet thinks that his poetry can ever be a ladder to God. I don't either. Writing can be a quest for transcendence: not an escape from this world, which no poet really wants, but a resistance to being engulfed in immanence. Charles wants to believe in "something beyond belief," as he says in one poem: not dogma but Tao. He admires the great Christian mystics, while also distancing himself from anything that smacks of heroic asceticism, anything that keeps people from being fully human. I see Charles as a pilgrim: he's already on the way, looking for illumination, but also, in a sense, he's looking for the right place to begin his pilgrimage. Much of the pathos in his poetry arises out of that tension.

You say I'm a religious poet "with religion," and of course you have good reason to put it that way. But I wouldn't want to give the impression that Christianity is something that one can have. It goes without saying, I suppose, that it's not simply a set of propositions to which one can subscribe, or a set of beliefs that one can make one's own. It's a path that opens before you only when you start to walk toward God. It doesn't feel like a straight and narrow path, because you're pulled here by your own experience and pulled there by the testimony of others, most of whom are not around to be questioned. Without being overly dark about it, I'd say that the verb "to be Christian" can be conjugated only in the future anterior: "I will have been Christian." You never really know in the present. Faith, hope, and love are ways of being, not ways of knowing.

Whatever you write comes in the wake of who you are. You cannot change your style, or even what you write about, without first changing who you are. At the same time, I wouldn't want to suggest that the poetry simply reflects the person who writes it. In poetry too the self is stretched. You find yourself feeling and thinking what you have never quite felt and thought before.

In a review of Wicked Heat *in the TLS, Brian Henry asserts that "Hart is not a religious poet; rather, his poems are spiritual and mystical, fulfilling Emerson's charge that 'the poet must be a rhapsodist.' (Hart's mysticism appears through his heightened vision and awareness of something 'a touch away, / Always about to pull the darkness back.').' If religion, in the formal sense, appears infrequently in your more recent work (perhaps less and less?), then this simply begs the question as to how the religious manifests itself in poetry. Clearly—your own work implicitly underlines this—the poetically spiritual has a relation to the formally religious, but the two cannot be conflated even when they are most germane to each other. What is this relation? What is the difference?*

Perhaps at times a poem can help you peel away the layers of skin that have grown over words like "soul" and "eternity." The line in which the word appears can do that. At other times you peel enough layers away and the word becomes another word, an image, a whole line, even a poem.

Your poetry, as it develops over time, uses obviously religious imagery more and more sparingly. And yet, paradoxically, it seems to me to grow more and more religious, not less.

Wasn't it Origen who said that prayer is like a game of hide and seek with God? At any rate, he's not always where you think he is.

You've an essay on Derrida in Phillip Blond's collection, Post-Secular Philosophy. *It strikes me that you write a poetry that could be called "post-secular."*

I don't think that the secular and the sacred can be related as the title of Phillip's book suggests. We're not in a "post-secular" society, because society is never just one thing or another, and because the secular and the sacred aren't related to one another periodically. No sooner had the French revolutionaries got rid of the Catholic clerics than they appropriated the Church's language with their talk about *"l'union sacrée"* and so on. Modern secularity partly derives from liberal trends in religion in the eighteenth and nineteenth centuries, and to the extent that it tolerates religion it also prizes liberality. Someone committed to radical orthodoxy like Phillip would be unhappy with that. He might regard the secular as an aberration, or even self-delusive, but it doesn't follow that we think in a post-secular way these days.

I can't help noting, too, that your imagination does not follow anything like that via negativa *or tradition of ascetic mysticism that we find in T.S. Eliot.*

Negative theology has sources in Greek philosophy and Jewish faith, and Eliot was very well aware of them. *Four Quartets* is rich and ripe with motifs from several negative theologies. It's a powerful set of poems, if not a work I warm to all that much. "You say I am repeating / Something I have said before. I shall say it again. / Shall I say it again?": that highly mannered, prosy aspect of the poetry doesn't appeal to me at all. You often find in negative theologies the image of a limit that runs between this world and another: we cannot speak adequately of that other world. As I said a while back, I think this limit does not run between this world and another but within this world. Thinking of things this way does not eliminate negative theology; it folds it another way. And so I'd be surprised if there aren't motifs of negative theology in some of my poems.

Your poetry is deeply quotidian.

I hope so. There is only experience, and God and poetry can be a part of any of it.

Yes. It's quite evident from your poetry too that you have embodied that kind of sense of the religious, even through — I'm speaking colloquially now — the sort of poetics of space that your work embodies. Things are always contained within, or they pass through rather than pass beyond. One could even look at your poetry simply in the way you use prepositions.

Oh, I hadn't noticed that.

In "Rain," for instance, you write, "I sit here, deep inside this April day"; in "How Hast Thou Counselled Him ..."" you have the lines, "as though night were always here / Inside me ..." The poetry, in other words, insists on a quality of presentness, on a kind of immanence rather than transcendence even in its prepositions. Its adverbs of time and place, too, I might add. Or perhaps it would be better to say that the space your poetry creates (and each and any writer has his characteristic way of building space in his or her work) is always the space of that which is indwelling.

I'll probably never be able to use a preposition again! [Laughter.] Again, though, I'd say that I don't think of the immanent and the transcendent as being opposed. Transcendence comes as an interruption of immanence, of being closed in on oneself or one's group. Being is being-in-relation, and the only way that being-in-relation is kept open, fluid, alive, is if the central relation is with God whose very act of being is generosity.

But you would nevertheless agree with someone like George Steiner who, writing about Heidegger, argues that it is still "the poet's calling … to bring creation into the neighborhood of the divine"?

I'd have to look at the context very carefully. I don't warm to the romantic assumption that poets, or artists, have special access to the divine, and I'm wary of what "divine" means for the later Heidegger. I'd need a lot of time to disentangle all this. My immediate response wouldn't be one that Heidegger would adopt. Since everyone is created in the image of God, everyone is creative; and people don't have to be told to make use of their creativity: it's an ache that we ignore at our peril, like the human ache for being with others.

Having said that, I think that the poet—the artist in general—can help to re-enchant the world. It's not a matter of returning us to the middle ages, or of discovering an alternate, pagan past. I don't like either of those projects, and both can come with horrible politics following behind, if not leading the wagon. It's a matter rather of attending to what is left unheard or has been silenced, of creating spaces and times when beauty can be celebrated and the truth can be explored. I said a while back when we were talking about Hölderlin that I don't like confusing poetry and the sacred. Yet I would say that these days the reading and writing of poetry, acts that have no instrumental values or that greatly exceed them, can themselves be the way in which other values can be glimpsed. To re-enchant the world, these days, is not to fill it with angels and demons but to stop it from becoming ever more narrow, to allow people to have an experience with experience.

Given that your work is aligned with being and with becoming—contemplative and meditative rather than a response to events—do you see a social function for a poetry like yours?

If poetry does any social work, it should be a relentless rejection of idolatry. All idolatry involves reduction, simplification, a denial of mystery, or even a refusal of complexity. As I said earlier, our times are idolatrous. Think of the media! Adorno says in one of his essays on music that modern society has rendered experience—*Erfahrung*—impossible. In its own ways and in its own time, poetry seeks to subvert that.

But poetry has another function, surely. Even the patient measure of most of your poetry, its predominant calm, effects a kind of deepening in one's experience of language itself. This, in turn, renders the possibility of meaningfulness as such that much more present. (It's also, I should add, what makes your poetry sound like the poetry of a believer, whether the reader or not has a clue as to your Catholicism.) Knowing all this through your work, experiencing the kind of primal underwriting (if you'll forgive the expression!) that your poetry engages in—and engages us, the readers, in—it seems to me that the work as a whole serves the purposes of making praise possible, and thankfulness possible, and worship by implication.

Well, I hope that is true. As you know, just recently I've been going through my poems in order to put them in some kind of order for a new selected poems coming out with Bloodaxe [*Flame Tree: Selected Poems*], and so I've re-read them all and thought about them all. And I was struck when I was putting the manuscript together how often the word "calm" comes up. In fact there is one that I called "The Calm."

It seems to me that one of the most remarkable features of your earlier poetry is its formal distancing of emotion. The work is remarkable for its conceptualizing of experience—and feeling, too. Whereas more recently, perhaps especially in sections of Wicked Heat, *you seem to me to be aiming at something more like "the true voice of feeling."*

Well, a number of my early poems—I'm thinking of "The Stone's Prayer," "The Horizon," "The Twenty-First Century"—try to work through and around a concept. I suspect younger poets are attracted to concepts in poetry, and I was already prone to that in studying philosophy.

But there is in your more recent work a much more concerted attempt to leave the more elaborately conceptual behind and to speak with a kind of self-disclosing (though not necessarily "confessional") directness of feeling. How would you chart your own sense of your development? Certainly, a sequence like "Nineteen Songs" (in Wicked Heat) *is more directly erotic than anything you've written in the past.*

One evening I wrote the first of those lyrics, then, as though they were waiting just behind the first poem, there came the second two. Over the next few weeks all nineteen came. I drew on some lines that I had scribbled in a notebook years before. My experience was of a voice writing the poems. Perhaps it's a matter of trusting a voice.

For someone like myself, who's lived most of his life in South Africa, a country which was literally at war with itself for decades, one is used to poetry being ascribed a vociferously political role. Poetry can, of course, be used to bring down governments, ferment revolutions, among much else. But why I responded at once to your work was precisely because it seemed to have very different ends in view. As soon as I read your work I thought of a sentence that Milosz also uses in his Nobel Prize lecture in 1980 to define his sense of the poet's mission. "The poet's true vocation," he wrote, "is to contemplate being." Would these words chime accurately with your own sense of the poet's vocation? In your "Wimmera Songs" (Wicked Heat), for one thing, you allude to "The stranger we call Being."

I find myself rebelling against sentences beginning, "The poet's true vocation is ..." There are all sorts of poets. Perhaps you can gather George Herbert and Walt Whitman together and say that they are both contemplating being, albeit in very different styles, but then "contemplating being" begins to seem a bit thin. If we're not to beat contemplation to "airy thinness" we must let it work alongside other dispositions, including curiosity. I can imagine a poet who might object to Milosz and say, "No, the poet's true vocation is to be curious about things." I doubt that one can be curious and contemplative at one and the same time. Or maybe one is just pulled in those two directions at once. It feels like that when writing poems.

It seems to me that there's always been a kind of alternative tradition in poetry itself—perhaps a real continuing underground. It carries, and is carried by, a certain conception of poetry itself and of a poet's role. There have, no doubt, been dozens of ways of putting these, in idioms varying according to time and language. But all of these tend to define the art itself, as well as the poet, in terms that are unmistakably religious in their idiom. I think of Heidegger's notion of the poet as "shepherd of Being"; of Montale; even of Octavio Paz's conception of poetry as "the other voice." I think of Milosz in his lecture again: "The poet's true vocation is to contemplate being."

Undoubtedly I'm at home in that alternative tradition. All the poets whose work I love are there. Thinking back to your previous question, I should add that this tradition doesn't exclude outrage against injustice. Far from it! Poetry can offer testimony against oppression, can give voice to a people's pain, and can object to idolatry, without abandoning its contemplative role. Akhmatova, Mandelstam, Celan, Yeats …

The poets and others I've just mentioned see their roles as poets, and that of poetry more broadly, not in socio-political terms. They're compelled to assume, with whatever disclaimers as to their fitness for the task, the burden of the mystery—the mystery of being itself, both in its radiance and its opacity.

Oh yes, I agree: to regard poetry solely in socio-political terms is to kill it. That's as bad as draining poetry of ethics. Today the problem is how to stop politics, especially identity politics, from determining what counts as ethics … Perhaps it's possible, though, to respond to the mystery of being in an almost wholly social way: Dryden and Robert Browning might be examples.

Improbable as it might sound, I think that this tradition I've just sketched (and which your own poetry both continues and extends) perhaps provides a more viable route for poetry to continue to follow than almost any other. Even now—and perhaps especially now. For it answers more fully, more satisfactorily, that interminable, vaguely despairing question, "Can poetry matter?"

You can never really tell what sort of work a poem will do. I've had mail over the years from people who have told me that reading one of my poems has helped them in times of desolation. A couple of years ago I was telephoned by a man who had been a political prisoner in Chile; he had been subjected to the most horrifying indignities. He called me to say that one thing that kept him going while in solitary confinement was a Spanish translation of my poem "The Room." He told me that some of my poems had encouraged his friends in their struggles. He wasn't talking about a poem like "Prague, 1968" that responds to a particular political situation but about those poems you associate with the contemplation of being. In a way, those poems did political work in helping that man and his friends to survive.

ALEŠ DEBELJAK

Aleš Debeljak was born in 1961 in Slovenia. He received a degree in compara-
tive literature and an MA in Cultural Studies from the University of Ljubljana
and a PhD in Social Thought from Syracuse University. He is the author of
seven books of poetry, including, in English translation, *The City and the
Child* (White Pine Press, 1999, cotranslated by Christopher Merrill), *Anxious
Moments* (White Pine Press, 1994, cotranslated by Christopher Merrill), and
The Dictionary of Silence (Lumen Press, 1999, translated by Sonja Kravanja).
He has won the Preseren Prize—the Slovenian national book award—and the
Miriam Lindberg Israel Poetry for Peace Prize. His books are translated into a
dozen languages. Debeljak has published several books of cultural criticism,
edited numerous anthologies, and translated John Ashbery into Slovenian. His
nonfiction published in the U.S. includes *Reluctant Modernity: The Institu-
tion of Art and its Historical Forms* (Rowman & Littlefield, 1998), *Twilight of
the Idols: Recollections of a Lost Yugoslavia* (White Pine Press, 1994), and *The
Hidden Handshake: National Identity and European Postcommunism* (Rowman
& Littlefield, 2004). This interview, conducted by Andrew Zawacki, was begun
October 29, 1999, at the "Three Lands, Three Generations: Russia, Poland,
Slovenia" conference at Northwestern University, and continued over email.

In Twilight of the Idols *you state that "the collective memory of any nation
clings to the experience of the past, without which there can be no vision of the
future." How would you characterize the collective memory of Slovenia, and
what possible visions of the future might it engender?*

The collective memory immediately brings us to a rather slippery terrain,
only to the extent that collective memory is always a constructed memory, a
memory that is being culled from various sources, from various pockets and
sediments of linguistic, aesthetic, political, social, and historical experiences
that coalesce to make up public representation of what the nation stands for.
I am very well aware of broad generalizations when I use the terms "collective
memory" and "nation." Yet I do believe that the life of a nation, insofar as it
is embedded in not only civic institutions but in the cultural web of everyday
habits and language of that nation, is something that propels us toward the
future, provided—and this is an important emphasis—that an individual is
able to work her way through that collective memory, being able to inherit

yet not uncritically praise certain images, phrases, and stereotypes, and at the same time to grapple with the centripetal force wherein one can carve out a space of individual freedom within the collective memory—that is, freedom for idiosyncratic speech.

The Slovenian nation has been traditionally characterized by the absence of political institutions in the nineteenth century, the period in which political institutions had to be replaced by the linguistic usage that was first and foremost pushed to its true aesthetically, highly accomplished extreme by France Preseren, a Romantic poet who, in the mid-nineteenth century, succeeded in articulating a vision of a unified nation, the segments of which at the time lived under different regimes. Particularly the Austro-Hungarian Empire had exerted a heavy influence on the ways the Slovenian nation came to see itself, which was always already positioned on the periphery not only of the Empire but also of the vital cultural life, while Vienna remained a powerful source of inspiration and a draw for many intellectuals of Slovenian extraction that were educated there. It also represented both the very seat of the regime—the House of Habsburgs—and a source of admittedly marginal possibilities for resistance against the regime. When I speak of collective memory I also speak of the preeminence of the Slovenian language, which, as I said before, in the absence of other political institutions which have been either poorly developed or simply did not exist, took on a lot larger role than just the means of expression of the individual self. The language was practically the only umbrella, the only common thread that united Slovenians who had lived in different landscapes and countries, although predominantly under the Austro-Hungarian Empire.

Collective memory also implies the production of those figures that may, in negotiations through time, inspire people who adhere to that memory. In the case of Slovenians, it is interesting to note that we simply did not have any longstanding, age-old mythological figures. Most figures that exist and have made their way into everyday life or everyday linguistic use have been produced in the nineteenth century. So in very many ways, Slovenians do cling, less and less so particularly in the post-independence period, to the Romantic notion of a poetic genius. Such genius is, in the case of Preseren, sadly unable to win the beloved [Preseren's lifelong love for Julia went unrequited] yet succeeded in providing the unifying vision for the entire nation. Up until Preseren's time, Slovenians really saw themselves first and foremost as the denizens of their respective landscapes, respective regions that made them develop numerous distinct and sometimes even mutually incomprehensible dialects. It was only since Preseren's work that Slovenians came to contemplate their common fate under the sign of a common denominator, and that was, again, primarily the language. No wonder, then, that the literary arts, so desperately existing in language alone, assumed a vital importance for the sustenance and nourishment of Slovenian political resistance vis-à-vis the ruling regimes. So one would not be too excessive in claiming that the life of the Slovenian nation has been, for the longest time, articulated along the lines of resistance. Even the guerilla struggle against oppressors and foreign powers has almost never been expressed in terms of the actual fight with guns, yet it had assumed serious traits of a linguistic guerilla warfare. Therein are the sources of the relevance that Slovenian poetry, fiction, and literature at large have continued to exert upon the life of the nation.

We've been talking at the conference this weekend about interactions between Anglo-American and Eastern European poetries. If, as you suggest, Slovenian collective memory is relatively recent—a distinction between Slovenia and other parts of Eastern Europe perhaps—then it's not all that dissimilar from the situation of mythological figuration in the United States, is it?

That's a very intriguing observation. It never occurred to me that one could draw this sort of parallel, but there is some validity to it. To a degree, it is indeed possible to argue that the American invention of the nation and the Slovenian invention of the nation have much in common, at least in the sense of being rather recent phenomena. Yet there is also an important distinction that needs to be drawn here, and that is that American public discourse is permeated by references to real figures, figures with a concrete historical existence, such as Abraham Lincoln, Benjamin Franklin, the Founding Fathers, and of course even going back to the Pilgrims and John Winthrop, etcetera. All those are historical occurrences that have been remodeled, reshaped to fit contemporary purposes. Whereas in Slovenia it was mostly mythological figures, unless one claims writers such as France Preseren and Ivan Cankar, our pre-eminent fiction writer who was active before World War I, as being already mythologized or undergoing the process of mythologization. But the important distinction is in the fact that our mythological figures have taught us, if anything, a suspicion toward power, toward the ruling regimes, regardless what stripe they may be, and an adherence to the highly private, inward-directed type of personality. (No wonder Slovenians have such a high rate of suicide.) On the other hand, American figures that provide the frame of reference for public discourse in this country have succeeded in giving civic institutions to the American public life, thus providing that particular sphere—which we in Slovenia are still struggling to attain—that allows for the separation of public and private. The distinction between public and private life is only gradually being made in Slovenia because of our being steeped in a sort of fabricated mythological tradition that, however produced and artificial, continues to exert a powerful influence on the collective imagination of Slovenians and the way we perceive ourselves. Even a rejection of this heritage, convulsive as it is, falls into its gravitational pull: *negatio est determinatio.*

Only after the velvet revolutions, after the changes in 1989 and, in the case of Slovenia, particularly after the assent to independent statehood in 1991, are we beginning to grapple with the issues that have long been resolved, at least in terms of foundations of public life, in America. So while the mythological tradition, or the mythologized historical tradition in Slovenian life, has been emancipating, it may be that it is increasingly seen as a burden, as something that cripples the individual imagination because it continues to impose certain collective habits of mind and collective forms of behavior. This is something increasingly seen as, if not obsolete, then at least in dire need of re-articulation and restructuring. I don't think there is any need whatsoever to do away with the tradition *per se*. That's in fact impossible, because every time one utters a word one also refers to the entire body of the language, which encompasses not only strictly linguistic aspects, expressive aspects, but also historical and cultural sediments, mores and affective frames, in which we almost subconsciously see ourselves as a subjugated people. It will take some time before we'll be able to shed that burden and to come from under the yoke of our own collective memory, which has, until the acquisition of independence, proven to be such a vital source of emancipatory impetus. So what had been liberating up until independence may very well prove to be paralyzing during the life of an independent state. But as that's something we currently undergo, I find it rather difficult to put any definitive form to it—though, my lord, I do run up against this process every day.

In much of your poetry there persists a strong current of nostalgia, which appears to exist both on a national level and on a personal scale, playing itself out as a political drama as well as an affair of the heart. What is the nature of this nostalgia?

If anything, my work reveals nostalgia for the lost time of childhood, not only on a personal level but also, once again, on the level of the collective.

Childhood is the only thing that remains real for an artist, I think, because that was the time when it was possible to speak with the authority of naiveté while able to discover things anew, not hampered by the analytical tools of language one acquires later. Childhood: certainly not as an Edenic place but as a continuous channel of inspiration that opens at random, wherein it was possible to aspire to, if not attain, a comprehensive experience of the world in which discourses were not separate, in which to speak of minerals also meant to speak of constellations in the sky. When, in other words, it was possible to experience the world in its bodily aspect. So I think there is a certain nostalgia, a certain proliferation of farewells, of bidding goodbye to the time that beckons from the past, yet we know it's irrevocably gone. And that past I have imbued with the meaning that may attempt to be redemptive. I want to say that redemption in our highly fragmented time stems from a belief that it is possible to speak in a powerful, urgent, authoritative voice in which the disparate, often conflicting discourses are united in the sense of, if you will, magical incantation. It is hardly a surprise that many of my poems refer or implicitly make use of religious vocabulary, because in many ways religion and—I would like to hope—art preserve some of the power that was retained by the pre-modern imagination, the imagination before the separation of various spheres that comes with the late Renaissance and modernity.

I think pretty much every artist aspires to speak about the world in the most tangible way, not removed from it but steeped in it, so that you don't speak *about* the world but that you speak the world itself. That you—pardon the sentimental expression—that you sing the world into existence. This is the continuous temptation and anguished challenge that poetry presents to the writer: the beckoning hope that it is possible, by the use and manipulation of images and various registers of language, to sing the world into existence as if it hasn't been done before. That you are basically creating the world anew. And you know that with every failed effort to do so, you only approximate that ideal where the world and the word merge. I have read too many books on hermeneutics and structural linguistics to safely say this is possible, but I would be loathe to let go of the hope that that particular possibility resides in certain recesses of one's imagination. Poetry at its best moments does lead us, as writers and as readers, into those recesses wherein we would probably be unable to go were we to resort to more analytical tools of linguistic expression. That's why I need to emphasize my belief, my *credo qui absurdum est*, in the redeeming power of poetic imagination, which brings together various discourses. Moreover: it is articulated as if the division of discourses did not occur.

In this sense, nostalgia is a valid term to describe my poetry, but certainly not nostalgia in any facile, flattened-out sense of longing for something that has been lost. I do acknowledge loss, but writing about loss, writing through loss, allows me to hope for what is beyond hope. I cannot do otherwise but to think that that is what is ultimately redeeming, the hope that can be glimpsed in the folds of nostalgia. The peeled bricks on the corner of the street in a small town are repositories of value and give support even for those lovers that never used or never knew the wall: this is the kind of nostalgia that conceals, not strangles hope.

You have been very much a citizen of the world that you speak about singing into existence. Elsewhere you've suggested that emigration is integral to being a "Yugoslav" citizen, and in the late 1970s and early 1980s you spent time in Paris, Vienna, Trieste, Munich, New York. To what extent does one need to leave one's country, at least for a time, to feel perhaps more at home in that same country later?

I have no qualms with subscribing to that particular Romantic tradition that calls for the necessity of *die Wanderjahre,* the "wandering years," during which one carries out an apprenticeship in the service of larger means. In my case it certainly was *die Wanderjahre* in the service of what, at the time, I did not know would more and more assert itself with the authority of a vocation, that is, the writing of poetry. I also want to distinguish between profession and vocation. Poetry cannot be a profession, although it certainly would appear so to a superficial eye. Poetry is first and foremost a vocation; it's something you don't choose to do but are chosen to do. I think that sort of drive to write poetry also drives one beyond—at least, it drove me beyond the confines of the often comfortable but more frequently ossifying and crippling cradle of my own culture, in which I certainly felt at home, but at home so much that I felt I needed to get out in order to appreciate what home can offer.

When I spoke of the necessity or the inevitability of migration and isolation as being part and parcel of my experience of being Yugoslav, I only meant that my frequent and comprehensive travels across the landscapes and republics of the former Yugoslavia taught me a valuable lesson, the lesson of constant migration between languages and cultures, between linguistic and social traditions. After all, this was the country that encompassed, in a rather small space, not only the great divide between Western Christianity and Eastern Christianity but also had, as an integral part, the Islamic tradition. I did not have to go to

Turkey to experience the vertiginous verticals of the mosque and the minaret; I only had to go to Sarajevo. In a very important and very real way, that was also my country. I was born a Yugoslav, and while one could be a Yugoslav, one was also a member of one's immediate ethnic tradition. So I like to say I have benefited immensely by being Yugoslav because I migrated between three frames of identification. Sure, I am ethnically Slovenian and culturally Yugoslav, but I would also like to see myself as a citizen of the global—which often means Anglo-American—mass culture. In other words, that I dwell in manifold distinct realms at the same time. The experience of my early travels, first as a sportsman—I was practicing judo, I was on a national Yugoslav team, I was a vice-champion of Yugoslavia at the time—and then later as a fledgling literati, taught me the dangers of ethnic grandeur, which are all the easier to be realized, to come out in the open, if one only sits in the lap of one's own culture. "He who knows one knows none": I think I had learned that early on, simply because I had a keen desire to experience myself from the outside.

After all, what is poetry if not about turning infinity into finite words, expressing what is inexpressible in a definitive set of words? What is poetry if not the expression of what resists expression? In that expressive effort you also see yourself, and your failing yet continuous efforts are akin to extricating yourself from the folds of your own culture so that you can see yourself in a clearer light. But also the drawbacks and advantages of belonging to your ethnic community, you can see those better too. I was taught that lesson early, throughout the late '70s and early '80s, when I was pretty much constantly on the move across Yugoslavia, to say nothing about the obligatory travels in Western Europe, North Africa, and Asia Minor. Those are of course important aspects of my personality, but certainly not crucial. Crucial was my growing up Yugoslav, because it taught me that it is indeed possible—current turmoil and the violent breakup of my former country notwithstanding—to dwell simultaneously in more than one tradition. I'd like to think that I continue that tradition not only by having married an American who lives with me now in Slovenia but also by continuing to write poetry and essays in which I try to address that manifold experience, this continuous circuit of migration between various registers of language, between various experiences and stocks of metaphor I use in my work. So I think we translate, we exit and re-enter edifices of language constantly in our daily life—except poetry makes us aware of that transition. Poetry, at its best moments, can provide a useful, invigorating awareness of this constant migration between registers of language, teaching us also the benefits of solitude and the solace of communal experience.

You've spoken of the reality of the imagination. I know that both Borges and Kis have been important writers to you. In what ways exactly?

Both writers had been important to my coming of age as a writer in the 1980s. I had avidly read the collected works of Borges as they were available in Croatian translation. I had read the entire *ouevre* of Danilo Kis, had written extensively about Kis in particular. I'd only like to say there is a major difference separating the two authors, and that is the difference of reality, if you will. Danilo Kis clearly uses the ecumenical, catholic, eclectic stylistic devices that Borges invented, the ease with which Borges moved between various layers of civilizational experience in order to reach for the mystery of existence. Yet unlike Borges, Kis used stylistic devices not as a highly sophisticated exercise in pursuit of the impossible but remained firmly rooted in the concrete social and political reality of life under Communism. Kis rendered that ever so brilliantly and in a very sophisticated manner and had shown me how it is possible to remain politically engaged with everyday life without resorting to the stereotypes and formulas of an otherwise flat, one-dimensional political discourse. Kis, particularly in *A Tomb for Boris Davidovich*, had demonstrated the possibilities, indeed redeeming possibilities, of a poetic imagination that does not need to be separate from everyday reality but which speaks through reality itself, thus not only bearing witness but also transcending it in a visionary manner, pointing outward to those realms that are inaccessible to other genres of discourse. In this regard Kis remains a very powerful writer, even though Communism as a political regime collapsed. But the forms of oppression continue in different shapes, and I think one is still able to cull glimpses of possibilities for literary writing in the work of Kis, precisely because he resisted the otherwise comfortable and sanitized version of literary writing that sometimes afflicted Borges, and that was the neat separation of social-historic reality on the one hand and the sheer play of imagination on the other. I think the imagination can only benefit from being engaged with reality, and Kis demonstrated that. And that sort of ethical commitment to the anxieties and joys of the other are clearly manifest in the work of Kis, who had of course benefited from Borges but had pushed his poetical protocols to a higher degree of a poetics of witness and visionary transcendence at the same time. That sort of ambiguity between witnessing reality and going beyond it remains inspirational for me.

Anxious Moments is a book of prose poems, which you wrote in the U.S. In Slovenia the tradition of the prose poem began with Ivan Cankar. Does your experience of prose poetry come out of any particular national heritage?

I found the prose poem to be a liberating form because it allowed me to chart an escape route from under the pressures and imperatives of the often very formalist poetic tradition in my culture. While Cankar had certainly been an inspiration for me because of his weaving together of political and aesthetic concerns and, particularly in his late work, his grappling with the notion of absolute reality and with God, he had not made any impact whatsoever on my writing in terms of his early efforts at the prose poem. I think I had simply been liberated by living on the American shores, the vast immensity of the continent that had at first thwarted me and dwarfed my youthful ambitions, but then, in a paradoxical way, allowed me to open up to sources of imagination that I might not otherwise have been able to tap or was not aware were dormant and latent in my mind. So I don't think the American prose poem as such had been particularly inspiring for me, because I simply didn't read that many American prose poets at the time. On the other hand, Baudelaire has been a source of inspiration because he had brought to bear some vestiges of the Romantic tradition on his poems that he acutely attuned to the nascent urban landscape. I think that sort of tension is something that animates my work.

On one hand there is, again, this nostalgia for the natural world as it was before the advent of the urban cosmopolis of the nineteenth century, while on the other there is also an awareness that a return to the unblemished, unspoiled, uncontaminated natural world is impossible, that humans are so fully present in the environment that they have radically modified it. And if the natural environment has been radically modified, then our language, which would allow us to capture it, has also had to be modified. Which is not to say that nature ceases to provide an inspiration for the pursuit of the impossible, for the pursuit of absolute reality, but I think it takes on a different form. One way of addressing the problem of speaking in a highly personal voice about the issues that transcend me as an individual human being was found in the prose poem, because it was looser, more vital because less explored. It offered tremendous possibilities for me, and it was a great—I remember clearly—a great pleasure to write that book, which I finished in a matter of a month and a half, in the wasteland of upstate New York, where I was a doctoral candidate in social theory at Syracuse in the late '80s. But I would be hard pressed to name any American writers of prose poems who would have had any influence on me, simply because I was not aware of their writing at the time.

In answer to Frost's statement that poetry is what is lost in translation, you've said that poetry is in fact what survives translation. Can you elaborate on what's lost and what remains when your work is translated from Slovenian into English?

I obviously do not believe that poetry is lost in translation, though the imperatives and strictures of poetic language, with its highly sophisticated use of linguistic devices, do present an anguished problem. But I don't think it's insoluble, because after all, we would all be impoverished if we were to read only poems written in our respective linguistic traditions. I mean, I simply cannot conceive of myself without the work of, say, Gabriel García Marquez or Borges or Baudelaire or Paul Valéry—to say nothing of the German tradition—even though I don't necessarily read all the original languages in which these works were written. Because I think that poetry, if it really matters, if it's not just inconsequential play at words, needs to reveal a message or its meaning to a reader, even though the reading of poetry in translation might be akin to kissing a bride through her veil—but you still get around to kissing her, as Turkish poet Nazim Hikmet suggested. That sort of not-fully-consummated experience of a kiss compels you to seek out more and more, you keep returning to get more of that experience, even though it may be at times frustrating. If poetry is so utterly dependent on the form that it ceases to have any inherent meaning that survives translation, then it may be but a very complex yet nonetheless irrelevant decoration. Hence I don't subscribe to Frost's dictum of poetry as that which "gets lost in translation," even though it has been often invoked.

To the contrary, I would like to emphasize the fact that poetry in translation has often animated readers around the world precisely because it is not embedded in the "natural" tradition of a particular nation from which individual poems float, because that gives one a sense of freedom to get to poems in translation from any desired angle, unburdened by the established protocols of reading that might be valid in the tradition in which the originals were written. That sort of freedom is something to be cherished and nurtured, because it allows not only readers but also the poets themselves to understand the responses of various cultural milieux in which poems in translation are read. Those responses certainly enrich and enhance the inherent meaning that poetry carries across the linguistic divide. And of course, just like in carrying water from the well to your home, something does get spilled, but ultimately we quench our thirst if we are successful. Success largely depends on the generosity not only of translators and poets but also of readers. If we are taught a generosity of spirit by reading poetry in translation, a lot has been accomplished.

So who were some of your early, strictly poetic sources? What sort of poetics were you pursuing?

Shortly before *The Dictionary of Silence* was written, Slovene poets Srecko Kosovel and Edvard Kocbek became my constant reading companions; also at that time I continued to draw from authors with a more international following, such as Rilke and Czeslaw Milosz. It is fascinating that Milosz—a living author whom I had the honor to meet—holds such esteem in my personal pantheon, and to me it makes no difference whether a particular Milosz poem was written in the Krakow underground during the Second World War or just recently in the hills above Berkeley while overlooking San Francisco Bay. The freedom contained in the authority of his artistic revelation is the freedom which contains the agony of the wound as well as the ordeal of Catholic theology, yet in such a fashion that it is predominated by a concentration on the truth in a certain—for a lack of a better word—"Zen" way, in a permitting manner of fulfillment. With his lyrical attempts to materialize the emptiness in his verse, with celestial translucency and his melancholic voice, with his solemn pledge to the impact of the word, Rilke, too, seldom fails to satisfy.

If writing poetry is, to some extent, a process in which the emotional—the irrational force of inspiration—is not the exclusive ruling force, but it is rather combined with a reflection of form and composition, then it must be noted that, from the very beginning of my poetic creativity (my first collection was entitled *Exchanges, Exchanges*), I have been of the firm belief that the spirit of individual poetics addresses the reader not through the power of individual poems but through the collection as a whole. The first impression is that the dramaturgical scheme of my poetry books follows a formalistic legacy that demands that a book be divided into individual cycles because it is not held together by an evident "red thread" of narrative impulse. Yet, from the very beginning and regardless of the actual outcome, the concept behind this collection was one of a solid, single composition that would stand like a single tree. This tree is nurtured from the somber feeling which was later to be confirmed by my fervid reading of, if not direct modeling on, Kosovel, a Slovenian poet between the two world wars, and also Georg Trakl, that dark prophet of Central European anxieties.

My first book of poetry describes a relatively predictable though aesthetically disguised psychical condition in which two opposites meet: on the one side there is a certain lack of personal existential foundation, while on the other there is a shy erotic inkling of the endless vertigo of orgasm foretelling the finality of death. A verse from this collection — "Astonished, the thought follows the cry into speech" — perhaps even suggests the entire sphere of self-awareness, in which the creative writing process is investigated and priority is gradually being given to the more important and fateful eruption of images which burst into speech spontaneously from the guts and physical experience of this world. Yet I was not able to let this stream speak out more or less directly; it remained a waterfall of images. The search for balance between the existential quiver and the form meant to restrain those unregulated outbursts began with pre-meditation, with conscious effort dedicated to the form, in my book *The Names of Death* (1985).

You used the phrase "single composition" to describe how you conceive and assemble each poetry volume. Why is it important to you that a poetry book be a "book" and not just a collection of individual poems? What sort of formal constraints or permissions do you encounter en route to writing such a "book"?

A concept of a book as an integral project — which is distinct from the incidental piling up of individual poems written at different times — has, in my case, no conscious connection with Mallarmé's intentional orientation toward an abstract totality which is itself unattainable and consequently lives off its impossible struggle, in which a successful artistic style is already conditioned through the defeat of the form. Instead, I was, and indeed still am, interested in the much more "pragmatic" integrity of a book as a world of its own. It is only such a world that knows its own narration, a dramaturgical curve and the filigree precision of overlooked details, the true meaning of which can be experienced only if individual poems are not read separately. To my mind, poetry must be read within a perspective in which the book of poetry is, above all, a lyrical document of time and space, yet at the same moment a direct testimony which discovers the inspiration for a vision of utopic landscapes and nostalgic concentration. Poetry explores modes of being in which today, yesterday, and tomorrow — albeit only during the moments of reading — become the same thing. Driven by an immodest ambition to inscribe the desire and the recollection of a fleeting moment into a metaphorical picture, I carefully search for a lyrical structure that would thicken and, at the same time, knead the palpability of light which, for a brief moment, for a transient throb, exposes the contour of an angel's wings on the face of a passerby. I search for a lyrical structure which could halt — as if captured in amber — the sense of loss growing out of mourning and a humble hymn, that fraction of a second when the menacing demonic gaze of a shadow looks into us before rushing across the bedroom wall, in that no-man time zone when the night is coming to its end and the day has not yet begun.

What I wish to say here is: if the art of lyrical words is to be as essential as food, then some of this existential essentiality must also be revealed in the instruments of the poetic language. This is, I suppose, the reason for my bashful flirtation with form in *Exchanges, Exchanges*, a work in which I tried to harness—at least partially—the pulsating movement of images with rhyme, strong rhythm, and a sonorous melody. Subconsciously, I wanted to provide outer order to an inner "sweet confusion" of psychical states. I was first drawn to the sonnet form in *The Names of Death*, where I developed the "sonnetoid," a sonnet only remotely reminiscent of the traditional sonnet structure, while seeking to correspond with the contemporary pulse. It is with the sonnet that modern Slovene poetry begins; therefore, a return to its roots represented a challenge that could not be avoided. I showed regard for the form, and through the application of rhyme and meter I strove to demonstrate my commitment to tradition and, consequently, to recognizable spiritual positions. At the same time, I aspired to make room for my own lyrical voice.

Here, in the dialectics of the acceptance and rejection of tradition, is the key to an understanding of my poetics. I tried to avoid the *en bloc* shaking off of those impulses that we all receive from our cultural inheritance; rather, I tried to search for the contemporary living spirit within them. Hence my application of characteristic verse schemes in *The Dictionary of Silence*, in which the form of three four-line stanzas corresponds with that of Slovene folk poetry. In terms of the form of my poems, on the one hand I endeavored to approach the universal states of fear, anxiety, and violence, while on the other I aimed to confront loneliness, so typical of our age.

"Responsibility of form," as Roland Barthes named it, requires both repetition as well as innovation. Repetition of given verse schemes assures the minimum possibility of recognition and secures the spontaneous conditions for reading empathy, while the innovative shaping of psychic states drives the poem beyond the framework of that which has already been heard or written. Formal discipline inevitably suggests the feeling of order which, for the most part, we miss in everyday life. After all, isn't art driven by the need to give a semblance of order to our most intimate and least articulated explosions of dreams, impressions, stimuli? It would be too simple to respond to the challenge of contemporary chaos in a chaotic way, particularly so today, after a quarter-century-long revolt against the straitjacket of sentimental humanism, as well as the revolt against versification for its own sake. The very repetition of given forms and genre formulae can be easily reduced to kitsch, while innovation requires the background of a strong tradition against which the revolt can be recognized. For instance, in the works of Tomaž Šalamun, the great magus of Slovene free verse, such a fundamental critical charge is clearly evident. It is directed against the ossified ideal of verse discipline and is opposed to existential attitudes which are themselves doomed to sterility behind formal bars.

Your essays, from the pair that comprise Twilight of the Idols *through the intro-duction to your more scholarly and more recent* Reluctant Modernity, *seek to elaborate a notion of "Yugoslav experience." I put both "Yugoslav" and "experi-ence" in quotation marks here, of course, as each of them represents a moving target. Can you say something about your own experience in this context?*

The Yugoslav perspective was exceedingly important for my personal as well as creative biography. For instance, my very first "big city" experience was Belgrade, in the east of what was once Yugoslavia. I imagine I can still remember the excitement I felt when entering this new territory. The streets of Belgrade seduced me with promises of romantic encounters and the allure of eastern—more specifically, Balkan—wisdom. How well I remember my first ascent from the central railroad station in this capital city of the former Yugoslavia, walking through the canyon of fading elegant buildings and up to the broad-shouldered Terazije Boulevard. Strolling along the boulevard, taking delight in the colorful, relaxed attitude of the passersby, I passed the Hotel Moskva where, following his return from England after decades of exile, the aged giant of Serbian literature, Milos Crnjanski, spent his final years. Maybe it was the depressive predicament of exile in his *The London Novel*, which struck me with awe and horror, that years later prevented me from staying in America when I likewise followed the call of foreign lands. I continued to the building called Albania to glance in a bookshop window at titles not yet available in Slovene translation; among these were the volumes in which I was later to sense the depths of Lautréamont's inferno of desire and the cold ironical perfection of the poems by Joseph Brodsky. I zigzagged among the beer-spilled tables of an open-air café set out around the statue of Prince Mihajlo and felt my way through the bon-vivant atmosphere of the main Knez Mihajlova Street, to finally take a rest under the trees in the cool Kalemegdan park, where a naïve provincial man had just been fleeced by two devilishly fast gypsies in a game involving three match boxes.

No doubt about it, this city absolutely fascinated me. It embodied everything that my native Ljubljana was not. Belgrade gave me my first experience of a dangerous and vibrantly appealing cosmopolis, something that even Vienna had not given, even though it is a former Habsburg city close to Slovenian lands historically and geographically, and thus familiar. Belgrade might not have been particularly sophisticated by western standards, which were still unknown to me then, in the early '80s, but it exuded a special urban self-confidence which truly swept me off my feet. Maybe it was because of the pure innocence of these first memories of Belgrade that I have never mustered enough energy or conviction to revisit it since the beginning of the wars that led to the violent disintegration of Yugoslavia. It may sound sentimental, but I don't want to spoil the memory.

It is only in the context of great tectonic changes that the lyrical ear for the poet's own destiny becomes finely tuned. By way of this it also assumes the fateful weight of the collective experience. All things considered, it is my impression that through an early acquaintance with the treasury of modern Serbian poetry—in this context, I was undoubtedly under the influence of discussions and social relations with Serbian poets and literary critics—I subconsciously desired to surpass the limitation that presses like a nightmare on twentieth-century Slovene literature, namely, the lack of cosmopolitan mentality that the sovereignty of a big city and a self-confident stroll through the library of world constellations would bring! How few Slovene writers and poets actually lived and worked, for example, in Paris! Let's think: Vladimir Bartol—a virtually unknown novelist until quite recently—and Joze Javorsek—the notorious lounge lizard. Edvard Kocbek only got as far as Lyon. There were some who reached Vienna or maybe studied in Prague, a few visited Munich, briefly, and … that's the sad end of mostly crumpled biographies. In terms of biography, the modest nature of Slovenia's literary tradition is demonstrated in the fact that a young poet wishing to get inspired by the adventurous, eventful, and risky passage of a chosen artist can but rely either on his/her own imagination or draw from the annals of other national traditions. Every poet must create such a mythology by himself.

Tomaž Šalamun stood by my side when my own orientation was slowly becoming defined. He was a constant source of encouragement and support and, using his personal connections, opened some important doors for me. And this is precisely it: personal attitude. After all, Tomaž also managed to transgress the national context, not merely in the spiritual but also in the physical sense. Despite the twenty-year time gap that separates me from my friend, as well as thoroughly different personal and poetic preferences, Šalamun's imagining of America served as an inspirational model for my own. My inclusion in the chain of the national poetic tradition—fragile in some, yet more solid in other times—can be perceived in the book series which I, as editor, produced for White Pine Press, a small but enterprising American publisher, and which will hopefully encompass more than just a few books in the future. I am proud to say that the first book in the *Terra Incognita: Writings from Central Europe* series, published in 1997, was a selection of Šalamun's most recent poems, *The Four Questions of Melancholy*, edited by Christopher Merrill. In the spirit of a lyrical poem which I see as a given and returned gift, I am now able to modestly give back to Tomaž that which he gave me: the best he could, eagerly and with the liberated unselfishness of an accepted artist, at a time when I had no friends or connections in literary America.

As a student you were a magazine editor. Can you say something about that, and about journals in other parts of Yugoslavia?

During the early '80s I was the chief editor of *Tribuna*, a radical student magazine that published articles that were routinely problematic for the political authorities. Our board of editors searched for writers with similar opinions, and not only in Slovenia, where dissident texts were also being written for the *Nova revija* magazine by an older and, to us, somewhat unknown generation of writers. We looked for them in the wider framework of Yugoslavia. *Tribuna* writers often traveled to Belgrade and Zagreb to meet colleagues. These meetings invariably turned into exciting intellectual, erotic, and social adventures. Belgrade evenings included a stop at the Madera Café where we would hope to catch word as to where a party was to take place that particular night. I had the feeling that parties were thrown nonstop in Belgrade. It was also in that city that I attended my first "garden party," at which more than a hundred guests were present. True, this might well be deemed a "mere" social dimension, yet through it shines a flash of the animated faces of poets, anarchists, political dissidents, and braggarts. Here was sparkling conversation with new people and the allure of discovering the unknown. The choice of such venues was also extraordinarily rich in Belgrade. Comparing them to the few Ljubljana cafés, Union for instance and the underground FV Discotheque, where I spent my student days, I could not help but feel that being in the Yugoslav capital was like falling into a glamorous whirlpool of manifold possibilities.

The Zagreb-published *Quorum* magazine was the most important Croatian literary monthly of its time. The far-sighted and well-considered editorial policy of its chief editor, Branko Egec, supported the publication of work by the leading representatives of the younger generation of literary writers, as well as budding literary critics and essayists from all over the Yugoslav federation. Ever since its first issue in 1985 and its ascent onto the Yugoslav stage, this ecumenical journal published my essays and poems on a regular basis. Not surprisingly, I enjoyed Zagreb's literary circle, its performances and media coverage, maybe even more than I did Ljubljana's. To me, being in Zagreb, meant being "abroad" while, in a way, still remaining at home. And if being at home means feeling confident to move through space without constant concern about how to behave and what to say, I did feel at home in Zagreb. I spent more nights at the Dubrovnik Hotel in the main square than I did in any other hotel in the world. Literary travels often took me to Miroslav Krleza's city, and the historic streets of Zagreb's Upper Town are almost as familiar to me as the granite cobblestones of old Ljubljana. It was in Zagreb that my book *The Names of Death* was awarded Yugoslavia's *Sedem Sekretarjev SKOJ* literary prize, even though it had not been translated into Serbo-Croatian and had to be read in the original; indeed the Croats used to be far more attentive readers of Slovene literature than the Slovenes were of theirs.

You have given a great deal of thought to the political and ethical responsibilities of the "intellectual." What were some of those responsibilities, as you perceived them, during the third Balkan war? Did thinkers step up to the task or back off? More broadly, what do you think is the role of the intellectual during times of violent political crisis?

Not having had any personal experience of the Second World War, I beheld the violent disintegration of Yugoslavia as something verging on the apocalyptic, in much the same way as my parents' generation must have perceived the Fascist and Nazi occupation of their Slovene motherland. The disintegration of Yugoslavia represented an "epistemological break": in its wake, nothing was impossible any longer. If the town of Vukovar could be blown off the map and nobody be held responsible; if Sarajevo should live under a constant hail of shelling, in comparison with which even the siege of Leningrad lost the status of absolute entrapment in violence; if the little son of my Bosnian poet-friend Semezdin Mehmedinovic, who now lives in Washington, DC (see his 1999 book *Sarajevo Blues*, in Ammiel Alcalay's translation), desperately wanted to "move to Greenland because there are no people there"—then surely all metaphysical, moral, and political assumptions taken for granted before the war ceased to be valid. New ones are only coming into being with horrible pains.

Here, in my opinion, lies the central responsibility of intellectuals. In the illumination of Balkan conflagration, which is now integrated into our history and has become our "second nature," we cannot discuss only such matters as the function of mirrors in the fiction of Borges, or a celebrity anchorperson switching television stations. True, such discussions are necessary. However, they cannot be the sole focus of the public interest of intellectuals, unless their aspirations don't reach beyond academia. Both disciplines—the intellectual and being a professor in academia—differ considerably. I myself have striven, to the best of my knowledge and ability, to practice intellectual responsibility. This responsibility is far from simple, though. The "wise men" who would like to dismiss such a responsible attitude as the last *Masada* of moralism must, time and time again, be told that it is better to be naïve than corrupt, to quote Josip Osti, a Bosnian writer who now lives in Ljubljana.

In my formation as an intellectual and literary critic, I was inspired by the homeless Weimar left, i.e., by Benjamin and Adorno, and for me the pitiful response of the majority of European leftist and post-structuralist theoreticians to the recent Balkan wars was entirely shocking. I detected no sense of responsibility in their feeble responses. Faced by the war in the Balkans, the leftist community, well-versed only in the empty conjuring of formulae about non-interventionism, pacifism, and anti-Americanism, were naturally perplexed. The intellectual community, which uses euphemistic rhetoric and applies the term *ethnic cleansing* in order to avoid using the term *genocide*—even when the occurrence of such is more than obvious—is unfortunately unaware that, by doing so, it has sunk below the level of elementary discourse on dignity in life *and* in death. Antigone, at the rise of western civilization, was the first to speak of such dignity with passionate strength when she, in respect for the unwritten rule, defied the written laws of Creon's *polis* in order to bury her brother Polyneicus. Austrian writer Peter Handke and consorts obviously could not care less for the fact that to pay attention to political loyalties constructed on the media-promoted illusion about the tradition of general Serbian alliance against the axis powers during World War II means to reject the *universal metaphysical right to be.*

It is only the unspeakable suffering under a military jackboot that constitutes the fundamental test of moral imagination, as it examines the suitability of principles in everyday life and the practical value of ideas. The compendium of progressive theories has failed this test and failed it miserably. Political attitudes like abstract humanism, which is blind to actual relations and consequently perceives both the executioner and the victim equally culpable; radical peace activism, which fails to realize that by preaching non-violence to the party that is being attacked, the aggressor's job is made even easier—such political attitudes are nowadays successful merely because they are an expression of popular cynicism, washing of hands. This Pilate-like behavior was unintentionally described in *Verbatim II*, a book published in 1995 by Jacques Attali, the often lucid "analyst of noise" who, for many years, served as an advisor to French president François Mitterand. Attali recalls how he once asked Mitterand the question that is frequently asked by those of us who have heartfelt feelings about war in the Balkans: "What is the most important characteristic of a good politician?" Mitterand refused to be confused: "I would like to say it's honesty. In fact it is indifference." Mitterand's *mot juste* is demonstrative of a spirit in which the republican tradition of solidarity has long been lost. The *common good*, as the supreme goal of society, has been supplanted by the assertion of one's own interest, the dark side of which is indifference.

What, if anything, have the Balkan wars taught us about moral fiber?

My position on this matter is simple. I believe that an ethical attitude and a moral fiber—in its thoroughly elementary form—are innate in every human being. After all, in everyday life we constantly make moral decisions, be it on the professional, personal, or social level. The status of a moral decision is not only attributable to grand topics, such as the efforts to advocate the rights of victims of the third Balkan war. However, for me this military nightmare represents a kind of milestone and a prism through which I perceive both the world and myself. War and childbirth are the two keystones of my existential orientation, now that I'm in my early forties. From this perspective, it is probably understandable, although possibly sentimental in the opinion of masters of press-promulgated superficiality, if I say that a moral attitude is important simply because I want to bring up my children in a world where a man is not a wolf to another man, and where the cynicism of the "status quo" as the natural order of things won't be the only metaphysical explanation a child might receive. I feel that it's a natural desire to want to bring up children in a world where it is possible to walk the streets and feel safe. In a world where, for instance, rape won't be dismissed with a shrug of the shoulders as if to say "she was looking for it."

It was the repercussion of this armed cataclysm to have successfully and radically relativized all these seemingly obvious convictions. For this reason, the human dimension and the golden rule of not doing to others what one would not want done to oneself—known in a variety of forms, in all civilizations and religious imaginations—should not be renounced so easily. Eager servants of the post-modern "anything goes" philosophy will cry out that such an attitude represents the imposition of one particular perspective, and consequently is an attack upon the happy pluralism of models. Yet I cannot but express aloud my doubts as to how productive indifference is. To the best of my belief, indifference is necessarily in opposition to the conviction that, despite relativism, there are nevertheless moral and symbolic values worth striving for.

To avoid saying that the mass rape of Muslim women (as a form of military aggression) in Bosnia is wrong, merely because one is afraid that such a denouncement might leave the impression of supporting a particular side in the conflict, is repulsive. As is the belief that it is better to abstain from moral evaluation for the sake of upholding some utopian ideal of "neutrality" and "equidistance." I find the viewpoint of silence abhorrent, and impossible to accept. To me it represents a commonly practiced mode of opportunistic conformism, which claims that nothing can be done and that striving for truth and justice is beyond the power of the individual. The perspective that such "actions" may only be presided over by state councils and strategic cabinets, among a handful of world political powers, and that the eventual outcomes are regulated and determined within the impenetrable secrecy of great diplomatic machinations, I find difficult to reconcile for a number of reasons. First, this perspective silently presumes that the practicalities of *realpolitik*—the politics of that which is possible and attainable, a concept exceptionally well-promoted by the media—shall also, at the same time, become the automatic basis for our personal and individual reflections. Furthermore, I cannot agree with such a viewpoint because it gradually scales from the individual those exceedingly vital layers of agitation, indignation, and anger, which in my opinion guarantee, among other things, the existence of our most intimate humanity.

It is these very feelings and emotions that are directed toward concern for the lives of others and not merely toward the cultivation of our own pleasures. Said perspective is most likely well-supported by public opinion believing that "nothing can be changed anyway." Writers who advocate such a viewpoint fail to notice that it is we who change the most: namely from active into passive personalities. From this specific aspect I find the constant, monotonous rattling about art which must, has, and can have no contact with outside, trans-literary reality to be a viewpoint that is far more cynical than it may appear at first glance. It is cynical precisely in the degree to which it *a priori* renders incapable our ability to form value judgments. In the soap bubble of literature the moral, political, social, historical, and erotic dimensions, which are characteristic of an undiminished human life, are easily lost. After all, if beauty were all we really enjoyed—and not the tension between beauty and pain—then we probably would not read the lyrics of troubadours or Roman elegies, because these poems, written such a long time ago, could hardly tell us anything about human life at the time. A sublime ear, however, can detect in them an echo of castle intrigues and the yearning to surpass topical limitations; it can listen to the buzz of the forum through which imperial grandeur is revealed in an intimate and authentic way. In this regard, the universal truth of poetry, as expounded in Aristotle's *Poetics*, is still valid. If poetry really provides the most integral crystallization of anthropological experience, then I feel it must be driven by an ambition to play all the strings: only a concert of emotional states, sensual perceptions, and mental concentration can reveal the entire agonizing richness of humanity. Playing only one string, no matter how virtuosic, sooner or later becomes monotonous in its reductionism.

Drawing attention to various forms of collective and individual barbarism does not represent the position of "a pure soul." The opposite is true: it is the pure soul which actually supports the social, cultural, political, and historical status quo precisely by refusing to comment on barbarism, even in a footnote, claiming instead that the matter is "well-known" and should be put to rest because it is aesthetic considerations that writers must be engaged with. To me, to remain silent means to become reconciled with damage to the moral nerve that propels us to distinguish between good and evil. We can, of course, argue about the definitions of good and evil, as well as about the ways the boundary between them shifts. However, there's no negotiating about how irreplaceable the difference between them is. If we accept the fashionable "postmodern" assertion that there is no difference between good and evil, it will lead us straight to radical moral relativism, an ideology which derives from the French "new philosophers" and German historical revisionists, a philosophy inspired by the *tout court* rejection of the Enlightenment tradition. Through the adoption of such a doctrine, it is impossible to preserve spontaneous humanity—even at the personal level—let alone create the conditions for the growth of new life, either in literature or real life.

Silence in the presence of terror is the silence that honors the logic of accomplished fact and the absolute prevalence of private interest. Above all, such silence must, by definition, be adopted by recruits of "cynical distance," i.e., economists, politicians, and businessmen. My essays, critical articles, and analyses of a Bosnian situation, which through my own catastrophic vision I perceive as something symptomatic of the mentality of the time, most certainly refuse to kneel before the yoke of accomplished fact. I cannot simply consider my lived world as "the best of all possible worlds" or as an amorphous mass of the natural tide of catastrophes. Oscillating between desire and memory, my writings try to isolate the message that can still be discerned from the burning bush that illuminates the bloody ruins that mark this *fin-de-millennium*. Make no mistake about it: such ruins are far from being limited solely to the razed territories of former Yugoslavia. Instead, they outline the structure of the western spirit as such. There is a significant difference between "public policy," i.e., the rhetoric of party programs and strategies for winning elections, on the one hand, and intellectual critique on the other. The essence of this difference lies in the fact that at a given moment the strategic thought must necessarily take into consideration the limited possibilities for change, as well as the public conditions for the consequences of the propositions it formulates.

Intellectual criticism is not committed to this topical imperative. Yet this does not necessarily mean that it is not topical, when such a critique reaches into the utopian lyrics of personal hope and—in the face of logical analysis—into the reservoirs of historical pessimism. Provided that it endorses the preservation of freedom and dignity and advocates the necessity of life (recall *Antigone*), it shall remain topical. Let me clearly stress here that I do not think that an intellectual, artistic, or literary critique of the "status quo" must necessarily bear directly quantifiable fruits—for instance, in visible changes of the geostrategic maps or in the policy suggestions about the political mechanisms of power. Suffice it to say, the right of expression of a critical spirit presupposes a confidence that individual ideas, attitudes, and visions ooze through into broader strata of a collective mentality.

I'm of a strong opinion that the balance of the world mosaic only ever shifts slightly. As a writer committed to an activity slowly losing its audience, I have to believe in this effect that writing entails. I believe that the tectonic plates of cultures shake for a tiny fraction of a second, if only one anonymous reader refuses to look up from the pages of a low-circulation literary journal, allowing a writer to take her on a travel into those recesses of imagination wherein a different perspective might be sensed. Such a perspective may expand the tissue of reality, enhance the reader's sensitivity, and fill her nostrils with a strong aroma of places which the reader will later recognize as her own, even though she didn't ever actually go there in person.

About the Editors

Brian Henry has published three books of poetry: *Astronaut* (Arc Publications, 2000/Carnegie Mellon University Press, 2002), *American Incident* (Salt Publishing, 2002), and *Graft* (New Issues Press, 2003). He edited *On James Tate* (University of Michigan Press, 2004), and is co-editing *The Salt Book of Contemporary American Poetry*. He teaches at the University of Richmond in Virginia.

Andrew Zawacki has published two books of poetry, *By Reason of Breakings* (University of Georgia Press, 2002) and *Anabranch* (Wesleyan University Press, 2004). He edited *Afterwards: Slovenian Writing 1945-1995* (White Pine Press, 1999). A former Rhodes Scholar, he is currently a doctoral student in the Committee on Social Thought at the University of Chicago.

Henry and Zawacki have been co-editors of *Verse* since 1995.